How to Start Your Own S Corporation

How to Start Your Own S Corporation

Second Edition

Robert A. Cooke

John Wiley & Sons, Inc.
New York • Chichester • Weinheim • Brisbane • Singapore • Toronto

This book is printed on acid-free paper. ♾

Published by John Wiley & Sons, Inc.

Published simultaneously in Canada.

Library of Congress Cataloging-in-Publication Data:
Cooke, Robert A., 1931–
How to start your own S corporation / Robert A. Cooke. — 2nd ed.
p. cm.
Rev. ed. of: How to start your own Subchapter S corporation. c1995.
Includes index.
ISBN 0-471-39812-8 (pbk. : alk. paper)
1. Subchapter S corporations—Popular works. 2. Small business—Law and legislation—United States—Popular works. 3. Subchapter S corporations—Taxation—Popular works. 4. Small business—Taxation—Law and legislation—United States—Popular works. I. Cooke, Robert A., 1931– How to start your own Subchapter S corporation. II. Title.
KF6491.Z9 C67 2001
343.7306'7—dc21 00-046265

Printed in the United States of America.

10 9 8 7 6 5 4 3 2 1

PREFACE

There have been many changes in the income tax rules since the first edition (written in 1994), and those that affect S corporations and limited liability companies (LLCs) are included in this second edition. The most notable changes for S corporations have been the expansion of the allowed number of stockholders to 75 and the rule that S corporations can now own subsidiary corporations. Also, there are many minor details that have been updated in this edition.

For LLCs, the greatest change was the fact that the IRS dropped the fight to try to classify LLCs as corporations and, thereby, collect corporation taxes. I've also included more details about the steps to take to set up one of these business forms.

The income tax laws have constantly changed for the past 77 years, so it's certain that they will continue to change. The best way to keep abreast of the changes would be a new edition of the book every week, but my publisher says that's impractical. So, when there are significant changes that affect S corporations and LLCs, I intend to post them on my Web site, so take a look now and then at www.robertcooke.com.

Of course, I'm always interested in knowing how my product meets the needs of readers. If you have comments or suggestions (up or down), please send them to me via e-mail: rob@robertcooke.com.

ROBERT A. COOKE

HOW THIS BOOK IS ARRANGED AND HOW TO USE IT

CHAPTER 1

S corporations have been around for only about 50 years, and they have gone through several mutations [tax simplification(?) acts] in those years. As, in essence, they are corporations that are taxed similarly to a partnership or sole proprietorship, the best way to understand the nature of S corporations is to first understand the older forms of business organization. So, Chapter 1 briefly covers the legalities of these other forms. Read this short chapter for some basic concepts.

CHAPTER 2

This chapter continues the basics in Chapter 1 by outlining how these business forms are taxed. Again, understanding the basics of the taxation of sole proprietorships, partnerships, and regular corporations makes understanding S corporation taxation much easier. This chapter is also short, covering just the essentials.

CHAPTER 3

Here are the various specifics of federal and state taxation of S corporations—at least those that would apply to an individual or a few individuals starting an S corporation from scratch or turning an existing simple business into an S corporation. What's here is enough to help you decide whether an S corporation fits your needs, without learning all the minutiae you'll need to know if you decide for an S corporation.

CHAPTER 4

Here's the minutiae of what steps you should take if you are forming an S corporation: the forms to file, meetings to hold, and records to keep. In other words, how to keep the bureaucrats (particularly those at the IRS) out of your hair as much as possible.

CHAPTER 5

This is more nitty-gritty of S corporation taxation. These are rules that apply to situations that most S corporation owners won't run into, but some will. Not knowing the rules might create disastrous tax bills and penalties. Read all of the headings. If you see something that may apply to you, read the details to be safe.

CHAPTER 6

Here's the popular alternative to S corporations, the LLC. Read this chapter to determine whether this might be a better route for your enterprise. The chapter also covers procedures you should take to set up an LLC and keep it operating in a manner that will continue its LLC status.

APPENDIXES

Here are aids to help you plan your own business future. Included are tax rates, some thoughts about just what does *limited liability* mean, as well as blank IRS forms and instructions that are essential for S corporations and limited liability companies.

CONTENTS

1 S CORPORATION—THE UNIVERSAL CURE—MAYBE

WHAT IS AN S CORPORATION?

Ask this at the beauty parlor, barber shop, social club, or your next party. You will hear:

"It's a corporation that is taxed like a partnership."

"It's a partnership with limited liability that protects you from being sued."

"It's a tax-saving device that used to be attractive, but now the rules are so complicated that it's no longer viable."

"It's a device that enables lawyers and accountants to charge more fees."

All of these answers are, to some extent, true. However, each one also has much myth and some fable built in. Except for the tax area, S corporations are like any other corporations. In the tax area, they are more like partnerships, but there are significant differences. S corporations, their configurations, and their tax aspects can be quite complicated, and that can mean high professional fees. However, those complications are often unnecessary and are brought about because the owners of S corporations did not take time to learn the basic rules. This book is designed to help you stay out of such quagmires and run a clean, uncomplicated S corporation. We are going to help you weed out the myths and fables to enable you to make wise decisions regarding incorporation.

THE ALTERNATIVE FORMS OF DOING BUSINESS

The best way to understand S corporations is to know what they are not and why. To do that, we should look at the various legal forms of doing business and why an S corporation may be your best choice (or, in some cases, not your best choice). Two short chapters cover this: This chapter describes each legal form in general; Chapter 2 covers the tax aspects of each. (Taxes are important enough to merit their own chapter.)

Sole Proprietorship

This is the form in which you operate if you do nothing to change your business to another form. That is, no one else is a part owner, you have not applied to your state government for a corporate charter, and you have not taken the steps to qualify as a limited liability company. In other words, one day you just hang out a sign that lets the public know that you sell platinum banana holders. That puts you in business. (Be aware, though, that even at this simple level, you will have some local government rules to worry about. Your city or county government will insist that you contribute to its treasury by at least purchasing an occupational license.)

Liability of a Sole Proprietor. If you follow this course of least resistance and hassle, you will have unlimited liability. If a banana falls off your holder onto the floor, and Aunt Emma slips on it, falls, breaks her hip, and successfully sues your banana holder business, you could end up having to sell your boat, sports car, and airplane in order to pay the judgment. If the award is exorbitant, you may even have to file for bankruptcy!

Transferability of a Sole Proprietorship. What if you want to sell the business or give it away to your child? This can be somewhat involved. What you sell are the machinery, desks, and other assets of the business. If the buyer is to assume the debts of the business, you'll need legal help to jump through the hoops.

Government Regulation of a Sole Proprietor. The bureaucrats will be prodding you no matter what form of business you choose. However, there is a little less hassle for a sole proprietor than for other business forms.

Partnership (General Partnership)

Like a sole proprietorship, this form of business often exists by default. If you and at least one other person decide to enter business together, you have formed a partnership. Who can be a partner? Almost any individual, corporation, limited liability company, association, government agency, another partnership, or any other legal or commercial entity. Even though your state or local government may expect you to register your partnership, the Internal Revenue Service (IRS) will recognize this entity as a partnership even if it is not registered or recorded as such with any government authority.

Liability of Partners. As are sole proprietors, each partner is liable for the debts of the partnership, and the liability is what the lawyers call *joint and several.* In other words, if the business is unable to pay its debts (which might include judgments resulting from a successful suit by a customer) each partner has liability for *all* the debts of the partnership. For example:

> *Doris, Eleanor, and Fred form a partnership. Doris is independently wealthy, but Eleanor and Fred have no investments and not much else that can be converted into cash. If the partnership falls on hard times, runs up debts of $1 million, and has only enough cash and other assets to pay $100,000 of the debts, the partners will have to cough up the other $900,000. Because Eleanor and Fred have no assets, Doris will have to pay the whole $900,000 from her resources.*

Watch out for the spendthrift partner:

> *What if Fred decides that the partnership could do more business if he could frequently fly around the world, contacting distributors of the product? So, he signs a contract for a long-term lease of an executive jet plane, obligating the partnership to monthly payments of $50,000. Now the debts of the partnership could total more than even Doris has in her investment account, wiping her out financially.*

So, if you are in Doris' shoes, be wary of forming a simple, or *general,* partnership. Choose another form of business that avoids this unlimited liability.

Transferability of a Partnership Interest. If all the partners sell the business to others, the transfer is similar to selling a sole proprietorship, with the added complication of which partners get how much of the proceeds of the sale. If one partner wants to sell his or her partnership interest, there can be more complications. For instance, if one partner is older than the others and wants to retire, how much should that partner receive for the partnership interest?

> *Because of your technical background, you have developed an efficient method of manufacturing platinum banana holders. However, you need some marketing help, so you enlist Elmo, your brother-in-law, who has a successful background in sales and marketing, plus a hoard of some cash that your business sorely needs. In exchange for his cash, expertise, and time, you give Elmo one-half the business. You have now established a partnership.*
>
> *Your agreement with Elmo may be nothing more than an oral agreement. However, it's foolish to rely only on an oral understanding. What if your sister divorces Elmo? What if you and Elmo have a major disagreement as to how the business should be operated? What if Elmo states that he should own more than one-half the business because (he thinks) he has contributed more to it? Without a written agreement as to how the partnership may be split up, you may be in for some lengthy and expensive litigation.*

The caveat here is that, at the formation of a partnership, the partners should draw up a partnership agreement that specifies the formula for valuing a partnership interest and how profits and proceeds of a sale of the business will be allocated among the partners.

Limited Partnership

The *limited* in the term *limited partnership* refers to the limited liability conferred on some of the partners, who are called limited partners. If properly set up, they cannot lose (be at risk for) more than they have invested in the partnership.* In order to create this limited liability for certain partners, specific rules have to be followed. The rules include:

1. At least one partner must be designated as a general partner, and that partner generally does not have limited liability.
2. An individual or entity who is to be a limited partner should be so designated in the partnership agreement and in any document filed with the state.
3. The limited partners can take part in the management of the business of the partnership to only a limited extent. Exactly how much of a management role they can have varies with the laws of each state.
4. The limited partnership must be registered with the proper state authority.

Limited partnerships are currently seldom used except in special circumstances. Why? The recent development of limited liability companies has created a business form that avoids some of the complexity of limited partnerships. Specifically, it avoids the confusion over the requirement that some partners have unlimited liability while other partners are protected by limited liability.

However, one of the circumstances that favor a limited partnership is the *family limited partnership*. Setting up one of these can significantly reduce federal estate taxes for an owner of a business with a worth of $1 million or more.

Corporation

A corporation is a separate entity, defined and created by a government. It is like another person, although it does not have the emotional needs that humans have. Neither does it have the same health problems and mortality humans have, although you can find corporations that are sick (financially), and many do eventually die. Theoretically, though, corporations can live forever.

The government does not create corporations willy-nilly, but only

*A limited partner could be at risk for more than his or her investment if that partner signs a note to the partnership or guarantees an obligation of the company (as a bank loan).

when one or more persons ask the government to authorize, or *charter*, a corporation. In the United States, most corporations are chartered by state governments. A few are chartered by the federal government, but these are created for specific needs of the federal government rather than for meeting the requirements of individuals.

Corporations that are formed for the purpose of earning profits* (it is hoped) are owned by stockholders. After a state charters a for-profit corporation, the stockholders fund the corporation by buying shares of stock from the corporation.

Four people set up a corporation to sell platinum letter openers. They anticipate that $10,000 will finance the inventory, advertising, and other initial expenses. They might, in their request to the state for a corporate charter, seek authority for the corporation to issue 50,000 shares with a stated value of one dollar per share. After the charter is issued, they then each buy 2,500 shares at one dollar each. The other 40,000 shares that are authorized are kept, as unissued stock, by the corporation, but they are available to be sold if more funds are needed later from the existing or additional owners of the corporation.

Although the operation of a sole proprietorship or partnership is almost always managed by the proprietor or partners, the corporation form provides an easy way for investors (the owners or stockholders) to hire others to manage the business. Historically, the stockholders hold meetings, at least annually, at which they elect several individuals to be *directors* of the corporation. These directors meet and elect *corporate officers* (president, vice president(s), secretary, and treasurer) who will actually manage the business. Generally, these directors and officers do not have to own any stock in the corporation, although they usually do.

The terms of chief executive officer (CEO), chief financial officer (CFO), chief operating officer (COO), and so on that have come into popular use are not formally recognized as pertaining to corporate officers, although they may be the same people. The popular terms are just more descriptive of the duties of the individuals than are president, vice president, and so on.

Obviously, this business of electing directors who elect officers works for large publicly held corporations. However, for Cedric, who is incorporating his bake shop, it's pretty ridiculous. Cedric will own all the stock, he will elect himself and other family members as directors, and they will elect Cedric as president. In the past few years, enlightened state legislatures have recognized this absurdity and passed laws that allow, in smaller corporations, the stockholders to directly designate a president, who can also act as all the other officers. Check with the proper authority in your state as to whether you can use this streamlining in setting up a corporation.

---

*Not all corporations are incorporated for the purpose of conducting a profit-making business. Some government operations and many charities are operated as nonprofit corporations. As nonprofit entities, they do not issue stock or have owners.

Liability of the Owners of a Corporation. The owners (stockholders) of corporations have limited liability that the state confers on them. Although a corporation may be sued, and, if the suit is successful, it may lose all of its assets and be forced into bankruptcy, the stockholders of the corporation would not lose their assets (other than the corporation's stock that they own). At least that is the theory. In real business life, directors and officers of corporations are often sued, along with the corporation, for damages allegedly caused by the negligence of the officers. That's why, in addition to incorporating a business, the owners need liability insurance to protect their personal assets. So why bother to incorporate your business?

Assume you are one of the four people who are stockholders and officers in the platinum letter opener business. A customer, William, buys one of the letter openers, trips over a curb on the way home, and in the process of falling manages to stab himself. The cost for the ambulance, surgeon, hospital, needle, and sutures is $25,000. William sues your corporation for the $25,000 plus $500,000 for pain and suffering. He wins a judgment of $200,000, but can collect only $10,000 from the corporation. (That's all the money the corporation has.) However, William also sues you and the three other officers, but culpability and the resulting liability of the four of you are far harder to prove in court. The chances are good that you will not be found liable, and if that is the case, you have saved yourself much grief by incorporating. Had you not done so, the four of you would have had to come up with the money to pay the $200,000 (or file for bankruptcy).

In other words, the risk of personal liability is far less for a corporate officer than for a sole proprietor or partner.

Transferability. Another reason for incorporating is that it bundles up your business in a tidy package that makes selling all or part of the business to other people an easy task. To transfer ownership of a corporation, all that must happen is that one owner sells his or her corporate stock to another new (or existing) owner. A sale of a sole proprietorship or partnership is generally much more complicated, particularly in the tax area. (More about that later in the book.)

Government Involvement. Because corporations are a creation of the state, it has carte blanche authority to regulate them and, unfortunately, levy whatever fees and taxes please the legislature. Again, check with your state's authority about fees and taxes. If you are starting a very tiny business, you might be well advised to avoid this additional expense by starting as a sole proprietor. Take the money you save on fees and taxes and use it to buy liability insurance for your business.

S Corporations. What's the difference between an S corporation and a plain-vanilla corporation? Except for income tax issues, there is none. You turn a C corporation into an S corporation by filing a form with the IRS, telling the folks there that you want your corporation to be an S corporation. Then, when the IRS acknowledges in writing that your corporation will be taxed or not taxed according to the rules in Subchapter S of the Internal Revenue Code, you really do have an S corporation. Sounds simple, but there are some picky rules involved, as covered throughout this book.

You may hear both the terms *S corporation* and *Subchapter S corporation*. Here again, there is no difference. These interchangeable terms came about this way:

When the concept of an S, or Subchapter S, corporation was enacted into our federal income tax code about 50 years ago, the pertinent section of the law was titled "Subchapter S." These small business corporations then became known as Subchapter S corporations not because the tax code itself gave them that name, but because tax professionals referred to them by the section of the law that instituted them. When the rules relating to these corporations were revised (read, made more complicated) in 1982, Congress recognized this name, shortened it to just "S corporations," and included that appellation in the tax code. In other words, the correct and most often used name now is S corporation. However, there is no law that forbids you to say "Subchapter S," and you can still find tax professionals who use that term. (The tax code sections covering S corporations are still in Subchapter S of the Internal Revenue Code.)

While the subject of chapters of the Internal Revenue Code is at hand, I should mention Chapter C of the IRC. That is the chapter that covers regular corporations that do not receive S corporation tax treatment. In the rest of this book and in other tax literature you'll read about "C corporations" and "S corporations," meaning conventional corporations and corporations that have S tax status.

Limited Liability Company (LLC)

This is a relatively new-kid-on-the-block form of business operation. Like corporations and limited partnerships, a limited liability company is created by the operation of state law. It is similar to a corporation, in that all the owners are protected by limited liability. However, the rest of the attributes are similar to those of a partnership. Although it would not be completely accurate, a limited liability company could be defined as a partnership in which all the partners have limited liability. The emergence of LLCs is, obviously, the reason that general and limited partnerships are much less used today. There is much more discussion in Chapter 6, which is devoted to this form of business structure.

Estates and Trusts

A discussion of entities would not be complete without a mention of estates and trusts. The only way to create an estate that operates your business is to die. Because this is not a desirable choice for most of us, we'll leave that subject to books on administration of estates.

Trusts can also be established by the act of dying, if the trust has been planned for and documented ahead of time, or trusts can also be established during a lifetime and can operate a business, be a partner, and sometimes be a corporate stockholder. However, the current income tax rates for trusts are not attractive, so there is no income tax reason to set one up. There may be estate-tax reasons to set up trusts, and there may be valid nontax reasons, such as providing for a spendthrift heir or avoiding probate.

SUMMARY

Table 1.1 is a summary comparison of the types of business forms we have discussed. Note that C corporations and S corporations are described in the same column, because the difference between them is in how they are taxed. That subject is covered in Chapter 2.

TABLE 1.1 Summary of Types of Business Organizations

	SOLE PROPRIETORSHIP	GENERAL PARTNERSHIP	LIMITED PARTNERSHIP	CORPORATION (C OR S)	LIMITED LIABILITY COMPANY (LLC)
Eligible owner	Any individual	Individuals, corporations, LLCs, other partnerships, trusts, estates	Individuals, corporations, LLCs, other partnerships, trusts, estates	Individuals, corporations, LLCs partnerships certain trusts, some estates[1]	Individuals, corporations, partnerships, other LLCs, trusts, estates
Evidence of ownership of business	Signs, letterhead, advertisements, city or county business license	Partnership agreement, written or oral	Partnership agreement, written as specified by state law; registration with state	Charter issued by state to corporation; stock certificates issued by corporation to stockholders	Agreement between owners written to comply with state law; registration with state
Number of owners	One individual	Any number	Any number	Any number (but see Chapter 2 as to limitation for S corporations)	Any number
Personal liability of owners	Unlimited	Unlimited	Limited for limited partners; unlimited for general partners	Limited to amount of investment (unless corporate veil can be pierced)	Limited for all owners (unless veil can be pierced)
Ease of entering organization	Very easy	Easy to start small partnership; later entry determined by existing partners and partnership agreement	Complex for organizer of partnership; purchase of limited partnership interest usually easy	Complexity varies with size of operation, but must comply with state law and administrative procedures	

[1]S corporations may be owned only by individuals, certain trusts, and estates.

(Continued)

TABLE 1.1 *(Continued)*

	SOLE PROPRIETORSHIP	GENERAL PARTNERSHIP	LIMITED PARTNERSHIP	CORPORATION (C OR S)	LIMITED LIABILITY COMPANY (LLC)
Continuity of life	Until owner closes business, sells assets, or dies	Usually until more than 50% of ownership changes, but varies with state laws and partnership agreements	Usually until some date or future event specified in partnership agreement	Forever, or until stockholders agree to merge, dissolve, or sell corporation	Usually until some specified date or future event; variation between states as to requirement
Management	Either owner or hired manager (with no ownership interest)	Some or all of partners or hired managers	General partners(s); management by limited partners may be limited by state law	Stockholders generally elect board of directors, which appoints corporate officers to manage business	Members (owners) of the LLC or hired managers

2 HOW FORMS OF BUSINESS ORGANIZATION ARE TAXED

Amazing, isn't it? Every business, and almost every individual, in the United States computes its tax burden and cheerfully(!) sends the money off to Congress and the president to spend on all kinds of programs, many of which we don't need and don't want. Almost all of us engage in this self-taxing idiocy, and some call it a "voluntary" tax system. Of course, the voluntary part is strongly encouraged by knowledge that the alternative to this volunteering is a few years in the Atlanta Federal Penitentiary!

Because we all "volunteer" to be taxed, we have a need to know how best to organize our lives in order to be taxed the least. For the businessperson, there are several alternatives: He or she can operate as a sole proprietor, or in a partnership, a limited partnership, a C corporation, an S corporation, or an LLC. The best choice is not always clear. Even if the choice is made after acquiring thorough knowledge of the tax rules, future events can often make it a poor choice. Nevertheless, it is still wise to spend the time and effort to try to pick the best option. You may luck out and find you made a good decision.

Although this book is about S corporations and LLCs, do not let that lead you into thinking that only one of these is the best business form to select in today's taxing environment. So that you can make an informed choice, we'll take a look at the whole selection that is available to most businesses.

In the following discussion, we'll use some examples. Unless otherwise noted, the assumption is that the individuals are married and file a joint return. (In some cases, the earnings of a spouse can affect the business owner's choice of business form.*) We also assume that the family

*As I write this, Congress is debating whether we will continue to have a marriage penalty in the tax code. However, this is not a significant factor in deciding on a business form, so this information will not become outdated regardless of the fate of this legislation.

claims the standard deduction and four exemptions (husband, wife, and two children).

Also, keep in mind that not only income tax but Social Security tax is now onerous enough to be a consideration in tax planning. In all fairness to our benevolent federal welfare government, I should point out that the self-employment tax may eventually come back to you in Social Security benefits. However, if you could avoid this tax and stash the same money in a private pension or 401(k) plan, your future retirement fund would most probably be much higher.

As you'll see, we spend some time discussing some of the income tax aspects of sole proprietorships, partnerships, limited partnerships, and regular C corporations before we cover S corporations and LLCs. Why? Proprietorships, partnerships, and corporations were on the scene long before the income tax, S corporations, and LLCs. Understanding the tax rules and concepts developed for these early forms of doing business makes understanding the taxation of S corporations and LLCs much easier.

SOLE PROPRIETORSHIP

Sole proprietors compute their net income by subtracting business expenses from business income. Then they add that net income or loss to any other family income, subtract itemized or standard deductions and exemption amounts to arrive at taxable income on the individual income tax form (Form 1040), and compute the tax. As noted in Chapter 1, this is the simplest form and the easiest with which to start a business. However, it may have some tax traps, which are discussed next.

Profits and Other Income

What if the spouse's income is high enough to put the family in the highest tax bracket (39.6 percent)? If the other spouse starts a sole proprietorship business, the profits from that business will be added to the existing income, so those profits will be taxed at 39.6 percent—from the first dollar to the last dollar of profits. To that, add the self-employment tax (Social Security and Medicare) of 15.3 percent, plus state income tax and various local taxes, and the prospective entrepreneur can wonder whether starting a business is worthwhile.

On the other hand, if the spouse has little or no other income, the new business can earn up to $54,000 before rising out of the 15 percent bracket. There would still be the 15.3 percent self-employment tax, but a total of 30.3 percent tax is better than the 54.9 percent incurred when the spouse already has a high income.

Would filing separate income tax returns, rather than jointly with a spouse, solve the problem of having to pay tax at a 39.6 percent rate on the business profits? Probably not, for deductions and exemptions have to be divided between the spouses depending on who paid for them, and other tax reductions, such as the child care credit, are not available unless a joint return is filed. Also, in the married filing separately tax rates, the higher brackets kick in at half the level of income at which they change in the married, joint-tax rate tables.

Losses, Limitations on Losses, and Loss Carryovers

If a sole proprietorship incurs a net loss, that loss is applied to other income on the owner's individual income tax return, thus reducing the total income tax of the individual or the married couple. However, there are some limitations on how much loss can be claimed.

At-Risk Limitations. You cannot deduct more than you have invested in the business or have at risk in the business. What's the difference between investment and money at risk? If you borrow money from the bank to start your sole proprietorship, The Seaside Cookie Factory, you will have to repay that loan, even if the cookies taste like seaweed and you can't sell any. You are at risk not only for your investment, but for the amount of the bank loan plus any other liabilities, such as amounts owed for the flour, chocolate chips, and imported seaweed. However, if your Uncle Charlie lends your business $60,000 and agrees that you would not have to repay unless the cookie factory was profitable, you will not be at risk for the $60,000.* If the business fails, you can claim a loss for your personal investment, but not for the $60,000 from Uncle Charlie. (However, Uncle Charlie should be able to claim a capital loss for the $60,000 he will never see again.) The numbers would look like Table 2.1.

Of course, in real life, you're unlikely to find a backer as benevolent as Uncle Charlie. Usually a sole proprietor is at risk for all the money he or she has invested as well as all the money the business has borrowed. That amounts to dubious advantage of a sole proprietorship: If the worst happens, the owner will have a large tax deduction (for the loss) to use in other years.

TABLE 2.1 Seaside Cookie Factory

Cash you invested in your business	$ 30,000
Borrowed from bank (with recourse)	40,000
Owed to suppliers	7,500
Subtotal	77,500
Loan (nonrecourse) from Uncle Charlie	60,000
Total investment in business	$137,000

Note: If the business fails, you can deduct $77,500 from other income, and Uncle Charlie may be able to deduct $60,000 as a capital loss.

*The technical term for Uncle Charlie's loan is *nonrecourse*. If the business can't pay him back, he has no recourse to your personal assets. On the other hand, if he can attach your yacht and sell it to pay off your debt, then the loan is *with recourse*.

Loss Carryovers. Another challenge: Your business generates a loss, but what good is that if you have no other income from which to deduct that loss? All is not lost. You can carry that loss back two years and forward 20 years, applying it to as much income as you had or will have in those years.* (If you do not have income in any of those 22 years, you have many problems, but income tax is not among them.)

The following example (Table 2.2) illustrates this carryback and carry-forward of loss concept.

Ethyl has a loss in her business (sole proprietorship) this year amounting to $270,000. Because she does not have any other income this year, she can carry that loss back to the second prior year (the line marked "–2"). She amends her tax return for the "–2" year. Originally, it showed income of $35,000 (column B), so she uses up $35,000 (column C) of the $270,000 loss to reduce the income in year –2 to zero. Her new income tax (column F) for that year is zero, so all of the original tax she paid ($4,400 in column E) will be cheerfully (?) refunded to her by the IRS.

She still has available loss of $235,000 to use in other years (the $270,000 loss minus the $35,000 used in year –2). In the same way, she applies $40,000 of the loss to the first previous (–1) year. Unlike real life, authors of books like this one can create crystal balls. So, we'll use ours to look ahead to Ethyl's tax returns for the next five years. Next year she will have taxable income of $50,000 and use the same amount of her loss from this year to reduce that taxable income to zero. Because she does that on her original tax return, she will not receive a refund, she will just pay no tax. That is, the loss carryover will result in a tax benefit of $6,400.

Ethyl continues this every year until all of that $270,000 loss is used up in future year 4. In that final year, the remaining loss does not wipe out her tax, but only reduces her taxable income to the point that it gives her a tax benefit of $6,500.†

If Ethyl had a larger loss this year, she could keep on wiping out future taxes through the future year 20. If she had another loss year before the original $270,000 loss was used up, she would add the new loss to what was left of the original and carry the total forward to offset future taxable income. The maximum carryforward period of the original $270,000 loss is still 20 years from the year the loss is incurred. The maximum carryforward period for the new loss would be 20 years from the date it is incurred. In other words, losses from separate years have to be kept in separate buckets so the 20-year period can be computed based on each loss year. (The earliest loss is applied first to future income years.)

Before leaving the subject of sole proprietorship, I should point out that using these business losses to offset other income is subject to *passive loss* rules. However, because passive losses seldom occur in a sole proprietorship, these rules are covered in the limited partnership section. (If a

*If your loss is related to casualty loss or a presidentially declared disaster, you may be eligible to carry back a loss for three years.

†The rules for applying loss carryovers on individual income tax returns are complex. In essence, however, you cannot deduct the personal exemption amounts and most itemized deductions in addition to the loss carryover. That is, you lose the benefits of exemptions and itemized deductions, but if the loss carryover is big enough, it's worth doing the complex calculations.

TABLE 2.2 Ethyl's Refunds and Tax Benefits Resulting from Net Operating Loss Carryback and Carryforward

A	B	C	D	E	F	G
YEAR	INCOME BEFORE APPLYING LOSS	LOSS CARRYOVER APPLIED	NEW TAXABLE INCOME	ORIGINAL TAX	NEW TAX	REFUND/ TAX BENEFIT
–2	$ 35,000	$ (35,000)	$ 0	$ 4,400	$ 0	$ 4,400
–1	40,000	(40,000)	0	5,800	0	5,800
This Year	(270,000)	0		0	0	0
1	50,000	(50,000)	0	8,600	0	8,600
2	55,000	(55,000)	0	10,000	0	10,000
3	60,000	(60,000)	0	11,400	0	11,400
4	75,000	(30,000)	45,000	15,700	9,200	6,500
Totals		$(270,000)		$55,900	$9,200	$46,700

sole proprietor has passive losses, these are likely to be in the area of poor investments in stocks, bonds, or real estate. Technically, investment activities are not part of a sole proprietorship business but are investment income and losses of the individual sole proprietor with one exception: a business of investing, such as a stockbroker or real estate professional.)

PARTNERSHIP (GENERAL PARTNERSHIP)

Including this as a choice is not really accurate. The change from a sole proprietorship to a partnership happens automatically if you sell or give part of your business to someone else, as explained in Chapter 1.

Profits—Who Pays the Tax?

A simple partnership is taxed much like a sole proprietorship. The net taxable income is split up among the individual partners and each of them reports his or her share of the income (or loss) on his or her individual income tax return (Form 1040). There is an added dimension in that the net income (or loss) of the partnership has to be split between the partners. That split should be specified in the partnership agreement, but if the partners have been so sloppy that there is no agreement, state law related to the division of profits would determine how profits are to be split. (Normally, the split would be in the same proportion as the partners' investments in the business.)

Besides splitting the profits, there is an item called *guaranteed payments* to partners. These are funds that are withdrawn by partners who perform work for the partnership, whereas investors share only in the profits that are left after the guaranteed payments. Usually, these guaranteed payments are substitutes for salaries and wages, because they are paid for work performed. However, unlike wages, they are not subject to withholding for income tax, nor does the partnership deduct social security tax from these payments. (Each partner is responsible for paying income tax and social security tax on any guaranteed payments received and on his or her share of the profits.)

Note that guaranteed payments can also be paid to inactive partners. In that case, the payments are in the nature of interest on the investment by the partner, although the partner reports them as his or her share of income from the partnership, not as interest income.

The mechanics of computing profits and losses and how they are shared among the partners works this way: The partnership files an income tax return (IRS Form 1065) on which it computes the *ordinary income or loss* of the partnership. It also computes some types of income that are not considered "ordinary" for a partnership, such as capital gains and losses, income from rental activities, and several other classes of income. Then it allocates these items on another IRS form (Schedule K-1).

Losses and Related Subjects

As with a sole proprietorship, losses can be applied to other income, or if there is no other income this year, they can be applied to the previous two years and forward to the next 20 years. Note that these losses are used on the individual income tax return of each partner (Form 1040), not on the tax return of the partnership (Form 1065). Also, partners cannot deduct losses that are more than the basis of their partnership interest (read on for an explanation of basis). The result is that the amount of tax saving resulting from a partnership loss will vary among the partners, depending on factors in each partner's individual tax return.

Basis. The at-risk rules, discussed under sole proprietorship, also apply to partnerships, and a related term creeps in here: *basis*. In most simple partnerships, basis is equivalent to investment. If you and Ralph start the Oily Coffee Company by each investing $50,000, your basis in your partnership interest is $50,000. However, it does not always remain $50,000. To explain, let's continue the example of the Oily Coffee Company partnership.

During the first year of business, the partnership earns $80,000. Your half is $40,000. If the partnership has the cash, and your partner, Ralph, agrees, you could take your $40,000 share out in cash. If Ralph does the same, the partnership has no cash on which to operate, so you each put $15,000 back into the partnership. Your investment, or basis, is now the total of your original investment of $50,000, plus your $40,000 share of the income, minus the withdrawal, or distribution, of $40,000, plus the additional investment of $15,000, or a total of $65,000. (In actual practice, you would probably not take a distribution of $40,000 and write a check to invest $15,000 back in the partnership. Instead, you would just take a net distribution of $25,000, leaving the other $15,000 in the business. The same basis would result.)

Schedule K-1 (Partner's Share of Income, Credits, Deductions, etc.) of Form

1065 (U.S. Partnership Return of Income), a copy of which is in Appendix D, would require a computation for the basis of your partnership interest as follows:

Basis at the beginning of the year	*$50,000*
Add net income for the year	*40,000*
Subtotal	*90,000*
Subtract distributions	*25,000*
Basis at the end of the year	*$65,000*

For a simple partnership based on the share-and-share-alike principle, this is fairly simple. However, in more complex partnerships it can become complicated and confusing. To illustrate:

Let's assume you and Ralph need expansion money and accept Teresa as a partner at the beginning of the second year. As you and Ralph have already built up some goodwill for the business, you require Teresa to invest $120,000, for which she will have only a one-third interest in profits and losses. Then, unfortunately, the partnership suffers a loss of $210,000 in the second year. Table 2.3 demonstrates the effect of the loss on partners' basis. The first five lines repeat what I laid out earlier. Then we add the effect of Teresa's investment and the effect of the $210,000 loss.

The result would appear to be that you and Ralph each have a basis of negative $5,000, and Teresa has a basis of positive $50,000. Because Teresa still has a positive basis, she can deduct her $70,000 share of the loss from other income. (If she does not have other income, she can carry it back or forward, as explained previously under sole proprietorship.) However, you and Ralph cannot deduct more than your basis before computation of the loss for the year, or $65,000, from other income or income of other years. Do you lose the tax benefit of this other $5,000 of loss you cannot deduct this year? Not necessarily. It can be carried forward and used in some year in which your basis turned positive. How could that happen? The partnership could earn a profit that was more than the partners withdrew, or you could make an additional investment in the partnership of $5,000.†*

Let's add another dimension to this. During the second year, the Oily Coffee Company partnership needs even more money to finance a big advertising campaign. It borrows $50,000 from the bank. As the partners are personally liable for the debts of the partnership, each partner's share of the bank loan is added to the person's basis, making the basis computation appear as in Table 2.4. Now, because each partner can add his or her share of the debt to his or her basis, your basis is positive and you can deduct your entire share of the loss ($70,000) from other income. (Note: This rule regarding bank debt as increasing basis applies to partnerships, but not to S corporations, as we shall see later.)

Nonrecourse Debt. This is a concept that arises only in the context of real estate investments, whether they are made by an individual, a part-

*Technically, the IRS does not permit a negative basis. However, the losses that cannot be used because the basis is zero can be held in suspension and used when there is basis in the partnership interest. That amounts to the same effect as a negative basis.

†This gives rise to a tax-planning maneuver that no partnership (or S corporation or LLC) should overlook. If you are an owner of a business that will generate a loss for this year, and you are planning to make an additional investment in the business soon, make it before the end of the year. That will raise your basis this year, so that you can deduct more of the loss on your individual income tax return.

TABLE 2.3 Computation of Basis, Oily Coffee Company Partnership

	TOTAL	YOU	RALPH	TERESA
Investment by original two partners	$100,000	$ 50,000	$50,000	
Net profit, first year	80,000	40,000	40,000	
Subtotal	180,000	90,000	90,000	
Subtract distributions	50,000	25,000	25,000	
Basis at end of first year (two partners)	130,000	65,000	65,000	
Additional investment by Teresa, first day of second year	120,000			$120,000
Basis first day of second year	250,000	65,000	65,000	120,000
Net loss, second year	(210,000)	(70,000)	(70,000)	(70,000)
Basis, end of second year	$ 40,000	$ (5,000)	$ (5,000)	$ 50,000

nership, or a limited liability company. The term *nonrecourse* means that the mortgage on the real estate is secured only by the property. If the owner(s) of the property default on the mortgage debt, the mortgagee (the bank, etc.) can seek its money only by foreclosure on the property. Even if sale of the property is not enough to pay off the debt, the mortgagee cannot collect the difference from the owners. Nevertheless, because none of the partners is individually liable for the debt, each of them can add his or her share of the debt to the basis of his or her partnership interest. Consequently, they can deduct more losses, if losses occur.

Mary, Nancy, Lucretia, and Oscar form a partnership called MNLO for the purpose of buying an apartment building for $1 million. They each invest $50,000 in MNLO for a total of $400,000 equity. Because their equity amounts to 40 percent, the bank agrees to lend MNLO the other $600,000 without recourse to Mary, Nancy, Lucretia, Oscar or the MNLO partnership. Although each member of the partnership is really at risk for only $50,000, each can add his or her share of the nonrecourse debt ($150,000) to that at-risk money in computing basis. That means that in the event of losses, each can deduct up to $200,000 of losses.

Why this exception to the at-risk limitation of deducting losses? The tax law is not always logical and the real estate lobby is strong.

LIMITED PARTNERSHIP

Limited partnerships are taxed in the same way as the general partnerships just discussed. That is, the profits and losses of the business are passed through to the individual partners, and each partner's share of those profits and losses appear on his or her income tax return. Because the limited partners are seeking to limit their liability, it is in limited partnerships that we most often find debts that are nonrecourse to the limited partners. That is, it is usually the general partner* who must pay the bank

*Every limited partnership must have at least one general partner.

TABLE 2.4 Computation of Basis, Oily Coffee Company Partnership after Bank Loan

	TOTAL	YOU	RALPH	TERESA
Investment by original two partners	$ 100,000	$ 50,000	$ 50,000	
Net profit, first year	80,000	40,000	40,000	
Subtotal	180,000	90,000	90,000	
Subtract distributions	50,000	25,000	25,000	
Basis at end of first year (two partners)	130,000	65,000	65,000	
Additional investment by Teresa, first day of second year	120,000			$120,000
Loan from bank	60,000	20,000	20,000	20,000
Basis before computation of loss for year	310,000	85,000	85,000	140,000
Net loss, second year	(210,000)	(70,000)	(70,000)	(70,000)
Basis, end of second year	$ 100,000	$ 15,000	$ 15,000	$ 70,000

or other creditors if the business fails, not the limited partners. Therefore, the limited partners are not at risk for these loans, so they cannot deduct losses that are larger than their basis in the partnership interest, exclusive of the nonrecourse debt.

Why these complicated rules? Until 1986, a large tax-shelter industry peddled limited partnership "investments" that would generate losses for the limited partners. Those people could then deduct their share of the partnership losses from their salaries or other income.

Why would anyone throw money into a losing business just to create a tax loss? That can be explained as follows:

The old rules allowed the partnership to borrow money to finance the business, with only the general partner being liable for the loan amount. Yet the limited partners could deduct the losses, even though they had not made major investments. That meant that for a small investment, a limited partner could deduct large losses, and those losses often resulted in tax savings that were far greater than the partner's investment. It was to prevent that maneuver that the rules about basis discussed previously were inserted into the income tax law. Now the limited partners cannot use their shares of the loans, for which only the general partner was at risk, to justify their deductions of losses.

However, Congress included this tidbit of tax shelter in the law: If no partner, including the general partner, was liable for the loan (beyond the amount of his or her investment), all partners could use their shares of the loan debt to increase their basis for the purpose of justifying their deductions of losses. Although unusual today, in the 1980s many banks were willing to make such nonrecourse loans, depending on the value of the real estate to ensure that the mortgage loan would be repaid.

There is one other requirement for this plan to be legal. The partnership had to be involved in the ownership of real estate as its major business. (The real estate lobby is effective.)

Passive Income and Losses

An additional tax factor for limited partners to consider is the nature of any profits or losses from the partnership. Generally, the tests about whether an item of income or loss is passive is applied to the individual, not to the passthrough entity from which he or she receives the income. However, because limited partners are restricted about how much they can participate in active management, the income and losses they receive are passive income and losses.

That can be an advantage or a disadvantage. If the partnership generates a loss, the limited partner will not be able to use that loss to reduce income unless he or she has other interests that generate passive income. (Passive losses may be applied to, and reduce the taxable income of, passive income.)

On the other hand, if the partnership generates passive income, the limited partner who has other interests that generate passive losses will be able to use those losses to offset the passive income from the partnership. If the limited partner has no other passive interests, he or she pays tax on that passive income, the same as on any income.

Passthrough of Income

In a simple business, a partnership is entirely a passthrough entity. That is, the partnership does not pay any income tax. Instead, the income is reported on the individual income tax forms of the partners. (Notice that the income shows up on the individuals' tax returns, regardless of payments of cash from the partnership to the stockholders.)

For example, Shirley, Tom, and Jennifer open a bowling ball cleaning business as a general partnership called the Brilliant Bowling Ball Company. Each of them invests $50,000 in the partnership for a one-third interest. During the first year, the business earns $90,000. Shirley, Tom, and Jennifer decide that cash distributions will be $10,000 to each of them. Even though they each received only $10,000, they each must report one-third of the earnings ($30,000 each) on their individual income tax returns.

One of the flaws of partnerships should be obvious from this example. If the partnership does not distribute some cash to the partners, those partners will be in the position of having to report taxable income from the partnership without receiving the cash with which they can pay the tax.

Suggestion: Put a clause in the partnership agreement that the partnership is required to distribute enough income to pay the tax.

If only partnership life were as simple as the affairs of Shirley, Tom, and Jennifer. If life were that simple, each partner would receive a one-line report from the partnership, stating his or her share of the income or loss that must be reported on his or her individual income tax return. However, this report to the partners actually takes up one-and-a-half pages. That's because most income items that do not arise in the basic operations of the business maintain their identity as they pass through to the stockholders. Why? Let's go back to our example.

Shirley earns $75,000 per year in her salaried job in advertising. She has invested in some rental real estate that generates a loss of $23,000 per year. As you may be aware, people who are not full-time real estate professionals cannot deduct more than $25,000 per year of real estate rental loss from their regular income. However, Shirley comes up with the idea that if the Brilliant Bowling Ball Company invests in some rental property, it could create a loss and pass that loss along to the partners. She supposes that if the partnership's rental property generates a loss of $21,000, Shirley can then deduct more than the $25,000 limitation allowed by the IRS. She can deduct the $23,000 loss from the property she owns directly, plus the $7,000 loss that is her share of the loss from the rental property the partnership owns.

Will this work for Shirley? Sorry, no, it won't! The tax law requires that the partnership identify real estate rental loss as a separate item in its report to the stockholders. Shirley would have to add the $7,000 rental loss from the partnership to her own $23,000 rental loss, making a total of a $30,000 loss. Then she could deduct only $25,000 from her regular income.

Among the more common passthroughs are:

- Income or loss from rental of real estate.
- Interest income.
- Dividend income.
- Royalties.
- Capital gains and losses.
- Charitable contributions made.
- Interest expense on investment debts.

The form on which a partnership reports these items to a partner is called a Schedule K-1 (Partner's Share of Income, Credits, Deductions, etc.). A copy of Schedule K-1 is in Appendix D. You might want to take a look at it now. Do not let it scare you unduly. Most partnerships do not have more than three or four of the items on the Schedules K-1 they prepare.

C CORPORATION

This is the plain, basic corporation covered in Chapter 1. As far as the IRS is concerned, it is the tax status you automatically have if you do nothing beyond applying for, and receiving, a corporate charter from one of the 50 states.

How the Corporation Is Taxed

A C corporation is taxed as a separate entity. A separate tax schedule applies to the taxable income, which is computed by deducting all allowable costs and expenses from income. In other words, there is little difference in determining net profit from a business whether it is a sole proprietorship, a partnership, or a corporation. The difference is in how it is taxed.

How the Owners (Stockholders) of a Corporation Are Taxed

Stockholders of small corporations, in which all the stock is owned by a family or a few families (*closely held* corporations) can take earnings out of the corporation in one of two ways:

1. *As salaries:* Stockholders who work for the corporation can be paid salaries and be treated just like any nonstockholder employee. The corporation withholds income tax and social security taxes from the paycheck and deducts the total salary and employment taxes in computing its taxable income. These stockholder-employees receive a Form W-2 at the end of the year, as do all employees, and should report the salaries received as income on their individual income tax returns (Form 1040). Note that the corporation deducts these salaries paid to stockholder-employees.
2. *As dividends:* Periodically, the board of directors of a corporation may declare that stockholders should receive a dividend, paid out of the profits that the corporation has earned, either currently or in prior years. (The owners of each share of stock who are employees would receive the same amount for each share of stock owned as do all the stockholders.) These dividends are taxable to the stockholders as dividend income, which is not subject to social security taxes and, usually, not subject to income tax withholding, but the stockholders receive a Form 1099-DIV indicating the amount of dividends they received, and they must report that amount as income and pay tax thereon.

   However, dividends are not deductible by the corporation, which leads us to the next subject.

Double Taxation

The biggest disadvantage of the C corporation is the double taxation of profits before they can show up in a stockholder's bank account. Dividends are not deductible in computing a corporation's taxable income, but instead come out of the after-tax profit. Then when they are received by stockholders, they must pay individual tax on that dividend income. Let's look at Mary's Marble Store, Incorporated, in Table 2.5.

Although Mary will have to pay individual income tax on her $60,000 salary, her salary is a deductible expense for the corporation. Similarly, she will have to pay individual income tax on the $50,000 dividend the corporation pays her, but notice that this dividend is not subtracted from income in computing the corporation taxable income and corporate income tax. In other words, the $50,000 dividend is still in the $85,000 corporate taxable income when the tax is computed, so the corporation pays income tax on it, and then, when Mary receives the dividend, she must also pay tax

TABLE 2.5 Mary's Marble Store, Incorporated (C Corporation): Computation of Taxable Income

Sales of marbles		$1,000,000
Minus cost of marbles sold		600,000
Gross profit		400,000
Subtract expenses:		
Advertising	$100,000	
Depreciation	15,000	
Insurance	15,000	
Rent, utilities, telephone	75,000	
Staff salaries	50,000	
Mary's salary	60,000	
Total expenses		315,000
Taxable income		85,000
Minus corporate income tax		10,000
Net income after income tax		75,000
Subtract dividend paid		50,000
Profits kept in business		$ 25,000

on that $50,000. As a worst-case scenario (when the corporation and Mary are both in the highest tax brackets), the corporation would pay tax of $19,000 on the $50,000 earmarked as a dividend and Mary would pay $12,276 on what was left, making a total of $31,276 tax on that $50,000 of earnings Mary worked so hard to make.

Could Mary avoid this double tax? Yes. When she realized during the year that there would be some money from which she could pay a dividend, she could have raised her salary or paid herself a bonus.

Caveat: Be careful in paying year-end bonuses to stockholders who are also employees. Because the IRS would stand to collect much more tax if a year-end bonus can be classified as a dividend, it will try to do just that. There is little that can ruin your day more than having an IRS agent tell you that you owe thousands more in tax because that year-end bonus is really a dividend.

Can you avoid this dismal possibility? This will usually work: At the *beginning* of the year, include in the minutes of a directors' meeting that you and other stockholder-employees are to receive a bonus in December based on the profitability of the company during the year.

In Mary's case (Table 2.5), she should have had a formal bonus plan in her minutes stating that the president of the company would receive a bonus of 59 percent of the pretax income of the corporation. That would have made the $50,000 payment to her deductible to the corporation and reduce corporate taxes by $4,750 to $5,250.

Passive Income

An advantage of the C corporation is that, generally, there are no rules limiting the deduction of passive income from ordinary income. However, this is of little benefit for the stockholders, as these losses cannot pass through to them. The losses are locked into and remain in the corporation, usable only to offset corporate income in this or other years. The same rules apply as apply to individuals—carryback two years and carry forward 20 years.

When a C Corporation Makes Sense

Why, with this negative aspect of double taxation in mind, would anyone set up a C corporation? Here are three good reasons why many entrepreneurs do just that.

1. If the manager(s) of the corporation want to keep most of the earnings in the corporation for expansion, the first $50,000 of corporate earnings is subject to a tax rate of only 15 percent, and the next $25,000 of profits is subject to 25 percent, both of which are lower than the 28 percent or higher bracket in which most small corporation owners probably find themselves. That is, if, to avoid the C corporation status, the owner(s) instead formed a sole proprietorship, partnership, S corporation, or limited liability company, that income would flow through to the owners, and they would pay the higher individual rate on those business earnings, even though they did not draw the earnings out of the business.
2. The stockholders want their personal liability limited, and alternative ways of providing that, such as limited partnerships, S corporations, and limited liability companies will not work for one reason or another.
3. There are fewer restrictions on fringe benefits for stockholder-employees. The stockholders of a C corporation can be covered by fringe benefit plans just as can all employees, whereas sole proprietors, partners, and S corporation stockholders are considered to be self-employed and, therefore, must set up benefit plans separately from employees. (Be aware, though, that there are fringe benefit limitations on highly compensated employees.)

   This makes little difference in pension and retirement plans, as the rules for corporate employees and self-employed individuals are almost identical. However, in the medical expense reimbursement area, there is still an advantage in being an employee of your C corporation, rather than of your S corporation. Employees of C corporations, even the employee who owns all the stock, can be covered by a medical plan that is a deduction from corporate income but not taxable to the employee.* However, an S corporation cannot deduct the medical

*There are some restrictions. The plan cannot discriminate in favor of highly compensated individuals, and the plan must not be top-heavy, which is determined by a formula comparing the benefits top managers receive to those received by other employees.

plan expense of an employee who owns more than 2 percent of the outstanding stock. The plan expense for that employee is added onto his W-2.

Is this fair? Congress has finally decided it might be inequitable. As recent changes to the law now stand, sole proprietors, partners, LLC members, and S corporation stockholders who own more than 2 percent of the outstanding stock can deduct some of their medical expense, and this is not an itemized deduction but an adjustment deducted in computing adjusted gross income. In other words, if you fit one of those business-owner categories, you could take the standard deductions and still deduct some of your medical expense. How much? You could deduct 60 percent of your medical expense in years 2000 and 2001, 70 percent in 2002, and 100 percent in 2003 and thereafter.*

PERSONAL SERVICE CORPORATIONS

Some of the information in the previous section will not apply to personal service corporations, particularly the comments about the lower C corporation rates on incomes up to $75,000. That's because this category of corporations is taxed at 35 percent on income, from the first dollar of income.

What is a personal service corporation? The federal tax law defines it as a corporation that engages in the performance of services in the fields of health, law, engineering, architecture, accounting, actuarial science, performing arts, or consulting. Also, the stock of the corporation is substantially held by employees, retired employees, or estates of former employees.

S CORPORATIONS

With exceptions, an S corporation is treated similarly to a partnership by the IRS rules. However, the exceptions and considerations peculiar to S corporations fill another chapter, so they are covered in Chapter 3.

LIMITED LIABILITY COMPANY (LLC)

Again, we have devoted an entire chapter to this business form (Chapter 6). Suffice it to say here that LLCs are usually taxed as general partnerships. However, LLCs are not partnerships, but a separate type of legal entity that computes and reports income just as does a partnership.

---

*Tax books used to suggest that a sole proprietor, a partner, an S corporation stockholder, or an LLC member hire his or her spouse as an employee, install a medical expense fringe benefit so the spouse would be covered by the plan and the business owner would be covered by the spouse's plan. So, the cost of medical insurance and other medical expenses would be deductible. The now-available deduction described here makes such maneuvering unnecessary.

The significant difference between LLCs and partnerships are (1) the liability aspect and (2) the fact that owners of LLCs are members, not partners, and that's particularly significant in the area of social security taxes levied on LLC members. That is covered in Chapter 6.

SUMMARY

One of the most confusing areas of business income tax is that of losses and how they may or may not be used to offset other income, so, here's a brief review. (*Owner*, as used here, refers to a sole proprietor, a partner, a member of an LLC, or an S corporation stockholder.)

Basis refers to the dollar amount of the business owner's interest in the business. It's normally computed as follows (for sole proprietorships, partnerships, and S corporations):

Amount originally invested in the ownership interest.

Add earnings of the business.

Subtract withdrawals of earnings (usually as cash).

Subtract losses of the business.

Add additional investments in the business (ownership interest or loans to the business).

Deduct reduction in owner's loans to the business.

Add amounts borrowed from banks or other unrelated parties by the business (not applicable to S corporations).

Subtract reduction of loans from banks and others (not applicable to S corporations).

Add or subtract other unusual items that may affect basis.

At-risk amount is the total of the liabilities of the business for which the owner is responsible. That is, the owner would have to pay off the liability if the business is unable to do so.

Nonrecourse debt consists of liabilities of the business for which the owner is not responsible (the opposite of at-risk amounts).

Passive income and losses generally refer to income and losses that a nonactive owner receives from a business. (The nonactive owner is an investor, rather than an active participant.)

Portfolio income and losses relate to stocks, bonds, and similar investments. This is a type of passive income and loss, but in parts of the tax code it is considered as a separate bucket of income and losses.

These attributes of income and loss attach to the owner of the business, not the business. For example, a partner in a real estate partnership who is not active would receive passive income or loss from it, whereas the partner who is actively running the partnership would receive ordinary income. Both partners receive their income out of the same cash box, but it has a different nature in each partner's hands.

Table 2.6 summarizes the taxation of the forms of enterprise covered in this chapter.

TABLE 2.6 Summary of Income Tax Rules for Types of Business Organization

	SOLE PROPRIETORSHIP	GENERAL AND LIMITED PARTNERSHIP	C CORPORATION	S CORPORATION	LIMITED LIABILITY COMPANY (LLC)
Entity that pays income tax on profits earned by the business	The owner pays, on his or her individual income tax return.	The partners pay, on their individual income tax returns.	The corporation pays. Stockholders pay income tax only on the dividends, if any.	Stockholders, like partners, pay income tax on their share of corporate income, with exceptions on which S corporation pays its own income tax.	Owners pay income tax on share of profits, just as do partners in partnership (assuming LLC elected to be taxed as a partnership).
Income items that maintain their identity if and as they flow through to owners	All income from business retains its type identity as it is passed through to the owner's income tax return.	Rental income and loss, most items of passive and portfolio (investment) income and loss, as well as expenses related to portfolio income. See Schedule K-1 in Appendix D for a more complete list.	No item of income retains its identity in dividend income to stockholders.	Rental income and loss, most items of passive and portfolio (investment) income and loss, as well as expenses related to portfolio income. See Schedule K-1 in Appendix D for a more complete list.	Same rules as for partnership (assuming LLC elected to be taxed as partnership).
Income subject to self-employment (social security) tax	Income from operations of the business.	Flow through of operating income is subject to self-employment tax on returns of active partners.	Salaries paid to stockholder-employees, but not dividends, are subject to social security tax.	Salaries paid to stockholder-employees, but not distributions, are subject to social security tax.	Same rules as for partnership (assuming LLC elected to be taxed as partnership).

3 WHEN TO BE AN S CORPORATION

There are several factors involved in the decision to be, or not to be, an S corporation, among them:

Do you need the protection from personal liability that a corporation may provide?

Will you be withdrawing most of the profits for your living expense, or will you be leaving most of the profits in the business to finance expansion?

Do you, or your spouse, have significant other income? Is that income from other employment or from investments?

Do you anticipate losses in the first year or two of operating your business?

Will others have an interest in your business as co-owners?

How these and other factors affect your choice of business organization is the subject of this chapter.

S CORPORATION TAXES, IN GENERAL

S corporations are in a tax posture with many similarities to partnerships. For the most part, an S corporation passes through the income to the stockholders, and the income retains its nature as it passes through. In other words, if the S corporation receives interest from an investment, the stockholders will report their share of the interest on their individual income tax returns as interest income. The partnership rules about basis, and at-risk amounts apply to S corporations, with exceptions. The most notable is the treatment of S corporation debt (as a bank loan) as the basis of a stockholder's investment. (It isn't. That, and other idiosyncrasies of

S corporation tax rules are covered as we pursue the good and the bad about S corporations.)

WHEN AN S CORPORATION MAY BE GOOD FOR YOU

Limited Liability

Have you ever met anyone who wants to pay a court-ordered judgment or an out-of-court settlement? Probably not. How can you avoid having to pay someone whom the court says you have damaged, or to whom you owe money? You could have someone else take the actions that might invite suit. Because it is hard to find an individual to be such a fall guy, the way to accomplish this transfer of responsibility is to set up a corporation to conduct your business. Then, if someone is hurt or otherwise damaged, or if business is bad and there is no money with which to pay bills, you can simply tell those people to sue the corporation, not you. If the corporation has no money, that's tough. The damaged individuals or creditors are out of luck.

Sound appealing? Of course. Because an S corporation, except for its income tax status, is like any other corporation, liability for its acts and debts does not extend to the stockholders. If someone sues your corporation for $10,000,000 and wins a judgment for that amount, they can attach the assets of your corporation, but they cannot get at your home, your Rolls Royce, or your $500,000 yacht.

That's the theory! In practice, plaintiffs sometimes are able to convince a court that personal actions by the stockholders/officers did the damage. Or the court discovers that the stockholders diverted corporate assets that should have gone to creditors. (The stockholders/officers have to give back those big bonuses that bought the cars and boats.) So, although setting up a corporation to act as a veil to protect you from damage awards is attractive, it is not foolproof. However, it is still well worth doing. Probably, more people have avoided personal bankruptcy by doing business as a corporation than have had their corporate veil pierced.

See Appendix B for more discussion of limited liability.

You Want to Pull Most of the Profit Out of the Business

If you need all the profit the business generates to support your family and sustain your hobbies, putting your business in an S corporation may be the way to go. If you need a large personal cash income, you will have to pay income tax on it in one way or another. Because the earnings of an S corporation pass through to the stockholder(s), you pay tax only once on those earnings if you elect that S status. Except for social security tax considerations, it matters little whether you take the profits out as dividend distributions or as salary.

Should you even consider a C corporation if you need all the profit in your pocket? In general, no. Those corporate profits would be taxed twice on their way to you—once as corporate profit and again as a dividend paid to you. You can avoid the double tax by taking profits out as salary and bonuses, but an IRS auditor can modify your plans, reclassifying some salary as a dividend. (See Chapter 2 for an explanation of this double tax and reclassification danger.)

There Are Only a Few Owners of the Business

If there are only a few owners (stockholders) and they are in agreement as to the goals of the business, the S corporation will work well. Such an agreement does need to be carefully thought out and written down at the same time the corporation is formed. Although one-size-fits-all stockholder agreements are available, make sure the one you choose is adapted to your needs. After all, stockholders are individuals, and individual needs vary, so make sure your needs are met in the agreement. On what do the stockholders need to agree? They need to assent to:

- How much of the profits of the business the stockholders will draw out in the form of cash distributions, as either a percentage or dollar amount.
- Keeping the S status for the corporation and doing all things necessary to prevent the IRS from disqualifying it as an S corporation. (See Chapters 4 and 5 about how an S corporation may lose its S status.)
- No stockholder's stock will be transferred to another individual without the consent of the other stockholders. This prevents admission of an ineligible stockholder or one who is not in agreement with the other stockholders about the goals of the business and how much of the profits will be distributed to the stockholders.
- Who will be president and have full authority as to the day-to-day operation of the business. Management by committee is a sure way to failure.

For a more complete list of what may need to be covered in a stockholders' agreement, see the example in the Appendix.

The Stockholders Have No Other Significant Income. If the stockholders have no other income, their relatively low personal 15 percent and 28 percent tax brackets are available to apply to the corporate profits as they flow to the stockholders. However, if the lower brackets have already been used (the stockholders have other income), a C corporation may be preferable. (See the discussion later in this chapter of when an S corporation may be bad for you.)

You'd Like to Pay Less Social Security Tax

Stockholders in an S corporation can withdraw earnings in one of two ways:

1. As salary, which is subject to payroll taxes, including social security tax.
2. As distributions (similar to a dividend), which are not subject to social security or other payroll taxes.

Obviously, the tax-saving procedure would seem to be to take distributions and no salary from the corporation. However, there are a couple of reasons not to do this.

The Pay-No-Salary Trap. This is best explained by example:

Let's say you want to start a company to manufacture e-mail whiteout. You set up an S corporation called Screen White, Inc. and invest $100,000 by buying 100,000 shares at one dollar each. However, the machinery you need costs $200,000 and your banker is dubious about your business plan. But Aunt Gertrude isn't. She thinks the product is a marvelous idea, so she invests $100,000 by also buying 100,000 shares at one dollar each. Operations begin: You slave away, seven days a week, squeezing white-out berry juice into little bottles. Because you wish to avoid the social security tax bite, you agree that you will be paid no salary. Aunt Gertrude stays home and watches soap operas.

At the end of the year, your accountant tells you that your corporation has net earnings of $60,000, which is available in cash from the bank account. The tax law requires that all stockholders be paid distributions pro rata their stockholdings. As you and Aunt Gertrude own an equal number of shares, you each receive $30,000 in distributions. You received a piddling amount for working as hard as you did, but Aunt Gertrude received a generous 30 percent return on her investment.

Lesson: Only by salaries can you compensate those stockholders who put more effort into the business.

The IRS Position. The tax law states that earnings from employment, whether you are employed by yourself or someone else, are subject to social security taxes (as well as lesser taxes such as unemployment insurance). So, if you are a stockholder in an S corporation, and you also work for the corporation, you should receive a salary for your efforts. Of course, you are also due some distributions as a stockholder, not for services but as a return on your investment, taking into consideration the initial risk of funding the company, and so on. The unresolved question about nearly every S corporation is how much there should be of each way of withdrawing funds. There is no clear answer, but there is some history that may help you decide, and that is covered in the details in Chapter 5.

The Business Will Be Conducted in Several States

As compared to partnerships and limited liability companies, registering to do business in other states is easier for a corporation and may be less expensive. Remember that the state authorities that oversee corporate registration have no interest in the IRS designation of C or S corporation, so there is no additional registration hassle because a corporation has elected S status. (Do not confuse this with the question of whether the state *tax* department recognizes S status.)

Personal Service Corporations

As mentioned under C corporations in Chapter 2, those corporations that render professional services cannot use the lower 15 and 25 percent rates on the first $75,000 of C corporation income. Without that advantage, an S corporation can look even more advantageous to a personal service corporation. For a definition of this category of corporations, see Chapter 2.

WHEN AN S CORPORATION MAY BE BAD FOR YOU

You Need to Keep Most of the Profits in the Business

If the stockholders have other income that puts them into the 39.6 percent income tax bracket, that is higher than the corporate tax rates. In other words, why elect S status and pay 39.6 percent on the profits that you are going to leave in the corporation, when the top corporation tax rate is 39 percent and, at most income levels, it is less, even as low as 15 percent (on the first $50,000). When I use the term "leave profits in the business," I am referring to the profits that are invested in buildings, machinery, and other assets that are long-term investments and for which you use cash that likely will never be distributed to the stockholders. If the profits kept in the corporation are temporary and are going to be distributed as dividends in the next year or two, then double taxation will be present. In that case, an S corporation would be preferable.

The Stockholders Do Not Fit the Requirements of the Tax Code

The Internal Revenue Code specifically limits the number of stockholders that may own an S corporation to 75. Although a husband and wife who own stock jointly are considered as one stockholder, partnerships are barred from being stockholders, so you can't circumvent the law with partnerships as owners.

However, the IRS has ruled that you can do the reverse. Several S corporations can form a partnership to conduct a business. It would work like this:

Two hundred ten people want to start the Punctured Balloon Company to manufacture hot air balloons. They would like to conduct the business as an S corporation, because they each want their liability limited to the amount of their investment, yet they want to avoid the double taxation of a C corporation. The solution: They split into three groups of 70 people each, and each group forms an S corporation. The three corporations, known as X Corporation, Y Corporation, and Z Corporation, file forms with the IRS to elect S status. Then the three corporations join together as a three-member partnership, called the Punctured Balloon Company, which is the entity that will actually manufacture the balloons.

If the partnership earns a profit of $180,000, it files a partnership tax return that reports the three partners (X, Y, and Z corporations) as each having taxable income of $60,000. Then each of the three partner-corporations files an S corporation tax return that reports that each of its 70 stockholders share the $60,000 income. That is, each S corporation stockholder reports income of $60,000 divided by 70 stockholders, or $857.

True, this makes the enterprise's accountants happy, as there are more tax returns to file and, therefore, higher accounting fees. However, those fees could be worth the price if substantial income tax is saved.

Until 1994, the IRS would have reclassified this set-up as one corporation and disallowed the S status, but in Revenue Ruling 94-43, the tax folk reversed their posture and decided to allow this method of circumventing the number-of-shareholders limit for S corporations.

(Before you rush out and create this pyramid, read Chapter 6 on limited liability companies. That form may better suit your needs.)

Besides partnerships, the law does not allow corporations, nonresident aliens, and many trusts to be stockholders. The principal trusts that can be stockholders are called QSSTs (Qualified Subchapter S Trusts). The essence of the rules that qualify a trust to be a QSST is that there be one beneficiary and that that beneficiary be considered the owner and report all the income from the S corporation as his or her own. Other trusts that may qualify are a trust set up by will for a limited time commencing at death, voting trusts (each beneficiary is considered an S corporation owner), and some other special cases of trusts. Stock held for a child under the Uniform Gifts to Minors Act might be considered a type of trust, but ownership for a child in that manner is acceptable to IRS. (The child is considered the stockholder.) In all cases of trusts, the beneficiaries must be individuals who qualify as S corporation stockholders. (For example, a beneficiary cannot be a nonresident alien.) In any event, the rules regarding trusts as S corporation stockholders are complicated. You should seek professional advice before allowing a trust to own shares in your S corporation.

There Is a Dissident Stockholder

If a stockholder who owns 50 percent or more of an S corporation's outstanding stock decides he or she no longer wants the S status for the corporation, he or she may terminate the S election (by notifying IRS) without the consent of the other stockholders. Consider this scenario.

Alvin, Betty, and Chris (a brother and two sisters) started the Beefy Bagel Corporation several years ago with each of them owning 300 of the 900 shares of common stock issued. They elected S corporation status. Three years ago, Alvin died, leaving his stock to his daughter, Alice. Last year, Betty (who had never married) died, leaving her stock to her niece, Alice. Now Alice owns 600 of the 900 shares of stock issued and outstanding.

The Beefy Bagel Corporation operates one bagel store that barely generated a living for the three siblings who were the original owners. As they never entertained serious thoughts of expansion, they made the corporation distribute most of the earnings to the stockholders. The S corporation election made sense, because it avoided the double taxation.

Now, after Alvin and Betty died, Alice owns 600 shares and Chris owns her original 300 shares. Chris still needs most of her share of the profits on which to live, although she is no longer active in the business, leaving the management to a hired manager. However, Alice is a successful lawyer with an income that puts her into the 39.6 percent bracket. Should the Beefy Bagel Corporation continue as an S corporation? Alice would rather that the corporation keep the profits and pay the lower C corporation tax rates. As Alice owns more than 50 percent of the stock, she can cancel the S corporation election without Chris' approval. Although this benefits Alice, it is indeed detrimental to Chris. Not only will Alice make the corporation drastically cut its dividend distributions, but any dividends paid will be subject to double taxation.

Moral: When you set up a corporation, particularly an S corporation, with more than one stockholder, look down the road. What will happen to ownership of the stock when an original stockholder dies or gives away his or her stock? Who will end up controlling the corporation? What sort of old-age income will surviving stockholders have? The solution lies in a carefully thought-out and drawn stockholder agreement. For instance, in the bagel example, a stockholder agreement could have provided that Alvin's and Betty's stock be offered for sale to the remaining stockholders before the estate could pass it on to an heir. The agreement should also contain a formula for setting the price at which the surviving stockholders could purchase the stock. Where do they get the money to purchase it? From the insurance they have held on each other. (The same thing can also be accomplished by having the corporation have the right to buy back the stock and be the beneficiary of the insurance policies.)

There Is a Need for Different Classes of Stock

For various reasons, you and your "partners" may want to share differently in the profits of the business. When the business is incorporated, this is accomplished by making the corporation issue two classes of stock. For instance:

Rudy has no money but lots of cooking experience. He wants to start Rudy's Rustic Restaurant. Margaret, his cousin, has lots of money on which she would like to earn a high return. She is willing to take some risk in order to earn that return, but she has no interest in cooking or managing the restaurant. In order to encourage Margaret to invest, Rudy tells her that after a modest salary for him, she will get first crack at her share of the profits. Specifically, if she invests $100,000, she will get $10,000 (10 percent of her investment) of dividends before Rudy receives any dividends. In corporate jargon, Margaret's stock will be preferred stock. That is, her stock will have preference when it comes to dividend declaration time. Rudy's stock will be common stock. Dividends are paid on common stock only if there is enough left in the profit kitty after the preferred stockholders have been paid.

This amounts to two classes of stock: common and preferred. If Rudy and Margaret attempt to obtain or to keep S corporation status for the restaurant, they will be turned down or lose the S status. The reason: S corporations may not issue two classes of stock.

The solution for Rudy and Margaret seems pretty simple. Do not issue two classes of stock if you are or want to be an S corporation. However, not all situations are that simple. The saga of Rudy and Margaret continues:

To avoid being denied the S status, Margaret does not receive stock from Rudy's Rustic Restaurant, Incorporated. Instead, she receives a promissory note from the corporation for her $100,000. The note specifies that Margaret will be paid $10,000 interest every year, provided there are profits from which it can be paid. If there are no profits, she does not receive her $10,000. Because Rudy can now tell IRS that there is only one class of stock, the corporation receives the IRS blessing of S status.

At the end of the first year of business, there are no profits, so Margaret receives no interest payment. At the end of the second year, there is a $75,000 profit. Margaret receives her $10,000 and Rudy takes a distribution of $50,000, leaving $15,000 in the business. As it is an S corporation, the corporation pays no income tax. Margaret pays income tax on her $10,000 interest income and Rudy pays income tax on the $65,000 S corporation profit that is passed through to his personal income tax return.

Then along comes the IRS auditor. His decision: Margaret does not have a valid note from the corporation. She, in effect, has been issued a second class of stock. If she had really made a loan, she would be due the interest every year, regardless of the profits of the business. The IRS auditor follows up with this computation:

The second class of stock disqualifies the S status election. Therefore, the corporation (now a C corporation) must pay corporate tax on the $75,000 profit, and Rudy and Margaret must pay individual tax on their respective distributions of $50,000 and $10,000. In other words, the IRS auditor's change has cost Rudy an additional $13,750 of corporation income tax!

Will the IRS finding stick if it is appealed to the courts? The history of court cases tells us that the courts are almost certain to back the IRS in a situation such as Rudy and Margaret set up.

The same reclassification problem can arise if the lender is also a stockholder in the corporation. In the Rudy and Margaret example, the result would be the same if Margaret also owned some of the stock of Rudy's Rustic Restaurant.

Moral: Make sure that in attempting to circumvent the no-second-class-of-stock rule you do not set up an arrangement that the IRS will consider to actually be a second class of stock (under another name).

Straight Debt. Does this mean that an S corporation cannot borrow except from a bank? Not since Congress passed a safe-harbor provision directing the IRS to accept a straight debt instrument as legitimate debt and not try to reclassify it as stock. The definition of this straight debt is as follows:

The debt instrument must be a written promise to pay a specific amount on a certain day.

The interest rate and payment of it is not contingent on profits of the corporation.

The debt is not convertible into stock.

The creditor would otherwise be eligible to be a stockholder.

This still leaves the door open for this sort of income shifting within a family:

Fanny operates an S corporation that generates a profit of $60,000 a year. Because of her husband's income, she is in the 39.6 percent tax bracket. Her 15-year-old son, Charlie, is still in school and works only occasionally, so he is in the 15 percent tax bracket.

Fanny could divert some of the income from the S corporation to Charlie by giving him some of the stock in her corporation. However, in order for the income attributable to Charlie's stock to be taxed to him and not to Fanny, the gift would have to be irrevocable. Because she does not know in what direction Charlie's future life may go, Fanny does not want to make a permanent gift of the stock to him when he is only 15.

Instead, she and her husband make a gift to him of $20,000, which is some of the money he will need for college. Charlie then lends the corporation $20,000 (with repayment due on a specific date), and the corporation pays him $2,000 per year interest.

The $2,000 per year interest is an expense to the corporation, reducing the income that flows through to Fanny by $2,000. The $2,000 is, of course, income to Charlie.

The result is a transfer of income from Fannie, who, with her husband, would pay $792 tax on it, to Charlie, who pays only $300 tax. That equates to a family tax saving of $492.

Voting Rights. You may have wondered, as we talked about 15-year-old Charlie, how he would vote as a stockholder? Interestingly, although the law is stringent in denying two classes of stock to an S corporation, it does not consider that lack of voting rights for certain stock creates a second class of stock. In other words, if Fannie did decide she wanted to give stock to Charlie, she could have the S corporation issue her nonvoting stock, in exchange for some of her voting stock, and give that nonvoting stock to Charlie. That would not cause a termination of the S status.

You Expect Initial Losses and, Therefore, Need All Basis Possible

S Corporation Debt as Basis. This is an area in which many unsuspecting S corporation stockholders get caught, unable to use losses from the corporation to offset other income. There is little difference in having a loss you can't use and throwing green currency in the river, so read on carefully.

If a partnership borrows money, as from a bank, that loan becomes part of the partners' at-risk basis. The cap on losses that the partners can apply to offset other individual income is the total of each partner's basis before the loan was made plus his or her share of the loan. The logic here is that the partners are all responsible for the loan, so they are at risk for the amount of the loan. (This assumes a general partnership, no limited partners.) As covered in Chapter 2, each general partner is liable for the full amount of partnership debts, not just his or her share. However, the IRS insists that the total of the debts be prorated among the partners for the purpose of computing the at-risk limitation on loss deductions from other income.

Stockholder Guarantees as Loans

In the case of an S corporation, loans made by others (as banks) to the corporation, even though they are also guaranteed by the stockholders, cannot be added to the at-risk basis ceiling on loss deductions. Is there logic to this rule that even though a stockholder might have to pay off a loan to the corporation with personal funds, he or she is not at risk? I don't see any, but the IRS has interpreted the law that way, and the courts have sided with the IRS on this issue.

Perhaps this story about Louise and Lem will help to clarify this situation:

Louise and Lem start the Luggable Luggage Company as a two-partner general partnership. Although they both have substantial other income and assets, they have little cash. Their cash investment in the luggage company is $5,000 each. To have enough cash to start the business, the partnership applies to the bank for a $100,000 loan. As general partners, Louise and Lem are liable for the debts of the partnership, they effectively guarantee the partnership debt to the bank. For that reason, the bank makes the loan to the partnership.

The basis of each of the partners, for purposes of a cap on losses, is $55,000 ($5,000 initial investment plus one-half of the bank loan). During the first year, the luggage operation loses $80,000. Louise and Lem can each deduct $40,000 from their other income. (This assumes they are both active in the luggage business. If either of them is simply a passive investor in the partnership interest, the passive loss rules come into play.)

Change the scene. Louise and Lem start the Luggable Luggage Company, but they form an S corporation to operate the business. Again, they each invest $5,000 cash and borrow a total of $100,000 from the bank. Because they are now stockholders, with limited liability, the bank insists that they each sign a personal guarantee of the corporation's debt to the bank, so that they must pay off the loan if the corporation is unable to make payment. It looks so similar to the partnership arrangement above, you would think the result would be the same limitation on loss deductions ($55,000), but that is not the case. Louise and Lem each have a basis of $5,000 in their stock. When the corporation loses $80,000, they can each deduct only $5,000 of that loss from other income. (They can carry that loss to future years and use it when they may have a larger basis, but a deduction now is far better than one sometime down the road.)

While you are contemplating these rules about the basis in your S corporation stock, you should be aware that loans *you* (*not the bank*) make to your corporation also have a basis, and that increases the amount of the basis ceiling on deducting losses. Initially, that basis is the amount of the loan, but like the basis in stock, loan basis can be reduced by corporation losses that you deduct on your income tax return.

The mechanics work this way: Once your share of the losses has been as much as the basis in your stock, the losses are applied toward reducing the basis in the loan. When losses have also wiped out that basis, you can deduct no more losses from the S corporation. The following example illustrates that how you handle loans to your corporation can affect how much loss you can deduct on your tax return.

Change the scene again. Everything is the same (S corporation, and so on) until Louise and Lem get to the bank. Instead of causing the S corporation to borrow $100,000, they each individually borrow $50,000 and then make individual loans of $50,000 to the corporation. What's their basis now? For each of them, it consists of the $5,000 original investment plus the $50,000 loan he or she made to the corporation. Now they can each deduct the full $40,000 share of the loss from other income.

Make sense? No. But it's the law, and tax law need not be logical.

Moral: Never have your S corporation borrow directly from a bank, institution, or other party. The stockholders should individually borrow the money and then, in turn, lend it to the corporation.

You Already Have a C Corporation with Losses to Carry Forward

If your C corporation has generated more loss than income, you probably have a net operating loss that can be applied to income in future years, thereby reducing or eliminating corporate tax on that income. If you keep the cash generated by that income in the business, you will effectively pay no income tax on that income.

However, if you elect S status, that prior loss is locked away, unavailable to your corporation or to you. Then, if you earn a profit, that profit will show up on your individual income tax return and you will pay individual income tax on that profit.

For example, look at Cynthia's Cinnamon Corporation:

Cynthia has operated her business as a C corporation for five years, generating a loss of $10,000 each year. She has accumulated a total loss of $50,000 that she can carry forward to future years.

This year she generates a profit of $30,000. If she continues as a C corporation, she can apply $30,000 of the $50,000 carryover loss to this year, reducing the taxable profit to zero, so the corporation pays no income tax. Unless she makes the corporation pay a dividend to her, she will pay no individual income tax on that $30,000 profit.

However, if she elected S corporation status for Cynthia's Cinnamon Corporation at the beginning of this year, her tax picture would look like this: The corporation would pay no income tax, because it is now an S corporation. However, that $30,000 profit would flow through to Cynthia, and she would have the privilege of paying individual income tax on it. If she were in the 28 percent tax bracket, that would cost her $8,400. An S corporation election at this time obviously would be bad for Cynthia.

You Convert from C Status to S Status and the Corporation Owns Appreciated Assets

If you are starting a new corporation and immediately electing S status, you can skip this section. However, if your C corporation has assets that have appreciated, and you maintain the C status, your corporation will have to pay capital gains tax on the gain when you sell those assets. If you now elect S status and sell those assets or transfer them to a stockholder(s) as a distribution, you still have to pay capital gains tax at 35 percent. For highly profitable corporations, this would not be a hindrance to changing to S status. However, if profits are under $75,000 and you expect to be selling or distributing appreciated assets next year, work out the numbers before you decide on an S election for next year.

This confusing area, called *built-in gains*, is explained further, with examples, in Chapter 5.

Loss of Some Fringe Benefits

At one time, there was a great disparity between various forms of business organizations with regard to retirement plans and other fringe benefits. A book such as this might have devoted a separate chapter to the subject. Allthough this area is still vast and whole books have been written about it, the disparity in fringe benefits between different forms of business have all but disappeared. However, a couple of comments are still pertinent.

Pension Plans. The rules for stockholders (those who own more than 2 percent of the outstanding stock) of S corporations are identical to the rules for partners. That is, they are treated as if they are self-employed for pension plan purposes. Pension plan contributions for employees who are not stockholders (or own less than 2 percent of the outstanding stock), if the plan is approved by IRS, are a deductible corporate expense. The contributions for stockholders' retirement plans (IRAs or Keogh plans) have to be deducted on their individual tax returns, not by the corporation.

Medical Expense Plans. For fringe benefit purposes, any stockholder who owns more than 2 percent of the outstanding stock of an S corporation is treated almost identically to a partner in a partnership. That means that while the corporation can pay for medical insurance of the stockholder-employee, and the corporation may deduct the expense, it must add the cost of the medical insurance onto the compensation on the stockholder-employee's W-2 form. Although the stockholder-employee may be able to deduct some of the insurance and other medical expenses as an itemized deduction, that is never as advantageous as receiving medical benefits that are not taxed from an employer.

That's a disadvantage of an S corporation compared to a C corporation. A stockholder in a C corporation, who is also an employee, can receive tax-free medical benefits, just as any employee can (provided the plan does not discriminate in favor of stockholder-employees or other highly paid individuals). However, it would be unusual for medical benefits to be significant enough to justify selecting a C corporation status instead of an S status when other factors indicate an S corporation is a better choice.

However, this disadvantage of an S corporation is about to disappear. In 2000, the stockholder-employee can deduct 60 percent of the medical insurance expense, and this percentage rises to 100 percent in 2003 and thereafter.

Watch this: There are situations in which an S corporation stockholder cannot deduct the cost of medical insurance:

- The deduction cannot be greater than the self-employment earnings of the stockholder, and self-employment earnings of an S corporation stockholder are defined as the salary that the stockholder receives from the corporation. So, if you take no salary from your S corporation, you cannot deduct the cost of medical insurance as a business expense.*
- For any month in which an S corporation stockholder or spouse is covered by the medical plan of another employer (i.e., day job) he or she cannot deduct the medical insurance furnished by his or her S corporation. However, conventional medical insurance and long-term care insurance are viewed as separate plans. Assume you are an S corporation stockholder and your day job employer offers conventional medical insurance, you could purchase long-term care insurance, or your S corporation could purchase it for you, and the cost of that insurance would be a medical insurance deduction as already discussed.

Need for Careful Attention to Details

Maintaining your status as an S corporation requires that at least one of the officers be a stickler for details. For the state, minutes of stockholders' and directors' meetings must be maintained. Although that is true of both C and S corporations, there are additional record-keeping requirements for S corporations, such as the nature of any new stockholders (do they qualify for S stock ownership), documentation of loans (make sure they are not disguised stock), and keeping track of the basis of stock for those stockholders who may fail to do it themselves. If the group of managing officers does not include such a detail person, you need an accountant whom you pay to do more than just prepare the annual corporate income tax return.

STATE INCOME TAXES

The tax laws vary from state to state. Some states recognize the federal S corporation status and treat S corporations the same way for state income

*The stockholder deducts it on the front of his or her personal tax form (Form 1040) as a negative adjustment to total income to arrive at adjusted gross income. That is better than an itemized medical deduction, because there is no reduction for 7.5 percent of adjusted gross income as there is on Schedule A, Itemized Deductions.

tax purposes. That is, they treat the S corporation generally as a passthrough entity and expect to see the S corporation income on the stockholders' individual income tax returns.

Other states do not recognize the S status. In those states, S corporations are taxed as if they were C corporations. The corporation must file an income tax return and pay state income tax, just as would a C corporation. At least, for federal tax purposes, the state corporate income tax is a deduction in computing the S corporation income that is passed along to stockholders.

In some states, if any of the S corporation stockholders are nonresidents of that state, the corporation must withhold state tax from distributions that it pays to those stockholders.

Like the Congress, state legislatures are constantly tinkering with the tax code. You can find out how your state treats S corporations by calling your state tax department, revenue service, or whatever it is called. I have not attempted to cover the tax rules of individual states here, because it is doubtful that the state tax situation would influence the choice of business entity, although it could. The best bet is to obtain your current state rules and work out the numbers as to the effect they would have if you elect S status.

SUMMARY AND EXAMPLES

Four examples can summarize the main points of this chapter. The first two examples consider businesses with moderate income, and the last two cover businesses with higher income. For each, we'll compare their choices, and the tax implications of those choices, as to how he or she should organize the business. In these four examples, I have assumed the individuals are married, have two children, file joint returns with their spouses, and take the standard deduction.* I have included sole proprietorship as an alternative, for its simplicity does have appeal. However, remember the unlimited liability involved.

The four examples are as follows, each one displayed in a table as follows:

Table 3.1: Fred expects to earn $50,000 operating Fred's Frankfurter Emporium next year. Although his wife earns $40,000 per year in her salaried job, Fred finds that he will have to take that $50,000 home to help support their family.† *As the table indicates, Fred would have the least tax burden if he elected S status for his corporation and paid himself all the profits as dividend distributions.*

---

*Admittedly, most higher income taxpayers will have enough deductible expenses to qualify for itemizing their deductions, but using the same standard deduction in all of these examples isolates the effect of the choice of business form.

†In this and the following three examples, we'll assume that all of the profit results in cash in the bank and can be taken home. Generally, this is not so, but let's not complicate the examples. However, the computations did consider that after paying corporate income tax, there would be less cash for Fred to take home.

TABLE 3.1 Fred's Frankfurter Emporium
$50,000 Profit before Income Tax—$40,000 Other Income
(Fred Draws All Profit Out of Business)

FORM OF BUSINESS	TOTAL SOCIAL SECURITY TAXES[a]	CORPORATE INCOME TAX	INDIVIDUAL INCOME TAX	TOTAL TAXES
Sole proprietorship	$7,065	0	13,197	$20,262
C corporation, pay out all profit as dividends	$ 0	7,500	12,086	$19,586
C corporation, pay out all profit as salary	$7,065	0	13,197	$20,262
C corporation, pay out profit 50% as salary, 50% as distributions	$3,532	3,750	12,641	$19,924
S corporation, pay out all profit as dividends	$ 0	0	14,186	$14,186
S corporation, pay out all profit as salary	$7,065	0	13,197	$20,262
S corporation, pay out profit 50% as salary, 50% as dividends	$3,532	0	13,691	$17,224

[a]In this and the following three tables, the social security tax figure is computed for the owner of the business. It does not include any social security tax that a spouse may pay on other employment.

However, the IRS and the Social Security Administration take a dim view of this procedure, because most of the tax saving is in avoiding the social security tax. If Fred goes to the other extreme and takes all the profit out of his S corporation as salary, he pays about the same total tax as he would as a sole proprietor or as a C corporation paying out all profit as salary.

Let's assume he would satisfy the IRS if he took out half of his profit as salary and half as dividend distributions. That saves him about $2,000 in social security tax.

Table 3.2: Bertha owns and runs Bertha's Boot Store. As her husband earns other income, she leaves her profits in the business, so she can increase her inventory and open additional stores. From the table, she is better off to be a C corporation. Her tax bill is about $4,700 less than it would be if her business were an S corporation, and she saves over $10,000 compared to operation as a sole proprietor. (This proves my point, at the beginning of Chapter 2, that an S corporation is not the cure-all for all tax problems.)

The reason she is better off as a C corporation is that she takes advantage of the 15 percent corporate rate on the first $50,000 of profit. Also, she incurs no social security tax on her own salary, because she takes no salary.

Table 3.3: Bill operates Bill's Boats dealership. As his tastes run to expensive automobiles and other luxuries, he takes the $500,000 annual profit out of the business, with which he maintains a large home, family, and a warehouse full of Porsches and Aston Martins. Like Fred and almost anyone who needs to draw most of the profit out of the business, taking it all as dividend distributions from an S corporation creates the least tax burden. Again, the IRS and the Social Security Administration won't like that procedure, so Bill should take some of the profit as salary. (Note that if he takes

TABLE 3.2 Bertha's Boot Store
$50,000 Profit before Income Tax—$40,000 Other Income
(Bertha Leaves All Profit in Business for Growth)

FORM OF BUSINESS	TOTAL SOCIAL SECURITY TAXES	CORPORATE INCOME TAX	INDIVIDUAL INCOME TAX	TOTAL TAXES
Sole proprietorship	$7,065	0	13,197	$20,262
C corporation. All profit retained in business	$ 0	7,500	3,218	$10,718
S corporation. All profit retained in business	$ 0	0	14,186	$14,186

half as salary and the rest as dividends, he increases the tax bite, compared to all dividends, by $5,500.)

Table 3.4: Sophia owns and runs the Soft Sofa Company. As her spouse holds down a job that generates $100,000 per year, she leaves all of the $500,000 annual profit in the business for the purchase of additional automated equipment.

Unlike Bertha, her best choice is the S corporation. At the $600,000 income level, the structure of income tax brackets is such that there is less tax paid as an individual than as a corporation.

Moral: There is no such thing as a general rule that any one form of business will always result in less tax. The scene varies with income level.

TABLE 3.3 Bill's Boats
$500,000 Profit before Income Tax—$100,000 Other Income
(Bill Draws All Profit Out of Business)

FORM OF BUSINESS	TOTAL SOCIAL SECURITY TAXES	CORPORATE INCOME TAX	INDIVIDUAL INCOME TAX	TOTAL TAXES
Sole proprietorship	$22,393	0	158,889	$181,282
C corporation, pay out all profit as dividends	$ 0	170,000	96,003	$266,003
C corporation, pay out all profit as salary	$22,393	0	158,889	$181,282
C corporation, pay out profit 50% as salary, 50% as dividends	$15,697	80,750	128,238	$224,685
S corporation, pay out all profit as distributions	$ 0	0	163,323	$163,323
S corporation, pay out all profit as salary	$22,293	0	158,889	$160,215
S corporation, pay out profit 50% as salary, 50% as distributions	$15,697	0	160,215	$175,912

TABLE 3.4 Soft Sofa Company
$500,000 Profit before Income Tax—$100,000 Other Income
(Sophia Leaves All Profit in Business for Growth)

FORM OF BUSINESS	TOTAL SOCIAL SECURITY TAXES	CORPORATE INCOME TAX	INDIVIDUAL INCOME TAX	TOTAL TAXES
Sole proprietorship	$22,393	0	198,489	$220,882
C corporation. All profit retained in business	$ 0	170,000	16,986	$186,986
S corporation. All profit retained in business	$ 0	0	202,923	$202,923

It will also vary with other tax laws that we have not considered in these examples, such as the Alternative Minimum Tax, passive income and losses, and various credits for certain business and investment activities.

To summarize, make your best guess of the future of your business and compute the probable tax bite for each type of organization, then pick the type you should have, which selection will be based on your guesses. (The buzz words for guesses of the future are projections and forecasts.)

4 PROCEDURES FOR BECOMING AND CONTINUING AS AN S CORPORATION

Operating a corporation requires specific procedures to ensure that the corporation will be recognized, and will continue to be recognized, as a corporation under the laws of the state(s) in which the corporation operates. In addition, a corporation operating as an S corporation not only has to satisfy state laws, but it must also satisfy several IRS requirements and file various forms with the IRS.

This chapter discusses both the state and IRS requirements. The first section of this chapter is directed to those who form a new corporation and immediately elect S status from day one, so that the corporation is never in C status. The second section covers those factors that are of concern if you change from a C corporation to an S corporation.

STARTING AS AN S CORPORATION FROM DAY ONE OF YOUR NEW CORPORATION

Many businesses are started as sole proprietorships or simple general partnerships and then incorporated later. If the liability protection of a corporation is of little concern when you start a small business, there is little wrong with that procedure. However, once you have decided to operate as a corporation, you can save some hassle and escape several onerous IRS rules if you make sure your corporation is an S corporation from day one.

If you already are operating as a C corporation, keep reading. Your procedures are also covered.

As we cover the steps to take, remember that we are dealing with incorporation and tax rules in 50 states, as well as those in possessions and territories. To list the different rules in each state would make this book too heavy to read comfortably, but we do try to suggest what questions you need to ask in your state.

Contact Your State's Corporation Authority and Obtain a Schedule of Fees

Corporations must pay fees, both on creation of the corporation and annually thereafter. Also, obtain blank forms that are discussed here. Most states now have Web sites where you can download the fee schedules and blank forms.

Hold a Meeting of All the Prospective Owners of the Corporation

Make various decisions, as follows: (Even if you are to be the sole owner of the corporation, you need to set aside some time to meet with yourself and make many of the same decisions.)

Who Will be the Initial Stockholders of the Corporation and How Much Will Each Invest? Make a list of stockholders and the amounts of their investments. Then, for computation purposes, assign a dollar value to each share of stock that is to be issued and divide that value into each stockholder's investment to determine how many shares of stock each will receive for his or her investment. That determines how many shares will be *issued* to each stockholder. You also need to determine how many shares will be *authorized*. It's a good idea to authorize much more stock that you initially issue. If your business prospers and grows fast, you may need additional working capital and decide to obtain the funds by selling stock to another investor. If you have stock that is authorized but not issued, you can issue the additional stock without having to obtain approval from the state. However, if you don't have that additional authorized stock available, you'll have to obtain the state's authorization to issue more stock. Although such state authorization is seldom withheld, it is more paperwork and hassle. Note that the state does not require or force a corporation to issue more stock. That decision is made by the board of directors or the existing stockholders.

Arlene, Ben, and Charlie plan to set up a corporation to manufacture implanted cell phones. (No more sagging belts.) Their investment schedule looks like this:

Arlene	*$3,000,000*
Ben	*$1,500,000*
Charlie	*$ 100,000*

They might decide that each share of stock would represent $100 of investment, so each would receive certificates for stock in the following amounts:

Arlene	*30,000 shares*
Ben	*15,000 shares*
Charlie	*1,000 shares*

As the corporation will therefore issue 46,000 shares, it might be prudent to request that the state authorize 100,000 shares.

Here's a caveat and why I suggested you obtain the fee schedule from the state as the first item in this list: The $100 per share is what is sometimes called the *stated value* or *par value*, and some states levy fees based on this value of the stock. Others levy fees based on the number of shares issued. If the latter is the case in your state, you may want to increase the value of each share and issue fewer shares, so check the fee schedule.

In the preceding comments and examples I have dealt only with common stock. There are other types or classes of stock, such as preferred stock. However, because S corporations cannot issue other classes of stock, they are not included in this discussion.

Who Will Fill the Statutory Offices of the Corporation? That is, who will be president, vice president(s), secretary, and treasurer, and who will be the directors, if your state still requires them in small corporations.

Who Will Be the *Incorporator(s)?* This is of low importance. The title goes to whoever signs the initial filing with the state. If you use an attorney to help you with this set-up, you'll probably find that he or she acts as the incorporator to save you a trip to the law office to sign the filing. In other words, there's no glory or symbol of authority that goes with being an incorporator.

Restrictions on the Stock That Is to Be Issued. You may want to decide that the future stockholders should agree that they will not sell their stock in the corporation until they have offered it to the other existing stockholders. That prevents a disgruntled stockholder from selling his or her share of stock to a mean individual who would make life miserable for you and the other remaining stockholders. Also, include a statement that all stockholders will agree to election of S corporation status.

Should You Incorporate in Your Home State or Some Other State? Several states, most notably Delaware and Nevada, make bold pitches to entrepreneurs, extolling the benefits of incorporating in that state. (The fees are obviously higher than the cost of cranking out forms, approvals, and advertising.) There are advantages to incorporating in those states if:

- You are going to sell the stock in your corporation nationally, to the public (in which case you cannot elect S corporation status).
- You are going to operate in several states as soon as you incorporate.*

*Selling by catalog or on the Internet to residents or businesses in other states generally does not mean that you are operating in those states, unless you have a physical site (such as a warehouse) there. If you have an agent or employee soliciting orders for you in those states, the rules are murky. Seek legal advice.

However, if you are starting or running a business that will operate only in your state, incorporating in another state will only subject you to double state annual corporation fees, require you to register your foreign (as in another state) corporation, and possibly incur unnecessary complications in filing state income tax returns. If your business grows beyond your wildest expectations and you go public, you can incorporate in Delaware later. (That can be done without creating a tax burden if certain rules are followed.)

Write Down Your Decisions

After these decisions have been made, reduce them to writing in the form of a *Preincorporation Agreement*. This does not go to the state or anywhere else, but each stockholder should keep a copy. Memories fade with time, but a written agreement can save many later arguments.

File the Paperwork with the Appropriate State Office

What is the appropriate state agency? In most states, it is the office of the Secretary of State, but some states have other names. Blank forms can usually be obtained by calling this state agency, or if you dislike busy signals and on-hold music, most states have the forms in downloadable form on their Web sites.

What Forms Should Be Filed?

These can vary somewhat among states, but generally the following may be required.

Application for Reservation of Name. If you've decided on a name but still have other decisions to make or details to work out, you can reserve your choice of a corporate name for some period (usually about 60 days). This lets you arrange for signs, letterhead, and so on without the danger that someone else will grab your corporate name while you develop your plans. If that is of no concern to you, you can skip this form. The procedure is simple: Obtain the form, fill it in, and send it to your state agency. Remember, you don't have a reserved name until the state confirms it to you in writing.

Want to know if a name has already been taken before you send in the name reservation form? You may be able to get your question answered by calling the agency or your state may have a list of existing corporations posted on its Web site.

Articles of Incorporation. Historically, this was a rather formal document in which the incorporators had to describe the business activities in which the corporation would engage, as well as some other extensive boilerplate. Now, this document is usually a one-page, fill-in-the-blanks affair. It does, however, require a statement about how many shares of stock are to be authorized and the names of the incorporators. It may also call for the names of the initial directors (who you can immediately vote out of office if you change your mind on who they will be).

If the form allows space for more details about the corporation, this is probably for the benefit of organizations such as banks and insurance companies, who operate under stricter regulation than general business corporations.

Designation of Resident Agent. All the directors and officers of a corporation could live out of state, with the day-to-day management left in the hands of a paid manager. If there were no corporate officer in state, the courts would have a problem in attempting to serve legal notices on the corporation. For that reason, all states require that someone who is a resident of the state be designated as the *resident agent,* and that someone should be either a director or officer of the corporation or a lawyer who is a member of the bar in that state. Other than accepting service and notifying the corporate officers, the resident agent has no other duties.

As this designation takes up only one line of a form, it is often included in the Articles of Incorporation form. The separate form version is used later, if the registered agent changes.

Certificate of Acceptance of Appointment of Resident Agent. Obviously, the person appointed resident agent has the option of accepting or rejecting the appointment. This is the form on which he or she can accept the designation. As already mentioned, it is often included as one line in the Articles of Incorporation.

Corporation Charter or Certificate. If you have filled in the Articles of Incorporation to the satisfaction of the people in the state agency, you should receive an acknowledgment that your corporation is officially in existence. This acknowledgment could be in the form of a letter or a fancier charter or certificate. Display it at your headquarters or keep it in a safe place.

SS-4, Application for Employer Identification Number. In our Big Brother society, not only must every individual have a number (Social Security), but every business must also have one. It is a nine-digit number, and you obtain one for your business by filing an SS-4 form with the IRS. (There is a blank SS-4 form in Appendix C.)

This is a relatively simple form, and it appears that the IRS uses it for no other activity than that of assigning an employer identification number to your business, so you make no binding elections by filing it with the IRS. However, you must file it. Without the number, you will not be able to comply with the many tax regulations and could end up being assessed substantial penalties.

Don't let the word "employer" in the name of the number throw you off track. Although the number is used for employment forms (reporting taxes withheld, for instance), it is also used for business income tax returns and various other forms that must be filed with the IRS. Indeed, many states will insist that the federal employer identification number appear on the state tax forms filed by a business.

If you already are operating as a C corporation, do not file an SS-4 form just because you are electing S status. It is still the same corporation, so it keeps the same employer identification number. However, if you are operating as a sole proprietor, partnership, or limited liability company and are incorporating your business, you will need a new employer identification number. The IRS views a corporation as separate from the former business form, so it requires a new number.

Item 17a on the form is often answered incorrectly. (It asks, "Has the applicant ever applied for an employer identification number for this or any other business?") For a new corporation, the answer would always be "no." It's the new corporation that is applicant for an identification number, not the owner of the corporation. So, the answer is "no," even if you had been operating as a sole proprietor or partnership and had applied for a number for that entity.

As for tax year (item number 11), selecting a calendar year (ending December 31) is the most expedient. If you have a compelling reason for a different tax year, see the pertinent section in Chapter 5.

You also need this employer identification number for the next form, which requests the IRS to recognize your corporation as an S corporation. Because there is a deadline for submitting the next form, it is critical that you receive the nine-digit identification number as soon as possible. To that end, note that, under "How to Apply" on page 2 of the instructions to the form, you can receive the number from the IRS by telephone. I strongly urge that you do this rather than wait for mail to and from the IRS.

IRS Form 2553, Election by a Small Business Corporation. This is the form by which you elect S status for your corporation. The form should be completed carefully, and must be submitted to the IRS within the first two-and-a-half months of starting the corporation. This document provides basic information about the corporation, along with the names of the stockholders. Each stockholder must sign the form (or a separate consent), indicating his or her agreement with the election. Note that this form does not guarantee that IRS will recognize your corporation as an S corporation. That is done, sort of, only by a letter from the IRS that accepts your election. I say "sort of" because, as the IRS does in many situations, it accepts an election by a taxpayer subject to possible later examination.

Meeting the deadline for filing this form, with all the information requested, is important.* If you miss the deadline for the first year of the corporation's life, you have a C, or regular corporation for that first year. (A Form 2553 election filed after the deadline could be effective for the next year, so your corporation would be under S status in the second year, but not in the first.) As discussed in Chapter 5, a corporation that had a C status before an S status has some additional tax complications.

Stockholders' Consent. Each stockholder in the corporation, whether it is a new corporation or a C corporation changing to S status, must consent to the election of S status. This can be accomplished by having each stockholder sign box K of Form 2553, or each stockholder may sign a separate consent form. There is no IRS form for the separate consent, but a signed statement that contains the following information will suffice:

Name, address, and employer identification number of the corporation.

Name of the stockholder, including spouse's if the stock is held jointly.

Number of shares owned and the date they were acquired.

Social Security number of the stockholder.

Day on which the stockholder's tax year ends (December 31, for most people).

If the stockholders live far apart, using this statement saves much time over sending Form 2553 around for each stockholder to sign. The post office could make you miss the filing deadline for the consents, which is the same as that for Form 2553; i.e., two-and-a-half months after the start of the corporation or the beginning of the tax year.

Note that all the same information as was just listed previously should be inserted on Form 2553, in columns J, L, M, and N. Only column K would be left blank if you use separate consent letters.

If, when you fill in the blanks on Form 2553, one of your stockholders is on safari or cooped up in a research station in Antarctica, you may have trouble securing his or her consent in time to meet the deadline. Nevertheless, you probably can still have your S election. The IRS usually will accept a request for extension of time to secure the consent of the stockholder if there is a reasonable cause.

If you acquire new stockholders after filing Form 2553 and before the

*Before 1998, the law required that IRS deny S status for the current year unless Form 2553 was filed on time. There were no exceptions. However, in 1998, Congress amended the law to give the IRS leeway in granting S status when the form is late, provided the corporate officers had a good reason for the tardiness. At this writing, the IRS has been quite liberal in accepting reasons for late filing and granting S status as if the form had been filed on time. However, will the kinder, gentler people at the IRS like your reason for belated filing? Don't risk it. File on time.

IRS accepts your election, you must secure the consents of those new stockholders and file them with the IRS.

File Form 2553 as early as you can after the corporation charter is issued. If the IRS rejects it for an error or omission, you will have time to correct it. Actually, the IRS can and sometimes does allow additional time for correction of errors and omissions on Form 2553. However, the IRS is not required to grant this extra time, so why take the risk? File it the day the corporation qualifies to file it. The corporation first qualifies to elect S corporation status and file Form 2553 on the earlier of:

The date the corporation first had assets.

The date the corporation first had shareholders.

The date the corporation first started doing business.

A final point about signing a consent to an S election. It may not be withdrawn after a valid S corporation election is made by the corporation. If you own less than 50 percent of a corporation that seeks your consent to an S election, consider the ramifications to you before you sign the consent. Once signed, you have no way to cause a revocation of the S status, unless you act with other stockholders and all of you together own 50 percent or more of the stock. For instance, you will have to pay income tax on your share of the corporate profits, even though the corporation may not distribute any cash.

SOLE PROPRIETORSHIP CHANGING TO AN S CORPORATION

The procedure for this change is almost identical to that for starting a new business as an S corporation, so only the differences are highlighted here.

Forms to File with Your State

You need to file the same forms with the state to receive a state charter of your corporation as those mentioned previously. The state corporation authority usually will not care whether you are putting an existing business in a corporation. (However, the state tax department, the unemployment insurance tax folks, and the professional licensing offices may care.)

Forms to File with the IRS

The Form SS-4, Application for Employer Identification Number, will look the same as the one for a new business in a new corporation, with the exception that question 9 should be answered by checking the box for "Changed type of organization" and the new type is, of course, a corporation.

The Form 2553, Election by a Small Business Corporation, will be identical to the form you would file for a new business in a new corporation.

However, there is a new wrinkle.

Avoid Tax When You Transfer Your Business to a Corporation (S or C). If you, as a sole proprietor, set up a corporation in which to continue your business, you could have a thorny problem. You own the business' assets (fixtures, machines, office equipment, etc.). When you transfer them to the corporation, you are, in effect, selling the equipment to the corporation in exchange for the stock of the corporation. Does selling this equipment generate gain on which you must pay tax?

Gertrude Greengrass operates a lawn maintenance business as a sole proprietorship but decides to incorporate her business as an S corporation for the various reasons covered in Chapter 3. Her only asset is a piece of equipment called a Scorched Lawn Machine. (It cuts grass, trims hedges, edges, and stomps on bugs all in one operation.) She originally paid $50,000 for the machine, but on her tax returns for the years she has owned it, she had deducted depreciation totaling $40,000. Her tax basis in the machine is then $10,000 ($50,000 original cost minus $40,000 depreciation deducted).

When she sets up her corporation, she transfers ownership of the machine to the corporation in exchange for stock the corporation will issue to her. Now, the more value that machine has on the books of the corporation, the more depreciation it can deduct on future corporate tax returns. Therefore, Gertrude arbitrarily assigns a value of $45,000 to the machine and has the corporation issue her 450 shares of stock at $100 per share. With the flick of a pen on some paper, she has created more basis in the machine, and that means she can deduct more depreciation expense, and that will benefit her, as an S corporation stockholder.

Then, behold, there comes a letter from the IRS, telling Gertrude that an IRS examiner will visit her corporate office (her den) and inspect her financial records. The IRS representative, Mr. Beady, is overjoyed soon after he arrives. He makes this calculation:

Machine sold to corporation for	*$45,000*
Subtract Gertrude's basis	*10,000*
Gertrude's gain	*$35,000*

Mr. Beady gets to assess Gertrude for the tax on $35,000 of gain. As this happens two years after Gertrude has filed the return on which she should have reported the income, she also is hit with penalties and interest!

Could Gertrude have avoided this scene? Yes. Section 351 of the Internal Revenue Code allows an individual or several individuals to transfer assets to a new corporation (C or S) with no tax effect if, after the transfers, these individuals own 80 percent or more of the corporation. As you might expect, the equipment so transferred has the same basis to the corporation as it did to the individual who transferred the equipment. In Gertrude's case, that would be $10,000, so the maneuver to increase depreciation deductions won't work. (Contrary to common perceptions, the IRS and, yes, the Congress have some pretty smart folks in the ranks. Over the years, they have plugged many loopholes such as this one—darn it.)

The rules under Section 351 also can delay income tax.

Gertrude owns an antique desk she uses every day in her office. She paid $50 for it at a garage sale in 1984, and recently she and the desk appeared on the Antiques Roadshow where she learned it was now worth $10,000. Without Section 351, she would, in effect, sell her desk to her corporation for its current value and have to pay tax on the gain of $9,950 ($10,000 minus $50). Now she says "hooray for Section 351." She won't pay tax on it until the corporation sells the desk, if it ever does.

To make sure that an IRS examiner cannot treat you as Gertrude was, make up what is called a *Section 351 Statement*. This is a statement that notifies the IRS that you are claiming that the transfer of assets and liabilities to the corporation qualifies for treatment under Section 351. Essentially, the statement lists the property you are transferring to the corporation, describes the property, describes the stock you are receiving in exchange, and provides some other details. The details of what must be included are in Regulation 1.351-3, which is reproduced in the Appendix with an example of a Section 351 Statement. (Note that the statement is actually two documents, one to be included with the stockholder's income tax return and one with the corporation's return.)

There is an alternative to consider: Keep the assets in your name and lease (rent) them to the corporation. Leasing to your own corporation should fly if you set the lease at the same rental that an unrelated leasing company would charge your corporation for the same assets and make sure the rental payment is made from the corporation to you every month. Properly structured, the rental payments should be deductible by the corporation and should be income to the owner. Because the corporation is an S corporation, that should be a wash; the expense to the S corporation will end up on the stockholder's individual income tax return as a deduction that offsets the rental income. Note that rental payments to a stockholder are not subject to social security taxes.

PARTNERSHIP OR LLC CHANGING TO AN S CORPORATION

As Section 351 applies to one or more persons, it applies to partnerships as well as sole proprietors. Be careful, though, to be sure that all the former partners who now own at least 80 percent of the outstanding stock of the corporation have an interest in the partnership property that is transferred. This should not be a problem for a simple general partnership that puts its business in a corporation. It can be a problem if the partnership is merged into an existing corporation with existing stockholder(s) who were not partners in the partnership. If you have an unusual situation, read Regulation 1.351-1 in the Appendix. It contains several explanatory examples that might fit your circumstances. Otherwise, it's a tricky area that deserves professional advice.

Corporations, estates, and trusts can be part of this transaction also, but if you want to elect S status right after incorporating, the corporate stockholder would disqualify your new corporation from S status. Also, there are special rules for estates and trusts owning shares of stock in an S corporation (see Chapter 5). If you do not meet the 80 percent test, and the fair market value of your assets is greater than your basis in them, you would have the privilege of paying tax on that difference.

CONVERTING A C CORPORATION TO AN S CORPORATION

As you read this section, you'll become aware that there are more complications to an S corporation that was formerly a C corporation. However, changing to an S corporation may be your best alternative if you want to bail out of a C corporation. That's because changing to anything else, such as an LLC or a partnership, involves liquidating the corporation. Unless you have a small corporation with virtually no assets, the liquidation will probably result in additional taxes to pay.

Here's a list of the tasks to perform in order to change from a C to an S corporation. It follows the order and refers to the preceding list of tasks for a new corporation electing S status.

Dealing with Your State Corporation Authority

Here's some good news: When you change from C to S corporation, you don't have to do a thing with the state office that regulates the establishment of corporations, such as the secretary of state. (That office is not concerned with how the corporation pays income taxes.) Similarly, if the name of the resident agent does not change, there is nothing relative to that title to file with the state.

This is not to say, however, that you don't have to deal with the state *income tax* office. See the section on state taxation of S corporations at the end of this chapter.

Hold a Directors' or Stockholders' Meeting

Pass a resolution to the effect that the corporation elects to be taxed under Subchapter S of the Internal Revenue Code. If there is no change in the number of stockholders or how much stock each owns, there is no need to issue any additional stock. The same certificates that represented ownership of the C corporation also represent ownership of the S corporation.

Get Right with the IRS

You do have some time-critical tasks to perform with regard to the IRS, as follows.

Employer Identification Number. Do *not* file another SS-4 for your corporation. Use the same employer identification number as you always have for your corporation. (That also means that you continue the reporting of *payroll* taxes as if there were no change in the *income* tax status of the corporation.)

IRS Form 2553, Election by a Small Business Corporation. This form *must* be filed with the IRS, and all the requirements covered in the previous paragraphs for a new corporation apply to an existing corporation. In other words, consent by all of the stockholders is necessary, and the same deadline of two-and-one-half months after the start of the tax year applies. Actually, you can file the Form 2553 at any time during the previous tax year and request that it be effective for a subsequent year. (You can file the form at any time during year 2001 and up to March 15, 2002 requesting that the S status be effective for 2002.) However, conditions can change, so prudence would dictate that you not file a Form 2553 until at least late in the year for a change to S corporation status in the following year.

The consents of the stockholders can be on separate documents, just as previously covered. Note, though, that if you file the form early in one year, to be effective the following year, you will need to take more action if there is a change in stockholders during the remainder of the year. If there are changes in stockholders, the new stockholders will have to file consents to the S election.

Tax Year for Your Corporation after Changing to S Status. As I pointed out when discussing new S corporations earlier, it makes practical sense to report your corporation income on a calendar year basis. To use a fiscal year ending on other than December 31 creates much more hassle and may involve estimated income tax payments to be made by the S corporation on behalf of the stockholders. (This requirement was adopted many years ago to defeat some significant tax deferral maneuvers through an S corporation on a fiscal year ending in January or February.) If your business is such that a December 31 year-end makes for cumbersome accounting problems, you can jump through hoops and perhaps use a fiscal year ending some other time. The details are in Chapter 5.

If your C corporation's fiscal year ends on other than December 31, you change to the December 31 year by filing a tax return for the short year of less than 12 months. In other words, if your present fiscal year as a C corporation ends on May 31, you would file a Form 2553 to elect S status by August 15. Provided your election is accepted by the IRS, your corporation would file a short-year return, as an S corporation, for the seven-month period from June 1 through December 31.

Plan ahead for the personal taxes of the stockholders. In this case, they will have taxable income from their salaries from the C corporation through May, salaries from the S corporation for the rest of the year, plus their share of the earnings of the S corporation for the seven months from June 1 through December 31.

Get Rid of Accumulated Earnings, If Possible. There are additional tax law hurdles for S corporations that were once C corporations, compared to corporations that have always been S corporations. These are explained in Chapter 5, but you can avoid them by making sure that the C corporation has no earnings and profits when it converts to an S corporation. How? The IRS would suggest that you pay dividends to the stockholders and make sure that the dividends equal the accumulated earnings at the date of conversion to S status. However, the payments of those dividends do result in double taxation, so try to accomplish this in other ways.

Perhaps you can reduce much of the accumulated earnings by paying higher salaries and bonuses to stockholder-employees, but don't overdo this. If, as CEO, you have always been paid yearly compensation (salary and bonus) of $250,000, and your corporation pays you a bonus of $2.5 million a week before the start of the new S corporation year, you can well expect a knock on your door by an IRS examiner. He or she will be intent on reclassifying your big bonus (deductible expense to your corporation when it was in C status) as a dividend (nondeductible) from the C corporation. That is, you'll end up paying double tax, corporate and individual, on that $2.5 million!

If possible, plan for a conversion to S status several years ahead of the event. Pay salaries that are on the high side of the reasonable range for two or three years before converting to S status, so you won't be waving a red flag by a lump-sum bonus at the wrong time.

Of course, getting rid of accumulated earnings may be impossible. If profits of your C corporation have been plowed back into the business, buying equipment and buildings, you probably do not have the cash to reduce accumulated earnings to zero. At least, you don't want to impair your working capital and credit lines by this procedure. If that is the case, you can live with the rules for S corporations that were once C corporations, if you're careful. The rules are in Chapter 5.

PROCEDURES TO KEEP YOUR S CORPORATION LEGAL OVER THE YEARS

If someone is injured by your corporation—financially, emotionally or physically—you can, of course, anticipate a lawsuit. You expect that the limited liability of your corporation will protect you, while the plaintiff's lawyer will try to prove that your corporation is not legitimate because you have failed to dot an *i* somewhere. In addition, if you let your corporation default in some area, the IRS may take this opportunity to decide that you have become whatever type of organization will net the most taxes for the government! So, you took the pains to set up the corporation and elect S status. Take the additional pains to keep it that way.

Bylaws

These are the rules by which the corporation will be operated. They should cover such items as:

Where and when stockholders' meetings will be held (at least annually).

Where and when directors' meetings will be held.

How stockholders and directors will be notified of meetings.

What constitutes a quorum.

How directors will be elected and for what term.

Who is entitled to vote.

What form voting proxies may take.

What powers the directors have.

How officers will be elected.

How directors and officers may be removed.

How the bylaws may be amended.

Any other rules you may want to include—as long as they don't conflict with state law.

Some states have streamlined their laws for small corporations such that a board of directors is unnecessary. If your state permits that, leave the director level out (unless you have so many stockholders that stockholder meetings are unwieldy).

You can find "boilerplate" corporate bylaws in office supply stores, libraries or on the Internet.* But beware. Use them as a guide. Don't just adopt them "as is."

You don't have to submit the bylaws to any government body, but if you don't have them, you may wish you did when some lawyer is trying to destroy your limited liability (corporate veil) by proving your corporation was never perfected. Just as horrible, the IRS may take the same tack to prove that the corporation never existed, if such a situation would result in your paying more taxes. In addition, the bylaws can help settle disputes that may arise between the stockholders.

Corporate Minutes of Meetings

Keep a written record of both stockholders' and directors' meetings. Include who was present, what proxies were submitted, the results of elections of directors and officers, and what major decisions were voted upon and approved. (In the first meeting of stockholders, include a resolution that the corporation elects to be taxed as an S corporation and that a Form 2553, Election by a Small Business Corporation, will be submitted in a timely manner to the IRS.)

As with the bylaws, failure to write up these minutes and keep them current can invite troubles in court as well as with the IRS.

Annual Reports to Your State

The state in which you incorporated (presumably your home state) will expect you to file an annual report with the office of the secretary of state (or its equivalent). The report usually consists of a list of officers and directors, as well as confirmation of the name and address of the resident agent. It should also be no surprise to you to learn that this report has to be accom-

*Try the Lectric Law Library at www.lectlaw.com/formb.htm.

panied by a check, payable to the state, for $100 or more. This is often called a franchise tax, but by any name, you have to pay it to stay legal.

In addition, it is the responsibility of the corporation officers and directors to notify the state if there is a change in resident agents. The resigning resident agent will probably notify the state of the change, but it is up to you, as a corporate officer, to notify the state of the new resident agent and be sure he or she has furnished the state with an acceptance of the appointment as resident agent.

Keep on Good Terms with the IRS

Form 1120S, U.S. Income Tax Return for an S Corporation. This is the annual income tax return that must be filed for your S corporation. The due date for a corporation filing on a calendar year basis is March 15, although you can file for an automatic extension on Form 7004, which will give you another six months, to October 15, to complete and file your corporate return. Remember that none of the stockholders of your S corporation can file a final individual return (Form 1040) until you have completed the corporate return, because they have to include their share of the corporate income (or loss) on their individual returns.

Depending on the nature of your operation, with Form 1120S you may have to file one or more of the following:

Schedule K-1 (Form 1120S). This is the form that goes to each stockholder, telling him or her how much income, and what type of income, has flowed to them from the corporation. Each stockholder then reports those numbers on their individual income tax return (Form 1040). Every S corporation must send these forms to the stockholders and include a copy with Form 1120S that goes to the IRS. The only exception would be if the corporation has no income and no loss of any kind for the year, and there have been no distributions or other activities that could affect a stockholder's basis in the stock.

Schedule D (Form 1120S). Capital Gains and Losses and Built-In Gains. Note that this Schedule D is a special Schedule D form for use by S corporations only. What are built-in gains? If your corporation has been in S corporation status since day one of its existence, it doesn't have any, so don't worry about it. If your corporation spent some time as a C corporation, you very well may have some and have to wrestle with this arcane section of the tax rules. Again the details are in Chapter 5.

Form 4562, Depreciation and Amortization. This is same depreciation form that is used to accompany a tax return for any type of entity that owned depreciable assets. This is another complex area on which there is some help in Chapter 5.

Form 4797, Sales of Business Property. Again, this is the standard form that is used to accompany a tax return for any type of entity that was involved in the sale of business property. Depreciation that the corporation deducted in previous years enters into these calculations, so the details are in Chapter 5.

Form 8825, Rental Real Estate and Expenses of a Partnership or S Corporation. Use this form to report income and loss from rental property owned by the S corporation.

There are other forms that may be required to accompany a particular Form 1120S, but these are the ones most often needed. Examples of these forms, filled in with an example, are in the Appendix.

Don't Neglect Your State's Tax Department

After all, your state tax department won't neglect you. So don't wait for the state people to come calling. Avoid penalties and interest by getting in contact with the tax department (or whatever your state calls it).

Most states impose corporate income taxes as well as other creative revenue sources on corporations. (For instance, as well as a corporate income tax, Florida imposes an intangible tax on the corporation's issued and outstanding stock.) As far as taxation of S corporations is concerned, there is much diversity among the states. Some recognize the federal status of an S corporation and levy no income tax on such an entity, depending on cash flow from the tax bite put on the shareholders. Other states do not recognize an S status and levy the same corporate income taxes on an S corporation that they collect from C corporations.

You will need to call your state tax department and ask for information. They will have a package that explains the state tax scheme and provides the necessary forms.

Many states now have a single form that gets a new business set up for income tax, payroll tax collection, sales tax collection, and other levies. If your corporation is new, these all-in-one forms can save a lot of time.

EXAMPLE OF A NEW S CORPORATION AND THE FORMS IT FILES

To end this chapter, filled-in forms are included for a fictitious company that forms a corporation and then elects Subchapter S tax status. There are also Section 351 forms that Gertrude Greengrass would have prepared. The same blank IRS forms are also reprinted in the Appendix.

The example is for one of three people, each with a different amount of investment in the company, who start a new business in Florida (perhaps inappropriately). The example covers filing the forms with the secretary of state and with the IRS, as well as the corporation's first income tax return. The forms are reproduced here, with comments, but we didn't want to clutter up the example with many instructions to the forms. The more important IRS instructions are in the Appendix.

TRANSMITTAL LETTER

Department of State
Division of Corporations
P.O. Box 6327
Tallahassee, FL 32314

SUBJECT: Wet'n Soggy Coal Co., Inc.
(PROPOSED CORPORATE NAME—MUST INCLUDE SUFFIX)

Enclosed is an original and one (1) copy of the articles of incorporation and a check for:

☑ $70.00 Filing Fee	❑ $78.75 Filing Fee & Certificate of Status	❑ $78.75 Filing Fee & Certified Copy	❑ $87.50 Filing Fee, Certified Copy & Certificate of Status
		ADDITIONAL COPY REQUIRED	

FROM: Joseph Firehouse
Name (Printed or typed)

60 Waterway Road
Address

Nearhere, FL 12399
City, State & Zip

999-888-7777
Daytime Telephone Number

NOTE: Please provide the original and one copy of the articles.

ARTICLES OF INCORPORATION

In compliance with Chapter 607 and/or Chapter 621, F.S. (Profit)

ARTICLE I NAME

The name of the corporation shall be:

Wet'n Soggy Coal Company, Inc.

ARTICLE II PRINCIPAL OFFICE

The principal place of business/mailing address is:

60 Waterway Road
Nearhere, FL 12399

ARTICLE III PURPOSE

The purpose for which the corporation is organized is:

General business

ARTICLE IV SHARES

The number of shares of stock is:

1,000

ARTICLE V INITIAL OFFICERS/DIRECTORS (optional)

The name(s) and address(es):

ARTICLE VI REGISTERED AGENT

The **name and Florida street address** of the registered agent is:

Joseph Firehouse
60 Waterway Road
Nearhere, FL 12399

ARTICLE VII INCORPORATOR

The **name and address** of the Incorporator is:

Joseph Firehouse
60 Waterway Road
Nearhere, FL 12399

****

Having been named as registered agent to accept service of process for the above stated corporation at the place designated in this certificate, I am familiar with and accept the appointment as registered agent and agree to act in this capacity.

s/Joseph Firehouse	June 5, 1999
Signature/Registered Agent	Date

s/Joseph Firehouse	June 5, 1999
Signature/Incorporator	Date

INSTRUCTIONS FOR A PROFIT CORPORATION

The following are instructions, a transmittal letter and sample articles of incorporation pursuant to Chapter 607 and 621 Florida Statutes (F.S.)

NOTE: THIS IS A BASIC FORM MEETING MIMIMAL REQUIREMENTS FOR FILING ARTICLES OF INCORPORATION.

The Division of Corporations strongly recommends that corporate documents be reviewed by your legal counsel. The Division is a filing agency and as such does not render any legal, accounting, or tax advice.

This office does not provide you with corporate seals, minute books, or stock certificates. It is the responsibility of the corporation to secure these items once the corporation has been filed with this office.

Questions concerning S Corporations should be directed to the Internal Revenue Service by telephoning 1-800-829-1040. This is an IRS designation which is not determined by this office.

A preliminary search for name availability can be made on the Internet through the Division's records at www.sunbiz.org. Preliminary name searches and name reservations are no longer available from the Division of Corporations. You are responsible for any name infringement that may result from your corporate name selection.

Pursuant to Chapter 607 or 621 F.S., the articles of incorporation must set forth the following:

Article I: The name of the corporation **must** include a corporate suffix such as Corporation, Corp., Incorporated, Inc., Company, or Co.

A Professional Association **must** contain the word "chartered" or "professional association" or "P.A.".

Article II: The principal place of business and mailing address of the corporation.

Article III: **Specific Purpose for a "Professional Corporation"**

Article IV: The number of shares of stock that this corporation is authorized to have **must** be stated.

Article V: The names and street addresses of the directors/officers **(optional)**. The names of officers/directors may be required to apply for a license, open a bank account, etc.

CR2E010 (3/00)

Article VI: The name and **Florida street address** of the initial Registered Agent. The Registered Agent **must** sign in the space provided and type or print his/her name accepting the designation as registered agent.

Article VII: The name and address of the Incorporator. The Incorporator must sign in the space provided and type or print his/her name below signature.

An Effective Date: **Add a separate article if applicable or necessary:** An effective date **may** be added to the Articles of Incorporation, otherwise the date of receipt will be the file date. (An effective date can not be more than five [5] business days prior to the date of receipt or ninety [90] days after the date of filing).

****

The fee for filing a profit corporation is:

Filing Fee	$35.00
Designation of Registered Agent	$35.00
Certified Copy (optional)	$ 8.75 (plus $1 per page for each page over 8, not to exceed a maximum of $52.50).
Certificate of Status (optional)	$ 8.75

(Make checks payable to Florida Department of State)

Mailing Address:
Department of State
Division of Corporations
P.O. Box 6327
Tallahassee, FL 32314
(850) 487-6052

Street Address:
Department of State
Division of Corporations
409 E. Gaines St.
Tallahassee, FL 32399
(850) 487-6052

Form **SS-4** (Rev. April 2000) Department of the Treasury Internal Revenue Service

Application for Employer Identification Number

(For use by employers, corporations, partnerships, trusts, estates, churches, government agencies, certain individuals, and others. See instructions.)

▶ Keep a copy for your records.

EIN

OMB No. 1545-0003

Please type or print clearly.

1 Name of applicant (legal name) (see instructions)
Wet'n Soggy Coal Co., Inc.

2 Fill in box 2 only if trade name different than corporate name

3 Executor, trustee, "care of" name

Leave 3, 5a, and 5b blank. Applies to trusts, not corporations.

4a **60 Waterway Road**

5a B

4b City, state, and ZIP code
Nearhere, FL 12399

5b City, state, and ZIP code

6 County and state where principal business is located
Beach County, Florida

7 Name of principal officer, general partner, grantor, owner, or trustor–SSN or ITIN may be required (see instructions) ▶ **555-55-5555**
Joseph D. Firehouse

8a Type of entity (Check only one box.) (see instructions)
Caution: *If applicant is a limited liability company, see the instructions for line 8a.*

- ☐ Sole proprietor (SSN)
- ☐ Partnership
- ☐ Personal service corp.
- ☐ REMIC
- ☐ National Guard
- ☐ State/local government
- ☐ Farmers' cooperative
- ☐ Church or church-controlled organization
- ☐ Other nonprofit organization (specify) ▶ (enter GEN if applicable)
- ☐ Other (specify) ▶
- ☐ Estate (SSN of decedent)
- ☐ Plan administrator (SSN)
- ☑ Other corporation (specify) ▶ **Retailer**
- ☐ Trust
- ☐ Federal government/military

8b If a corporation, name the state or foreign country (if applicable) where incorporated | State **Florida** | Foreign country

9 Reason for applying (Check only one box.) (see instructions)
- ☑ Started new business (specify type) ▶ **Coal retailer**
- ☐ Hired employees (Check the box and see line 12.)
- ☐ Created a pension plan (specify type) ▶
- ☐ Banking purpose (specify purpose) ▶
- ☐ Changed type of organization (specify new type) ▶
- ☐ Purchased going business
- ☐ Created a trust (specify type) ▶
- ☐ Other (specify) ▶

10 Date business started or acquired (month, day, year) (see instructions) **06/12/1999**

11 Closing month of accounting year (see instructions) **December**

12 First date wages or annuities were paid or will be paid (month, day, year). **Note:** *If applicant is a withholding agent, enter date income will firs* . . . . . . ▶ **7/6/1999**

Boxes 12 and 13: S Corporations should pay salaries, at least to stockholder/employees

13 Hig ... exp ... *the applicant does not ... tions)* . . . . ▶

Nonagricultural	Agricultural	Household
3	0	0

14 Principal activity (see instructions) ▶ **Retail sales of coal**

15 Is the principal business activity manufacturing? . . . . ☐ Yes ☑ No
If "Yes," principal product and raw material used ▶

16 To whom are most of the products or services sold? Please check one box. ☐ Business (wholesale)
☑ Public (retail) ☐ Other (specify) ▶ ☐ N/A

17a Has the applicant ever applied for an employer identification number for this or any other business? . . . . ☐ Yes ☑ No
Note: *If "Yes," please complete lines 17b and 17c.*

Answer "no." The corporation, not the stockholder, is the applicant.

17b If you checked "Yes" on line 17a, give applicant's legal name and trade name shown on prior application, if different from line 1 or 2 above.
Legal name ▶ Trade name ▶

17c Approximate date when and city and state where the application was filed. Enter previous employer identification number if known.
Approximate date when filed (mo., day, year) | City and state where filed | Previous EIN

Under penalties of perjury, I declare that I have examined this application, and to the best of my knowledge and belief, it is true, correct, and complete.

Business telephone number (include area code) (999) 888-7777

Fax telephone number (include area code) ( )

Name and title (Please type or print clearly.) ▶ **Joseph D. Firehouse, President**

Signature ▶ *s/ Joseph D. Firehouse* Date ▶ **6/15/2001**

Note: *Do not write below this line. For official use only.*

Please leave blank ▶	Geo.	Ind.	Class	Size	Reason for applying

For Privacy Act and Paperwork Reduction Act Notice, see page 4. Cat. No. 16055N Form **SS-4** (Rev. 4-2000)

Form **2553** (Rev. July 1999) Department of the Treasury Internal Revenue Service

Election by a Small Business Corporation

(Under section 1362 of the Internal Revenue Code)

▶ See Parts II and III on back and the separate instructions.

▶ The corporation may either send or fax this form to the IRS. See page 1 of the instructions.

OMB No. 1545-0146

Notes: 1. *This election to be an S corporation can be accepted only if all the tests are met under **Who may elect** on page 1 of the instructions; all signatures in Parts I and III are originals (no photocopies); and the exact name and address of the corporation ... provided.*

2. *Do not file **Form 1120S,** U.S. Income Tax Return for an S Corporation, for any tax year before the yea...*

3. *If the corporation was in existence before the effective date of this election, see **Taxes an S corporatio...***

Obtain the Employer ID number by phone, not mail, so you'll have it for this form. See IRS instructions for Form SS-4

Part I Election Information

Please Type or Print

Name of corporation (see instructions)
Wet'n Soggy Coal Co., Inc.

A Employer identification number
98 ⋮ 7654321

Number, street, and room or suite no. (If a P.O. box, see instructions.)
60 Waterway Road

B Date incorporated
June 10, 1999

City or town, state, and ZIP code
Nearhere, FL 12399

C State of incorporation
Florida

D Election is to be effective for tax year beginning (month, day, year) ▶ **06 / 12 / 2001**

E Name and title of officer or legal rep...
Joseph Firehouse, President

Question D: The tax year may start days after corporate charter is issued--see question H

Telephone number of officer or legal representative
(351) 555-4444

G If the corporation changed its name or address after applying for the EIN shown in **A** above, check this box ▶ ☐

H If this election takes effect for the first tax year the corporation exists, enter month, day, and year of the **earliest** of the following: (1) date the corporation first had shareholders, (2) date the corporation first had assets, or (3) date the corporation began doing business ▶ **06 / 12 / 1999**

I Selected tax year: Annual return will be filed for tax year ending (month and day) ▶ **December 31**

If the tax year ends on any date other than December 31, except for an automatic 52-53-week tax year ending with reference to the month of December, you **must** complete Part II on the back. If the date you enter is the ending date of an automatic 52-53-week tax year, write "52-53-week year" to the right of the date. See Temporary Regulations section 1.441-2T(e)(3).

J Name and address of each shareholder; shareholder's spouse having a community property interest in the corporation's stock; and each tenant in common, joint tenant, and tenant by the entirety. (A husband and wife (and their estates) are counted as one shareholder in determining the number of shareholders without regard to the manner in which the stock is owned.)	K Shareholders' Consent Statement. Under penalties of perjury, we declare that we consent to the election of the above-named corporation to be an S corporation under section 1362(a) and that we have examined this consent statement, including accompanying schedules and statements, and to the best of our knowledge and belief, it is true, correct, and complete. We understand our consent is binding and may not be withdrawn after the corporation has made a valid election. (Shareholders sign and date below.)		L Stock owned		M Social security number or employer identification number (see instructions)	N Share-holder's tax year ends (month and day)
	Signature	Date	Number of shares	Dates acquired		
Joseph Firehouse 1235 Canal Road Nearhere, FL 12398	*s/Joseph Firehouse*	**6/15/1999**	**150**	**6/12/1999**	**555-55-5555**	**12/31**
Julie Firehouse 1235 Canal Road Nearhere, FL 12398	*s/Julie Firehouse*	**6/15/1999**	**Jointly with above**	**6/12/1999**	**333-33-3333**	**12/31**
Karen Coolwater 2 Main Street Somewhere, FL 44444	**Stockholder's consent is forthcoming on separate document. See letter attached.**		**100**	**6/12/1999**	**888-88-8888**	**12/31**
Larry Hotland 76 Firey Place Somewhere, FL 44443	*s/Larry Hotland*	**6/20/1999**	**50**	**6/12/1999**	**444-44-4444**	**12/31**

Caren Coolwater is exploring the Australian Outback, so mail takes several weeks to turn around. Therefore, the other stockholders are sending the Form 2553 without Fred's signature in the signature block. The accompany letter to the IRS and the the separate consent are on the pages that follow this form.

...edge and belief,

Signature of officer ▶ **s/Joseph Firehouse** Title ▶ **President** Date ▶ **8/5/1999**

For Paperwork Reduction Act Notice, see page 2 of the instructions. Cat. No. 18629R Form **2553** (Rev. 7-99)

Form 2553 (Rev. 7-99) Page **2**

Part II **Selection of Fiscal Tax Year** (All corporations using this part must complete item O and item P, Q, or R.)

O Check the applicable box to indicate whether the corporation is:

1. ☐ A
2. ☐ Ar
3. ☐ Ar

> Unless you must have a fiscal year (tax year) ending on other than December 31 or a Qualified Subchapter S Trust is a stockholder, there is nothing to complete on this page.

P Complete ... to request **(1)** a natural business year (as defined in section 4.01(1) of Rev. Proc. 87-32) or **(2)** a year that satisfies the ownership tax year test in section 4.01(2) of Rev. Proc. 87-32. Check the applicable box below to indicate the representation statement the corporation is making as required under section 4 of Rev. Proc. 87-32.

1. Natural Business Year ▶ ☐ I represent that the corporation is retaining or changing to a tax year that coincides with its natural business year as defined in section 4.01(1) of Rev. Proc. 87-32 and as verified by its satisfaction of the requirements of section 4.02(1) of Rev. Proc. 87-32. In addition, if the corporation is changing to a natural business year as defined in section 4.01(1), I further represent that such tax year results in less deferral of income to the owners than the corporation's present tax year. I also represent that the corporation is not described in section 3.01(2) of Rev. Proc. 87-32. (See instructions for additional information that must be attached.)

2. Ownership Tax Year ▶ ☐ I represent that shareholders holding more than half of the shares of the stock (as of the first day of the tax year to which the request relates) of the corporation have the same tax year or are concurrently changing to the tax year that the corporation adopts, retains, or changes to per item I, Part I. I also represent that the corporation is not described in section 3.01(2) of Rev. Proc. 87-32.

Note: *If you do not use item P and the corporation wants a fiscal tax year, complete either item Q or R below. Item Q is used to request a fiscal tax year based on a business purpose and to make a back-up section 444 election. Item R is used to make a regular section 444 election.*

Q Business Purpose—To request a fiscal tax year based on a business purpose, you must check box Q1 and pay a user fee. See instructions for details. You may also check box Q2 and/or box Q3.

1. Check here ▶ ☐ if the fiscal year entered in item I, Part I, is requested under the provisions of section 6.03 of Rev. Proc. 87-32. Attach to Form 2553 a statement showing the business purpose for the requested fiscal year. See instructions for additional information that must be attached.

2. Check here ▶ ☐ to show that the corporation intends to make a back-up section 444 election in the event the corporation's business purpose request is not approved by the IRS. (See instructions for more information.)

3. Check here ▶ ☐ to show that the corporation agrees to adopt or change to a tax year ending December 31 if necessary for the IRS to accept this election for S corporation status in the event (1) the corporation's business purpose request is not approved and the corporation makes a back-up section 444 election, but is ultimately not qualified to make a section 444 election, or (2) the corporation's business purpose request is not approved and the corporation did not make a back-up section 444 election.

R Section 444 Election—To make a section 444 election, you must check box R1 and you may also check box R2.

1. Check here ▶ ☐ to show the corporation will make, if qualified, a section 444 election to have the fiscal tax year shown in item I, Part I. To make the election, you must complete **Form 8716,** Election To Have a Tax Year Other Than a Required Tax Year, and either attach it to Form 2553 or file it separately.

2. Check here ▶ ☐ to show that the corporation agrees to adopt or change to a tax year ending December 31 if necessary for the IRS to accept this election for S corporation status in the event the corporation is ultimately not qualified to make a section 444 election.

Part III **Qualified Subchapter S Trust (QSST) Election Under Section 1361(d)(2)***

Income beneficiary's name and address	Social security number
Trust's name and address	Employer identification number

Date on which stock of the corporation was transferred to the trust (month, day, year) . . . . ▶ / /

In order for the trust named above to be a QSST and thus a qualifying shareholder of the S corporation for which this Form 2553 is filed, I hereby make the election under section 1361(d)(2). Under penalties of perjury, I certify that the trust meets the definitional requirements of section 1361(d)(3) and that all other information provided in Part III is true, correct, and complete.

Signature of income beneficiary or signature and title of legal representative or other qualified person making the election   Date

*Use Part III to make the QSST election only if stock of the corporation has been transferred to the trust on or before the date on which the corporation makes its election to be an S corporation. The QSST election must be made and filed separately if stock of the corporation is transferred to the trust after the date on which the corporation makes the S election.

CONSENT STATEMENT
(Under Regulation Sec. 1.1361-6)

Corporation: Wet'n Soggy Coal Co., Inc.
60 Waterway Road
Nearhere, FL 12399
Telephone: 555-444-5555
Taxpayer ID number: 98-7654321

Shareholder: Karen Coldwater
52 Main Street
Somewhere, FL 44444
Telephone: 333-444-7777
Social security number: 888-88-8888

Number of shares of stock owned: 100

Date on which stock was acquired: June 12, 1999

Shareholder's taxable year ends on December 31

Under penalties of perjury, I declare that I consent to the election of the above-named corporation to be an S corporation under section 1362(a) and that I have examined this Consent Statement and the Form 2553, Election by a Small Business Corporation and to the best of my knowledge and belief, it is true, correct, and complete. I understand my consent is binding and may not be withdrawn after the corporation has made a valid election.

______________________________ Date:____________________

Karen Coldwater

Joseph Firehouse
1235 Canal Road
Nearhere, FL 12398
555-444-5555

March 10, 2001

Internal Revenue Service Center
Atlanta, GA 39901

Re: Request for extension of time for filing stockholder's consent
Wet'n Soggy Coal Co., Inc.
Employer identification number 98-7654321

Dear Sir or Madam:

Enclosed is Form 2553, Election by a Small Business Corporation (under Section 1362 of the Internal Revenue Code).

This form includes the signed consent of all but one stockholder. Karen Holland has been on a sabbatical leave of absence from her employment by the University of Lake Okeechobee, exploring the Outback in Australia, where she has been since before the formation of the corporation on June 10, 1999. I am informed that she has received the Shareholder's consent form that was sent to her, that she has signed it, and it is in transit back to our corporate office. We will forward the original to you as soon as we receive it.

We therefore request an extension of time in which to file this consent, until April 30, 2001. (She is scheduled to return to civilization on April 2, so if we have not received her consent by then, the April 30 date would provide time to obtain it by express package service and forward it to you.)

Thank you for your consideration.

Yours sincerely,

s/Joseph Firehouse

Joseph Firehouse
President

Form **1120S** | **U.S. Income Tax Return for an S Corporation** | OMB No. 1545-0130

Department of the Treasury
Internal Revenue Service

▶ Do not file this form unless the corporation has timely filed Form 2553 to elect to be an S corporation.
▶ See separate instructions.

2000

For calendar year 2000, or tax year beginning **June 12**, 2000, and ending **December 31**, 20**00**

A Effective date of election as an S corporation **June 12, 2000**	Use IRS label. Otherwise, print or type.	Name **Wet'n Soggy Coal Co., Inc.**	C Employer identification number **98 7654321**
		Number, street, and room or suite no. (If a P.O. box, see page 11 of the instructions.) **60 Waterway Road**	D Date incorporated **June 10, 2000**
B Business code no. (see pages 29-31) **454319**		City or town, state, and ZIP code **Nearhere, FL 12399**	E Total assets (see page 11) $ **264000**

F Check applicable boxes: (1) ☑ Initial return (2) ☐ Final return (3) ☐ Change in address (4) ☐ Amended return

G Enter number of shareholders in the corporation at end of the tax year . . . ▶ **3**

Caution: *Include **only** trade or business income and expenses on lines 1a through 21. See page 11 of the instructions for more information.*

Section	Line	Description			Line	Amount
Income	1a	Gross receipts or sales **255000** b Less returns and allowances **5000** c Bal ▶			1c	250000
	2	Cost of goods sold (Schedule A, line 8)			2	140000
	3	Gross profit. Subtract line 2 from line 1c			3	110000
	4	Net gain (loss) from Form 4797, Part II, line 18 *(attach Form 4797)*			4	
	5	Other income (loss) *(attach schedule)*			5	
	6	**Total income (loss).** Combine lines 3 through 5 ▶			6	110000
Deductions (see page 12 of the instructions for limitations)	7	Compensation of officers			7	50000
	8	Salaries and wages (less employment credits)			8	
	9	Repairs and maintenance			9	1500
	10	Bad debts			10	
	11	Rents			11	14000
	12	Taxes and licenses			12	1000
	13	Interest			13	10000
	14a	Depreciation *(if required, attach Form 4562)*	14a	2625		
	b	Depreciation claimed on Schedule A and elsewhere on return	14b			
	c	Subtract line 14b from line 14a			14c	2625
	15	Depletion **(Do not deduct oil and gas depletion.)**			15	
	16	Advertising			16	5000
	17	Pension, profit-sharing, etc., plans			17	
	18	Employee benefit programs			18	
	19	Other deductions *(attach schedule)* (schedule omitted)			19	1875
	20	**Total deductions.** Add the amounts shown in the far right column for lines 7 through 19 ▶			20	86000
	21	Ordinary income (loss) from trade or business activities. Subtract line 20 from line 6			21	24000
Tax and Payments	22	**Tax: a** Excess net passive income tax *(attach schedule)*	22a			
	b	Tax from Schedule D (Form 1120S)	22b			
	c	Ad[...]tional taxes)			22c	
	23	Pa[...]	23a			
	b	Ta[...]	23b			
	c	Cr[...]	23c			
	d	Ad[...]			23d	
	24	Estimated tax penalty. Check if Form 2220 is attached ▶☐			24	
	25	**Tax due.** If the total of lines 22c and 24 is larger than line 23d, enter amount owed. See page 4 of the instructions for depository method of payment ▶			25	
	26	**Overpayment.** If line 23d is larger than the total of lines 22c and 24, enter amount overpaid ▶			26	
	27	Enter amount of line 26 you want: **Credited to 2001 estimated tax** ▶ **Refunded** ▶			27	

There are no numbers to go in this section. As is the situation for most S corporations, the stockholders pay all the income tax from their personal funds

Sign Here

Under penalties of perjury, I declare that I have examined this return, including accompanying schedules and statements, and to the best of my knowledge and belief, it is true, correct, and complete. Declaration of preparer (other than taxpayer) is based on all information of which preparer has any knowledge.

s/Joseph Firehouse | *3/14/2001* | **President**
Signature of officer | Date | Title

Paid Preparer's Use Only

Preparer's signature ▶	Date	Check if self-employed ☐	Preparer's SSN or PTIN
Firm's name (or yours if self-employed), address, and ZIP code ▶		EIN	
		Phone no. ( )	

For Paperwork Reduction Act Notice, see the separate instructions. Cat. No. 11510H Form **1120S** (2000)

Form 1120S (2000) Page 2

Schedule A — Cost of Goods Sold (see page 16 of the instructions)

1	Inventory at beginning of year	1	0
2	Purchases	2	300000
3	Cost of labor	3	40000
4	Additional section 263A costs *(attach schedule)*	4	
5	Other costs *(attach schedule)*	5	
6	**Total.** Add lines 1 through 5	6	340000
7	Inventory at end of year	7	200000
8	**Cost of goods sold.** Subtract line 7 from line 6. Enter here and on page 1, line 2	8	140000

9a Check all methods used for valuing closing inventory:
(i) ☐ Cost as described in Regulations section 1.471-3
(ii) ☐ Lower of cost or market as described in Regulations section 1.471-4
(iii) ☐ Other (specify method used and attach explanation) ▶

b Check if there was a writedown of "subnormal" goods as described in Regulations section 1.471-2(c) ▶ ☐

c Check if the LIFO inventory method was adopted this tax year for any goods *(if checked, attach Form 970)* ▶ ☐

d If the LIFO inventory method was used for this tax year, enter percentage (or amounts) of closing inventory computed under LIFO | 9d |

e Do the rules of section 263A (for property produced or acquired for resale) apply to the corporation? ☐ Yes ☑ No

f Was there any change in determining quantities, cost, or valuations between opening and closing inventory? ☐ Yes ☑ No
If "Yes," attach explanation.

Schedule B — Other Information

		Yes	No
1	Check method of accounting: **(a)** ☑ Cash **(b)** ☐ Accrual **(c)** ☐ Other (specify) ▶		
2	Refer to the list on pages 29 through 31 of the instructions and state the corporation's principal: **(a)** Business activity ▶ Retail **(b)** Product or service ▶ Coal		
3	Did the corporation at the end of the tax year own, directly or indirectly, 50% or more of the voting stock of a domestic corporation? (For rules of attribution, see section 267(c).) If "Yes," attach a schedule showing: **(a)** name, address, and employer identification number and **(b)** percentage owned		✔
4	Was the corporation a member of a controlled group subject to the provisions of section 1561?		✔
5	Check ... Shelte... of a Tax ▶ ☐		
6	Check ... ▶ ☐ If so, ... Discount Instruments.		
7	If the corporation: **(a)** filed its election to be an S corporation after 1986, **(b)** was a C corporation before it elected to be an S corporation **or** the corporation acquired an asset with a basis determined by reference to its basis (or the basis of any other property) in the hands of a C corporation, and **(c)** has net unrealized built-in gain (defined in section 1374(d)(1)) in excess of the net recognized built-in gain from prior years, enter the net unrealized built-in gain reduced by net recognized built-in gain from prior years (see page 17 of the instructions) ▶ $		
8	Check this box if the corporation had accumulated earnings and profits at the close of the tax year (see page 18 of the instructions) ▶ ☐		

An S coporation that was once a C corporation may have a number to insert after the "$" sign in line 7 and will very likely have accumulated ernings and profits, in which case it should check the box at the end of line 8.

Note: *If the corporation had assets or operated a business in a foreign country or U.S. possession, it may be required to attach* ***Schedule N (Form 1120),*** *Foreign Operations of U.S. Corporations, to this return. See Schedule N for details.*

Schedule K — Shareholders' Shares of Income, Credits, Deductions, etc.

Income (Loss)

	(a) Pro rata share items		(b) Total amount
1	Ordinary income (loss) from trade or business activities (page 1, line 21)	1	24000
2	Net income (loss) from rental real estate activities *(attach Form 8825)*	2	
3a	Gross income from other rental activities — 3a		
b	Expenses from other rental activities *(attach schedule)* — 3b		
c	Net income (loss) from other rental activities. Subtract line 3b from line 3a	3c	
4	Portfolio income (loss):		
a	Interest income	4a	
b	Ordinary dividends	4b	
c	Royalty income	4c	
d	Net short-term capital gain (loss) *(attach Schedule D (Form 1120S))*	4d	
e	Net long-term capital gain (loss) *(attach Schedule D (Form 1120S))*: **(1)** 28% rate gain (loss) ▶ **(2)** Total for year ▶	4e(2)	
f	Other portfolio income (loss) *(attach schedule)*	4f	
5	Net section 1231 gain (loss) (other than due to casualty or theft) *(attach Form 4797)*	5	
6	Other income (loss) *(attach schedule)*	6	

Form **1120S** (2000)

Form 1120S (2000) Page **3**

Schedule K **Shareholders' Shares of Income, Credits, Deductions, etc.** *(continued)*

		(a) Pro rata share items		(b) Total amount
Deductions	7	Charitable contributions *(attach schedule)*	7	1000
	8	Section 179 expense deduction *(attach Form 4562)*	8	
	9	Deductions related to portfolio income (loss) (itemize)	9	
	10	Other deductions *(attach schedule)*	10	
Investment Interest	11a	Interest expense on investment debts	11a	
	b (1)	Investment income included on lines 4a, 4b, 4c, and 4f above	11b(1)	
	(2)	Investment expenses included on line 9 above	11b(2)	
Credits	12a	Credit for alcohol used as a fuel *(attach Form 6478)*	12a	
			12b(1)	
			12b(2)	
			12b(3)	
			12b(4)	
			12c	
		...es	12d	
	e	Credits related to other rental activities	12e	
	13	Other credits	13	
Adjustments and Tax Preference Items	14a	Depreciation adjustment on property placed in service after 1986	14a	
	b	Adjusted gain or loss	14b	
	c	Depletion (other than oil and gas)	14c	
	d (1)	Gross income from oil, gas, or geothermal properties	14d(1)	
	(2)	Deductions allocable to oil, gas, or geothermal properties	14d(2)	
	e	Other adjustments and tax preference items *(attach schedule)*	14e	
Foreign Taxes	15a	Name of foreign country or U.S. possession ▶		
	b	Gross income sourced at shareholder level	15b	
	c	Foreign gross income sourced at corporate level:		
	(1)	Passive	15c(1)	
	(2)	Listed categories *(attach schedule)*	15c(2)	
	(3)	General limitation	15c(3)	
	d	Deductions allocated and apportioned at shareholder level:		
	(1)	Interest expense	15d(1)	
	(2)	Other	15d(2)	
	e	Deductions allocated and apportioned at corporate level to foreign source income:		
	(1)	Passive	15e(1)	
	(2)	Listed categories *(attach schedule)*	15e(2)	
	(3)	General limitation	15e(3)	
	f	Total foreign taxes (check one): ▶ ☐ Paid ☐ Accrued	15f	
	g	Reduction in taxes available for credit and gross income from all sources *(attach schedule)*	15g	
Other	16	Section 59(e)(2) expenditures: **a** Type ▶ .... **b** Amount ▶	16b	
	17	Tax-exempt interest income	17	
	18	Other tax-exempt income	18	
	19	Nondeductible expenses	19	
	20	Total property distributions (including cash) other than dividends reported on line 22 below	20	
	21	Other items and amounts required to be reported separately to shareholders *(attach schedule)*		
	22	Total dividend distributions paid from accumulated earnings and profits	22	
	23	**Income (loss).** (Required only if Schedule M-1 must be completed.) Combine lines 1 through 6 in column (b). From the result, subtract the sum of lines 7 through 11a, 15f, and 16b	23	23000

The profit per the accounting books for this corporation is the $24,000 minus the $1,000 charitiable contributions expense. So each stockholder reports his or her share of the $24,000 income ($8,000 each) on Schedule A (itemized deductions) of Form 1040. The kicker is in the teeth for stockholders that don't amortize, but use the standard deduction. They lose any benefit from the charitable contribution.

Form **1120S** (2000)

Form 1120S (2000) Page 4

Schedule L **Balance Sheets per Books**

Assets	Beginning of tax year (a)	(b)	End of tax year (c)	(d)
1 Cash		30000		15000
2a Trade notes and accounts receivable			3975	
b Less allowance for bad debts				3975
3 Inventories				200000
4 U.S. Government obligations				
5 Tax-exempt securities				
6 Other current assets *(attach schedule)*				
7 Loans to shareholders				
8 Mortgage and real estate loans				
9 Other investments *(attach schedule)*				
10a Buildings and other depreciable assets			45000	
b Less accumulated depreciation			2625	42375
11a Depletable assets				
b Less accumulated depletion				
12 Land (net of any amortization)				
13a Intangible assets (amortizable only)			3000	
b Less accumulated amortization			350	2650
14 Other assets *(attach schedule)*				
15 Total assets		30000		264000
Liabilities and Shareholders' Equity				
16 Accounts payable				3000
17 Mortgages, notes, bonds payable in less than 1 year				30000
18 Other current liabilities *(attach schedule)*				
19 Loans from shareholders				
20 Mortgages, notes, bonds payable in 1 year or more				190000
21 Other liabilities *(attach schedule)*				
22 Capital stock		30000		30000
23 Additional paid-in capital				
24 Retained earnings				11000
25 Adjustments to shareholders' equity *(attach schedule)*				
26 Less cost of treasury stock		( )		( )
27 Total liabilities and shareholders' equity		30000		264000

Line 24 may not equal the totals of M-2, line 8, if the corporation was ever a C corporation.

Schedule M-1 **Reconciliation of Income (Loss) per Books With Income (Loss) per Return** (You are not required to complete this schedule if the total assets on line 15, column (d), of Schedule L are less than $25,000.)

1 Net income (loss) per books	23000	5 Income recorded on books this year not included on Schedule K, lines 1 through 6 (itemize):	
2 Income included on Schedule K, lines 1 through 6, not recorded on books this year (itemize):		a Tax-exempt interest $	
3 Expenses recorded on books this year not included on Schedule K, lines 1 through 11a, 15f, and 16b (itemize):		6 Deductions included on Schedule K, lines 1 through 11a, 15f, and 16b, not charged against book income this year (itemize):	
a Depreciation $		a Depreciation $	
b Travel and entertainment $			
		7 Add lines 5 and 6	
4 Add lines 1 through 3	23000	8 Income (loss) (Schedule K, line 23). Line 4 less line 7	23000

Schedule M-2 **Analysis of Accumulated Adjustments Account, Other Adjustments Account, and Shareholders' Undistributed Taxable Income Previously Taxed** (see page 27 of the instructions)

	(a) Accumulated adjustments account	(b) Other adjustments account	(c) Shareholders' undistributed taxable income previously taxed
1 Balance at beginning of tax year	0		
2 Ordinary income from page 1, line 21	24000		
3 Other additions			
4 Loss from page 1, line 21	( )		
5 Other reductions Charitable contributions	1000)	(	
6 Combine lines 1 through 5			
7 Distributions other than dividend distributions	23000		
8 Balance at end of tax year. Subtract line 7 from line 6	12000		

This column applies to non-taxable items, such as tax-exempt income

This column applies only to corporations that were in S status before 1982

Form **1120S** (2000)

SCHEDULE K-1 (Form 1120S)
Department of the Treasury
Internal Revenue Service

Shareholder's Share of Income, Credits, Deductions, etc.

▶ See separate instructions.

For calendar year 2000 or tax year beginning June 12, 2000, and ending December 31, 20 00

OMB No. 1545-0130

2000

Shareholder's identifying number ▶ 555-55-5555

Corporation's identifying number ▶ 98 : 7654321

Shareholder's name, address, and ZIP code
Joseph & Julie Firehouse
1235 Canal Road
Nearhere, FL 12398

Corporation's name, address, and ZIP code
Wet'n Soggy Coal Co., Inc.
60 Waterway Road
Nearhere, FL 12399

A Shareholder's percentage of stock ownership for tax year (see instructions for Schedule K-1) . . . . ▶ 50 %
B Internal Revenue Service Center where corporation filed its return ▶ Atlanta, GA
C Tax shelter registration number (see instructions for Schedule K-1) . . . .
D Check applicable boxes: (1) ☐ Final K-1 (2) ☐ Amended K-1

Tax shelter number not required for this corporation, as it's not a tax shelter.

		(a) Pro rata share items		(b) Amount	(c) Form 1040 filers enter the amount in column (b) on:
Income (Loss)	1	Ordinary income (loss) from trade or business activities	1	12000	See pages 4 and 5 of the Shareholder's Instructions for Schedule K-1 (Form 1120S).
	2	Net income (loss) from rental real estate activities	2		
	3	Net income (loss) from other rental activities	3		
	4	Portfolio income (loss):			
	a	Interest	4a		Sch. B, Part I, line 1
	b	Ordinary dividends	4b		Sch. B, Part II, line 5
	c	Royalties	4c		Sch. E, Part I, line 4
	d	Net short-term capital gain (loss)	4d		Sch. D, line 5, col. (f)
	e	Net long-term capital gain (loss):			
		(1) 28% rate gain (loss)	4e(1)		Sch. D, line 12, col. (g)
		(2) Total for year	4e(2)		Sch. D, line 12, col. (f)
	f	Other portfolio income (loss) *(attach schedule)*	4f		(Enter on applicable line of your return.)
	5	Net section 1231 gain (loss) (other than due to casualty or theft)	5		See Shareholder's Instructions for Schedule K-1 (Form 1120S).
	6	Other income (loss) *(attach schedule)*	6		(Enter on applicable line of your return.)
Deductions	7	Charitable contributions *(attach schedule)*	7	500	Sch. A, line 15 or 16
	8	Section 179 expense deduction	8		See page 6 of the Shareholder's Instructions for Schedule K-1 (Form 1120S).
	9	Deductions related to portfolio income (loss) *(attach schedule)*	9		
	10	Other deductions *(attach schedule)*	10		
Investment Interest	11a	Interest expense on investment debts	11a		Form 4952, line 1
	b	(1) Investment income included on lines 4a, 4b, 4c, and 4f above	11b(1)		See Shareholder's Instructions for Schedule K-1 (Form 1120S).
		(2) Investment expenses included on line 9 above	11b(2)		
Credits	12a	Cre[illegible]			Form 6478, line 10
	b	Low[illegible]			
		(1) [illegible] service before 1990			Form 8586, line 5
		(2) Other than on line 12b(1) for property placed in service before 1990	12b(2)		
		(3) From section 42(j)(5) partnerships for property placed in service after 1989	12b(3)		
		[illegible] ...e after	12b(4)		
	c	Qualified rehabilitation expenditures related to rental real estate activities	12c		See page 7 of the Shareholder's Instructions for Schedule K-1 (Form 1120S).
	d	Credits (other than credits shown on lines 12b and 12c) related to rental real estate activities	12d		
	e	Credits related to other rental activities	12e		
	13	Other credits	13		

For each line, the figures on the three Schedules K-1 add up to the figures on the Schedule K (page 3 of the Form 1120S).

Page 2 of this Schedule K-1 is not shown, as nothing on that page applies to this corporation.

For Paperwork Reduction Act Notice, see the Instructions for Form 1120S. Cat. No. 11520D **Schedule K-1 (Form 1120S) 2000**

SCHEDULE K-1 (Form 1120S)

Department of the Treasury
Internal Revenue Service

Shareholder's Share of Income, Credits, Deductions, etc.

▶ See separate instructions.

For calendar year 2000 or tax year beginning June 12, 2000, and ending December 31, 20 00

OMB No. 1545-0130

2000

Shareholder's identifying number ▶ 888-88-8888

Corporation's identifying number ▶ 98 : 7654321

Shareholder's name, address, and ZIP code
Karen Coolwater
52 Main Street
Somewhere, FL 44444

Corporation's name, address, and ZIP code
Wet'n Soggy Coal Co., Inc.
60 Waterway Road
Nearhere, FL 12399

A Shareholder's percentage of stock ownership for tax year (see instructions for Schedule K-1) . . . . ▶ 33.3 %
B Internal Revenue Service Center where corporation filed its return ▶ Atlanta, GA
C Tax shelter registration number (see instructions for Schedule K-1) . . . .
D Check applicable boxes: (1) ☐ Final K-1 (2) ☐ Amended K-1

Tax shelter number not required for this corporation, as it's not a tax shelter.

		(a) Pro rata share items		(b) Amount	(c) Form 1040 filers enter the amount in column (b) on:
Income (Loss)	1	Ordinary income (loss) from trade or business activities	1	8000	See pages 4 and 5 of the Shareholder's Instructions for Schedule K-1 (Form 1120S).
	2	Net income (loss) from rental real estate activities	2		
	3	Net income (loss) from other rental activities	3		
	4	Portfolio income (loss):			
	a	Interest	4a		Sch. B, Part I, line 1
	b	Ordinary dividends	4b		Sch. B, Part II, line 5
	c	Royalties	4c		Sch. E, Part I, line 4
	d	Net short-term capital gain (loss)	4d		Sch. D, line 5, col. (f)
	e	Net long-term capital gain (loss):			
		(1) 28% rate gain (loss)	4e(1)		Sch. D, line 12, col. (g)
		(2) Total for year	4e(2)		Sch. D, line 12, col. (f)
	f	Other portfolio income (loss) *(attach schedule)*	4f		(Enter on applicable line of your return.)
	5	Net section 1231 gain (loss) (other than due to casualty or theft)	5		See Shareholder's Instructions for Schedule K-1 (Form 1120S).
	6	Other income (loss) *(attach schedule)*	6		(Enter on applicable line of your return.)
Deductions	7	Charitable contributions *(attach schedule)*	7	333	Sch. A, line 15 or 16
	8	Section 179 expense deduction	8		See page 6 of the Shareholder's Instructions for Schedule K-1 (Form 1120S).
	9	Deductions related to portfolio income (loss) *(attach schedule)*	9		
	10	Other deductions *(attach schedule)*	10		
Investment Interest	11a	Interest expense on investment debts	11a		Form 4952, line 1
	b	(1) Investment income included on lines 4a, 4b, 4c, and 4f above	11b(1)		See Shareholder's Instructions for Schedule K-1 (Form 1120S).
		(2) Investment expenses included on line 9 above	11b(2)		
Credits	12a	Cred...			Form 6478, line 10
	b	Low...			
		(1) ... service before 1990			Form 8586, line 5
		(2) Other than on line 12b(1) for property placed in service before 1990	12b(2)		
		(3) From section 42(j)(5) partnerships for property placed in service after 1989	12b(3)		
		...ce after ...	12b(4)		
	c	Qualified rehabilitation expenditures related to rental real estate activities	12c		See page 7 of the Shareholder's Instructions for Schedule K-1 (Form 1120S).
	d	Credits (other than credits shown on lines 12b and 12c) related to rental real estate activities	12d		
	e	Credits related to other rental activities	12e		
	13	Other credits	13		

For each line, the figures on the three Schedules K-1 add up to the figures on the Schedule K (page 3 of the Form 1120S).

Page 2 of this Schedule K-1 is not shown, as nothing on that page applies to this corporation.

For Paperwork Reduction Act Notice, see the Instructions for Form 1120S. Cat. No. 11520D **Schedule K-1 (Form 1120S) 2000**

SCHEDULE K-1 (Form 1120S)

Department of the Treasury
Internal Revenue Service

Shareholder's Share of Income, Credits, Deductions, etc.

▶ See separate instructions.

For calendar year 2000 or tax year beginning June 12, 2000, and ending December 31, 20 00

OMB No. 1545-0130

2000

Shareholder's identifying number ▶ 444-44-4444

Corporation's identifying number ▶ 98 : 7654321

Shareholder's name, address, and ZIP code
Larry Hotland
76 Firey Place
Somewhere, FL 44443

Corporation's name, address, and ZIP code
Wet'n Soggy Coal Co., Inc.
60 Waterway Road
Nearhere, FL 12399

A Shareholder's percentage of stock ownership for tax year (see instructions for Schedule K-1) . . . . ▶ 16.7 %
B Internal Revenue Service Center where corporation filed its return ▶ Atlanta, GA
C Tax shelter registration number (see instructions for Schedule K-1) . . . .
D Check applicable boxes: (1) ☐ Final K-1 (2) ☐ Amended K-1

Tax shelter number not required for this corporation, as it's not a tax shelter.

	(a) Pro rata share items		(b) Amount	(c) Form 1040 filers enter the amount in column (b) on:
Income (Loss)	1 Ordinary income (loss) from trade or business activities	1	4000	See pages 4 and 5 of the Shareholder's Instructions for Schedule K-1 (Form 1120S).
	2 Net income (loss) from rental real estate activities	2		
	3 Net income (loss) from other rental activities	3		
	4 Portfolio income (loss):			
	a Interest	4a		Sch. B, Part I, line 1
	b Ordinary dividends	4b		Sch. B, Part II, line 5
	c Royalties	4c		Sch. E, Part I, line 4
	d Net short-term capital gain (loss)	4d		Sch. D, line 5, col. (f)
	e Net long-term capital gain (loss):			
	(1) 28% rate gain (loss)	4e(1)		Sch. D, line 12, col. (g)
	(2) Total for year	4e(2)		Sch. D, line 12, col. (f)
	f Other portfolio income (loss) *(attach schedule)*	4f		(Enter on applicable line of your return.)
	5 Net section 1231 gain (loss) (other than due to casualty or theft)	5		See Shareholder's Instructions for Schedule K-1 (Form 1120S).
	6 Other income (loss) *(attach schedule)*	6		(Enter on applicable line of your return.)
Deductions	7 Charitable contributions *(attach schedule)*	7	167	Sch. A, line 15 or 16
	8 Section 179 expense deduction	8		See page 6 of the Shareholder's Instructions for Schedule K-1 (Form 1120S).
	9 Deductions related to portfolio income (loss) *(attach schedule)*	9		
	10 Other deductions *(attach schedule)*	10		
Investment Interest	11a Interest expense on investment debts	11a		Form 4952, line 1
	b (1) Investment income included on lines 4a, 4b, 4c, and 4f above	11b(1)		See Shareholder's Instructions for Schedule K-1 (Form 1120S).
	(2) Investment expenses included on line 9 above	11b(2)		
Credits	12a Cred[illegible]			Form 6478, line 10
	b Low[illegible]			
	(1) [illegible]			Form 8586, line 5
	(2) Other than on line 12b(1) for property placed in service before 1990	12b(2)		
	(3) From section 42(j)(5) partnerships for property placed in service after 1989	12b(3)		
	[illegible] ce after [illegible]	12b(4)		
	c Qualified rehabilitation expenditures related to rental real estate activities	12c		See page 7 of the Shareholder's Instructions for Schedule K-1 (Form 1120S).
	d Credits (other than credits shown on lines 12b and 12c) related to rental real estate activities	12d		
	e Credits related to other rental activities	12e		
	13 Other credits	13		

For each line, the figures on the three Schedules K-1 add up to the figures on the Schedule K (page 3 of the Form 1120S).

Page 2 of this Schedule K-1 is not shown, as nothing on that page applies to this corporation.

For Paperwork Reduction Act Notice, see the Instructions for Form 1120S. Cat. No. 11520D **Schedule K-1 (Form 1120S) 2000**

The next three pages are the forms covered in the Gertrude Greengrass example of a Section 351 transfer of assets to a corporation. You can save taxes if you avail yourself of this procedure when you incorporate the business, if you have significant assets that you use in your sole proprietorship or partnership.

[Statement to be included in stockholder's tax return. The numbers in () refer to the numbering system in the regulation (Sec. 1.351-3) requiring this statement]

Transferor's I.R.C. Section 351 Statement
Information filed in accordance with Sec. 1.351-3

Transfer date: March 1, 2001

Stockholder: Gertrude Greengrass
18 Rocky Boulevard
Denver, Colorado 22222
Social Security number 111-11-1111

Corporation: Greengrass Lawn & Garden Maintenance, Inc.
18 Rocky Boulevard
Denver, Colorado 22222
Employer I.D. number: 55-5555555

(1) Property transferred in exchange for stock:	
Scorched Lawn Machine.	
Original cost	$50,000
Adjusted basis	10,000
Supplies: original cost and adjusted basis	$2,000
(2) Stock of the corporation received:	
Common stock, the only class of stock issued by the corporation	
110 shares of stated value of $100	$11,000
Fair market value of each share	$100
No preferences as no other class of stock issued	
(3) Other securities of the corporation received	None
(4) Amount of money received from the corporation	None
(5) Other property received from the corporation	None
(6) Liabilities of the transferor assumed by the controlled corporation:	
Accounts payable for supplies	$1,000
Created in normal operating cycle	
Corporation assumed with transfer of supplies	
Assumption does not eliminate transferor's liability	

[Statement to be included in corporation's tax return. The numbers in () refer to the numbering system in the regulation (Sec. 1.351-3) requiring this statement]

Transferee's I.R.C. Section 351 Statement
Information filed in accordance with Sec. 1.351-3

Transfer date: March 1, 2001

Stockholder:	Gertrude Greengrass 18 Rocky Boulevard Denver, Colorado 22222 Social Security number 111-11-1111
Corporation:	Greengrass Lawn & Garden Maintenance, Inc. 18 Rocky Boulevard Denver, Colorado 22222 Employer I.D. number: 55-5555555

(1) Property received from transferor:

Scorched Lawn Machine, manufactured by Scorch, Inc. Gasoline-powered machine that mows lawn, edges, and fertilizes customers' lawns and gardens. Purchased new in 1996 by transferor.

Fertilizer and other supplies required for the business.

(2) Cost of property received from the transferor:

Scorched Lawn Machine.	
Original cost	$50,000
Adjusted basis on date of transfer	10,000
Supplies: original cost and adjusted basis	$2,000

(3) Information with respect to the capital stock of the corporation.

Total issued and outstanding shares of capital stock immediately prior to the exchange	None
Total issued and outstanding shares of capital stock immediately after the exchange	1,100 shares
All stock is common. No other classes authorized	
1,100 shares of common stock issued to Gertrude Greengrass:	
She owned, prior to transfer	None
She owns, after transfer	1,100 shares
Fair market value of the capital stock as of date of exchange	$100 per share

(4) Information with respect to securities of the corporation No securities, other than common stock, have been issued	
(5) Amount of money which passed to the transferor	None
(6) Other property which passed to the transferor	None
(7) Transferor's liabilities assumed by the corporation: Accounts payable	$1,000
Created by the purchase of business supplies	
Corporation assumed the accounts payable as it also received the supplies that gave rise to the accounts payable from the transferor.	

5 MORE NIT-PICKING RULES—SOME GOOD/SOME BAD

In the first four chapters, we have discussed many rules pertaining to S corporations and whether each would or would not be good for you. As you can surmise by the title of this chapter, there are more rules. I did not include them, in what might be the logical place, in the earlier discussions, because rule overload can render brains useless.

Some of what follows may be repetition of what has been discussed in the earlier chapters. However, although Chapter 3, for instance, grouped aspects of S corporations into advantages and disadvantages, this chapter is in the form of a recitation of the rules, so it's more of a reference.

REQUIREMENTS FOR A CORPORATION TO BE AN S CORPORATION

Of course, the corporation must elect S status, by filing Form 2553 with the IRS, as discussed in Chapter 4, and it must be a domestic corporation. (A domestic corporation is one chartered by any state or the federal government.) S corporation status is denied to certain banks, insurance companies, possession corporations, and DISCs (domestic international sales corporations). Other requirements follow.

Who May Own Stock in an S Corporation

The rules about who may own an S corporation's stock are as follows:

- Individuals must be citizens or resident aliens.
- Estates.
- Certain trusts.

- Certain tax-exempt organizations.
- Another S corporation, if it owns 100 percent of the stock (see the discussion of QSubs later in this chapter).

How to Count the Individual Stockholders for the Maximum of 75 Rule

- Husbands and wives are counted as one stockholder, whether they both own stock, own it jointly, or whether or not they live in a community-property state. If one or both should die, the estates or an estate and the living spouse continue as one stockholder. If they divorce, they are then treated as two individuals.
- Joint tenants who are not married are counted as individuals. (If Ethyl, Frances, and Gloria own stock in an S corporation as any type of joint tenants, they count as three stockholders.)
- Grantor trusts count as one stockholder.
- Voting trusts, but each beneficiary counts as one stockholder.
- A testamentary trust counts as one stockholder, but may hold the stock for only two years after the death of the testator.
- Estates, including bankruptcy estates.
- Qualified Subchapter S trusts (QSSTs): the beneficiary is deemed to be the owner of the stock and counts as one stockholder.
- Electing Small Business Trusts.

Rules for Qualified Subchapter S Trusts (QSSTs)

- Only one income beneficiary allowed.
- Corpus (the principal) may be distributed only to the income beneficiary.
- Upon termination of the trust, all of its assets must be distributed to the income beneficiary.

Electing Small Business Trusts. These trusts are not as restricted as QSSTs, but the trust, rather than the beneficiary, pays tax on the income at a 39.6 percent tax rate. Exception: Capital gains are taxed at individual capital gain rates.

SUBSIDIARY S CORPORATIONS

There is the possibility, particularly in our sue-sue-sue society, that the owners of an S corporation would like to have segments of their business in separate subsidiary corporations, so if a large judgment sinks one of the segments, the whole enterprise doesn't slide into the murky bankruptcy waters. To help small businesses so arrange their affairs, the law now allows S corporations to own other S corporations. Those subsidiary corporations have a legal posture of separate entities (under state law), but for federal income tax, the parent and all the subsidiary corporations are treated as one. Therefore, there is only one tax return to file for the whole operation.

Some terminology: The S corporation that owns the stock in other S corporations is usually referred to as the *parent* corporation, whereas the subsidiary corporations are usually called *subs*. When a sub has become a valid qualified subchapter S subsidiary, the tax code, and the rest of us, call it a *QSub*.

Rules to Follow to Have Subsidiary S Corporation(s)

- 100 percent of the outstanding stock of a subsidiary corporation must be owned by the parent S corporation.
- The parent must make an election for the subsidiary to be classified as a QSub by filing *Form 8869, Qualified Subchapter S Subsidiary Election* with the IRS. If a parent forms a sub and immediately elects QSub status for it, Form 8869 should be filed with the same IRS service center where the parent files its tax form. If the parent purchased all the outstanding stock of an existing corporation and elects QSub status for it, Form 8869 should be filed with the IRS service center where the sub formerly filed its tax returns.
- The rules regarding the type of corporation that can be a QSub are the same as the rules about what type of corporation can be an S corporation.
- The exception, of course, is that a QSub is owned by a corporation.

When to File a QSub Election

If you form a subsidiary with the intention that it be a QSub, file the election immediately. The deadline is actually two months and 15 days after the subsidiary is formed, if you want to avoid the sub spending some time as a C corporation.

Care Needed When an S Corporation Buys an Existing C Corporation

You can select an effective date for the QSub election ranging from two months and 15 days prior to the election to one year after the election. However, be sure you are following the best procedure for your tax bill.

When you elect QSub for an existing C corporation, the tax law regards that event as the sub having been "liquidated into the parent S corporation." That is, for tax purposes, the sub ceases to exist, and all its assets are transferred to the parent. Usually, this should result in no tax to either the parent or the sub, but there are exceptions. The area of parent corporations, subsidiaries, liquidations, reorganization, and so on is another tax area that is beyond the scope of this book. Although you can be reasonably assured that starting a new corporation, selling all its stock to a parent S corporation, and electing QSub status for the sub will not generate any taxes other than from the future operations of both corporations, buying an existing corporation and electing QSub status for it can be fraught with tax traps.

Sally, as sole stockholder of Sally's Salads, an S corporation, had the corporation purchase Dan's Desserts, Inc., a C corporation. Checking with her state's secretary of state indicated that Dan's Desserts, Inc. had only one class of stock outstanding. She also examined (so she thought) Dan's books, so when she bought all of Dan's Desserts, Inc. stock, she was aware that the corporation has signed a promissory note to Dan's uncle, to be paid monthly at $1,000 per month.

Sally elected QSub status for Dan's Desserts, Inc. Then, two years later, Mr. Beady from the IRS arrived in her store. He rummaged through her records and found a copy of an agreement with Dan's uncle that stated that the monthly payment did not have to be paid in any month in which sales were below $50,000. It also provided that Dan's uncle could exchange the notes for common stock if he ever chose to do so.

*"That note," said Mr. Beady, "amounts to a second class of stock, and that means Dan's Desserts, Inc. is not a QSub." So, Sally had to use up all the cash, and then some, in Dan's Desserts to pay the C corporation taxes for two years. There was also much hassle in removing Dan's Desserts' transactions from the S corporation tax return and preparing the C corporation tax returns for Dan's Desserts, Inc.**

Moral: Hand-holding by a tax professional is necessary in a situation like Sally's. At the very least, Sally should have had her favorite accountant examine the records of Dan's Desserts, Inc.

QSub status is not limited to just one or more corporations whose stock is owned by a parent S corporation. You could have a parent-child-grandchild situation, in which the Acme Corporation owns the Bounce Corporation, which owns the Crunch Corporation. If the Acme Corporation is an S corporation, it could elect QSub status for the Bounce Corporation, and, assuming it does, Acme could elect QSub status for the Crunch Corporation.

ACCUMULATION OF UNDISTRIBUTED PROFITS

If you look at the federal income tax form for S corporations (1120S), you will see, on page 4 of the form, a box called Schedule M-2. That is the place in which the corporation (and the IRS) keep track of the accumulated adjustments account (AAA). As you will note, there are two other columns, called Other Adjustments Account and Shareholders' Undistributed Taxable Income Previously Taxed. These three accounts all relate to earnings of the corporation while it was an S corporation and distributions to the stockholders while it was an S corporation or within one year (usually) after termination of S status.

There is another classification of earnings and distributions that is

*It's conceivable, under today's "friendlier" environment, that the IRS would have decided Sally's situation was an inadvertent termination and let her rectify the fault by buying the note from Dan's uncle. But she can't be sure the IRS would do that. Why take chances?

called earnings and profits (E&P). It does not appear in Schedule M-2, for it pertains to years in which the corporation was in C status. (To be technical, it also could arise for S corporations that have always been S corporations and were in existence before 1983.)

What is the reason, beyond the need to fill in the tax form, for worrying about these accounts? If an officer of an S corporation is not aware of the distinctions in this classification of accumulated earnings, some serious tax bills could be incurred without realizing it. If a corporate officer does not understand this complex area, he or she at least should be aware of the need for professional advice before making profit distributions.

Let's review the AAA and discuss the other classifications. If you keep a bookmark at the page where page 4 of Form 1120S is reproduced, this may be a little easier to follow.

Accumulated Adjustments Account

This is a running total of income (profits) minus distributions of those profits to the stockholders. The Schedule M-2 lists line items of ordinary income, other additions, and other reductions. If you want to figure out which items of income, expense, and loss go on which line, it is explained in the instructions to the form. My advice is to let your accountant worry about that detail. It is sufficient to realize that this account contains the items that have an impact on the taxes that the stockholders pay.

What is important is the concept that the bottom line (line 8) essentially is the balance of the S corporation profits that have not been distributed to the stockholders. As long as the corporation remains in S status and distributions are less than the balance in this account, the stockholders should not have to pay any additional taxes on the distributions they receive. (The tax has already been paid by the stockholders for the year in which the corporation earned the profits.) Beyond that, if there is a balance at the bottom of either or both of the other two accounts in Schedule M-2, the corporation can distribute more than the balance of the AAA without tax consequences.

Other Adjustments Account

This pot holds just the tax-exempt income (such as tax-exempt bond interest) and related expenses. Logic prevails here. Because the underlying income was tax-exempt, distributions can be made from this account without incurring any tax liability.

Shareholders' Undistributed Taxable Income Previously Taxed

Before 1983, S corporations operated under another set of rules. It would be pointless to discuss the details of those regulations from long ago. Suffice it to say that this account was, in those old rules, almost the equivalent of the AAA account today. However, for various technical reasons, the IRS wants S corporations who were in business before 1983 to keep the undistributed earnings from those years separate from the undistributed profits earned after 1982.

Because the stockholders paid those taxes years ago, distributions can be made from this account balance without incurring additional taxes.

Earnings and Profits (E&P)

Although this account is not displayed in the tax return, it is a balance that the corporation should keep track of. It consists of earnings of the corporation while it was in C status, minus dividends that were paid to the stockholders. (There could be other items in this computation, but the explanation here is enough to digest now.)

Inasmuch as these earnings arose when C status was in effect, the earnings are subject to double taxation. That is, even though the corporation paid corporate taxes on the profits, stockholders have to again pay tax on those earnings when they are distributed to them as dividends. (See Chapter 2 for more discussion of this double-tax rule.)

Corporations that were in Subchapter S status before 1983 could also generate E&P. That was because certain items of income were not passed through to the stockholders, but the tax on those items was paid by the corporation, just as if it were a C corporation.

There are two reasons this account is important. One, as mentioned before, if any dividend distributions are made from it, they are taxable to the stockholders, even though the corporation is presently in S status. Two, if there is any balance in the E&P account, it changes the rules as to whether an S corporation can have substantial passive income. (See the section in this chapter on passive income.)

Order of Distributions

Now comes this question: "If my corporation pays distributions to me, out of which pot of earnings does that money come?" The IRS has set up a precedence for determining the source of distributions. The accumulated earnings pots are used in this numeric order:

1. Accumulated adjustments account.
2. Shareholders' undistributed taxable income previously taxed.
3. Other adjustments account.
4. Earnings and profits.

That would seem to be the way most S corporation stockholders would want the distribution hierarchy to be. There is no dipping into the pot that would create a tax bill unless there is nowhere else to dip.

However, if your S corporation has E&P, but it is not a large number, you might want to distribute out of that pot to get rid of all E&P. That would change the rules about passive income for your S corporation.

Amazingly, the tax rules do allow you to do just that. You can elect to distribute earnings from the E&P before you distribute from the other pots. (On second thought, that is not amazing. Of course, the IRS will approve of anything that generates more taxes!)

Please do not feel that you must have a thorough understanding of this accumulated-earnings area if you are to operate an S corporation. It is enough that you are aware of the complications and seek advice from your tax professional before making distributions to shareholders.

PASSIVE INVESTMENT INCOME

If you are just starting an S corporation, or you have an S corporation that has never been a C corporation, this section will not affect you. However, if you do have an S corporation with E&P left over from your C corporation days, you should be wary of what passive investment income can do to you and your corporation, so read on.

The tax rules about passive income are murky and, as are most tax rules, complicated. The complication is not helped by the fact that the rules use the term *passive* with different meanings in different areas. Let's try for some clarification.

Passive income, as it is used in the 1986 law (Internal Revenue Code Section 469) that blew many tax shelters out of the water, generally refers to income from a business activity (and most rental activities) in which the part-owner of a business is not active. It does not include portfolio income, which is income from interest, dividends, annuities, and gain or loss on property held for investment.

In the area of S corporations (Internal Revenue Code Section 1375), the rules refer to passive investment income. This term includes income from royalties, rents, dividends, interest (with some exceptions), annuities, and gains from sales or exchanges of securities. Notice that this use of the word *passive* includes portfolio income but excludes passive business income, whereas the rules about tax shelters exclude portfolio income but include passive business income. No wonder we stay so confused about tax rules!

There are still more terms involved here. The first is *net passive income.* This number is passive investment income minus expenses directly connected with the production of that income. The definition of the second term, *excess net passive income,* takes longer to define and is complicated, to say the least. If you do not understand the definition (most of us don't), don't worry. You can skip it if you remember that the trouble starts when passive investment income exceeds 25 percent of the gross receipts of the corporation. The definition is, "Excess net passive income is that portion of the S corporation's net passive income that bears the same ratio to the total net passive income for the tax year as the excess gross passive income bears to the total gross passive investment income for the year." Do you like formulas? This convoluted rule can be expressed this way:

$$ENPI = NPI \times \frac{PII - (.25 \times GR)}{PII}$$

Where:

$ENPI$ = excess net passive income
NPI = net passive income
PII = passive investment income
GR = total gross receipts

The Tax on Excess Net Passive Investment Income of an S Corporation

Yes, there are taxes that are levied directly on an S corporation rather than on the stockholders, and this is one of them.* Fortunately, you do not have to understand that definition in order to compute the resulting tax. You can use the worksheet for line 22a in the instructions to Form 1120S, page 14 (see the Appendix). Again, this tax applies only if the S corporation has E&P from its C corporation days.

As this tax is computed at the maximum corporate rate (35 percent at this writing), it behooves the directors of an S corporation to take steps to avoid it. Those steps can be to declare dividends that would distribute all of the E&P to stockholders or the passive investments could be distributed to the stockholders.

Escape Hatches: Excess net passive income cannot exceed the corporation's taxable income for the year, so if the corporation suffered a loss for the year (counting both operating income and passive income), there would be no excess net passive income and, therefore, no tax on it.

The IRS may waive the tax if the officers of the corporation can establish that, in good faith, they believed the corporation had no E&P left from its C status time. When it is discovered that there is E&P, it must distribute those accumulated earnings to the stockholders within a reasonable time.

TAX YEARS

At one time, you could select any fiscal or tax year you wished, as long as it ended on the last day of a month. Many of us took advantage of that to defer income, and the resulting income tax, from one year to the next. (A year ending on January 31 did best. It put 11 months of corporate income on the tax returns of the stockholders for the following year.)

Again, the IRS has slammed the door on a tax-deferring gimmick. Now, S corporations generally must be on the same tax year as are the majority of its stockholders. As stockholders of S corporations usually are individuals, and most individuals are on a calendar year (a year ending on December 31), most S corporations must be on a calendar tax year.

---

*The other tax is that on built-in gains of appreciated assets. See the discussion later in this chapter.

There are a couple of exceptions: First, an S corporation can adopt a tax year in which the gross receipts of the last two months of the year represent 25 percent or more of the gross receipts for 12 months. This has to be the situation for three consecutive years. This is not an alternative for a new corporation, for there is no history on which to base the 25 percent test. (This exception to the rule could work for a seasonal business in a summer resort area. July and August could well represent more than 25 percent of annual sales, so the year could end on August 31. Would that generate much tax advantage? Probably not, for it would defer only the income in the slow fall months to the following year.)

Second, an S corporation may request the IRS to approve a tax year other than the calendar year based upon facts and circumstances. This is sort of a roulette wheel situation: how understanding the IRS person is who reviews your request. Also, remember that when you base a request on facts and circumstances, the IRS person is very likely to review your prior tax returns. Do you really want them to do that? Also, you will incur IRS user fees of several hundred dollars for processing your application, whether it's approved or not.

If an S corporation cannot pass the 25 percent of gross income test or gain IRS approval of a different tax year, it still may be able to elect a fiscal year ending on the last day of September, October or November. Again, the rules are complex, but they usually result in this: If you are a new corporation electing S status, those fiscal years are available to you. If you are an existing corporation with a fiscal year ending in those months, you can keep the same fiscal year. If you are an existing corporation with a December 31 year-end, you're stuck with it.

In short, most S corporations will have less hassle and receive less notice from the inquisitive people at the IRS if they file their tax returns on a calendar-year basis.

If you still insist on a fiscal year ending on a date other than December 31 (or within a few days for a corporation on a 52/53-week year), you can study the appropriate forms and instructions available from your friendly IRS at 1-800-TAX-FORM.

Form 8716, Election to Have a Tax Year Other Than a Required Tax Year.

(This is to elect a tax year ending in September, October, or November)

Form 8752, Required Payment or Refund Under Section 7519

(This is how you send money to the IRS to offset the tax advantage you get from deferring up to three months' worth of taxes on the stockholders)

Form 1128, Application to Adopt, Change, or Retain a Tax Year

(This is to avail yourself of the 25-percent-of-gross-receipts-in-two-months test)

IRS Publication 538, Accounting Period and Methods

CHANGE OF STOCKHOLDERS

For a C corporation, change of ownership (change of number of shares of stock owned by one or more individuals) has no effect on the income tax filings of the corporation, because the corporation pays its own taxes. However, the taxable earnings of an S corporation attach themselves to the stockholders, who then pay the tax. So, if a stockholder sells some or all of his or her stock during the year to another individual, who pays tax on how much? The IRS regulations provide some guidance. They state:

> *For purposes of subchapter S of chapter 1 of the Internal Revenue Code and this section, each shareholder's pro rata share of any S corporation item described in section 1366(a) for any taxable year is the sum of the amounts determined with respect to the shareholder by assigning an equal portion of the item to each day of the S corporation's taxable year, and then dividing that portion pro rata among the shares outstanding on that day. See paragraph (b) of this section for rules pertaining to the computation of each shareholder's pro rata share when an election is made under section 1377(a)(2) to treat the taxable year of an S corporation as if it consisted of two taxable years in the case of a termination of a shareholder's entire interest in the corporation.**

On first reading, about all one can get out of this is that there are two methods of allocating taxable income to stockholders involved in a changing ownership situation. For explanation, take a look now at Table 5.1 and the story about the BUG Corporation. Then come back to these comments.

Using the first method, Ulysses could be clobbered with a tax bill on income of $251,598 that he never saw in a check to him. Using the second method, he would have a loss (negative income) that he could apply to other income, and thereby save some taxes. Our first impulse, of course, is to deem it obvious that he should demand the corporation use the second method. However, if Ulysses has little other income and none in the prior two years to which he could carry the loss, the loss from the corporation of $83,333 might be of little benefit. Instead, he could demand, before he sold his stock, an agreement from the two remaining stockholders that they will cause the corporation to pay him a pro rata share of the funds that ensue from any profits at any time during the year. In that case, he might be better off with the first method.

Also, the second method can be used only if there is a complete divestiture of stock by a stockholder. If a stockholder sells only some stock that he or she owns, only the first method can be used to allocate taxable income.

TAX ON BUILT-IN GAINS

This sounds like a tax on the group of us who flunked out of the weight-loss class. Unfortunately, it's a bit more complicated and could be much more expensive. It is, however, an area that affects only those S corporations who

*Regulation Section 1.1377-1, Pro rata share (see the Appendix).

TABLE 5.1 Determining Allocation of Income When Stockholder Sells Out

BUG, Inc., an S Corporation, is owned by Butterfly, Ulysses, and Grunt, each of whom hold ten of the 30 outstanding shares of stock in BUG, Inc. On May 31, Ulysses sells his 10 shares to the remaining stockholders. (Butterfly and Grunt each buy five shares.) BUG, Inc. is engaged in the business of selling used cruise ships and other vessels. During this year, the corporation made one sale in October on which it collected a commission of $2.5 million, and that was its only income for the year. The corporation incurred expenses of $50,000 per month, so the monthly income statements looked like the column to the right. There are two ways to determine how much of the corporation's income each stockholder must report on his or her individual income tax return.

January	$	(50,000)
February		(50,000)
March		(50,000)
April		(50,000)
May		(50,000)
June		(50,000)
July		(50,000)
August		(50,000)
September		(50,000)
October		2,450,000
November		(50,000)
December		(50,000)
	$	1,900,000

Method #1: This is the method that must be used unless all of the stockholders involved in the sale and purchase agree to use method number 2.

Compute earnings per share for the year:	
Earnings ($1,900,000) divided by the number of shares (30)	$63,333.33333
Divide by the number of days in the year	365
Result: Earnings per share per day	$ 173.51598

Allocate the earnings-per-share-per day to the three stockholders:

	Butterfly	Ulysses	Grunt
145 days through May 31, times $173.51598, times the 10 shares that each held	$ 251,598	$ 251,598	$ 251,598
220 remaining days of the year, times $173.51598 times 15 shares that Butterfly and Grunt each now own	572,603		572,603
Income allocated to each shareholder	$ 824,201	$ 251,598	$ 824,201

Method #2: Treat the period before the transfer of stock as one short taxable year and treat the period after the transfer of stock as a separate short taxable year.

	Monthly Net Taxable Income Total	Butterfly	Ulysses	Grunt
January	$ (50,000)	$ (16,667)	$ (16,667)	$ (16,667)
February	(50,000)	(16,667)	(16,667)	(16,667)
March	(50,000)	(16,667)	(16,667)	(16,667)
April	(50,000)	(16,667)	(16,666)	(16,666)
May	(50,000)	(16,666)	(16,666)	(16,666)
Total first short year	(250,000)	(83,334)	(83,333)	(83,333)
June	(50,000)	(25,000)		(25,000)
July	(50,000)	(25,000)		(25,000)
August	(50,000)	(25,000)		(25,000)
September	(50,000)	(25,000)		(25,000)
October	2,450,000	1,225,000		1,225,000
November	(50,000)	(25,000)		(25,000)
December	(50,000)	(25,000)		(25,000)
Total second short year	2,150,000	1,075,000		1,075,000
Total entire year	$ 1,900,000	$ 991,666	$ (83,333)	$ 991,667

spent some years as C corporations before changing to S status. (If this does not apply to your situation, you can skip this section.)

The subject concerns assets that a C corporation has acquired, if those assets have appreciated above their basis, and then only if the C corporation changes to S status. What appreciates over its basis? Most of us would think first of real estate. The building that your business bought ten years ago for $300,000 is now worth $500,000. However, do not overlook plain old desks, chairs, drill presses, and forklifts. These things usually are not worth as much as you paid for them, but they are worth more than their basis. The basis of assets, such as real estate and equipment, is the original cost minus all that depreciation you claimed as an expense. (The depreciation did reduce your tax bill back when you claimed it, but now you may have to pay back that tax saving to the IRS. At least, you were able to use the saved money in the meantime.)

A little history and what-if might help set the stage for the explanation of this tax. Before a change in the S corporation laws in 1986, S corporations had to pay taxes on capital gains of over $25,000. Then the stockholders had to pay tax on most of the capital gain. In other words, in the capital gains area, S corporations were taxed almost like C corporations.

In the revised law, this capital gains tax on S corporations was dropped. This would leave the door open for a C corporation with appreciated assets to elect S status, sell the assets or distribute them to the stockholders, and thereby avoid the C corporation capital gains tax on the appreciation that had occurred within the C corporation. To prevent that, the law also set up a tax, payable by an S corporation, on that pre–S-status appreciation, now called built-in gains. The tax applies when those assets are sold or distributed to the stockholders, if such a transaction occurs within 10 years of the shift to S status.

An example may help to clarify this. See Table 5.2.

There is some minor relief from the built-in gain tax. Any unused net operating loss and business credits from C corporation days can be used to reduce this tax. Also, after the corporation has been an S corporation for 10 years, the tax goes away. After that, all of the gain on sale of assets flows to the stockholders' individual tax returns.

Moral: Wait until your corporation is in S status before you have it buy assets that are likely to appreciate (be worth more than the basis after depreciation), unless you plan to keep the assets for more than 10 years. Also, when you convert to S status, spend the money for appraisals of all significant assets. Any of this tax you might avoid in the future will probably pay for the appraisal several times over.

LIFO RECAPTURE TAX

You can skip this section unless you are operating as a C corporation, you are planning to elect S status, and the corporation is using the LIFO (last-in, first-out) system for valuing its inventory. In a way, this is a special built-in gain situation. As long as we have some inflation, the LIFO inven-

TABLE 5.2 Example of Built-in Gains

The Dusty Dirt Land Corporation was a C corporation until 1991, when it changed to S status, and we'll assume it is now 1995. It purchased land in 1987 for $100,000. In 1991, the land was worth $150,000 and, in 1995, when the corporation sells the land, it receives $225,000. The total gain on the land is:

Sales proceeds, 1995	$225,000
Minus cost of land in 1987	100,000
Total gain	$125,000

We can break the gain down into two parts:

Gain while C corporation	
Value of land in 1991 when status changed from C to S	$150,000
Minus cost of land in 1987	100,000
Gain while C corporation (built-in gain)	$ 50,000
Gain while S corporation	
Sale proceeds in 1995	$225,000
Minus value of land in 1991	150,000
Gain while S corporation	$ 75,000

The tax is computed on the gain while the corporation was a C corporation, labeled "built-in gain," at 35 percent. ($50,000 × 35% = $17,500)

tory method will cause the inventory left on hand to be undervalued. As such, it will generate higher profit when it is sold. To prevent a corporation from moving that higher profit from a C to an S status and thereby escaping double tax on it, this section of the law was enacted.

The tax is computed in this manner: In the last year of the C status, the value of inventory on LIFO method is subtracted from the value of the inventory on the FIFO (first-in, first-out) method. This LIFO recapture amount is added to the gross income of the C corporation, resulting, of course, in additional C corporation tax. However, this additional tax is payable over four years, with no interest charged on the spread-out of payments.

SECTION 1244 STOCK

Generally, the tax rules state that a loss on investments, such as stock in a corporation, is a capital loss. As such, it can only be used to offset capital gains, with this minor exception: If there is more capital loss than capital gain, it can be used to offset (be a deduction from) ordinary income at a rate of only $3,000 per year.

However, Section 1244 of the Internal Revenue Code allows an investor to take a deduction for up to $50,000 of capital loss on stock in certain small business corporations under specific circumstances. These include the following:

- It must be stock or preferred stock, not bonds or other instruments of debt. Nonvoting stock does qualify.
- The corporation must be a domestic corporation (either C or S).
- The stock must have been issued in exchange for money or property (but not for other stocks or bonds).
- During the corporation's five most recent tax years, not more than 50 percent of its income may have come from royalties, rents, dividends, interest, annuities, or the gains from sales of securities. Exception: This does not apply to a year in which the corporation shows a loss.
- The stock must have been issued directly to the individual investor or a partnership in which he is a member, and the individual or member must have held the stock since it was issued to him, her, or it. Corporations, including S corporations, cannot take a Section 1244 deduction for Section 1244 stock they own in other corporations.
- The maximum amount of Section 1244 stock that the corporation can issue is $1,000,000. (It can have other stock outstanding.)

As long as it comes within the above parameters, the issue of S corporation stock qualifies for this treatment. When you start your corporation, you hope that the value of the stock will increase. However, you have nothing to lose by issuing stock that will qualify for Section 1244 treatment if bad things happen and the stock loses value. In fact, most attorneys, in the minutes of the organizational meeting, will include a recitation that the stock qualify for Section 1244 treatment. Such a clause is not required, but it doesn't hurt.

Remember that the capital or Section 1244 loss on stock is the difference between the basis of the stock and the lower price for which you can sell it. If the stock becomes worthless, the loss is your basis in the stock. Because the basis for your S corporation stock is reduced by losses that you have deducted on your tax return, it often happens that there is little or no basis for it by the time you sell the stock or it becomes worthless. So Section 1244 may or may not be a significant tax-saving tool for S corporation stock, but you have nothing to lose by making sure it qualifies for this treatment.

TERMINATION OF S CORPORATION STATUS

An S corporation can be terminated in one of two ways:

1. Stockholders who own more than 50 percent of the outstanding stock (including nonvoting stock) of the corporation may elect to revoke the S status.
2. The IRS may determine that the corporation is no longer an S corporation (uh-oh!).

If the termination is voluntary, as in the first case, the actual termination date can be any date from the day of notifying the IRS to the last day of the corporation's tax year (December 31, for most S corporations). There is also a window for electing to revoke the S election for the current year: If the revocation is filed before the fifteenth day of the third month after the start of the tax year, it can be effective as of the first of the year. In other words, if the Billowy Biscuit Corporation (an S corporation) has a tax year ending December 31, 2001, it can elect to revoke the S status for the entire year of 2002 if it files a revocation by March 15, 2002. Except for that two-and-a-half month window, the termination cannot be as of a day in the past. Note that although the Billowy Biscuit Corporation could have elected some other effective revocation date, such as May 31, 2002, it was wise not to do that without a compelling reason. Why? If the revocation occurs during the tax year, the corporation ends up with two short-year periods and needs to close the books twice during the year and to prepare two tax returns. In the case of our biscuit corporation's electing May 31, it would have two short years. January through May transactions would be reported on a Form 1120S (as an S corporation) and from June 1 though December 31 transactions would be on Form 1120 (as a C corporation). Does anyone want to devote extra time and incur more expense preparing tax returns? As I said, you should have a compelling reason to change your tax horse in midstream.

There is no specific form for notifying the IRS of the termination, but written notices to the IRS should include the following:

For the corporation:

- The name, address, and taxpayer identification number of the corporation.
- The number of shares of stock (including nonvoting stock) issued and outstanding at the time the revocation is made.
- The notice or statement must be filed with the IRS service center where the election for S corporation status was filed.

For each stockholder assenting to the revocation of the S corporation status:

- The name, address, and taxpayer identification number of the stockholder.
- The number of shares of stock owned by the stockholder.
- The date (or dates) on which the stock was acquired.
- The date on which the stockholder's taxable year ends.
- The name and taxpayer identification number of the corporation.
- The election to which the stockholder consents.
- The signature of the stockholder, signed under penalties of perjury.
- The statement should be attached to the corporation's statement.

Of course, it's good policy to send all notices, statements, elections, etc. by certified mail with a return receipt requested or comparable service by a private express company.

A sample of a revocation statement is shown at the end of this chapter.

Special situations: The consent of a minor must be made by the minor or by the legal representative of the minor (or by a natural or an adoptive parent of the minor if no legal representative has been appointed). The consent of an estate must be made by an executor or administrator thereof, or by any other fiduciary appointed by testamentary instrument or appointed by the court having jurisdiction over the administration of the estate. In the case of a trust, only the person treated as the shareholder must consent to the election. When stock of the corporation is held by a married couple, both husband and wife must consent to any election if the husband and wife have a community or joint interest in the trust property.

If you have an "uh-oh" and the IRS revokes your S status because it discovered that you did something wrong, the IRS will notify you, rather than you having to notify the IRS. Life isn't fair: Although you cannot revoke your S election as of some date several months ago, the IRS can. Suppose it's now June 2004. The IRS comes calling for the purpose of looking at your records. And, behold, they find you let your Uncle Alexander's corporation buy some stock in your S corporation back on September 2, 2002. What's the effective date of your revocation? Of course, September 2, 2002. Now you not only have to file new tax returns, your C corporation, if it's profitable, will have taxes, penalties, and interest to pay.

However, that story could have a happy ending. If your sale of the stock to another corporation, or any other disqualifying act, was truly inadvertent, the IRS *may* forgive your transgression and let you continue as an S corporation, provided you almost immediately correct the error by buying back the stock, in this case. For that reason, and to save the accumulation of penalties and interest, when you discover your corporation has done some disqualifying act, notify the people at the IRS and ask that they allow you to correct the error and continue as an S corporation.*

CARRYOVERS OF TAX ITEMS WHEN A CORPORATION CHANGES FROM S TO C OR C TO S

Generally, items that relate to C corporations cannot be used if a corporation changes to S status, and vice versa. Following are some of the specifics.

Net Operating Losses Incurred by C Corporations

First, review the description of net operating losses (NOLs) for sole proprietors in Chapter 1. C corporations can create and use NOLs in a similar manner, first carrying the loss back two years, which reduces or eliminates the taxable income in one or both years. (Carrybacks require amend-

---

*Only recently has Congress given the IRS significant authority to allow taxpayers to correct inadvertent errors, rather than immediately levying penalties or forcing unintended tax situations.

ing the prior years' tax returns to generate refunds.) They can also carry any remaining loss forward 20 years, and, like individuals, they can forgo the carryback and simply carry the loss forward.

Unfortunately, if the corporation elects to change to S corporation status, it will not be able to use the loss carryforward to apply to income while it is an S corporation. However, the loss doesn't disappear. It remains there, locked away in the background, until the corporation changes back to a C corporation status. Provided it changes back within 20 years, that loss is still there and can be used to offset C corporation income. Note that the 20-year time limit runs even while the corporation is in S status.

The Rock Hard Pillow Corporation had taxable income as follows:

1998	*$50,000*
1999	*$30,000*

In 2000, it has a loss of $200,000. It can carry $80,000 of that loss back to 1998 and 1999, reducing taxable income in both of those years to zero. The remaining $120,000 of income is available to carry forward. However, the corporation decides to elect to be an S corporation, starting on January 1, 2001, and it earns $250,000 in 2001. As happens with an S corporation, the stockholders get to pay individual income taxes on each one's share of the $250,000. The loss carryover of $120,000 cannot be used.

In 2010, the corporation revokes its S corporation election and earns $130,000 in that year. It now can apply that old NOL carryover of $120,000, reducing taxable income to only $10,000. If the corporation did not revert to C status until 2030, the 20-year period would be over, and the NOL carryforward would be lost forever.

The moral here, of course, is to not change from a C corporation status until the NOL carryforward is used up. NOLs represent money in the bank. Don't give the funds to the federal government.

Net Operating Losses Incurred by S Corporations

When an S corporation incurs an NOL, it does not carry it back or forward to other tax years. Rather, it allocates the loss to the individual stockholders, by listing it as a negative income on the Schedule K-1 that goes to each stockholder. It is the situation of each stockholder that determines how his or her share of the loss can be used. If they have other income (and sufficient basis in their stock holdings) in the current year, it is used to offset that income. Having sufficient basis in the stock that each stockholder owns is just as limiting as the other-income requirement. See Chapter 3 for the discussion of *basis*.

If there is more loss than current other income, or there is insufficient basis in the stock, the loss can be carried forward to the last day of the next year and treated just as if the loss occurred on that day.

In 2000, Alice invested $10,000 in stock of Bent Benches Corporation, an S corporation. Her share of the S corporation's income in 2000 was $1,000, but the corporation did not distribute any cash to the stockholders, so Alice's basis now became *the sum of her investment ($10,000) plus her share of the 2000 income ($1,000) or $11,000.*

In 2001, Alice earned $50,000 from her job as a Web page designer. Bent Benches Corporation suffered a large loss, and Alice's share of the loss was $20,000. Alice would like to deduct that loss from her income of $50,000, but she can't do that. She's limited to deducting no more than her basis in the stock, so she can deduct only $11,000 of the loss. The other $9,000 is carried over to 2002. Her basis at this point is zero. ($11,000 basis at the end of the year minus the $11,000 loss she used.)

In 2002 Bent Benches Corporation made a profit. Alice's share of the taxable income was $5,000. In addition, she lent the corporation $10,000, so her basis in her stock is now $15,000. As she again earned $50,000 from her job, she can now deduct the other $9,000 loss from the corporation in 2001.

(Remember, Alice's direct loan to the corporation increases her basis. If she only guaranteed a loan from the bank to the corporation, it would not increase her basis.)

Watch out for this trap. If a stockholder sells all of his or her stock in an S corporation, he or she can never deduct any losses that have carried over from previous years. If, in the preceding example, Alice had sold her stock in the Bent Benches Corporation instead of adding to her investment in it, she would never be able to deduct the $9,000 loss that carried over from 2001. The rationale is that she cannot deduct any loss from the S corporation that reduces her basis in the stock to lower than zero. If she has sold the stock, she has no basis, so she cannot deduct the loss. (The loss carryover is treated as if it occurred on the last day of the next year.)

Disposition of S Corporation Income on Which Stockholders Have Paid Income Tax

When an S corporation revokes its S election, it probably will have a balance in its accumulated adjustments account and may have a balance in its other adjustments, and previously taxed income accounts. These all represent balances that could be distributed to stockholders without paying income tax thereon; this is an area that deserves careful planning.

On the date that the revocation of S corporation status is effective, there starts a period called the *post-termination transition period*. In the case of a revocation elected voluntarily by the corporation, that period is one year from the last day of the S status. In the case of determination by the IRS that the corporation was no longer eligible as of some date in the past, it is only 120 days after that determination.

The importance of this period is that during it, the corporation may distribute money to those stockholders who were stockholders on the last day of the S corporation period. That money will represent distributions from the accumulated adjustments account (AAA), on which tax has already been paid, rather than a taxable dividend from a C corporation. Notice that this applies only to a distribution of *money*, not other property.

Again, there is a moral. Plan ahead for conversion from an S to a C corporation. If there is a significant balance in the AAA, make any planned distributions of property before the S period ends, and make all possible cash distributions before the post-termination transition period ends. After that time, cash paid to stockholders (as stockholders, not employees or lessors) will not be *distributions*, but *dividends*, on which the stockholders again pay income tax.

While we're in the planning mode, think about this. As the corporation prospers and earns profits, you will probably want to buy additional equipment and possibly a building in which to operate, instead of paying rent. Consider buying these assets with personal funds and renting them to the corporation. Then the accumulated income, on which you, as a stockholder, pay income taxes, will not be locked in the corporation and its "already taxed" status won't be lost when you revoke the S election.

Jeremy operates his jewelry manufacturing company as an S corporation, Jeremy's Jewelry, Inc. (He is the only stockholder.) As the end of the first year of business, which has been good, the AAA has a balance of $100,000, representing the taxable income of the corporation for the year. As Jeremy's Jewelry sells for cash, the AAA is reflected in the corporation's bank account of $100,000.

Jeremy decides that the business needs an automatic jewelry-making machine that will cost $80,000. He has two choices:

1 *He can use the corporation's cash this way:*	
Pay the equipment supplier	*$ 80,000*
Pay a distribution to himself	*20,000*
Total cash disbursed	*$100,000*
2 *Or this way:*	
Pay himself a distribution of	*$100,000*
Buy the equipment to rent to the corporation	*80,000*
Left for his personal use	*$ 20,000*

If he uses method 1, he will have $80,000 worth of property in the corporation that was purchased with money on which he paid tax. Yet, he probably will never be able to withdraw that in cash from the corporation, because he bought equipment with it.

If he uses method 2, he has been able to distribute all of his AAA.

You can argue that it makes little difference, as Jeremy still has only $20,000 to use personally. There are other factors, as covered in the next section.

SHOULD STOCKHOLDERS BUY ASSETS PERSONALLY AND LEASE TO THE CORPORATION?

There are several reasons to do this:

- You can keep the balance of the AAA low, as discussed in the previous section.
- Rental payments from the corporation to the stockholders are not subject to self-employment tax.
- Record-keeping and tax return preparation when you sell equipment is a little easier if it's done individually, rather than in the corporation.

A reason not to do this:

- Income that accumulates in the AAA, without being distributed, has the effect of increasing the basis of the stock in the hand of the stockholder(s). The benefit is that if the corporation has a significant loss in a later year, the amount of loss that the stockholders can claim on their individual returns is limited to the basis of the stock. If that basis is high, because all of the AAA was not distributed, more of the loss can be used on their individual returns to offset other income. (Or it can be carried back two years and forward 20 years.)

OFFICE-IN-HOME EXPENSE

If you have been working in or from your home as a sole proprietor and now decide to incorporate and function as an S corporation, you'll run into new rules. That's because you are no longer using your home office for your own business, but are using it as an *employee* of the S corporation. In effect, you are letting your employer (your S corporation) use your home office. The obvious set-up, then, would be to have the corporation rent your office space. It would deduct the expense, you would report the rental income, and deduct your home-office expense from your rental income.

Unfortunately, the IRS and the Congress decided this would be a no-no. Section 280A(c)(6) reads as follows:

> *Treatment of rental to employer*
>
> *[Deduction of home office expenses] shall not apply to any item which is attributable to the rental of the dwelling unit (or any portion thereof) by the taxpayer to his employer during any period in which the taxpayer uses the dwelling unit (or portion) in performing services as an employee of the employer.*

There are, however, some offsetting factors. The most obvious is that you can still deduct mortgage interest and real estate taxes as itemized deductions. Also, by not claiming a deduction for a home office, you have preserved the residence nature of the whole building. That's important if and when you sell your residence. The gain on the residence part is not taxed (up to the $250,000/$500,000 limit), while any gain on the business portion of the residence (what you claimed as an office) is subject to capital gains tax.

Expenses of Your Home-Based Business

As for office equipment, supplies, and so on, have the corporation make those purchases. If you make them personally, you would be able to deduct them only as itemized deductions and they would be subject to the two-percent-of-gross-income floor. For the same reason, if you are changing from a sole proprietorship to an S corporation, transfer any equipment that is not fully depreciated to the corporation. Otherwise, the depreciation deductions might be lost in that two percent rule.

Larry has been operating his business from his home as a sole proprietor and decides to incorporate as an S corporation. For the first year, the corporation earns, before Larry's salary, an income of $100,000. Out of that, it pays Larry a salary of $75,000 and keeps the rest of the earnings for future growth.

Larry keeps the copy machine in his name, buys a new computer soon after the corporation starts business, and he buys $1,000 of office supplies during the year. His itemized deduction, as an employee of his corporation, looks like Table 5.3, where he ends up with a deduction of only $1,500.

On the other hand, if Larry had transferred the copy machine to the corporation and had made the corporation buy the computer and pay for office supplies, the total expense of $3,500 would have flowed, though the S corporation, to Larry.

Watch out for this: Computers, photographic, phonographic and similar equipment is considered to be listed property. Your employer, your S corporation, is providing you a computer for business use. However, as the space in which it is used is not the S corporation's office (it doesn't have one), but a residence, the computer is listed property. That means you should keep a log of its use, in order to prove it was used only for business. Or, if it's used partly for personal pursuits, the value of that personal use becomes income to you.

Set Up an Accountable Plan in Your Corporation

If you spend money out of your pocket for various supplies for your business, you can still make them corporate expenses, and, thereby, fully deductible, if your corporation has an *accountable plan* for employee expenses. Such a plan allows your corporation to reimburse you (its employee) and other employees for money paid out of pocket for business expenses. The reimbursement must be for the exact amount the employee spent. (A monthly stipend of $100 "for expenses" won't cut it.)

How do you set up the plan? A resolution, passed by the board of directors or the stockholders should do the trick. It just needs to specify that employees are authorized to make purchases of goods and services needed by the corporation for business purposes and that they will be reimbursed for the exact amount spent. If your corporation has other employees, authorize a trusted few to be covered by this plan. Set a dollar

TABLE 5.3 Employee Expense vs. Corporation Expense

Depreciation on the copy machine and computer		$2,500
Office supplies		1,000
Total employee business expense		3,500
Adjusted gross income (AGI):		
Salary	$ 75,000	
Net income of S corporation	25,000	
Total AGI	100,000	
Subtract 2% of AGI		2,000
Net deduction as an employee		$1,500

limit for all, including yourself. If the purchase is large, write a corporate check.

SOCIAL SECURITY TAXES, THE IRS, AND CONGRESS

A significant advantage of S corporations are the rules about how self-employment taxes (social security taxes) are levied. Consider the amount of this tax and the part of one's income on which it is levied.

As any employee who has ever looked at his or her paycheck stub knows, the social security tax that is withheld from a salary check is 7.65 percent of the first $76,200* of earnings, and the employer also pays a tax of 7.65 percent of the employee's first $76,200 of salaries and wages. In the case of a self-employed individual, he or she gets to pay both the employer and the employee share, for a total of 15.3 percent of earnings. Technically, this tax is composed of two taxes, and that affects those who earn more than $76,200. The old-age pension part (OASDI) is 12.4 percent, assessed on the first $76,200 of earnings, and the Medicare tax is 2.9 percent of *all* earnings, without limit.

Note that this tax applies to *all* earnings of a sole proprietorship, regardless of whether the earnings are from the owner's personal labor or from return on the owner's investment in the business.

Oscar labors long hours at an Internet service provider (ISP), for which work he is paid a few dollars and many stock options. The Amalgamated Electronic Media company buys Oscar's employer and his stock options suddenly become worth $1 million. Although that's nice pocket change in this industry, it's hardly great wealth, so Oscar decides to start his own ISP. And, as he failed to read this book, he operated his business as a sole proprietorship.

Oscar invested his $1 million in the business, buying servers and paying initial payroll and advertising expenses. By hard work and some luck, he was able to make the business earn $150,000 for his first year. How much self-employment tax will he pay? Here's the computation:

$ 76,200 ×	*12.4% =*	*$ 9,449*
150,000 ×	*2.9% =*	*4,350*
Total =		*$13,799*

As an alternative, Oscar could have incorporated his business, elected S corporation status, paid himself a salary of $50,000 per year and incurred self-employment tax as follows:

$50,000 ×	*12.4% =*	*$6,200*
50,000 ×	*2.9% =*	*1,450*
Total =		*$7,650*

Oscar's Uncle Aldrich argued that Oscar was better off in the first scenario—paying $13,799 in self-employment tax rather than $7,650—because it would increase Oscar's Social Security retirement income. However, Oscar realized the error of his way,

*This figure of $76,200 increases each year—the amount depending on the increase in the consumer price index.

incorporated as an S corporation for his second year in business, and invested the $6,000 annual savings. The result: a much higher retirement income than he could ever get from Social Security.

There is another tactic that has been tried by many, a few of whom have been caught by the IRS and met their doom in tax court or other dispensaries of federal justice. In Oscar's case, it would work like this:

Oscar would cause his S corporation to pay zero salary to himself and, instead, declare a distribution to Oscar of $50,000 per year, payable in monthly payments of $4,167. As S corporation distributions are not subject to self-employment tax, Oscar's self-employment tax would be zero.

Warning: this is illegal. The tax law defines *self-employment income* this way:

The term net earnings from self-employment *means the gross income derived by an individual from any trade or business carried on by such individual, less the deductions allowed by this subtitle which are attributable to such trade or business. . . .*

The courts have interpreted this and other sections of the federal tax code to mean that any payments made to a corporate officer, who is active in the business of the corporation, to be compensation subject to social security (and unemployment) taxes.

There are several federal court cases where S corporation stockholders have paid themselves no salary but have caused the corporation to pay substantial dividend distributions instead of salaries. Generally, the scene is that the stockholder is the sole stockholder of the corporation. Otherwise, he or she runs into the same inequity as with Aunt Gertrude in the example in Chapter 3.

So, what should you, as a stockholder of your own S corporation, do? Follow some IRS guidelines? You could, if there were any, but there aren't any—at least, not any real ones.

In 1997, the IRS issued proposed regulations that would have determined how much of the income of a limited partner in a limited partnership would be subject to social security tax, and it extended the same concepts to members of an LLC. Although the regulation didn't cover S corporations, many tax professionals thought that the concepts could be used to safely determine how much of the cash withdrawn by stockholders would be subject to social security taxes (i.e., salaries), and how much would not be so subject (cash distributions). There was much controversy over the regulations. Concerned members of Congress felt that the IRS was overstepping its authority and trying to legislate, rather than administer current law, by the proposed regulations. Congress then specifically forbade the IRS from implementing the regulations until July 1, 1998, which has now passed. Since then, the IRS has not implemented the regulation, and Congress has passed no new tax law covering this area. The best we can do is suggest the pros and cons of alternatives.

- You could follow the tests for partners' income being subject to social security taxes as in the proposed regulations. (Proposed regulations are just what the name implies. They have no weight and can't be enforced. They are only proposals, but they may indicate the thinking of the IRS executives.) The pertinent part of the proposed rules reads as follows:

> *Generally, an individual will be treated as a limited partner under the proposed regulations unless the individual (1) has personal liability for the debts of or claims against the partnership by reason of being a partner; (2) has authority to contract on behalf of the partnership under the statute or law pursuant to which the partnership is organized; or, (3) participates in the partnership's trade or business for more than 500 hours during the taxable year. If, however, substantially all of the activities of a partnership involve the performance of services in the fields of health, law, engineering, architecture, accounting, actuarial science, or consulting, any individual who provides services as part of that trade or business will not be considered a limited partner.*

So, if you are conservative in computing your taxes and work more than 500 hours a year in your S corporation business, you will cause the corporation to pay you a high salary and little in cash distributions.

- An aggressive stance would be to consider that the cases the IRS has pursued and won in court generally involve S corporations that paid their sole stockholder no salary. So if you pay some salary, you've changed the question from one of "why didn't you pay any salary?" to one of "did you pay enough salary?" It's easy for the IRS to prove your corporation paid no salary, as the checkbook reveals that. Proving your corporation didn't pay *enough* salary gets into judgment area, which is much more difficult to pursue. Of course, don't be ridiculous and set your salary at $100 per year. Make it enough so its adequacy is a fair question.
- You could determine your salary somewhere between the above alternatives. If your corporation's business is one that requires a heavy capital investment, and much of that comes from your original investment and taxable income that has not been distributed in cash, you certainly should not have to pay social security tax on the portion of the corporation's income that represents return on investment.

Your investment in your S corporation totals $500,000. The net taxable income of the corporation, before deduction of your salary, is $100,000. The reasonable return on your investment, given the risk involved, is 12 percent.

Income, before salary	*$100,000*
Subtract return on investment (12% × $500,000)	*60,000*
Left for salary	*$ 40,000*

In summary, here is what is defined as self-employment income, and, therefore, subject to social security tax at a total of 15.3 percent, in the various forms of business entities:

- Sole Proprietorships: All of the net taxable income is taxed. It makes no difference that some of the earnings are left in the business for purchase of equipment and working capital. How much cash the entrepreneur draws out is ignored.

- Partnerships: Those partners who are active in the business pay tax on their entire share of the partnership net taxable income, regardless of how much cash they take home. Those partners (general and limited) who are not active in the business escape this tax. The theory is that they are reaping returns on their investment in the partnership, and investment returns (dividends, interest, capital gains, etc.) are not subject to social security taxes. The general partners also have investment in the partnership, but their investment returns, contrary to good tax theory, are subject to social security tax. (It's not fair, but there is no requirement that tax law be evenhanded or logical.)
- Limited Liability Companies: Reread the forgoing, but substitute *members* for *general partners*. The same rules apply.
- C Corporations: Only the salaries that are paid to stockholder-employees are subject to social security taxes. Cash that is left in the business escapes that tax. However, the double taxation of C corporation dividends may offset this advantage.
- S Corporations: The salaries that are paid to stockholder-employees are subject to social security taxes, but the distributions that are paid to stockholders are not subject to those taxes.

OTHER RULES

There are more rules, more what-ifs, and more obscure rules for special situations. These rules should give you some idea of the basics of S corporation formation and operation. If your situation is complex, you may run afoul of rules that were too esoteric to include here. The advice, of course, is to run your proposed procedure by a tax professional. If you check with two tax professionals (e.g., a tax lawyer and a CPA) you may find a difference of opinion among the knowledgeable. If that be the case, you may be well advised to seek a private letter ruling from the IRS. That commits the IRS to accept what you do, taxwise, if it consists of applying the ruling. Unfortunately, it costs, but it could be well worth the price to know that you won't suffer major penalties and interest if it's two years later when the IRS says your S election was invalid or pronounces some other sickening after-the-fact decision.

As an addendum to this chapter, Form 8869 is reproduced, Qualified Subchapter S Subsidiary Election. At this writing, it is still in design status at the IRS, so call for or download an up-to-date copy before you use it.

Because dissolution of S corporations was covered in this chapter, included here are the forms for voluntarily terminating an S corporation or a QSub. There is no official form, but these documents contain what the IRS wants to know, per its regulations.

Form **8869** (September 2000) Department of the Treasury Internal Revenue Service

Qualified Subchapter S Subsidiary Election

(Under section 1361(b)(3) of the Internal Revenue Code)

OMB No. 1545-1700

Part I — Parent S Corporation Making the Election

1a Name of parent	2 **Employer identification number** (EIN)
b Number, street, and room or suite no. (if a P.O. box, see instructions)	3 Tax year ending (month and day)
c City or town, state, and ZIP code	4 Service center where last return was filed
5 Name of officer or legal representative whom the IRS may call for more information	6 Telephone number of officer or legal representative ( )

Part II — Subsidiary Corporation for Which Election is Made (For additional subsidiaries, see instructions.)

7a Name of subsidiary	8 EIN (if any)
b Number, street, and room or suite no. (if a P.O. box, see instructions)	9 Date incorporated
c City or town, state, and ZIP code	10 State of incorporation

11 Date election is to take effect (month, day, year) (see instructions) . . . . ▶ / /

12 Did the subsidiary previously file a Federal income tax return? If "Yes," complete lines **13a**, **13b**, and **13c** . . . . ▶ ☐ Yes ☐ No

13a Service center where last return was filed	**13b** Tax year ending date of last return (month, day, year) ▶ / /	**13c** Check type of return filed: ☐ Form 1120 ☐ Form 1120S ☐ Other ▶

14 Was the subsidiary's last return filed as part of a consolidated return? If "Yes," complete lines **15a**, **15b**, and **15c** . . . . . . ▶ ☐ Yes ☐ No

15a Name of common parent	**15b** EIN of common parent	**15c** Service center where consolidated return was filed

Under penalties of perjury, I declare that I have examined this election, including accompanying schedules and statements, and to the best of my knowledge and belief, it is true, correct, and complete.

Signature of officer of parent corporation ▶	**Title ▶**	**Date ▶**

General Instructions

Section references are to the Internal Revenue Code unless otherwise noted.

Purpose of Form

A parent S corporation uses Form 8869 to elect to treat one or more of its eligible subsidiaries as a qualified subchapter S subsidiary (QSub).

The QSub election results in a deemed liquidation of the subsidiary into the parent. Following the deemed liquidation the QSub is not treated as a separate corporation; all of the subsidiary's assets, liabilities, and items of income, deduction, and credit are treated as those of the parent.

Because the liquidation is a deemed liquidation, ***do not*** *file a* ***Form 966,*** *Corporate Dissolution or Liquidation. However, a final return for the subsidiary may have to be filed if it was a separate corporation prior to the date of liquidation.*

Eligible Subsidiaries

An eligible subsidiary is a domestic corporation whose stock is owned 100% by an S corporation and is **not** one of the following ineligible corporations:

- A bank or thrift institution that uses the reserve method of accounting for bad debts under section 585;
- An insurance company subject to tax under the rules of subchapter L of the Code;
- A corporation that has elected to be treated as a possessions corporation under section 936; or
- A domestic international sales corporation (DISC) or former DISC.

When To Make the Election

The parent S corporation can make the QSub election at any time during the tax year. However, the effective date of the election depends upon when it is filed. See **Effective Date of Election** on page 2.

Where To File

File Form 8869 with the service center where the subsidiary filed its most recent return. However, if the parent S corporation forms a subsidiary, and makes a valid election effective upon formation, submit Form 8869 to the service center where the parent S corporation filed its most recent return.

Acceptance of Election

The service center will notify the corporation if the QSub election is **(a)** accepted and when it will take effect or **(b)** not accepted.

The corporation should generally receive a determination on its election within 60 days after it has filed Form 8869. However, if the corporation is not notified of acceptance or nonacceptance of its election within 3 months of the date of filing (date mailed), take follow-up action by corresponding with the service center where the corporation filed the election.

If the IRS questions whether Form 8869 was filed, an acceptable proof of filing is: **(a)** a certified or registered mail receipt (timely postmarked) from the U.S. Postal Service, or its equivalent from a designated private delivery service (see Notice

For Paperwork Reduction Act Notice, see back of form. Cat. No. 28755K Form **8869** (9-2000)

Form 8869 (9-2000) Page **2**

99-41, 1999-35 I.R.B. 325); **(b)** a Form 8869 with an accepted stamp; **(c)** a Form 8869 with a stamped IRS received date; or **(d)** an IRS letter stating that Form 8869 has been accepted.

Termination of Election

Once the QSub election is made, it remains in effect until terminated. If the election is terminated, IRS consent is generally required for another QSub election with regard to the former QSub (or its successor) for any tax year before the 5th tax year after the 1st tax year in which the termination took effect. See Regulations section 1.1361-5 for more details.

Specific Instructions

Address

Include the suite, room, or other unit number after the street address. If the Post Office does not deliver to the street address and the corporation has a P.O. box, show the box number instead of the street address.

If the subsidiary has the same address as the parent S corporation, enter "Same as parent" in Part II.

If either the parent or subsidiary corporation changes its mailing address after the election is filed, it should notify the IRS by filing **Form 8822,** Change of Address.

Part II

If the QSub election is being made for more than one subsidiary, attach a separate sheet for each subsidiary. Use the same size, format, and line numbers as in Part II of the printed form. Put the parent corporation's name and employer identification number at the top of each sheet.

If the QSub elections are being made effective on the same date for a tiered group of subsidiaries, the parent S corporation may specify the order of the deemed liquidations on an attachment. If no order is specified, the deemed liquidations will be treated as occurring first for the lowest tier subsidiary and proceeding successively upward. See Regulations section 1.1361-4(b)(2).

Note: *A QSub election for a tiered group of subsidiaries may, in certain circumstances, result in the recognition of income. A primary example is excess loss accounts (see Regulations section 1.1502-19).*

Employer Identification Number (EIN)

A QSub is not required to have or use an EIN for Federal tax purposes. If the QSub does not have an EIN, enter "N/A" on line 8.

However, if the QSub has previously filed a return, separately or as part of a consolidated return, and used an EIN, enter that EIN on line 8 and (if applicable) the EIN of its common parent on line 15b. **Note:** *Failure to enter the subsidiary's EIN may result in the service center sending a notice of delinquent filing to the QSub.*

If the QSub wants its own EIN, but does not have one, get **Form SS-4,** Application for Employer Identification Number, for details on how to obtain an EIN immediately by telephone. (**Caution:** *The QSub may use its own EIN only under limited circumstances; see Notice 99-6, 1999-3 I.R.B. 12, for guidance.)* If the QSub has previously applied for an EIN, but has not received it by the time the election is made, write "Applied for" on line 8. **Do not** apply for an EIN more than once. See **Pub. 583,** Starting a Business and Keeping Records, for details.

Effective Date of Election

The effective date of the QSub election entered on line 11 cannot be more than:

1. Two months and 15 days prior to the date of filing the election or

2. Twelve months after the date of filing the election.

If the election specifies a date falling earlier than the date in **1,** it will be treated as being effective 2 months and 15 days prior to the date of filing the election. If the election specifies a date falling later than the date in **2,** it will be treated as being effective 12 months after the date of filing the election.

If no date is specified, the election is effective on the date Form 8869 is filed.

Late Filed Election

If the QSub election is not timely filed for the desired effective date, Rev. Proc. 98-55, 1998-2 C.B. 643, provides relief if the failure to file on time is due to reasonable cause. A corporation with a valid and timely filed S corporation election may be granted additional time to file the QSub election if **all** of the following conditions are met:

- The QSub election is filed within 12 months of the required due date for the desired effective date;
- On the desired effective date, the subsidiary qualifies for QSub status in all respects other than the timeliness of the election; and
- The parent's S corporation tax return due date (excluding extensions) for its first tax year it intended to treat the subsidiary as a QSub has not passed.

If all of the above conditions are met, then file Form 8869, write "FILED PURSUANT TO REV. PROC. 98-55" at the top of page 1, and attach a statement explaining the reason for failing to file the QSub election on time. The service center will review the request for relief and notify the parent corporation if the requirements for granting an extension of time to file the QSub election are satisfied.

If the parent's S corporation election and QSub election are both late, the parent corporation may request relief if the eligibility requirements of Section 4 of Rev. Proc. 98-55 are met. See the revenue procedure for details.

If Rev. Proc. 98-55 does not apply, to obtain relief for a late QSub election the parent corporation must request a private letter ruling and pay a user fee in accordance with Rev. Proc. 2000-1, 2000-1 I.R.B. 4 (or its successor).

Signature

Form 8869 must be signed by the president, treasurer, assistant treasurer, chief accounting officer, or other corporate officer (such as tax officer) authorized to sign the parent's S corporation return.

Paperwork Reduction Act Notice. We ask for the information on this form to carry out the Internal Revenue laws of the United States. You are required to give us the information. We need it to ensure that you are complying with these laws.

You are not required to provide the information requested on a form that is subject to the Paperwork Reduction Act unless the form displays a valid OMB control number. Books or records relating to a form or its instructions must be retained as long as their contents may become material in the administration of any Internal Revenue law. Generally, tax returns and return information are confidential, as required by section 6103.

The time needed to complete and file this form will vary depending on individual circumstances. The estimated average time is:

Recordkeeping	6 hr., 3 min.
Learning about the law or the form	59 min.
Preparing, copying, assembling, and sending the form to the IRS	56 min.

If you have comments concerning the accuracy of these time estimates or suggestions for making this form simpler, we would be happy to hear from you. You can write to the Tax Forms Committee, Western Area Distribution Center, Rancho Cordova, CA 95743-0001. **Do not** send the form to this address. Instead, see **Where To File** on page 1.

REVOCATION OF ELECTION TO BE TAXED AS AN S CORPORATION

Name of corporation: Wet'n Soggy Coal Co., Inc.
Address of corporation: 60 Waterway Road
Nearhere, FL 12399

Tax ID number: 98-7654321

The corporation hereby elects to revoke the S Corporation election under Section 1362 of the Internal Revenue Code.

Number of shares of stock (including non-voting stock): 300 shares

Number of stockholder assents to revocation attached: 2 (representing 200 shares)

Effective date of revocation: January 1, 2003

Corporation's taxable year ends: December 31

Under penalties of perjury, I declare that I have examined this election, including accompanying schedules and statements, and to the best of my knowledge and belief, it is true, correct, and complete.

s/Joseph Firehouse, President

Joseph Firehouse, President Date: February 2, 2003

[Send to the IRS service center where the Form 2553 was filed, with the stockholder consents attached, via certified mail, return receipt requested, or similar private delivery service.]

STOCKHOLDERS CONSENT TO REVOCATION OF ELECTION TO BE TAXED AS AN S CORPORATION

Name, address, and taxpayer identification number of the stockholders.

Joseph Firehouse, joint tenant
1235 Canal Road
Nearhere, FL 12398
Social security number 555-55-5555

Julie Firehouse, joint tenant
1235 Canal Road
Nearhere, FL 12398
Social Security number 333-33-3333

Number of shares of stock owned jointly: 100

Date on which the 100 shares were acquired: June 12, 1999

Taxable year of both stockholders ends on December 31

Name of corporation: Wet'n Soggy Coal Co., Inc.
60 Waterway Road
Nearhere, FL 12399

EIN number of corporation: 98-7654321

Under penalties of perjury, I declare that I consent to the revocation of the election of the above-named corporation to be an S corporation under section 1362 and that I have examined this Consent Statement and to the best of my knowledge and belief, it is true, correct, and complete.

s/Joseph Firehouse Date *February 2, 2003*

s/Julie Firehouse Date *February 2, 2003*

STOCKHOLDERS CONSENT TO REVOCATION OF ELECTION TO BE TAXED AS AN S CORPORATION

Name, address, and taxpayer identification number of the stockholders.

Karen Coolwater
52 Main Street
Somewhere, FL 44444

Number of shares of stock owned: 100

Date on which the 100 shares were acquired: June 12, 1999

Taxable year of stockholder ends on December 31

Name of corporation: Wet'n Soggy Coal Co., Inc.
60 Waterway Road
Nearhere, FL 12399

EIN number of corporation: 98-7654321

Under penalties of perjury, I declare that I consent to the revocation of the election of the above-named corporation to be an S corporation under section 1362 and that I have examined this Consent Statement and to the best of my knowledge and belief, it is true, correct, and complete.

s/Karen Coolwater Date *February 2, 2003*

6 AN ALTERNATIVE—THE LIMITED LIABILITY COMPANY (LLC)

DEFINITION OF AN LLC

From the preceding chapters, it should be clear that running an S corporation is not all fun and games. There are rules that can trip you up, and restrictions that can impair attracting additional capital and talent with different classes of stock. If a corporation wants to invest in your C corporation, you have to turn it down or lose your S corporation status. However, until recently, if you wanted to avoid the double taxation of C corporations and still be protected against unlimited liability for your active business, you had no choice other than an S corporation.

Within the last few years, however, several rulings by the IRS and the action of many state legislatures have made the LLC a viable alternative. A definition of this entity can be short: It is a general partnership with limited liability. How can you do that, when general partners have unlimited liability? That's easy: Change the law.

All states have now done just that. They have passed statutes that enable the formation of LLCs. Why? No doubt it is the result of lobbying from business associations and other interested parties.

Besides the limited liability, a requirement for registration with the state, there is a difference in terminology. The owners of the LLC are not partners, but *members*.

VARIATIONS IN STATE LAWS

Of course, life is not as simple as my six word definition of an LLC. The enabling acts that state legislatures have passed run on for many pages, and nearly all of them are different to some degree. As the National Conference of Commissioners on Uniform State Laws has produced a document called The Uniform Limited Liability Company Act, you might assume that the states have adopted that model act as their own law. That would make sense, for it would enable an LLC to operate in any or all states with the knowledge that it was obeying the law in those states. However, that's not the case. Only nine states have adopted the model act as their own law, while the other states have modified it or created their own act to incorporate the ideas (and possibly to assuage the egos) of the members of the legislatures.

The income tax laws regarding LLCs are long established by the IRS and fairly consistent in the 50 states, due to the fact that LLCs usually are taxed as general partnerships, even though they have limited liability. The variation on state laws is probably due to the fact that LLCs have only recently attained legal stature in the United States. Although Wyoming and Florida were early in the LLC arena (1977 and 1982, respectively), most of the other states adopted LLC laws in the 1990s. This was when the model act was still under design by the Conference of Commissioners on Uniform State Laws, so state legislatures felt free to put their own spin on their statutes. Keep in mind that state legislatures are under no requirement to adopt "model acts." The Commission hopes they will, as it makes life easier for all, but it has no way to force such adoption.

TAXATION OF LLCS AND CHECK-THE-BOX REGULATIONS

The first edition of this book devoted several pages to this subject, because the IRS was trying to develop some esoteric rules to determine whether an LLC should be taxed as a partnership or a C corporation. These rules measured various attributes of a corporation and the attributes of a partnership and tried to use those measurements to determine whether each LLC was more like a corporation than a partnership. Obviously, taxpayers were nervous about setting up an LLC and then gambling with the IRS, when that organization was the house, or at least held the trump card. The fear, of course, was that the IRS would find most LLCs to be corporations and, therefore, subject to the double taxation of C corporations.

Check-the-Box Regulations

Then, in 1996, the IRS gave in and published its check-the-box regulations. This ended IRS regulations and rules that attempted to determine which LLCs would be taxed as corporations and which as partnerships, and good riddance. Now, the way it falls out for all business organizations is this:

- A sole proprietorship can be taxed as a sole proprietor or as a corporation. That's right, an individual doing business could elect to be taxed as a corporation, although why one would do that without formally incorporating and gaining the limited liability protection is certainly not self-evident.
- Some states allow single-member LLCs. If you live in such a state and file the necessary paperwork with the state to be an LLC, the IRS will ignore that designation and tax you as a sole proprietor. That makes sense; one individual can't be a partnership, so his or her LLC is essentially a sole proprietorship with limited liability.

- A partnership can elect to be taxed as a corporation or a partnership.
- An LLC composed of two or more members can elect to be taxed as a partnership or a corporation.

This election is submitted to the IRS on Form 8832, Entity Classification Election. If an LLC, partnership, or sole proprietor elects to be taxed as a corporation and does nothing further, it will be taxed as a C corporation. To be taxed as an S corporation, it would still have to file Form 2553, Election by a Small Business Corporation.

What Happens If an LLC Does Not File a Form 8832?

If you are already operating as a corporation, filing this form would be meaningless. A corporation cannot "check the box."

For other types of entities, the IRS has prescribed *default* classifications. They are as follows:

- A sole proprietor is classified as a sole proprietor.
- A single-member LLC is classified as a sole proprietor.
- A partnership will be classified as a partnership.
- An LLC composed of two or more members will be classified as a general partnership.

If you wondered why we spent time on partnerships in earlier chapters, this is the reason. It all applies to LLCs.

WHEN AN LLC MAY BE GOOD FOR YOU

No Limit on the Number of Owners (Members)

Do you have 90 prospective equity investors for your enterprise? As explained in Chapter 3, you could set up a partnership of three S corporations with 30 stockholders each. That entails the filing of four annual income tax returns with lots of extra underlying computations. However, you can have 90 members in an LLC, or you can have 90,000 or more members. There is a practical limit in terms of administrative record keeping and communication with all of the members. (It's somewhere between 90 and 90,000.) Also, be aware that if you sell memberships to the general public, the Securities and Exchange Commission and/or the state security authorities will view it as a public offering of limited partnership interests, and that subjects you to a whole new set of rules.

Types of Entities That Can Be Members of an LLC

Almost any type of entity can be a member of an LLC. The prototype plan in the report from the ABA working group defines *members* as "persons" and defines *persons* as "an individual, a general partnership, a limited partnership, a domestic or foreign limited liability company, a trust, an estate, an association, a corporation, or any other legal entity." This gives an LLC far more flexibility than the S corporation rules, which limit membership to individuals and certain trusts.

This flexibility can help you attract capital and talent into your organization from any source. For example:

Uncle Oscar has made millions in his chicken business, which is operated as a C corporation. He would like to help you get started in the ostrich-raising business by investing $500,000 in your business, as an owner. If you are operating as an S corporation, he would have to take that $500,000 out of his corporation as a dividend, pay individual income tax on it, and would have only $302,000 left to invest in your business. (He is in the 39.6 percent tax bracket.)

However, if you are operating as an LLC, Uncle Oscar can have his corporation invest the $500,000 directly in your business. You would have almost $200,000 more cash with which to work if you form an LLC.

An LLC Can Own Other Business Entities

An LLC can own stock in a C corporation, be a general or limited partner in a partnership, or be a member in another LLC, even to the extent of owning 100 percent of that entity. For example:

Your ostrich LLC is doing well, whereas your neighbor, Alvin, who raises alligators, has come upon hard times. You and Uncle Oscar think you could run his operation (a C corporation) profitably, but you do not want to put the alligators in the same (financial) pot with the ostriches. Neither do you want your ostrich operation to be subject to the debts of the alligator operation. Your LLC can buy the stock in the alligator farm from Alvin. If you are not successful in alligators, your LLC would be protected from the debts of that corporation by virtue of the limited liability of corporation stockholders.

As an alternative, you could buy just the assets from Alvin's corporation. That would leave the debts for Alvin to worry about. Then you could put the alligators and their equipment into an LLC owned by you and/or the ostrich LLC. Both you and the ostrich LLC would be protected from the liabilities of the alligator operation by the limited liability of the alligator LLC.

An LLC Can Have Different Classes of Membership

Unlike an S corporation, an LLC can create different classes of ownership with each class having different rights about sharing profits, gains, losses, in any way that makes economic sense.*

Continuing the above example. Suppose that, in your negotiation with Alvin, you found he would accept less cash if you gave him a piece of the future alligator profits. So, his deal is that if there are any profits, he would receive $20,000 per year and you

*Assigning different rights to different owners solely for tax-saving reasons will not fly with the IRS. If an examining agent thinks that is the case, he or she will restructure the division of profits and other tax attributes to be in proportion to the investment of each LLC member.

and Uncle Oscar (as individual stockholders) would have the right to all the remaining profits. If the alligator operation is an S corporation, Alvin's deal would be the equivalent of preferred stock, and the issuance of that creature terminates an S election. However, if the alligator operation is in an LLC, there is no problem in one member (Alvin) receiving a definite amount of any profit before the other members receive any. Also, you and Uncle Oscar can own your interests in the alligators either individually or your ostrich LLC can own that interest.

You Want to Attract Venture Capitalists

A prospective venture capitalist, who could be the source of capital you need, will usually want to have an equity position and some say in the management of your business, as well as limited liability. As the venture capitalist is often a partnership or corporation, you cannot issue that organization stock in an S corporation. Your operation as a partnership would not provide limited liability to this source of capital. However, an LLC would provide limited liability, and the venture capitalist organization can be an LLC member, regardless of its business form.

WHEN AN LLC MAY BE BAD FOR YOU

Are You a Sole Owner of Your Business?

If so, and you operate as an LLC, you may have problems if you do business outside your state. Some states do not recognize single-member LLCs, so in those states you would be only a sole proprietor. That could mean that you do not have any limit on your liability in those states. You could, of course, set up a corporation to do business in those states, but that becomes more administrative hassle.

Do You Plan to Do Business in Many or All States?

As covered earlier in this chapter, there is much diversity in state LLC laws, registration, and registration fees, and state statutes are being amended and changed. Keep this administrative challenge in mind.

Earnings of Your LLC May Be Subject to Social Security Taxes

In Chapter 5 we discussed the details of the murky area of self-employment (social security) taxes as they applied to S corporations, with only a comment about LLCs. What follows is a review of some of that information and how it applies to LLCs.

In a limited partnership, those partners with limited liability (the limited partners) do not pay social security taxes on their share of the profits. General partners, who are active in the business, do pay social security taxes on their share. Some tax professionals argue that, inasmuch as members of an LLC have limited liability, their share of the earnings should not be subject to social security taxes. It follows that, because there is no general partner in an LLC, no partner pays social security taxes, no matter how active he or she is in the business.

The IRS and the courts have taken a narrow view of the law and held to a strict interpretation. The Internal Revenue Code states that limited partners are not subject to self-employment (social security) taxes. This is stated as an exception to the general rule that the income that is subject to social security tax is "gross income derived by an individual from any trade or business carried on by such individual, less the deductions allowed . . . which are attributable to such trade or business, plus his distributive share . . . of income or loss . . . from any trade or business carried on by a partnership of which he is a member . . ." [IRC Section 1402(a)].

The exception is worded, "there shall be excluded the distributive share of any item of income or loss of a limited partner, as such, other than guaranteed payments described in section 707(c) to that partner for services actually rendered to or on behalf of the partnership to the extent that those payments are established to be in the nature of remuneration for those services" [IRC Section 1402(a)(13)].

The courts have sided with the IRS: *members* of an LLC may have limited liability, but they are not *limited partners*. Notice that this strict interpretation means that those members who are only investors are subject to social security taxes.

Also, all the earnings of an LLC are subject to social security taxes, whether or not those earnings are distributed to the members. Conversely, the earnings of an S corporation are not subject to social security taxes, provided that, if there are distributions to stockholders who are also employees, there are also reasonable salaries paid to them. Only the salaries are subject to social security taxes. (See the more detailed explanation in Chapter 4.)

UNRESOLVED QUESTIONS

Some aspects of LLCs cannot be categorized as either advantages or disadvantages. As yet, we do not know, because we do not know the IRS position. What follows is one of these areas. Other unresolved areas are discussed later.

Basis, Loan Guarantees, and Loans from Banks and Other Sources

Although LLCs generally follow rules for partnership taxation, this may be an exception. The reason: General partners are at-risk for the partnership debt, whereas members of an LLC are limited in their liability, so they are not at-risk for debts of the LLC. That is, the members of an LLC may suffer the same limitations on deduction of losses as do stockholders of S corporations.

What, you might ask, is the status if the LLC members guarantee, as individuals, a debt of the LLC to a bank? (For a small business, banks, more often than not, require this guarantee.) The answer is technical and basically unresolved. There are no specific IRS rules issued yet, although some are in the development, or proposed, stage. Even though not guaranteed, it may be that nonrecourse financing of real estate (discussed in Chapter 2) by a third party would qualify as increasing the basis of an LLC member, thereby permitting an equivalent deduction of LLC losses.

Probably the best procedure for LLC members at this point is the same as that for stockholders in an S corporation. Borrow from the bank as individuals and, in turn, lend the cash to the LLC.

PROFESSIONAL LIMITED LIABILITY COMPANY (PLLC OR PLC)

Professionals in such fields as medicine, architecture, engineering, law, accounting, and similar activities* often join together in a business organization. That permits them some economy in overhead and individual specialization that can mean better service to clients. For years, the only legal avenue for this was a general partnership. The disadvantage of this business form is that each professional was responsible for not only general liability (slip on a pencil) but professional liability for malpractice (oops, I amputated the wrong leg).

To placate professionals, during the last 25 years most states have enacted laws that allowed for the formation of professional corporations. The limited liability sections of these laws are not as comprehensive as for general business corporations. Although they protect the stockholder-employees from general liability and professional liability for acts of other professionals in the corporation, they do not protect the professional against his own malpractice acts. (Legislators do want professionals to be responsible for their own acts.)

Until recently, that left two choices for professionals in a partnership that wanted this protection: Incorporate as either a C or an S corporation. If they formed a C corporation, they would be subject to the personal-service corporation rate of 35 percent from the first dollar of earnings. Admittedly, as the professionals are also employees, much of the profit could be distributed as salaries. (That procedure reduces the double tax, as explained in Chapter 2.) However, deciding on salary amounts makes for some pretty fancy financial games toward the end of the year, and there is always the danger that the IRS could reclassify part of the salaries as dividends. If professionals form an S corporation, they are hit by the limitation of only one class of stock. This makes it difficult to reward junior associates by a different formula than that used for the old hands that started the firm.

---

*For example, Virginia law relative to PLLCs defines professional service as that "rendered by pharmacists, optometrists, practitioners of the healing arts, practitioners of the behavioral science professions, veterinarians, surgeons, dentists, architects, professional engineers, land surveyors, certified landscape architects, public accountants, certified public accountants, attorneys at law, and insurance consultants." Check the law in your state.

The solution to the professionals' quandary is emerging in the form of the LLC. Because the state lawmakers do not want to imbue professionals with complete limited liability, most states prohibit these folk from forming an LLC for the practice of the profession. However, some enlightened states have enacted statutes that permit the formation of professional limited liability companies (PLLC or PLC). The liability sections of these statutes parallel the liability sections of professional corporation laws in that a professional is still liable for his own professional misdeeds, but not for those of his fellow members of the LLC. Otherwise, the rules are much the same as for any LLC: Meet the IRS tests to be considered a partnership, so the income is taxed only once. Also, each partner may share in the profits by a different formula without terminating the LLC.

Again, the states vary in nomenclature. Some call these professional vehicles *limited liability partnerships*, and some use that term to describe a business form that can be used by any group starting a business. How to tell what's what in your state? Read the state code or ask your neighborhood corporate attorney.

PROCEDURE TO SET UP AN LLC AND KEEP IT ALIVE

Procedures for creating an LLC vary from state to state, as does some of the terminology, such as names of forms and other documents. You can obtain the forms, with the terminology used in your state, by contacting the proper state authority (Secretary of State, State Corporation Commission, or whatever). Most of the terms used here, and the examples of forms in the Appendix, are those used in Virginia. (Virginia enacted a comprehensive Limited Liability Company Act in 1991 and has fine-tuned it with some later amendments. To those readers who live in New York or California and are used to seeing documents from those states as examples in business books, I apologize. However, your states have been slow to jump on the LLC bandwagon. Besides, Virginia is a great place to live, and its laws are, for the most part, friendly to business.)

Articles of Organization

This is the document that starts to put the LLC into existence. Some states provide a preprinted form that can be filled in, although an individually drafted form may be acceptable in your state. As to what should be contained in the articles, that also varies. Virginia requires the following five items:

1. The name of the LLC.
2. Registered office address.
3. Registered agent's name.
4. Address where the records will be maintained.
5. The latest date on which the LLC is to be dissolved and its affairs wound up.

Other states require more information in the articles, such as how new members are admitted and who will manage the operation (all members or a management committee).

LLC Operating Agreement

There is much on which members of a new LLC must agree, and very few of those matters are addressed in the articles of organization. One of the most important is how profits and losses are to be allocated to which members. Because profits of an LLC do not have to be shared in proportion to ownership, as they do in an S corporation, the formula for dividing up the profits is one item that needs to be in a separate operating agreement. This is an agreement, or contract, between the members of the LLC. This compact should also address voting rights, method of selecting management, method of determining distributions, and how to distribute a member's capital account to him or her upon withdrawal or death. (See the checklist in the Appendix.)

Although filling in a preprinted form that will satisfy the state as articles of incorporation could be an easy do-it-yourself task, drafting the operating agreement does not fall into that category. Once prospective members of an LLC have come to agreement on how the business will operate, they should engage the services of a business-oriented attorney. The operating agreement is a legal document, and you need an attorney to be sure that it sets out your agreement as you intended and that it does not contain anything that would destroy your limited liability.

If the attorney is not conversant with the income tax area, engage a CPA or other tax professional who is knowledgeable in partnership taxation and the IRS rulings to which an LLC must adapt in order to be taxed as a partnership.

Filing Fee

Most states will want some money from you, along with the articles of organization. The amount varies greatly from state to state, with some as low as $50 and some, varying with the amount of capital invested, that go as high as $25,000. Again, check with your state authority.

Annual Report and Annual Fees

Once an LLC is formed, many states require annual reports and charge annual fees. The report may be little more than a document that transmits the fee or it may require information such as the names and addresses of present members and managers.

Be sure you file these reports and pay the fees. If you fail to do so, the state may administratively terminate your LLC. That would put you in the status of a general partnership with unlimited liability!

WHEN DOES YOUR LLC COME INTO EXISTENCE?

Watch this. If you start doing business as an LLC before the state recognizes your operation to be one, you are violating the law. Also, you are doing business as a partnership, complete with unlimited liability.

Some states recognize the existence of the LLC as soon as the articles of organization are filed with the proper state authority. If there are errors in the articles, they can be corrected later (within a time limit). Other states have statutes that decree that an LLC does not exist until the state authority sends the organizers a certificate that states the LLC does exist.

CONVERTING YOUR PRESENT FORM OF BUSINESS TO AN LLC

So, an LLC sounds like the best choice for a form in which to organize your business. If this is a brand new business, a start-up enterprise, go to it. You can even skip reading this section.

However, if your business is presently operating, the route to an LLC may be easy, or the costs of converting to an LLC may be prohibitive. If your business is a candidate for conversion to an LLC, you are, in all probability, operating as a C corporation, an S corporation, a general partnership, or a limited partnership. We'll look at each in turn.

C Corporation

Stockholders in C corporations are those who may find the cost of converting to an LLC too high to justify such a maneuver. Generally, the technical steps that are involved consist of liquidating the corporation. That is, the assets and the liabilities of the corporation are distributed to the stockholders, and the corporation ceases to exist. Then the former stockholders turn over the assets to the LLC, in exchange for their interests in the LLC. This can trigger two levels of income tax. (The old C corporation double taxation again.)

The first tax is on the corporation. When the assets of the corporation are distributed to the stockholders, the IRS rules treat the transaction as if the corporation sold the assets to the stockholders for the fair market value of the assets. If that fair market value is more than the basis of the asset, the corporation will pay tax on that gain. For example:

National Hole, Inc. started business nine years ago by purchasing an automated drill press for $1,000 and selling its services of drilling holes for anyone who needed a hole. Over the nine years, it has claimed depreciation of $100 per year, so the total depreciation claimed is $900. That makes the basis of the machine now to be $100. (Basis is the cost minus the accumulated depreciation, or $1,000 – $900 = $100.) Now National Hole, Inc. is going to convert to National Hole, LLC, and the fair market value of the drill press is $400. The corporation will pay tax on the gain, computed as follows:

Fair market value of drill press	*$400*
Subtract basis	*100*
Taxable gain	*$300*

The second tax is levied on the stockholders. Mary and Morty each own 50 percent of the outstanding stock of National Hole, Inc. Originally, they each paid $50 for their stock. Now, they each receive one-half interest in the drill press with a fair market value of $200 for each interest. Mary and Morty each have taxable gain as follows:

Fair market value of one-half interest in the drill press	*$200*
Minus basis in stock	*50*
Taxable gain	*$150*

Is it worth paying both corporate and individual income tax on that gain in order to move to an LLC set-up? Probably not. The corporation could elect an alternative, that of an S corporation, without paying this tax.

However, there are some situations that may be exceptions. Among them are:

- The corporation, or the stockholders, or preferably both, have capital losses that they can apply to the gain, thereby eliminating the tax.
- The corporation has a net operating loss that it can carryback to a previous profitable year, thereby generating a refund that may offset the capital gains tax on the sale of assets to stockholders.
- The fair market value of the corporation's assets is less than the basis of the assets, so there would be no taxable gain for the corporation.
- The fair market value of the assets is less than the stockholders' basis in their stock, so there would be no gain to the stockholders.

S Corporation

Changing from an S corporation may be a little less expensive than making the switch from a C corporation. If the corporation has always been in S status, there will not be any corporate tax to pay on the excess of fair market value over basis. However, if the corporation has ever been in C status, there may be some tax to pay on the built-in gains. (This sneaky tax is explained in Chapter 4.)

As for the tax that the stockholders may have to pay on the gain on the stock they own, they are in the same boat as are C corporation stockholders. If the fair market value of the assets is greater than their basis in the stock, then there is taxable capital gain. Note that the basis of the S corporation stock is not just the purchase price. It also includes the net results of all the income, losses, and distributions over the years the individual owned the stock. (See Chapter 3 for more explanation of the computation of basis in S corporation stock.)

In other words, changing from an S corporation to an LLC would be viable if the corporation has always been in S status and there is little or no gain for the stockholders. It may also be viable in other circumstances. You have to work out the numbers.

Partnerships

Because an LLC is essentially a partnership with limited liability, the IRS has ruled that there is no dissolution of one form of business and the creation of another, but just a change in liability status. The result: This switch is tax free. States with the more comprehensive LLC statutes have included a clause that states, definitely, that a change from partnership to LLC is not considered to be a change from one business form to another. (This reinforces the concept in the IRS ruling. If the IRS rule makers changed their minds, this might help you in an argument with the feds.)

The exception to this no-tax result of the switch to LLC would be if the conversion is accompanied by a change in the percentage of ownership by any of the partners/members. The rules that would then come into play are the same as those for any change in any partner's share or withdrawal of a partner. That is, there may be some gain on which a partner is taxed, or it might be avoided if the partnership elects to change the basis of its assets to reflect the ownership change.

Limited Partnerships

The same comments made about general partnerships apply here. The one significant complication that may arise in limited partnerships is when the position of general partner has been filled by a corporation. Presumably, the stockholder(s) in that corporation set it up in order to have a liability shield. Now that they can have that shield in an LLC without the hassle of a corporate intermediary and corporate taxes, they would probably want to dissolve the corporation. As in the case of a corporation changing to an LLC, that could involve some heavy tax expense.

Sole Proprietorship

There is not much to say about a change from sole proprietor to LLC. Inasmuch as the IRS does not recognize a single-member LLC and will tax it as a sole proprietorship, there has been no change of form in the eyes of the IRS.

SUMMARY

An LLC may be just what the economic doctor ordered for you, or it may be more hassle than it is worth, particularly if you operate in several states. Try to reach a conclusion, based on what you read here and elsewhere. Write down the reasons for your decision, then run it by your attorney for another opinion. (Save money: You do all the preliminary work, just pay him or her for knowledge.)

You and your friends could create your own LLC, without any help. Should you? I do not recommend it as a do-it-yourself job nor as an any-attorney-can-do-it job. Find an attorney and an accountant who not only know what the initials LLC stand for, but are familiar with your state law and the IRS rulings regarding LLCs. Depending on factors regarding your future business and the individual situations of your prospective members, you may need to seek an attorney who stays up to date on LLC laws in all states in which you will do business.

EXAMPLE OF SETTING UP A NEW LLC

Again, we end a chapter with some filled-in forms. For an example, we have used the same company as the example at the end of Chapter 4: the same people, the same investment, the same product, etc. The only change is that the members of this LLC took an additional cash distribution of $12,000. Also, there were no salaries paid to members. Rather, there were guaranteed payments totalling the same $50,000. Of that, Joseph received $30,000 and Larry received $20,000. (Karen was off on another sabbatical and performed no services for the LLC.)

The Form 8832, Entity Classification Election, is included here for information only. On page two of the form, under "Domestic Default Rule," rule 2 indicates that this LLC will be classified as a partnership if it makes no election. So, there is no need to fill it in and submit it.

Also, I didn't include the Form SS-4, Application for Employer Identification Number, which should be filed with the IRS for a newly formed LLC. It will be identical to the one filed for the corporation at the end of Chapter 4, with the exception that the type of entity (item 8a) should read "Other: LLC" instead of "Other corporation."

ARTICLES OF ORGANIZATION FOR FLORIDA LIMITED LIABILITY COMPANY

Article I—Name:

The name of the Limited Liability Company is:
Wet'n Soggy Coal Co., LLC

Article II—Address:

The mailing address and street address of the principal office of the Limited Liability Company is:
60 Waterway Road
Nearhere, FL 12399

Article III—Registered Agent, Registered Office, & Registered Agent's Signature:

The name and the Florida street address of the registered agent are:

Joseph Firehouse
Name

60 Waterway Road
Florida street address (P.O. Box **NOT** acceptable)

Nearhere FL 12399
City, State, and Zip

Having been named as registered agent and to accept service of process for the above stated limited liability company at the place designated in this certificate, I hereby accept the appointment as registered agent and agree to act in this capacity. I further agree to comply with the provisions of all statutes relating to the proper and complete performance of my duties, and I am familiar with and accept the obligations of my position as registered agent as provided for in Chapter 608, F.S..

s/Joseph Firehouse
Registered Agent's Signature

Article IV—Management (Check box if applicable)

☑ The Limited Liability Company is to be managed by one manager or more managers and is, therefore, a manager-managed company.

Article V—Effective Date

The effective date of these Articles of Organization is June 12, 1999.
(An additional article must be added if an effective date is requested)

s/Joseph Firehouse
Signature of a member or an authorized representative of a member.
(In accordance with section 608.408(3), Florida Statutes, the execution of this document constitutes an affirmation under the penalties of perjury that the facts stated herein are true.)

Joseph Firehouse
Typed or printed name of signee

FILING FEES:

$100.00 Filing Fee for Articles of Organization
$ 25.00 Designation of Registered Agent
$ 30.00 Certified Copy (OPTIONAL)
$ 5.00 Certificate of Status (OPTIONAL)

Attached are the forms and instructions to form a Florida Limited Liability Company pursuant to Chapter 608, Florida Statutes. All information included in the articles of organization must be in English and must be typewritten or printed legibly. If this requirement is not met, the document will be returned for correction(s). The Division of Corporations suggests using the sample articles merely as a guideline. Pursuant to s. 608.407, Florida Statutes, additional information may be contained in the articles of organization.

Pursuant to section 608.406(2), the name of the limited liability company shall be filed with the Department of State for public notice only and shall not alone create any presumption of ownership beyond that which is created under the common law. The Department of State shall record the name without regard to any other name recorded.

NOTE: This form for filing Articles of Organization is basic. Each limited liability company is a separate entity and as such has specific goals, needs, and requirements. Additionally, the tax consequences arising from the structure of a limited liability company can be significant. The Division of Corporations recommends that all documents be reviewed by your legal counsel. The Division is a filing agency and as such does not render any legal, accounting, or tax advice. The professional advice of your legal counsel to ascertain exact compliance with all statutory requirements is strongly recommended.

Pursuant to s. 608.407, Florida Statutes, the articles of organization must set forth the following:

ARTICLE I:

The name of the limited liability company, which **must** end with the words "limited liability company" or "limited company" or their abbreviation "L.L.C.", "L.C.", "LLC" or "LC." (The word "limited" may be abbreviated as "Ltd." And the word "company" may be abbreviated as "Co.")

ARTICLE II:

The mailing address and the street address of the principal office of the limited liability company.

ARTICLE III:

The name and Florida street address of the limited liability company company's registered agent. The registered agent must sign and state that he/she is familiar with and accepts the obligations of the position.

ARTICLE IV:

If the limited liability company is to be managed by one or more managers, you must state the limited liability company is a manager-managed company.

Articles of organization must be executed by at least one member or authorized representative of a member, and the execution of the document constitutes an affirmation under the penalties of perjury that the facts stated therein are true.

If an effective date is listed, the date must be specific and cannot be more than five business days prior to or 90 days after the date of filing.

FILING FEES:

$100.00 Filing Fee for Articles of Organization
$ 25.00 Designation of Registered Agent
$ 30.00 Certified Copy (OPTIONAL)
$ 5.00 Certificate of Status (OPTIONAL)

A letter of acknowledgment will be issued free of charge upon registration. Please submit one check made payable to the Florida Department of State for the total amount of the filing fees and any optional certificate or copy.

A cover letter containing your name, address and daytime telephone number should be submitted along with the articles of organization and the check. The mailing address and courier address are:

Mailing Address	Street Address
Registration Section	Registration Section
Division of Corporations	Division of Corporations
Post Office Box 6327	409 E. Gaines St.
Tallahassee, FL 32314	Tallahassee, FL 32399
(850) 487-6051	(850) 487-6051

Any further inquiries concerning this matter should be directed to the Registration Section by calling (850) 487-6051.

Form **1065** — Department of the Treasury, Internal Revenue Service

U.S. Return of Partnership Income

For calendar year 2000, or tax year beginning June 12, 2000, and ending Dec 31, 20 00.
▶ See separate instructions.

OMB No. 1545-0099 — **2000**

A Principal business activity: **Retail sales**	Name of partnership: **Wet'n Soggy Coal Co., LLC**	D Employer identification number: **98 7654321**
B Principal product or service: **Coal**	Number, street, and room or suite no. If a P.O. box, see page 13 of the instructions.: **60 Waterway Road**	E Date business started: **June 10, 2000**
C Business code number: **454319**	City or town, state, and ZIP code: **Nearhere, FL 12399**	F Total assets (see page 13 of the instructions): $ **264000**

Use the IRS label. Otherwise, print or type.

G Check applicable boxes: (1) ☐ Initial return (2) ☐ Final return (3) ☐ Change in address (4) ☐ Amended return

H Check accounting method: (1) ☐ Cash (2) ☐ Accrual (3) ☐ Other (specify) ▶

I Number of Schedules K-1. Attach one for each person who was a partner at any time during the tax year ▶

Caution: *Include **only** trade or business income and expenses on lines 1a through 22 below. See the instructions for more information.*

Section	Line	Description	Sub-line	Sub-amount	Line	Amount
Income	1a	Gross receipts or sales	1a	255000		
	b	Less returns and allowances	1b	5000	1c	250000
	2	Cost of goods sold (Schedule A, line 8)			2	140000
	3	Gross profit. Subtract line 2 from line 1c			3	110000
	4	Ordinary income (loss) from other partnerships, estates, and trusts *(attach schedule)*			4	
	5	Net farm profit (loss) *(attach Schedule F (Form 1040))*			5	
	6	Net gain (loss) from Form 4797, Part II, line 18			6	
	7	Other income (loss) *(attach schedule)*			7	
	8	**Total income (loss).** Combine lines 3 through 7			8	110000
Deductions (see page 14 of the instructions for limitations)	9	Salaries and wages (other than to partners) (less employment credits)			9	
	10	Guaranteed payments to partners			10	50000
	11	Repairs and maintenance			11	1500
	12	Bad debts			12	
	13	Rent			13	14000
	14	Taxes and licenses			14	1000
	15	Interest			15	10000
	16a	Depreciation (if required, attach Form 4562)	16a	2625		
	b	Less depreciation reported on Schedule A and elsewhere on return	16b		16c	2625
	17	Depletion **(Do not deduct oil and gas depletion.)**			17	
	18	Retirement plans, etc.			18	
	19	Employee benefit programs			19	
	20	Other deductions *(attach schedule)*			20	6875
	21	**Total deductions.** Add the amounts shown in the far right column for lines 9 through 20			21	86000
	22	**Ordinary income (loss)** from trade or business activities. Subtract line 21 from line 8			22	24000

Sign Here

Under penalties of perjury, I declare that I have examined this return, including accompanying schedules and statements, and to the best of my knowledge and belief, it is true, correct, and complete. Declaration of preparer (other than general partner or limited liability company member) is based on all information of which preparer has any knowledge.

s/Joseph Firehouse — Signature of general partner or limited liability company member

3/14/2000 — Date

Paid Preparer's Use Only

Preparer's signature ▶ | Date | Check if self-employed ▶ ☐ | Preparer's SSN or PTIN

Firm's name (or yours if self-employed), address, and ZIP code ▶ | EIN ▶ | Phone no. ( )

For Paperwork Reduction Act Notice, see separate instructions. Cat. No. 11390Z Form **1065** (2000)

Form 1065 (2000) Page 2

Schedule A **Cost of Goods Sold** (see page 17 of the instructions)

		Line	Amount
1	Inventory at beginning of year	1	0
2	Purchases less cost of items withdrawn for personal use	2	300000
3	Cost of labor	3	40000
4	Additional section 263A costs *(attach schedule)*	4	
5	Other costs *(attach schedule)*	5	
6	**Total.** Add lines 1 through 5	6	340000
7	Inventory at end of year	7	200000
8	**Cost of goods sold.** Subtract line 7 from line 6. Enter here and on page 1, line 2	8	140000

9a Check all methods used for valuing closing inventory:
- **(i)** ☐ Cost as described in Regulations section 1.471-3
- **(ii)** ☐ Lower of cost or market as described in Regulations section 1.471-4
- **(iii)** ☐ Other (specify method used and attach explanation) ▶

b Check this box if there was a writedown of "subnormal" goods as described in Regulations section 1.471-2(c) ▶ ☐

c Check this box if the LIFO inventory method was adopted this tax year for any goods *(if checked, attach Form 970)* ▶ ☐

d Do the rules of section 263A (for property produced or acquired for resale) apply to the partnership? ☐ **Yes** ☑ **No**

e Was there any change in determining quantities, cost, or valuations between opening and closing inventory? ☐ **Yes** ☑ **No**
If "Yes," attach explanation.

Schedule B **Other Information**

		Yes	No
1	What type of entity is filing this return? Check the applicable box: **a** ☐ Domestic general partnership **b** ☐ Domestic limited partnership **c** ☑ Domestic limited liability company **d** ☐ Domestic limited liability partnership **e** ☐ Foreign partnership **f** ☐ Other ▶		
2	Are any partners in this partnership also partnerships?		✔
3	During the partnership's tax year, did the partnership own any interest in another partnership or in any foreign entity that was disregarded as an entity separate from its owner under Regulations sections 301.7701-2 and 301.7701-3? If yes, see instructions for required attachment		✔
4	Is this partnership subject to the consolidated audit procedures of sections 6221 through 6233? If "Yes," see **Designation of Tax Matters Partner** below		✔
5	Does this partnership meet **all three** of the following requirements? **a** The partnership's total receipts for the tax year were less than $250,000; **b** The partnership's total assets at the end of the tax year were less than $600,000; **and** **c** Schedules K-1 are filed with the return and furnished to the partners on or before the due date (including extensions) for the partnership return. If "Yes," the partnership is not required to complete Schedules L, M-1, and M-2; Item F on page 1 of Form 1065; or Item J on Schedule K-1		✔
6	Does this partnership have any foreign partners?		✔
7	Is this partnership a publicly traded partnership as defined in section 469(k)(2)?		✔
8	Has this partnership filed, or is it required to file, **Form 8264,** Application for Registration of a Tax Shelter?		
9	At any time during calendar year 2000, did the partnership have an interest in or a signature or other authority over a financial account in a foreign country (such as a bank account, securities account, or other financial account)? See page 19 of the instructions for exceptions and filing requirements for Form TD F 90-22.1. If "Yes," enter the name of the foreign country. ▶		✔
10	During the tax year, did the partnership receive a distribution from, or was it the grantor of, or transferor to, a foreign trust? If "Yes," the partnership may have to file Form 3520. See page 19 of the instructions		✔
11	Was there a distribution of property or a transfer (e.g., by sale or death) of a partnership interest during the tax year? If "Yes," you may elect to adjust the basis of the partnership's assets under section 754 by attaching the statement described under **Elections Made By the Partnership** on page 7 of the instructions		✔
12	Enter the number of Forms 8865 attached to this return ▶		

Designation of Tax Matters Partner (see page 19 of the instructions)

Enter below the general partner designated as the tax matters partner (TMP) for the tax year of this return:

Name of designated TMP ▶	**Joseph Firehouse**	Identifying number of TMP ▶	**555-55-5555**
Address of designated TMP ▶	**60 Waterway Road** **Nearhere, FL 12399**		

Form **1065** (2000)

Form 1065 (2000) Page **3**

Schedule K **Partners' Shares of Income, Credits, Deductions, etc.**

		(a) Distributive share items			(b) Total amount
Income (Loss)	1	Ordinary income (loss) from trade or business activities (page 1, line 22)		1	24000
	2	Net income (loss) from rental real estate activities *(attach Form 8825)*		2	
	3a	Gross income from other rental activities	3a		
	b	Expenses from other rental activities *(attach schedule)*	3b		
	c	Net income (loss) from other rental activities. Subtract line 3b from line 3a		3c	
	4	Portfolio income (loss): **a** Interest income		4a	
	b	Ordinary dividends		4b	
	c	Royalty income		4c	
	d	Net short-term capital gain (loss) *(attach Schedule D (Form 1065))*		4d	
	e	Net long-term capital gain (loss) *(attach Schedule D (Form 1065)):*			
		(1) 28% rate gain (loss) ▶ .... **(2)** Total for year ▶		4e(2)	
	f	Other portfolio income (loss) *(attach schedule)*		4f	
	5	Guaranteed payments to partners		5	50000
	6	Net section 1231 gain (loss) (other than due to casualty or theft) *(attach Form 4797)*		6	
	7	Other income (loss) *(attach schedule)*		7	
Deductions	8	Charitable contributions *(attach schedule)*		8	1000
	9	Section 179 expense deduction *(attach Form 4562)*		9	
	10	Deductions related to portfolio income (itemize)		10	
	11	Other deductions *(attach schedule)*		11	
Credits	12a	Low-income housing credit:			
		(1) From partnerships to which section 42(j)(5) applies for property placed in service before 1990		12a(1)	
		(2) Other than on line 12a(1) for property placed in service before 1990		12a(2)	
		(3) From partnerships to which section 42(j)(5) applies for property placed in service after 1989		12a(3)	
		(4) Other than on line 12a(3) for property placed in service after 1989		12a(4)	
	b	Qualified rehabilitation expenditures related to rental real estate activities *(attach Form 3468)*		12b	
	c	Credits (other than credits shown on lines 12a and 12b) related to rental real estate activities		12c	
	d	Credits related to other rental activities		12d	
	13	Other credits		13	
Investment Interest	14a	Interest expense on investment debts		14a	
	b	**(1)** Investment income included on lines 4a, 4b, 4c, and 4f above		14b(1)	
		(2) Investment expenses included on line 10 above		14b(2)	
Self-Employment	15a	Net earnings (loss) from self-employment		15a	74000
	b	Gross farming or fishing income		15b	
	c	Gross nonfarm income		15c	
Adjustments and Tax Preference Items	16a	Depreciation adjustment on property placed in service after 1986		16a	
	b	Adjusted gain or loss		16b	
	c	Depletion (other than oil and gas)		16c	
	d	**(1)** Gross income from oil, gas, and geothermal properties		16d(1)	
		(2) Deductions allocable to oil, gas, and geothermal properties		16d(2)	
	e	Other adjustments and tax preference items *(attach schedule)*		16e	
Foreign Taxes	17a	Name of foreign country or U.S. possession ▶			
	b	Gross income sourced at partner level		17b	
	c	Foreign gross income sourced at partnership level:			
		(1) Passive ▶ .... **(2)** Listed categories *(attach schedule)* ▶ .... **(3)** General limitation ▶		17c(3)	
	d	Deductions allocated and apportioned at partner level:			
		(1) Interest expense ▶ .... **(2)** Other ▶		17d(2)	
	e	Deductions allocated and apportioned at partnership level to foreign source income:			
		(1) Passive ▶ .... **(2)** Listed categories *(attach schedule)* ▶ .... **(3)** General limitation ▶		17e(3)	
	f	Total foreign taxes (check one): ▶ Paid ☐ Accrued ☐		17f	
	g	Reduction in taxes available for credit and gross income from all sources *(attach schedule)*		17g	
Other	18	Section 59(e)(2) expenditures: **a** Type ▶ .... **b** Amount ▶		18b	
	19	Tax-exempt interest income		19	
	20	Other tax-exempt income		20	
	21	Nondeductible expenses		21	
	22	Distributions of money (cash and marketable securities)		22	
	23	Distributions of property other than money		23	
	24	Other items and amounts required to be reported separately to partners *(attach schedule)*			

Form **1065** (2000)

Form 1065 (2000) Page **4**

Analysis of Net Income (Loss)

1	Net income (loss). Combine Schedule K, lines 1 through 7 in column (b). From the result, subtract the sum of Schedule K, lines 8 through 11, 14a, 17f, and 18b	1	

2 Analysis by partner type:	(i) Corporate	(ii) Individual (active)	(iii) Individual (passive)	(iv) Partnership	(v) Exempt organization	(vi) Nominee/Other
a General partners		23000				
b Limited partners						

Schedule L **Balance Sheets per Books** (Not required if Question 5 on Schedule B is answered "Yes.")

Assets	Beginning of tax year (a)	(b)	End of tax year (c)	(d)
1 Cash		30000		15000
2a Trade notes and accounts receivable			3975	
b Less allowance for bad debts				3975
3 Inventories				200000
4 U.S. government obligations				
5 Tax-exempt securities				
6 Other current assets *(attach schedule)* . . .				
7 Mortgage and real estate loans				
8 Other investments *(attach schedule)*				
9a Buildings and other depreciable assets . . .			45000	
b Less accumulated depreciation			2625	42375
10a Depletable assets				
b Less accumulated depletion				
11 Land (net of any amortization)				
12a Intangible assets (amortizable only).			3000	
b Less accumulated amortization			350	2650
13 Other assets *(attach schedule)*				
14 **Total** assets		30000		264000
Liabilities and Capital				
15 Accounts payable				3000
16 Mortgages, notes, bonds payable in less than 1 year.				30000
17 Other current liabilities *(attach schedule)* . . .				
18 All nonrecourse loans				
19 Mortgages, notes, bonds payable in 1 year or more .				190000
20 Other liabilities *(attach schedule)*				
21 Partners' capital accounts		30000		41000
22 **Total** liabilities and capital		30000		264000

Schedule M-1 **Reconciliation of Income (Loss) per Books With Income (Loss) per Return**
(Not required if Question 5 on Schedule B is answered "Yes." See page 30 of the instructions.)

1 Net income (loss) per books	23000	6 Income recorded on books this year not included on Schedule K, lines 1 through 7 (itemize):	
2 Income included on Schedule K, lines 1 through 4, 6, and 7, not recorded on books this year (itemize):		a Tax-exempt interest $	
3 Guaranteed payments (other than health insurance)	50000	7 Deductions included on Schedule K, lines 1 through 11, 14a, 17f, and 18b, not charged against book income this year (itemize):	
4 Expenses recorded on books this year not included on Schedule K, lines 1 through 11, 14a, 17f, and 18b (itemize):		a Depreciation $	
a Depreciation $			
b Travel and entertainment $		8 Add lines 6 and 7	
5 Add lines 1 through 4	73000	9 Income (loss) (Analysis of Net Income (Loss), line 1). Subtract line 8 from line 5	73000

Schedule M-2 **Analysis of Partners' Capital Accounts** (Not required if Question 5 on Schedule B is answered "Yes.")

1 Balance at beginning of year	30000	6 Distributions: a Cash	12000
2 Capital contributed during year		b Property	
3 Net income (loss) per books	23000	7 Other decreases (itemize):	
4 Other increases (itemize):		8 Add lines 6 and 7	12000
5 Add lines 1 through 4	53000	9 Balance at end of year. Subtract line 8 from line 5	41000

Form **1065** (2000)

SCHEDULE K-1 (Form 1065)
Department of the Treasury
Internal Revenue Service

Partner's Share of Income, Credits, Deductions, etc.

▶ See separate instructions.

For calendar year 2000 or tax year beginning June 12, 2000, and ending Dec. 31, 20 00

OMB No. 1545-0099

2000

Partner's identifying number ▶ 555-55-5555

Partnership's identifying number ▶ 98 : 7654321

Partner's name, address, and ZIP code
Joseph & Julie Firehouse
1235 Canal Road
Nearhere, FL 12398

Partnership's name, address, and ZIP code
Wet'n Soggy Coal Co., LLC
60 Waterway Road
Nearhere, FL 12399

A This partner is a ☐ general partner ☐ limited partner ☑ limited liability company member

B What type of entity is this partner? ▶ Individual

C Is this partner a ☑ domestic or a ☐ foreign partner?

D Enter partner's percentage of:

	(i) Before change or termination	(ii) End of year
Profit sharing	50 %	50 %
Loss sharing	50 %	50 %
Ownership of capital	50 %	50 %

E IRS Center where partnership filed return: Atlanta

F Partner's share of liabilities (see instructions):
Nonrecourse . . . $
Qualified nonrecourse financing . $
Other . . . $ 111500

G Tax shelter registration number . ▶

H Check here if this partnership is a publicly traded partnership as defined in section 469(k)(2) . . . ☐

I Check applicable boxes: (1) ☐ Final K-1 (2) ☐ Amended K-1

J Analysis of partner's capital account:

(a) Capital account at beginning of year	(b) Capital contributed during year	(c) Partner's share of lines 3, 4, and 7, Form 1065, Schedule M-2	(d) Withdrawals and distributions	(e) Capital account at end of year (combine columns (a) through (d))
15000		11500	(6000)	20500

		(a) Distributive share item		(b) Amount	(c) 1040 filers enter the amount in column (b) on:
Income (Loss)	1	Ordinary income (loss) from trade or business activities	1	12000	See page 6 of Partner's Instructions for Schedule K-1 (Form 1065).
	2	Net income (loss) from rental real estate activities	2		
	3	Net income (loss) from other rental activities	3		
	4	Portfolio income (loss):			
	a	Interest	4a		Sch. B, Part I, line 1
	b	Ordinary dividends	4b		Sch. B, Part II, line 5
	c	Royalties	4c		Sch. E, Part I, line 4
	d	Net short-term capital gain (loss)	4d		Sch. D, line 5, col. (f)
	e	Net long-term capital gain (loss):			
		(1) 28% rate gain (loss)	4e(1)		Sch. D, line 12, col. (g)
		(2) Total for year	4e(2)		Sch. D, line 12, col. (f)
	f	Other portfolio income (loss) *(attach schedule)*	4f		Enter on applicable line of your return.
	5	Guaranteed payments to partner	5	30000	See page 6 of Partner's Instructions for Schedule K-1 (Form 1065).
	6	Net section 1231 gain (loss) (other than due to casualty or theft)	6		
	7	Other income (loss) *(attach schedule)*	7		Enter on applicable line of your return.
Deductions	8	Charitable contributions (see instructions) *(attach schedule)*	8	500	Sch. A, line 15 or 16
	9	Section 179 expense deduction	9		See pages 7 and 8 of Partner's Instructions for Schedule K-1 (Form 1065).
	10	Deductions related to portfolio income *(attach schedule)*	10		
	11	Other deductions *(attach schedule)*	11		
Credits	12a	Low-income housing credit:			
		(1) From section 42(j)(5) partnerships for property placed in service before 1990	12a(1)		Form 8586, line 5
		(2) Other than on line 12a(1) for property placed in service before 1990	12a(2)		
		(3) From section 42(j)(5) partnerships for property placed in service after 1989	12a(3)		
		(4) Other than on line 12a(3) for property placed in service after 1989	12a(4)		
	b	Qualified rehabilitation expenditures related to rental real estate activities	12b		See page 8 of Partner's Instructions for Schedule K-1 (Form 1065).
	c	Credits (other than credits shown on lines 12a and 12b) related to rental real estate activities	12c		
	d	Credits related to other rental activities	12d		
	13	Other credits	13		

For Paperwork Reduction Act Notice, see Instructions for Form 1065. Cat. No. 11394R **Schedule K-1 (Form 1065) 2000**

Schedule K-1 (Form 1065) 2000 Page **2**

Section		(a) Distributive share item	Line	(b) Amount	(c) 1040 filers enter the amount in column (b) on:
Investment Interest	14a	Interest expense on investment debts	14a		Form 4952, line 1
	b	(1) Investment income included on lines 4a, 4b, 4c, and 4f	14b(1)		See page 9 of Partner's Instructions for Schedule K-1 (Form 1065).
		(2) Investment expenses included on line 10	14b(2)		
Self-employment	15a	Net earnings (loss) from self-employment	15a	42000	Sch. SE, Section A or B
	b	Gross farming or fishing income	15b		See page 9 of Partner's Instructions for Schedule K-1 (Form 1065).
	c	Gross nonfarm income	15c		
Adjustments and Tax Preference Items	16a	Depreciation adjustment on property placed in service after 1986	16a		See page 9 of Partner's Instructions for Schedule K-1 (Form 1065) and Instructions for Form 6251.
	b	Adjusted gain or loss	16b		
	c	Depletion (other than oil and gas)	16c		
	d	(1) Gross income from oil, gas, and geothermal properties	16d(1)		
		(2) Deductions allocable to oil, gas, and geothermal properties	16d(2)		
	e	Other adjustments and tax preference items *(attach schedule)*	16e		
Foreign Taxes	17a	Name of foreign country or U.S. possession ▶			Form 1116, Part I
	b	Gross income sourced at partner level	17b		
	c	Foreign gross income sourced at partnership level:			
		(1) Passive	17c(1)		
		(2) Listed categories *(attach schedule)*	17c(2)		
		(3) General limitation	17c(3)		
	d	Deductions allocated and apportioned at partner level:			
		(1) Interest expense	17d(1)		
		(2) Other	17d(2)		
	e	Deductions allocated and apportioned at partnership level to foreign source income:			
		(1) Passive	17e(1)		
		(2) Listed categories *(attach schedule)*	17e(2)		
		(3) General limitation	17e(3)		
	f	Total foreign taxes (check one): ▶ ☐ Paid ☐ Accrued	17f		Form 1116, Part II
	g	Reduction in taxes available for credit and gross income from all sources *(attach schedule)*	17g		See Instructions for Form 1116.
Other	18	Section 59(e)(2) expenditures: **a** Type ▶			See page 9 of Partner's Instructions for Schedule K-1 (Form 1065).
	b	Amount	18b		
	19	Tax-exempt interest income	19		Form 1040, line 8b
	20	Other tax-exempt income	20		See pages 9 and 10 of Partner's Instructions for Schedule K-1 (Form 1065).
	21	Nondeductible expenses	21		
	22	Distributions of money (cash and marketable securities)	22		
	23	Distributions of property other than money	23		
	24	Recapture of low-income housing credit:			
	a	From section 42(j)(5) partnerships	24a		Form 8611, line 8
	b	Other than on line 24a	24b		

Supplemental Information

25 Supplemental information required to be reported separately to each partner *(attach additional schedules if more space is needed):*

Schedule K-1 (Form 1065) 2000

SCHEDULE K-1 (Form 1065)
Department of the Treasury
Internal Revenue Service

Partner's Share of Income, Credits, Deductions, etc.

▶ See separate instructions.

For calendar year 2000 or tax year beginning June 12, 2000, and ending Dec. 31, 20 00

OMB No. 1545-0099

2000

Partner's identifying number ▶ 888-88-8888

Partnership's identifying number ▶ 98 : 7654321

Partner's name, address, and ZIP code
Karen Coolwater
52 Main Street
Somewhere, FL 44444

Partnership's name, address, and ZIP code
Wet'n Soggy Coal Co., LLC
60 Waterway Road
Nearhere, FL 12399

A This partner is a ☐ general partner ☐ limited partner ☑ limited liability company member

B What type of entity is this partner? ▶ Individual

C Is this partner a ☑ domestic or a ☐ foreign partner?

D Enter partner's percentage of:

	(i) Before change or termination	(ii) End of year
Profit sharing	33.3 %	33.3 %
Loss sharing	33.3 %	33.3 %
Ownership of capital	33.3 %	33.3 %

E IRS Center where partnership filed return: Atlanta

F Partner's share of liabilities (see instructions):
Nonrecourse . . . $
Qualified nonrecourse financing . $
Other . . . $ 74326

G Tax shelter registration number ▶

H Check here if this partnership is a publicly traded partnership as defined in section 469(k)(2) ☐

I Check applicable boxes: (1) ☐ Final K-1 (2) ☐ Amended K-1

J Analysis of partner's capital account:

(a) Capital account at beginning of year	(b) Capital contributed during year	(c) Partner's share of lines 3, 4, and 7, Form 1065, Schedule M-2	(d) Withdrawals and distributions	(e) Capital account at end of year (combine columns (a) through (d))
10000		7666	(4000)	13666

	(a) Distributive share item		(b) Amount	(c) 1040 filers enter the amount in column (b) on:
Income (Loss)	1 Ordinary income (loss) from trade or business activities	1	8000	See page 6 of Partner's Instructions for Schedule K-1 (Form 1065).
	2 Net income (loss) from rental real estate activities	2		
	3 Net income (loss) from other rental activities	3		
	4 Portfolio income (loss):			
	a Interest	4a		Sch. B, Part I, line 1
	b Ordinary dividends	4b		Sch. B, Part II, line 5
	c Royalties	4c		Sch. E, Part I, line 4
	d Net short-term capital gain (loss)	4d		Sch. D, line 5, col. (f)
	e Net long-term capital gain (loss):			
	(1) 28% rate gain (loss)	4e(1)		Sch. D, line 12, col. (g)
	(2) Total for year	4e(2)		Sch. D, line 12, col. (f)
	f Other portfolio income (loss) *(attach schedule)*	4f		Enter on applicable line of your return.
	5 Guaranteed payments to partner	5		See page 6 of Partner's Instructions for Schedule K-1 (Form 1065).
	6 Net section 1231 gain (loss) (other than due to casualty or theft)	6		
	7 Other income (loss) *(attach schedule)*	7		Enter on applicable line of your return.
Deductions	8 Charitable contributions (see instructions) *(attach schedule)*	8	333	Sch. A, line 15 or 16
	9 Section 179 expense deduction	9		See pages 7 and 8 of Partner's Instructions for Schedule K-1 (Form 1065).
	10 Deductions related to portfolio income *(attach schedule)*	10		
	11 Other deductions *(attach schedule)*	11		
Credits	12a Low-income housing credit:			
	(1) From section 42(j)(5) partnerships for property placed in service before 1990	12a(1)		Form 8586, line 5
	(2) Other than on line 12a(1) for property placed in service before 1990	12a(2)		
	(3) From section 42(j)(5) partnerships for property placed in service after 1989	12a(3)		
	(4) Other than on line 12a(3) for property placed in service after 1989	12a(4)		
	b Qualified rehabilitation expenditures related to rental real estate activities	12b		See page 8 of Partner's Instructions for Schedule K-1 (Form 1065).
	c Credits (other than credits shown on lines 12a and 12b) related to rental real estate activities	12c		
	d Credits related to other rental activities	12d		
	13 Other credits	13		

For Paperwork Reduction Act Notice, see Instructions for Form 1065. Cat. No. 11394R **Schedule K-1 (Form 1065) 2000**

Schedule K-1 (Form 1065) 2000 Page 2

		(a) Distributive share item		(b) Amount	(c) 1040 filers enter the amount in column (b) on:
Investment Interest	14a	Interest expense on investment debts	14a		Form 4952, line 1
	b	(1) Investment income included on lines 4a, 4b, 4c, and 4f	14b(1)		See page 9 of Partner's Instructions for Schedule K-1 (Form 1065).
		(2) Investment expenses included on line 10	14b(2)		
Self-employment	15a	Net earnings (loss) from self-employment	15a	8000	Sch. SE, Section A or B
	b	Gross farming or fishing income	15b		See page 9 of Partner's Instructions for Schedule K-1 (Form 1065).
	c	Gross nonfarm income	15c		
Adjustments and Tax Preference Items	16a	Depreciation adjustment on property placed in service after 1986	16a		See page 9 of Partner's Instructions for Schedule K-1 (Form 1065) and Instructions for Form 6251.
	b	Adjusted gain or loss	16b		
	c	Depletion (other than oil and gas)	16c		
	d	(1) Gross income from oil, gas, and geothermal properties	16d(1)		
		(2) Deductions allocable to oil, gas, and geothermal properties	16d(2)		
	e	Other adjustments and tax preference items *(attach schedule)*	16e		
Foreign Taxes	17a	Name of foreign country or U.S. possession ▶			Form 1116, Part I
	b	Gross income sourced at partner level	17b		
	c	Foreign gross income sourced at partnership level:			
		(1) Passive	17c(1)		
		(2) Listed categories *(attach schedule)*	17c(2)		
		(3) General limitation	17c(3)		
	d	Deductions allocated and apportioned at partner level:			
		(1) Interest expense	17d(1)		
		(2) Other	17d(2)		
	e	Deductions allocated and apportioned at partnership level to foreign source income:			
		(1) Passive	17e(1)		
		(2) Listed categories *(attach schedule)*	17e(2)		
		(3) General limitation	17e(3)		
	f	Total foreign taxes (check one): ▶ ☐ Paid ☐ Accrued	17f		Form 1116, Part II
	g	Reduction in taxes available for credit and gross income from all sources *(attach schedule)*	17g		See Instructions for Form 1116.
Other	18	Section 59(e)(2) expenditures: **a** Type ▶			See page 9 of Partner's Instructions for Schedule K-1 (Form 1065).
	b	Amount	18b		
	19	Tax-exempt interest income	19		Form 1040, line 8b
	20	Other tax-exempt income	20		See pages 9 and 10 of Partner's Instructions for Schedule K-1 (Form 1065).
	21	Nondeductible expenses	21		
	22	Distributions of money (cash and marketable securities)	22		
	23	Distributions of property other than money	23		
	24	Recapture of low-income housing credit:			
	a	From section 42(j)(5) partnerships	24a		Form 8611, line 8
	b	Other than on line 24a	24b		

Supplemental Information

25 Supplemental information required to be reported separately to each partner *(attach additional schedules if more space is needed):*

Schedule K-1 (Form 1065) 2000

SCHEDULE K-1 (Form 1065)
Department of the Treasury
Internal Revenue Service

Partner's Share of Income, Credits, Deductions, etc.

▶ See separate instructions.

For calendar year 2000 or tax year beginning June 12, 2000, and ending Dec. 31, 20 00

OMB No. 1545-0099

2000

Partner's identifying number ▶ 444-44-4444

Partnership's identifying number ▶ 98 : 7654321

Partner's name, address, and ZIP code
Larry Hotland
76 Firey Place
Somewhere, FL 44443

Partnership's name, address, and ZIP code
Wet'n Soggy Coal Co., LLC
60 Waterway Road
Nearhere, FL 12399

A This partner is a ☐ general partner ☐ limited partner ☑ limited liability company member

B What type of entity is this partner? ▶ Individual

C Is this partner a ☑ domestic or a ☐ foreign partner?

D Enter partner's percentage of:

	(i) Before change or termination	(ii) End of year
Profit sharing	16.7 %	16.7 %
Loss sharing	16.7 %	16.7 %
Ownership of capital	16.7 %	16.7 %

E IRS Center where partnership filed return: Atlanta

F Partner's share of liabilities (see instructions):
Nonrecourse . . . $
Qualified nonrecourse financing . $
Other . . . $ 37174

G Tax shelter registration number . ▶

H Check here if this partnership is a publicly traded partnership as defined in section 469(k)(2) . . . ☐

I Check applicable boxes: **(1)** ☐ Final K-1 **(2)** ☐ Amended K-1

J **Analysis of partner's capital account:**

(a) Capital account at beginning of year	(b) Capital contributed during year	(c) Partner's share of lines 3, 4, and 7, Form 1065, Schedule M-2	(d) Withdrawals and distributions	(e) Capital account at end of year (combine columns (a) through (d))
5000		3834	(2000)	6834

		(a) Distributive share item		(b) Amount	(c) 1040 filers enter the amount in column (b) on:
Income (Loss)	1	Ordinary income (loss) from trade or business activities	1	4000	See page 6 of Partner's Instructions for Schedule K-1 (Form 1065).
	2	Net income (loss) from rental real estate activities	2		
	3	Net income (loss) from other rental activities	3		
	4	Portfolio income (loss):			
	a	Interest	4a		Sch. B, Part I, line 1
	b	Ordinary dividends	4b		Sch. B, Part II, line 5
	c	Royalties	4c		Sch. E, Part I, line 4
	d	Net short-term capital gain (loss)	4d		Sch. D, line 5, col. (f)
	e	Net long-term capital gain (loss):			
		(1) 28% rate gain (loss)	4e(1)		Sch. D, line 12, col. (g)
		(2) Total for year	4e(2)		Sch. D, line 12, col. (f)
	f	Other portfolio income (loss) *(attach schedule)*	4f		Enter on applicable line of your return.
	5	Guaranteed payments to partner	5	20000	See page 6 of Partner's Instructions for Schedule K-1 (Form 1065).
	6	Net section 1231 gain (loss) (other than due to casualty or theft)	6		
	7	Other income (loss) *(attach schedule)*	7		Enter on applicable line of your return.
Deductions	8	Charitable contributions (see instructions) *(attach schedule)*	8	167	Sch. A, line 15 or 16
	9	Section 179 expense deduction	9		See pages 7 and 8 of Partner's Instructions for Schedule K-1 (Form 1065).
	10	Deductions related to portfolio income *(attach schedule)*	10		
	11	Other deductions *(attach schedule)*	11		
Credits	12a	Low-income housing credit:			Form 8586, line 5
		(1) From section 42(j)(5) partnerships for property placed in service before 1990	12a(1)		
		(2) Other than on line 12a(1) for property placed in service before 1990	12a(2)		
		(3) From section 42(j)(5) partnerships for property placed in service after 1989	12a(3)		
		(4) Other than on line 12a(3) for property placed in service after 1989	12a(4)		
	b	Qualified rehabilitation expenditures related to rental real estate activities	12b		See page 8 of Partner's Instructions for Schedule K-1 (Form 1065).
	c	Credits (other than credits shown on lines 12a and 12b) related to rental real estate activities	12c		
	d	Credits related to other rental activities	12d		
	13	Other credits	13		

For Paperwork Reduction Act Notice, see Instructions for Form 1065. Cat. No. 11394R **Schedule K-1 (Form 1065) 2000**

Schedule K-1 (Form 1065) 2000 — Page 2

		(a) Distributive share item		(b) Amount	(c) 1040 filers enter the amount in column (b) on:
Investment Interest	14a	Interest expense on investment debts	14a		Form 4952, line 1
	b	(1) Investment income included on lines 4a, 4b, 4c, and 4f	14b(1)		See page 9 of Partner's Instructions for Schedule K-1 (Form 1065).
		(2) Investment expenses included on line 10	14b(2)		
Self-employment	15a	Net earnings (loss) from self-employment	15a	24000	Sch. SE, Section A or B
	b	Gross farming or fishing income	15b		See page 9 of Partner's Instructions for Schedule K-1 (Form 1065).
	c	Gross nonfarm income	15c		
Adjustments and Tax Preference Items	16a	Depreciation adjustment on property placed in service after 1986	16a		See page 9 of Partner's Instructions for Schedule K-1 (Form 1065) and Instructions for Form 6251.
	b	Adjusted gain or loss	16b		
	c	Depletion (other than oil and gas)	16c		
	d	(1) Gross income from oil, gas, and geothermal properties	16d(1)		
		(2) Deductions allocable to oil, gas, and geothermal properties	16d(2)		
	e	Other adjustments and tax preference items *(attach schedule)*	16e		
Foreign Taxes	17a	Name of foreign country or U.S. possession ▶			Form 1116, Part I
	b	Gross income sourced at partner level	17b		
	c	Foreign gross income sourced at partnership level:			
		(1) Passive	17c(1)		
		(2) Listed categories *(attach schedule)*	17c(2)		
		(3) General limitation	17c(3)		
	d	Deductions allocated and apportioned at partner level:			
		(1) Interest expense	17d(1)		
		(2) Other	17d(2)		
	e	Deductions allocated and apportioned at partnership level to foreign source income:			
		(1) Passive	17e(1)		
		(2) Listed categories *(attach schedule)*	17e(2)		
		(3) General limitation	17e(3)		
	f	Total foreign taxes (check one): ▶ ☐ Paid ☐ Accrued	17f		Form 1116, Part II
	g	Reduction in taxes available for credit and gross income from all sources *(attach schedule)*	17g		See Instructions for Form 1116.
Other	18	Section 59(e)(2) expenditures: a Type ▶			See page 9 of Partner's Instructions for Schedule K-1 (Form 1065).
	b	Amount	18b		
	19	Tax-exempt interest income	19		Form 1040, line 8b
	20	Other tax-exempt income	20		See pages 9 and 10 of Partner's Instructions for Schedule K-1 (Form 1065).
	21	Nondeductible expenses	21		
	22	Distributions of money (cash and marketable securities)	22		
	23	Distributions of property other than money	23		
	24	Recapture of low-income housing credit:			
	a	From section 42(j)(5) partnerships	24a		Form 8611, line 8
	b	Other than on line 24a	24b		

Supplemental Information

25 Supplemental information required to be reported separately to each partner *(attach additional schedules if more space is needed):*

Schedule K-1 (Form 1065) 2000

Form **8832**
(December 1996)
Department of the Treasury
Internal Revenue Service

Entity Classification Election

OMB No. 1545-1516

Please Type or Print	Name of entity	Employer identification number (EIN)
	Number, street, and room or suite no. If a P.O. box, see instructions.	
	City or town, state, and ZIP code. If a foreign address, enter city, province or state, postal code and country.	

1 **Type of election** (see instructions):

a ☐ Initial classification by a newly-formed entity (or change in current classification of an existing entity to take effect on January 1, 1997)

b ☐ Change in current classification (to take effect later than January 1, 1997)

2 **Form of entity** (see instructions):

a ☐ A domestic eligible entity electing to be classified as an association taxable as a corporation.

b ☐ A domestic eligible entity electing to be classified as a partnership.

c ☐ A domestic eligible entity with a single owner electing to be disregarded as a separate entity.

d ☐ A foreign eligible entity electing to be classified as an association taxable as a corporation.

e ☐ A foreign eligible entity electing to be classified as a partnership.

f ☐ A foreign eligible entity with a single owner electing to be disregarded as a separate entity.

3 Election is to be effective beginning (month, day, year) (see instructions) . . . . ▶ ____/____/____

4 Name and title of person whom the IRS may call for more information	**5** That person's telephone number

Consent Statement and Signature(s) (see instructions)

Under penalties of perjury, I (we) declare that I (we) consent to the election of the above-named entity to be classified as indicated above, and that I (we) have examined this consent statement, and to the best of my (our) knowledge and belief, it is true, correct, and complete. If I am an officer, manager, or member signing for all members of the entity, I further declare that I am authorized to execute this consent statement on their behalf.

Signature(s)	Date	Title

For Paperwork Reduction Act Notice, see page 2. Cat. No. 22598R Form **8832** (12-96)

Form 8832 (12-96) Page 2

General Instructions

Section references are to the Internal Revenue Code unless otherwise noted.

Paperwork Reduction Act Notice

We ask for the information on this form to carry out the Internal Revenue laws of the United States. You are required to give us the information. We need it to ensure that you are complying with these laws and to allow us to figure and collect the right amount of tax.

You are not required to provide the information requested on a form that is subject to the Paperwork Reduction Act unless the form displays a valid OMB control number. Books or records relating to a form or its instructions must be retained as long as their contents may become material in the administration of any Internal Revenue law. Generally, tax returns and return information are confidential, as required by section 6103.

The time needed to complete and file this form will vary depending on individual circumstances. The estimated average time is:

Recordkeeping . . . 1 hr., 20 min.
Learning about the law or the form . . . 1 hr., 41 min.
Preparing and sending the form to the IRS . . . . 17 min.

If you have comments concerning the accuracy of these time estimates or suggestions for making this form simpler, we would be happy to hear from you. You can write to the Tax Forms Committee, Western Area Distribution Center, Rancho Cordova, CA 95743-0001. **DO NOT** send the form to this address. Instead, see **Where To File** on page 3.

Purpose of Form

For Federal tax purposes, certain business entities automatically are classified as corporations. See items **1** and **3** through **8** under the definition of corporation on this page. Other business entities may choose how they are classified for Federal tax purposes. Except for a business entity automatically classified as a corporation, a business entity with at least two members can choose to be classified as either an association taxable as a corporation or a partnership, and a business entity with a single member can choose to be classified as either an association taxable as a corporation or disregarded as an entity separate from its owner.

Generally, an eligible entity that does not file this form will be classified under the default rules described below. An eligible entity that chooses not to be classified under the default rules or that wishes to change its current classification must file Form 8832 to elect a classification. The IRS will use the information entered on this form to establish the entity's filing and reporting requirements for Federal tax purposes.

Default Rules

Existing entity default rule.— Certain domestic and foreign entities that are already in existence before January 1, 1997, and have an established Federal tax classification, generally do not need to make an election to continue that classification. However, for an eligible entity with a single owner that claimed to be a partnership under the law in effect before January 1, 1997, that entity will now be disregarded as an entity separate from its owner. If an existing entity decides to change its classification, it may do so subject to the rules in Regulations section 301.7701-3(c)(1)(iv). A foreign eligible entity is treated as being in existence prior to the effective date of this section only if the entity's classification is relevant at any time during the 60 months prior to January 1, 1997.

Domestic default rule.—Unless an election is made on Form 8832, a domestic eligible entity is:

1. A partnership if it has two or more members.

2. Disregarded as an entity separate from its owner if it has a single owner.

Foreign default rule.—Unless an election is made on Form 8832, a foreign eligible entity is:

1. A partnership if it has two or more members and at least one member does not have limited liability.

2. An association if all members have limited liability.

3. Disregarded as an entity separate from its owner if it has a single owner that does not have limited liability.

Definitions

Business entity.—A business entity is any entity recognized for Federal tax purposes that is not properly classified as a trust under Regulations section 301.7701-4 or otherwise subject to special treatment under the Code. See Regulations section 301.7701-2(a).

Corporation.—For Federal tax purposes, a corporation is any of the following:

1. A business entity organized under a Federal or state statute, or under a statute of a federally recognized Indian tribe, if the statute describes or refers to the entity as incorporated or as a corporation, body corporate, or body politic.

2. An association (as determined under Regulations section 301.7701-3).

3. A business entity organized under a state statute, if the statute describes or refers to the entity as a joint-stock company or joint-stock association.

4. An insurance company.

5. A state-chartered business entity conducting banking activities, if any of its deposits are insured under the Federal Deposit Insurance Act, as amended, 12 U.S.C. 1811 et seq., or a similar Federal statute.

6. A business entity wholly owned by a state or any political subdivision thereof.

7. A business entity that is taxable as a corporation under a provision of the Code other than section 7701(a)(3).

8. A foreign business entity listed in Regulations section 301.7701-2(b)(8). However, a foreign business entity listed in those regulations generally will not be treated as a corporation if all of the following apply:

a. The entity was in existence on May 8, 1996.

b. The entity's classification was relevant (as defined below) on May 8, 1996.

c. No person (including the entity) for whom the entity's classification was relevant on May 8, 1996, treats the entity as a corporation for purposes of filing that person's Federal income tax returns, information returns, and withholding documents for the tax year including May 8, 1996.

d. Any change in the entity's claimed classification within the 60 months prior to May 8, 1996, was a result of a change in the organizational documents of the entity, and the entity and all members of the entity recognized the Federal tax consequences of any change in the entity's classification within the 60 months prior to May 8, 1996.

e. The entity had a reasonable basis (within the meaning of section 6662) for treating the entity as other than a corporation on May 8, 1996.

f. Neither the entity nor any member was notified in writing on or before May 8, 1996, that the classification of the entity was under examination (in which case the entity's classification will be determined in the examination).

Binding contract rule.- If a foreign business entity described in Regulations section 301.7701-2(b)(8)(i) is formed after May 8, 1996, under a written binding contract (including an accepted bid to develop a project) in effect on May 8, 1996, and all times thereafter, in which the parties agreed to engage (directly or indirectly) in an active and substantial business operation in the jurisdiction in which the entity is formed, **8** on page 2 is applied by substituting the date of the entity's formation for May 8, 1996.

Eligible entity.—An eligible entity is a business entity that is not included in items **1** or **3** through **8** under the definition of corporation on page 2.

Limited liability.—A member of a foreign eligible entity has limited liability if the member has no personal liability for any debts of or claims against the entity by reason of being a member. This determination is based solely on the statute or law under which the entity is organized (and, if relevant, the entity's organizational documents). A member has personal liability if the creditors of the entity may seek satisfaction of all or any part of the debts or claims against the entity from the member as such. A member has personal liability even if the member makes an agreement under which another person (whether or not a member of the entity) assumes that liability or agrees to indemnify that member for that liability.

Partnership.—A partnership is a business entity that has **at least** two members and is not a corporation as defined on page 2.

Relevant.—A foreign eligible entity's classification is relevant when its classification affects the liability of any person for Federal tax or information purposes. The date the classification of a foreign eligible entity is relevant is the date an event occurs that creates an obligation to file a Federal tax return, information return, or statement for which the classification of the entity must be determined.

Effect of Election

The resulting tax consequences of a change in classification remain the same no matter how a change in entity classification is achieved. For example, if an organization classified as an association elects to be classified as a partnership, the organization and its owners must recognize gain, if any, under the rules applicable to liquidations of corporations.

Who Must File

File this form for an **eligible entity** that is one of the following:

- A domestic entity electing to be classified as an association taxable as a corporation.
- A domestic entity electing to change its current classification (even if it is currently classified under the default rule).
- A foreign entity that has more than one owner, all owners have limited liability, and it elects to be classified as a partnership.
- A foreign entity that has at least one owner without limited liability, and it elects to be classified as an association taxable as a corporation.
- A foreign entity with a single owner having limited liability, and it elects to have the entity disregarded as an entity separate from its owner.
- A foreign entity electing to change its current classification (even if it is currently classified under the default rule).

Do not file this form for an eligible entity that is:

- Tax-exempt under section 501(a), or
- A real estate investment trust (REIT), as defined in section 856.

When To File

See the instructions for line 3.

Where To File

File Form 8832 with the Internal Revenue Service Center, Philadelphia, PA 19255. Also attach a copy of Form 8832 to the entity's Federal income tax or information return for the tax year of the election. If the entity is not required to file a return for that year, a copy of its Form 8832 must be attached to the Federal income tax or information returns of all direct or indirect owners of the entity for the tax year of the owner that includes the date on which the election took effect. Although failure to attach a copy will not invalidate an otherwise valid election, each member of the entity is required to file returns that are consistent with the entity's election. In addition, penalties may be assessed against persons who are required to, but who do not, attach Form 8832 to their returns. Other penalties may apply for filing Federal income tax or information returns inconsistent with the entity's election.

Form 8832 (12-96) Page **4**

Specific Instructions

Employer Identification Number (EIN)

Show the correct EIN on Form 8832. If the entity does not have an EIN, it generally must apply for one on **Form SS-4,** Application for Employer Identification Number. If the filing of Form 8832 is the only reason the entity is applying for an EIN, check the "Other" box on line 9 of Form SS-4 and write "Form 8832" to the right of that box. If the entity has not received an EIN by the time Form 8832 is due, write "Applied for" in the space for the EIN. **Do not** apply for a new EIN for an existing entity that is changing its classification. If you are electing to disregard an entity as separate from its owner, enter the owner's EIN.

Address

Include the suite, room, or other unit number after the street address. If the Post Office does not deliver mail to the street address and the entity has a P.O. box, show the box number instead of the street address.

Line 1

Check box 1a if the entity is choosing a classification for the first time **and** the entity does not want to be classified under the applicable default classification. **Do not** file this form if the entity wants to be classified under the default rules.

Check box 1b if the entity is changing its current classification to take effect later than January 1, 1997, whether or not the entity's current classification is the default classification. However, once an eligible entity makes an election to change its classification (other than an election made by an existing entity to change its classification as of January 1, 1997), the entity cannot change its classification by election again during the 60 months after the effective date of the election. However, the IRS may permit (by private letter ruling) the entity to change its classification by election within the 60-month period if more than 50% of the ownership interests in the entity as of the effective date of the election are owned by persons that did not own any interests in the entity on the effective date of the entity's prior election.

Line 2

Check the appropriate box if you are changing a current classification (no matter how achieved), or are electing out of a default classification. **Do not** file this form if you fall within a default classification that is the desired classification for the new entity.

Line 3

Generally, the election will take effect on the date you enter on line 3 of this form or on the date filed if no date is entered on line 3. However, an election specifying an entity's classification for Federal tax purposes can take effect no more than 75 days prior to the date the election is filed, nor can it take effect later than 12 months after the date on which the election is filed. If line 3 shows a date more than 75 days prior to the date on which the election is filed, the election will take effect 75 days before the date it is filed. If line 3 shows an effective date more than 12 months from the filing date, the election will take effect 12 months after the date the election was filed.

Regardless of the date filed, an election will in no event take effect before January 1, 1997.

Consent Statement and Signatures

Form 8832 must be signed by:

1. Each member of the electing entity who is an owner at the time the election is filed; or

2. Any officer, manager, or member of the electing entity who is authorized (under local law or the organizational documents) to make the election and who represents to having such authorization under penalties of perjury.

If an election is to be effective for any period prior to the time it is filed, each person who was an owner between the date the election is to be effective and the date the election is filed, and who is not an owner at the time the election is filed, must also sign.

If you need a continuation sheet or use a separate consent statement, attach it to Form 8832. The separate consent statement must contain the same information as shown on Form 8832.

APPENDIXES

APPENDIX A
TAX RATE SCHEDULES FOR 2000

INDIVIDUALS

Schedule X Single

IF TAXABLE INCOME IS OVER	BUT TAXABLE INCOME IS NOT OVER	THE TAX IS			OF THE AMOUNT OVER
$ 0	$ 26,250	$ 0	+	15.0%	$ 0
26,250	63,550	3,937.50	+	28.0%	26,250
63,550	132,600	14,381.50	+	31.0%	63,550
132,600	288,350	35,787.00	+	36.0%	132,600
288,350	—	90,200.50	+	39.6%	288,350

Schedule Z Head of Household

IF TAXABLE INCOME IS OVER	BUT TAXABLE INCOME IS NOT OVER	THE TAX IS			OF THE AMOUNT OVER
$ 0	$ 35,150	$ 0	+	15.0%	$ 0
35,150	90,800	5,272.50	+	28.0%	35,150
90,800	147,050	20,854.50	+	31.0%	90,800
147,050	288,350	38,292.00	+	36.0%	147,050
288,350	—	89,160.00	+	39.6%	288,350

Schedule Y-1 Married Filing Jointly or Qualifying Widow(er)

IF TAXABLE INCOME IS OVER	BUT TAXABLE INCOME IS NOT OVER	THE TAX IS			OF THE AMOUNT OVER
$ 0	$ 43,850	$ 0	+	15.0%	$ 0
43,850	105,950	6,457.50	+	28.0%	43,850
105,950	161,450	23,965.50	+	31.0%	105,950
161,450	288,350	41,170.00	+	36.0%	161,450
288,350	—	86,854.50	+	39.6%	288,350

Schedule Y-2 Married Filing Separate Returns

IF TAXABLE INCOME IS OVER	BUT TAXABLE INCOME IS NOT OVER	THE TAX IS			OF THE AMOUNT OVER
$ 0	$ 21,925	$ 0	+	15.0%	$ 0
21,925	52,975	3,288.75	+	28.0%	21,925
52,975	80,725	11,982.75	+	31.0%	52,975
80,725	144,175	20,585.25	+	36.0%	80,725
144,175	—	43,427.25	+	39.6%	144,175

Social Security Taxes

Old Age, Survivors, and Disability Insurance (OASDI) Tax. A total of 12.4 percent of compensation up to $76,200. Of this one-half (6.2%) is paid by employer and the other 6.2 percent paid by employee. Self-employed individuals pay 12.4 percent on first $60,600 of income from business.

Hospital Insurance (Medicare) Tax. A total of 2.9 percent on all compensation (no limit). Of this, one-half (1.45%) is paid by employer and the other half paid by employee. Self-employed individuals pay 2.9 percent on all income from business.

CORPORATIONS

C Corporations

IF TAXABLE INCOME IS OVER	BUT TAXABLE INCOME IS NOT OVER	THE TAX IS			OF THE AMOUNT OVER
$ 0	$ 50,000	$ 0	+	15.0%	$ 0
50,000	75,000	7,500	+	25.0%	50,000
75,000	100,000	13,750	+	34.0%	75,000
100,000	335,000	22,250	+	39.0%	100,000
335,000	10,000,000	113,900	+	34.0%	335,000
10,000,000	15,000,000	3,400,000	+	35.0%	10,000,000
15,000,000	18,333,333	5,150,000	+	38.0%	15,000,000
18,333,333	—	5,150,000	+	35.0%	0

The rate increase at $15,000,000 to 38 percent and then back to 35 percent on income over $18,333,333 may look like the largest corporations are getting a 3 percent tax break. However, that is not the case. The extra 3 percent is designed to erase the benefit of the lower tax brackets. Once taxable income has reached $18,333,333, the benefit of the lower brackets has been recaptured by the IRS, and the corporation pays 35 percent on all taxable income.

This convoluted tax rate schedule is a classic example of unnecessary complexity brought about by political shenanigans and bureaucratic complicity. Our lawmakers wanted to raise corporate taxes, and they apparently wanted to raise them on midsize corporations. In order to hide that wish, they raised the top corporate bracket rate only 1 percent, from 34 to 35 percent. However, they slid in a provision that the benefit of the lower rates on the first $75,000 of income would phase out as corporate income rose above $100,000. Similarly, the benefit of the 34 percent rate for incomes under $10,000,000 would phase out as income rose above $15,000,000. The result of converting this phase-out of lower rates as income rises results in the table above. Why didn't Congress just enact the resulting rate schedule, as in the preceding rate table?

This weird fluctuation in effective rates makes it imperative that owners of small corporations work out the tax for the expected profit before deciding on a C or S status for the corporation. There can be no viable rule of thumb in this environment.

APPENDIX B
LIMITED LIABILITY: HOW LIMITED IS IT?

The major reason for selecting one of the two types of organizations that are the subject of this book is limited liability. Both S corporations and limited liability companies provide some limitations on the liability of the owners, but it is not foolproof.

The following article* by Jane Easter Bahls in the August 1994 issue of *Entrepreneur* magazine covers the finer points of this area. Please pay particular attention to the last section, "Mind Your P's and Q's."

---

*Reprinted with permission from *Entrepreneur Magazine,* August 1994.

RETHINKING INC.

Incorporating Your Business
Won't Shield You from Becoming a Target
for Personal Liability.

by Jane Easter Bahls

When you were deciding whether to incorporate your business, chances are you talked it over with your advisors. They told you what you'd always heard: Setting up and operating a corporation could be a hassle, but it provided valuable liability protection. If someone sued your company, your personal assets would be safe.

Or so they told you. But incorporation has never been a guarantee against courts touching your personal assets, and it's getting to be even less so. The trend in recent cases is for courts to "pierce the corporate veil" far more often than they used to, allowing plaintiffs to go after business owners' houses, cars and personal bank accounts.

"Entrepreneurs believe the corporate form magically shields them from liability, but it doesn't," says Robert Thompson, a professor at Washington University School of Law in St. Louis.

Consider this recently decided case: A small corporation with a single stockholder manufactured rubber parts for cars. In the early 1970s, the company leased land from the owner's sister and used it as a dump for toxic sludge. In 1981, the owner of another manufacturing company bought the land. When he discovered the extent of the mess, he sued the rubber maker, its retired owner and the owner's sister.

The case had been in and out of court for years. The new owner claimed that under CERCLA, the Comprehensive Environmental Response Compensation and Liability Act, those responsible for creating the toxic mess should pay the cost of cleanup. The trial court ruled that the owner of the corporation was not responsible. Since the court found that he did not participate in the daily activities of the corporation and had no idea of the environmental contamination created by it, the corporation (now defunct) was responsible.

In May 1993, the Sixth Circuit U.S. Court of Appeals ruled that the former owner wasn't off the hook. Since he had had the authority to prevent his corporation from contaminating the property, he could be held at least partly responsible for cleanup costs—which are yet to be determined but certain to be enormous.

Thompson contends that the danger is growing for shareholders of closely held corporations to be held liable in lawsuits against the corporation, especially in the areas of environmental and pension laws. In an empirical study conducted last year, he found that the number of lawsuits attempting to go after shareholders had increased 75 percent in the past decade. Thompson found 286 such cases, with 60 percent being brought against privately owned companies. Although it's not yet clear how many of those were successful, one of his earlier studies in 1992 showed that courts decided against sole shareholders in nearly half of the 276 cases he examined.

"Limited liability is in grave danger," agrees Stephen Presser, a professor at Northwestern University School of Law in Chicago. Increasingly, he says, federal courts are ignoring state standards that attempt to protect owners by restricting the circumstances under which shareholders may be held liable.

"Respect for the corporate form is not as great as it used to be," Presser complains. He blames anti-business hostility left over from the 1960s. If the trend continues, he warns, the corporate form as we know it may be killed off as laws aimed at promoting social goals take precedence over laws established to encourage investment.

Presser explains that early in the 19th century, state courts held corporate shareholders personally liable for nearly every contract their corporations entered into or any wrong their corporation committed. Evidently, he says, the goal was to provide security for creditors so they'd lend money to growing corporations. By 1850, though, states had reversed their positions through legislation. Hoping to encourage people to invest in corporations, most states began limiting the liability of shareholders to the amount they'd invested.

"Protecting the corporate veil is critical for staying competitive," Presser argues. "There are good reasons for courts to hesitate before undercutting the policy of limited liability in the interest of some other public goal."

SLOVENLY MANAGEMENT

When might the owners of a corporation face personal liability? Thompson distinguishes two broad categories of cases. The first, he says, is nothing new. Although the shareholders of a corporation are normally not liable for its debts, courts will ignore the existence of the corporation if its owners reject corporate formalities or use the corporation as their personal plaything. If a shareholder who controls the corporation's daily affairs apparently uses the corporation merely as a shield, the court may allow a creditor to recover damages from the shareholder.

To obtain the protection afforded to corporations, business owners and managers must play by the rules. That includes providing sufficient capital to carry out the corporation's business, electing officers and a board of directors, holding annual meetings, keeping separate records, signing documents properly, and making sure transactions are approved by the board.

The second major category of cases is the one that's changing, Thompson says. "If you directly participate in a wrongful action, you will be held liable," he says. Just because your business is incorporated doesn't mean you can break laws or misreat employees.

An extreme example would be murder. The landmark case in this area involved a firm that recovered silver from photographic film. The company's employees worked day after day with a substance described only as "the chemical." It turned out to be cyanide. Company officials scraped off the warning labels, provided no hazardous materials training, and told the workers the substance was harmless. In 1985, after a 61-year-old Polish immigrant succumbed to the fumes and died, a county prosecutor indicted three officers of the corporation for murder and sent them to jail.

Not all the misconduct in these cases is so clear-cut. "The number of direct actions for which you can be held liable is increasing," Thompson says.

As in the toxic waste case cited earlier, if a corporation fails to follow regulations in the way it disposes of hazardous wastes, the owners may be liable for the cleanup. If a radio station violates copyright law by failing to pay royalties on the songs it plays, the owners may be liable for damages. If a corporation withdraws union dues or pension contributions from employees' paychecks but fails to transfer the funds as agreed, the owners may be held liable.

Presser notes that state courts have traditionally used two tests to determine whether to pierce the corporate veil: whether the shareholder controls the corporation and whether the controlling shareholder uses that corporation to perpetrate an injustice or aviod a law. "The state tests try to find real injustices, but the federal courts can get you whether or not there's an injustice," he says. "Some federal courts uphold the state tests, but some say, 'There's an important federal goal here; let's go ahead and soak the shareholders.' "

WATCH YOUR P'S AND Q'S

Despite the increasing number of corporate actions for which owners can be held liable, the corporate form still provides more protection than a sole proprietorship or partnership. If you're running your corporation by the rules and being careful about how you sign contracts and checks, you shouldn't be held personally liable for ordinary business debts or for judgments against the corporation for your employees' mideeds—unless you were directly supervising those employees and aware of what they were doing.

"The corporate form insulates you from acts of others and contract obligations," Thompson says. "You remain liable for your own acts, as you always have."

The same goes for limited liability companies, a new option for business structure that many states now allow. The form offers the flexibility of a partnership and the protection of a corporation—no more, no less.

If you own a corporation, here's how to reduce your liability:

- Issue shares, even if you're the sole shareholder.
- At a duly called shareholders' meeting, elect a board of directors and a slate of officers—even if the shareholders, directors and officers are all the same people. Hold annual meetings, and make sure the board of directors approves major transactions. (Note: Some states have a simplified set of rules that closely held corporations may elect to follow. Ask your attorney.)
- Make sure the corporation is adequately capitalized. When you set up the corporation, have the owners contribute, in exchange for stock, enough cash or property to meet the corporation's expenses.
- Keep separate records for the corporation, and don't siphon money out to pay personal expenses. It's up to the board of directors whether to issue dividends.
- Make sure your suppliers know they're dealing with a corporation. All letters, contracts, notes and checks should include the full corporate name. Make sure any individual who executes contracts or signs checks on behalf of the corporation has been authorized to do so by the board, as recorded in the minutes.

Running a tight ship is simply good business, but when your business is incorporated, it's essential. Make sure your corporation meets its legal obligations—or you may end up holding the bag.

APPENDIX C
S CORPORATION DOCUMENTS AND FORMS

Here are the forms you are most likely to need in forming an S corporation and at the end of the year.

CORPORATION FORMS TO FILE WITH YOUR STATE

These are the forms you'd need if you incorporate in Virginia, including a list of available forms for almost every situation. All the forms listed are available on the Virginia government Web site and can be downloaded, filled in, and mailed to the State Corporation Commission. Why did we use Virginia for an example? Because they have a form for almost every purpose.

Compare Virginia's Articles of Incorporation with those for Florida, which we used in the example in Chapter 4. Obviously, there's much variation in what various states require and the forms available.

If you're among the majority who live in some other state, check with your secretary of state or similar department. Most states have an Internet address that takes you to a Web site from which you can download forms. (I considered listing the Internet addresses here, but they frequently change, so it's better to suggest you use your favorite search engine or directory. Of course, you can always call the state government—ask for the Internet address or just order the forms while you have the agency on the phone.)

SCC - OFFICE OF THE CLERK

OFFICE OF THE CLERK

Virginia State Corporation Commission

(07/2000)

Corporation Fee Schedule

The number of the form relates to the applicable statute in Title 13.1 (corporate and limited liability company forms) or in Title 50 (partnership, limited partnership and registered limited liability partnership forms).

All Fees should be made payable to the State Corporation Commission.

SCC FORM #	TITLE OF FORM CORPORATIONS	FILING FEE (IF APPLICABLE) & COMMENTS
SCC544	Guide for Articles of Incorporation–Professional Corporation	See attached Charter/Entrance Fee Schedule
SCC607/807	Guide for Articles of Correction	$25 Plus any additional charter or entrance fee because of an increase in shares
SCC619	Articles of Incorporation–Stock Corporation	See attached Charter/Entrance Fee Schedule
SCC631/830	Application for Reservation or for Renewal of Reservation of Corporate Name (domestic corporations)	$10 for Reservation, effective for 120 days. $10 for Renewal of Reservation, renewal can be filed up to 30 days prior to expiration of reservation
SCC632/831	Application for Registration or For Renewal of Registration of Corporate Name (foreign corporations)	$20 for Registration, effective for one year. $20 for Renewal of Registration, renewal can be filed up to 60 days prior to expiration of registration
SCC635/834	Statement of Change of Registered Office/Registered Agent of a Corporation	No fee. Contact the Clerk's Office to obtain a preprinted form SCC635/834.
SCC636/835	Statement of Resignation of Registered Agent of a Corporation	No fee.
SCC710	Guide for Articles of Amendment–Unanimous Consent of Shareholders–Stock Corporation	$25 Plus any additional charter or entrance fee because of an increase in shares

SCC - OFFICE OF THE CLERK

SCC720	Guide for Articles of Merger or Share Exchange – Stock Corporation	$25 Plus any additional charter or entrance fee because of an increase in shares
SCC743	Articles of Dissolution – By Unanimous Consent of Shareholders – Stock Corporation	$10
SCC744	Articles of Revocation of Dissolution – Stock Corporation	$10
SCC750	Articles of Termination of Corporate Existence – Stock Corporation	$10
SCC751	Articles of Termination of Corporate Existence – By the Initial Directors or the Incorporators – Stock Corporation	$10
SCC759/921	Application for a Certificate of Authority to Transact Business in Virginia	See attached charter/ entrance fee schedule
SCC760/922	Application for an Amended Certificate of Authority to Transact Business in Virginia	$25 Note: Form is used for amendments regarding name change and change of state of incorporation
SCC767/929	Application for Certificate of Withdrawal	$10
SCC819	Guide for Articles of Incorporation – Nonstock Corporation	$75
SCC888	Guide for Articles of Amendment Without Membership Action – Nonstock Corporation	$25
SCC896	Guide for Articles of Merger– Nonstock Corporation	$25
SCC904	Articles of Dissolution – Nonstock Corporation	$10
SCC905	Articles of Revocation of Dissolution – Nonstock Corporation	$10
SCC912	Articles of Termination of Corporate Existence – Nonstock Corporation	$10
SCC913	Articles of Termination of Corporate Existence by the Initial Directors or the Incorporators – Nonstock Corporation	$10

COMMONWEALTH OF VIRGINIA
STATE CORPORATION COMMISSION

SCC619
(07/00)

GUIDE FOR ARTICLES OF INCORPORATION
VIRGINIA STOCK CORPORATION

The undersigned, pursuant to Chapter 9 of Title 13.1 of the Code of Virginia, state(s) as follows:

1. The name of the corporation is:

____.

2. The number (and classes, if any) of shares the corporation is authorized to issue is (are):

Number of shares authorized	**Class(es)**
____________________	____________________
____________________	____________________

3. A. The name of the corporation's initial registered agent is ____.

   B. The initial registered agent is (mark appropriate box):
   (1) an individual who is a resident of Virginia **and**
   [ ] an initial director of the corporation
   [ ] a member of the Virginia State Bar
   OR
   (2) [ ] a professional corporation, professional limited liability company or registered limited liability partnership registered with the Virginia State Bar under § 54.1-3902 of the Code of Virginia.

4. A. The corporation's initial registered office address which is the business office of the initial registered agent, is:

   ______________________________, VA ______________.
   (number/street) (city or town) (ZIP code)

   B. The registered office is physically located in the [ ] City **or** [ ] County of ____________________.

5. The initial directors are:

NAME(S)	**ADDRESS(ES)**
____________________	____________________
	____________________
____________________	____________________
	____________________
____________________	____________________
	____________________

6. INCORPORATOR(S):

SIGNATURE(S)	**PRINTED NAME(S)**
____________________	____________________
____________________	____________________
____________________	____________________

See instructions on the reverse.

NOTE

When preparing articles of incorporation, the information must be in the English language, typewritten or printed in black, legible and reproducible.

This form contains the minimum number of provisions required by Virginia law to be set forth in the articles of incorporation of a stock corporation. If additional provisions are desired, then the **complete** articles of incorporation, including the additional provisions, should be typewritten on white, opaque paper 8 1/2" by 11" in size, using only one side of a page. A minimum of a 1" margin must be provided on the left, top and bottom margins of a page and 1/2" at the right margin.

INSTRUCTIONS

1. **Name:** The corporate name must contain the word "corporation," "incorporated," "company" or "limited"; or the abbreviation "corp.," "inc.," "co." or "ltd." See § 13.1-630 of the Code of Virginia.

2. **Shares:** List the total number of shares the corporation is authorized to issue. If more than one class of shares is to be authorized, list the number of authorized shares of each class and a distinguishing designation for each class (e.g., common, preferred, etc.) and state the relative rights, limitations & preferences of each class. See §§ 13.1-619, 13.1-638 of the Code of Virginia.

3. **Registered agent:** A. Provide the name of the registered agent, whose business address is the same as the corporation's registered office address. See §§ 13.1-619, 13.1-634 of the Code of Virginia.
   B. Check one of the boxes to indicate the status of the registered agent. The qualifications of the initial registered agent are set forth on the front of this form - no other person or entity may serve as the registered agent.

4. **Registered office:** A. Provide the complete post office address (which must include a street address, if any, or a rural route and box number in rural areas) of the corporation's registered office which is the same as the business address of the registered agent.
   B. Provide the name of the city **or** county where the registered office is physically located. (Cities and counties in Virginia are separate local jurisdictions.) See §§ 13.1-619, 13.1-634 of the Code of Virginia.

5. **Directors:** If the registered agent's status in 3.B. is that of initial director, then the names and addresses of the initial directors must be included in the articles of incorporation. A corporation can have directors immediately upon formation **only** if they are named in the articles.

6. **Incorporator(s):** One or more persons must sign the articles of incorporation in this capacity. See § 13.1-604 of the Code of Virginia.

   SEND THE ARTICLES OF INCORPORATION, ALONG WITH THE CHARTER AND FILING FEES, TO THE CLERK OF THE STATE CORPORATION COMMISSION, P. O. BOX 1197, RICHMOND, VA 23218-1197. (Street address: 1300 East Main Street, 1st floor, Richmond, VA 23219). IF YOU HAVE QUESTIONS, CALL (804) 371-9733.

   Charter fee: 1,000,000 or fewer authorized shares - $50 for each 25,000 shares or fraction thereof; more than 1 million shares - $2,500. **Filing fee**: $25.
   SEND BOTH FEES IN THE SAME CHECK, MADE PAYABLE TO THE STATE CORPORATION COMMISSION.

SCC544
(07/00)

COMMONWEALTH OF VIRGINIA
STATE CORPORATION COMMISSION

GUIDE FOR ARTICLES OF INCORPORATION
PROFESSIONAL CORPORATION

The undersigned, pursuant to Chapters 7 and 9 or 10 of Title 13.1 of the Code of Virginia, state(s) as follows:

1. The name of the corporation is:

   ____.

2. The corporation is organized for the sole and specific purpose of rendering the professional services of: ____.

3. The number (and classes, if any) of shares the corporation is authorized to issue is (are):

Number of shares authorized	Class(es)
____________________	____________________
____________________	____________________

4. A. The name of the corporation's initial registered agent is

   ____.

   B. The initial registered agent is (mark appropriate box):
   (1) An individual who is a resident of Virginia **and**
   [ ] an initial director of the corporation
   [ ] a member of the Virginia State Bar
   OR
   (2) [ ] a professional corporation, professional limited liability company or registered limited liability partnership registered with the Virginia State Bar under § 54.1-3902 of the Code of Virginia.

5. A. The corporation's initial registered office address, which is the business office of the initial registered agent, is:

   ______________________________, VA ____________.
   (number/street) (city or town) (zip code)

   B. The registered office is physically located in the [ ] City **or** [ ] County of

   ______________________________.

6. The first board of directors shall have __________ member(s).

7. The initial directors are:

NAME(S)	ADDRESS(ES)
____________________	____________________
	____________________
____________________	____________________
	____________________

8. The undersigned INCORPORATOR(s) is (are) duly licensed or legally authorized to render in Virginia the professional services of: ____.

SIGNATURE(S)	PRINTED NAME(S)
____________________	____________________
____________________	____________________

See instructions on the reverse.

NOTE

THIS FORM IS INTENDED FOR USE AS A GUIDE ONLY. Articles of incorporation must be in the English language and typewritten in black, on white opaque paper 8 ½" by 11" in size, using only one side of a page, legible and reproducible.

INSTRUCTIONS

1. **Name:** The corporate name must contain the word "corporation," "incorporated," "company" or "limited"; or the abbreviation "corp.," "inc.," "co." or "ltd."; or the initials "P.C." See §§ 13.1-544.1, 13.1-630 of the Code of Virginia.

2. **Professional services:** State the professional services the corporation is organized to render. The law limits such services to the personal services rendered by: pharmacists, optometrists, practitioners of the healing arts, nurse practitioners, practitioners of the behavioral science professions, veterinarians, surgeons, dentists, architects, professional engineers, land surveyors, certified interior designers, certified landscape architects, public accountants, certified public accountants, attorneys-at-law, insurance consultants, audiologists or speech pathologists and clinical nurse specialists. See § 13.1-543 of the Code of Virginia.

3. **Shares:** If a stock corporation, list the total number of shares the corporation is authorized to issue. If more than one class of shares is to be authorized, list the number of authorized shares of each class and a distinguishing designation for each class (e.g., common, preferred, etc.). See § 13.1-619, 13.1-638 of the Code of Virginia. For the percentage of shareholders that must be licensed or authorized to render the same services for which the corporation is organized, see §§ 13.1-549, 13.1-549.1 of the Code of Virginia.

4. **Registered agent:** A. Provide the name of the registered agent, whose business address is the same as the corporation's registered office address. See §§ 13.1-619, 13.1-634 of the Code of Virginia.
B. Indicate the status of the registered agent. The registered agent must be one of the options listed. No other person or entity may serve as the registered agent.

5. **Registered office:** A. Provide the complete post office address (which must include a street address, if any, or a rural route and box number in rural areas) of the corporation's registered office which is the same as the business office of the registered agent.
B. Provide the name of the city or county where the registered office is physically located. (Cities and counties in Virginia are separate local jurisdictions.) See § 13.1-619 of the Code of Virginia.

6&7. **Directors:** The articles must fix the number of the corporation's first board of directors. A corporation can have directors immediately upon formation only if they are named in the articles. Thus, if the registered agent's status in 4.B. is that of initial director, then the initial directors must be included. NOTE: The licensing restriction on shareholders referenced above in Instruction 3, also applies to directors. See § 13.1-553 of the Code of Virginia.

8. **Incorporator(s):** One or more persons must sign the articles in this capacity, and must be licensed or authorized to render the professional services involved. See §§ 13.1-544, 13.1-604 of the Code of Virginia.

SEND THE ARTICLES OF INCORPORATION, ALONG WITH CHARTER AND FILING FEES, TO THE CLERK OF THE STATE CORPORATION COMMISSION, P. O. BOX 1197, RICHMOND, VA 23218-1197. (Street address: 1300 East Main Street, 1st floor, Richmond, VA 23219). IF YOU HAVE QUESTIONS, CALL (804) 371-9733.

Charter fee: 1,000,000 or fewer authorized shares - $50 for each 25,000 shares or fraction thereof; more than 1 million shares - $2,500.
Filing fee: $25.
SEND BOTH FEES IN THE SAME CHECK, MADE PAYABLE TO THE STATE CORPORATION COMMISSION.

SHAREHOLDERS' AGREEMENT

AGREEMENT made this _________ day of ___________ , 19____ , between [name of corporation]____, having its principal office at ____________, [State]________, and ______[shareholder's name]______, of ______[shareholder's address]______, and ______[shareholder's name]______, of ______[shareholder's address]______, and ______[shareholder's name]______, ______[shareholder's address]______.

WHEREAS, the parties desire to promote their mutual interests and the interests of the Corporation by making provision to avoid future differences,

NOW, THEREFORE, it is mutually agreed as follows:

1. Each of the undersigned shareholders agrees that so long as he or she shall remain a shareholder in [name of corporation], he or she will vote his or her respective shares of stock in the corporation for each of the following named persons as a director, so long as that person remains a shareholder of the Corporation:

1. ____

2. ____

3. ____

Any of the foregoing directors who ceases to be a shareholder in the Corporation shall submit to the Corporation his or her resignation as a director when he or she transfers his or her shares.

2. For the best interest of [name of corporation], the undersigned shareholders agree to have each of the following persons appointed and elected as an officer of [name of corporation], as long as he or she remains a shareholder and performs faithfully, efficiently, and competently for the Corporation.

President ____________________________________

Vice-President________________________________

Secretary ____________________________________

Treasurer ____________________________________

Any of the foregoing officers who ceases to be a shareholder in the Corporation shall submit to the Corporation his or her resignation as an officer when he or she transfers his or her shares.

3. Each of the undersigned persons agrees that he or she will devote his or her best efforts to develop the best interests of the corporation.

4. (a) The undersigned shareholders agree that if any action be taken at a meeting of the shareholders or directors of the Corporation by a vote of less than ____% of the shareholders or directors, as the case may be, the dissenting shareholder may require the other shareholders or directors within ___ days either to (1) rescind the action dissented from, or (2) purchase the shares owned by the dissenter at a price per share computed on a pro rata basis according to Section 4(d) of this agreement. The individual shareholders party to this agreement agree that should their vote in favor of the action be dissented from, they will either (1) rescind it, or (2) purchase the dissenter's shares within ____ days.

(b) The undersigned shareholders agree that they will not transfer, assign, sell, pledge, hypothecate, or otherwise dispose of the shares of stock owned by any of them, or the certificates of stock representing their interests, unless such shares of stock shall have been first offered to the Corporation at a price per share computed on a pro rata basis according to the provisions of Section 4(d) of this agreement. Such offer shall be made in writing and shall remain open for the Corporation's acceptance for a period of _____ days. In the event the Corporation wishes to accept the offer, it must agree in writing to purchase the entire amount of stock offered and shall at that time make a down payment of ____% of the purchase price. The balance of the purchase price shall be paid as provided in section 4(e) of this agreement. If the Corporation should not choose to purchase the shares within ____ days, they shall then be offered to the remaining stockholders on a pro rata basis. Such offer shall be made in writing and shall remain open for a period of ____ days. In the event the stockholders wish to accept the offer, they must agree in writing to purchase any or all of their pro rata portion of shares, and make a down payment in the amount of ____% of the purchase price. The balance of the purchase price shall be paid as provided in Section 4(e) of this agreement. If any shareholder should elect not to purchase his or her pro rata portion, or should purchase less than the full amount, the remainder shall be offered to the other shareholders on a pro rata basis. The amount of stock that remains unpurchased after this offering to the shareholders shall be freely transferable and no longer subject to the provisions and limitations of this agreement. This agreement shall not bar a transfer, assignment, bequest, or sale of shares of stock by one of the undersigned shareholders to a member of his or her immediate family, who shall, however, take his or her stock subject to all the limitations of this agreement as if he or she were a party to it.

(c) The parties to this agreement agree that upon the death of [name of shareholders], ______________, or ______________, the executors, administrators, or legal representatives of the deceased shall, within ________ days after qualification as such, sell to [name of corporation], and the corporation agrees to buy, all the shares of stock in [name of corporation], owned by the deceased at the time of his or her death. It is the wish of the parties to this agreement that within the period specified above after the death of the shareholder, his or her family shall terminate all interest in the corporation, and all members of the family to whom any shares of stock have been or shall be transferred shall sell to the corporation all shares of its stock owned by them, within ________ days. The price per share shall be computed on a pro rata basis according to the provisions of Section 4(d) of this agreement.

(d) The parties to this agreement agree that as of the date hereof one share of stock in the corporation shall be worth $___________. It is the intention of the parties to review this figure ________ times a year, on ______[date]______, and that the last agreed-upon figure prior to a transfer described in Sections 4(a), (b), or (c) shall be conclusive as to the value of the stock for such purposes.

(e) The purchase price shall be paid as follows: ________% in cash within ________ days after the qualification of the legal representatives of the deceased shareholder. ________% of the unpaid balance shall be paid within the succeeding ________ days, and ________% of the still remaining unpaid balance within ________ days. Interest at the rate of _________% shall be calculated on the outstanding unpaid balance. The corporation reserves the right to prepay the whole or any part of the amount owed without the imposition of a premium or penalty therefore.

5. The parties hereto agree that they will take no action or dispose of their stock in such a way as to cause the termination of the corporation's ability to be taxed as an electing small business corporation under Subchapter S of the Internal Revenue Code of 1954.

6. Each stock certificate of the corporation shall contain the following information:

> Transfer or pledge of these shares is restricted under a shareholders' agreement dated ________________, 19____. A copy of the agreement, which affects other rights of the holder of these shares, is on file at the office of the corporation at [address of corporate offices].

7. Should any dispute arise between any one or more of the parties to this agreement as to their rights under any provisions of this agreement, the parties hereby agree to refer such dispute to the American Arbitration Association, whose decision on the questions shall be binding on the parties and shall be without appeal.

8. The corporation is authorized to enter into this agreement by a resolution adopted by the shareholders and directors, dated ____________, 19____.

9. This agreement or any of its provisions may be changed only by the mutual consent of the parties hereto, and unless so changed it remains binding upon all the parties, their heirs, executors, administrators, legal representatives, and assigns, who shall execute and deliver all necessary documents required to carry out the terms of this agreement.

IN WITNESS WHEREOF, the individual parties hereto set their hands and seals, and the corporation has caused this agreement to be signed by its duly authorized officers and the corporate seal affixed.

NAME OF CORPORATION

BY: ______________________________

President

[Names of shareholders] ____________

____

____

ATTEST:

____

Secretary

THE IRS FORMS

With Form 1120S, U.S Income Tax Return for an S Corporation, are many pages of instructions. Don't let that dissuade you from incorporating. The IRS used to put much of the information in a separate booklet for those who had unusual situations, but now it all goes in the instructions for the form. Don't try to read them cover to cover; use them as a reference.

If, after the discussion in Chapter 5 about a tax year that ends other than December 31 (or thereabouts), you still prefer to have such a fiscal year, the forms are here.

There are other forms you might need that are included here, but not their instructions. They're the forms that you encounter no matter what business form you select, such as those for depreciation and sale of assets. Because of space constraints, they aren't here, but you can order them from the IRS. The phone number is 800-TAX-FORM. The Internet address for forms download is http://www.irs.ustreas.gov/prod/forms_pubs/index.html. If that doesn't work, try getting there from http://www.irs.gov.

Form **SS-4**

(Rev. April 2000)

Department of the Treasury
Internal Revenue Service

Application for Employer Identification Number

(For use by employers, corporations, partnerships, trusts, estates, churches, government agencies, certain individuals, and others. See instructions.)

▶ Keep a copy for your records.

EIN

OMB No. 1545-0003

Please type or print clearly.

1 Name of applicant (legal name) (see instructions)

2 Trade name of business (if different from name on line 1)

3 Executor, trustee, "care of" name

4a Mailing address (street address) (room, apt., or suite no.)

5a Business address (if different from address on lines 4a and 4b)

4b City, state, and ZIP code

5b City, state, and ZIP code

6 County and state where principal business is located

7 Name of principal officer, general partner, grantor, owner, or trustor- SSN or ITIN may be required (see instructions) ▶

8a Type of entity (Check only one box.) (see instructions)
Caution: *If applicant is a limited liability company, see the instructions for line 8a.*

☐ Sole proprietor (SSN) ____
☐ Partnership
☐ REMIC
☐ State/local government
☐ Church or church-controlled organization
☐ Other nonprofit organization (specify) ▶ ____ (enter GEN if applicable) ____
☐ Other (specify) ▶
☐ Personal service corp.
☐ National Guard
☐ Farmers' cooperative
☐ Estate (SSN of decedent) ____
☐ Plan administrator (SSN) ____
☐ Other corporation (specify) ▶ ____
☐ Trust
☐ Federal government/military

8b If a corporation, name the state or foreign country (if applicable) where incorporated | State | Foreign country

9 Reason for applying (Check only one box.) (see instructions)
☐ Started new business (specify type) ▶ ____
☐ Hired employees (Check the box and see line 12.)
☐ Created a pension plan (specify type) ▶
☐ Banking purpose (specify purpose) ▶ ____
☐ Changed type of organization (specify new type) ▶ ____
☐ Purchased going business
☐ Created a trust (specify type) ▶ ____
☐ Other (specify) ▶

10 Date business started or acquired (month, day, year) (see instructions)

11 Closing month of accounting year (see instructions)

12 First date wages or annuities were paid or will be paid (month, day, year). **Note:** *If applicant is a withholding agent, enter date income will first be paid to nonresident alien. (month, day, year)* . . . . ▶

13 Highest number of employees expected in the next 12 months. **Note:** *If the applicant does not expect to have any employees during the period, enter -0-. (see instructions)* . . . . ▶	Nonagricultural	Agricultural	Household

14 Principal activity (see instructions) ▶

15 Is the principal business activity manufacturing? . . . . ☐ **Yes** ☐ **No**
If "Yes," principal product and raw material used ▶

16 To whom are most of the products or services sold? Please check one box. ☐ Business (wholesale)
☐ Public (retail) ☐ Other (specify) ▶ ☐ N/A

17a Has the applicant ever applied for an employer identification number for this or any other business? . . . . ☐ **Yes** ☐ **No**
Note: *If "Yes," please complete lines 17b and 17c.*

17b If you checked "Yes" on line 17a, give applicant's legal name and trade name shown on prior application, if different from line 1 or 2 above.
Legal name ▶ Trade name ▶

17c Approximate date when and city and state where the application was filed. Enter previous employer identification number if known.

Approximate date when filed (mo., day, year)	City and state where filed	Previous EIN

Under penalties of perjury, I declare that I have examined this application, and to the best of my knowledge and belief, it is true, correct, and complete.

Business telephone number (include area code)
( )

Fax telephone number (include area code)
( )

Name and title (Please type or print clearly.) ▶

Signature ▶ Date ▶

Note: *Do not write below this line. For official use only.*

Please leave blank ▶	Geo.	Ind.	Class	Size	Reason for applying

For Privacy Act and Paperwork Reduction Act Notice, see page 4. Cat. No. 16055N Form **SS-4** (Rev. 4-2000)

Form SS-4 (Rev. 4-2000) Page **2**

General Instructions

Section references are to the Internal Revenue Code unless otherwise noted.

Purpose of Form

Use Form SS-4 to apply for an employer identification number (EIN). An EIN is a nine-digit number (for example, 12-3456789) assigned to sole proprietors, corporations, partnerships, estates, trusts, and other entities for tax filing and reporting purposes. The information you provide on this form will establish your business tax account.

Caution: *An EIN is for use in connection with your business activities only. Do **not** use your EIN in place of your social security number (SSN).*

Who Must File

You must file this form if you have not been assigned an EIN before and:

- You pay wages to one or more employees including household employees.
- You are required to have an EIN to use on any return, statement, or other document, even if you are not an employer.
- You are a withholding agent required to withhold taxes on income, other than wages, paid to a nonresident alien (individual, corporation, partnership, etc.). A withholding agent may be an agent, broker, fiduciary, manager, tenant, or spouse, and is required to file **Form 1042,** Annual Withholding Tax Return for U.S. Source Income of Foreign Persons.
- You file **Schedule C,** Profit or Loss From Business, **Schedule C-EZ,** Net Profit From Business, or **Schedule F,** Profit or Loss From Farming, of **Form 1040,** U.S. Individual Income Tax Return, **and** have a Keogh plan or are required to file excise, employment, or alcohol, tobacco, or firearms returns.

The following must use EINs even if they do not have any employees:

- State and local agencies who serve as tax reporting agents for public assistance recipients, under Rev. Proc. 80-4, 1980-1 C.B. 581, should obtain a separate EIN for this reporting. See **Household employer** on page 3.
- Trusts, except the following:

1. Certain grantor-owned trusts. (See the **Instructions for Form 1041,** U.S. Income Tax Return for Estates and Trusts.)

2. Individual retirement arrangement (IRA) trusts, unless the trust has to file **Form 990-T,** Exempt Organization Business Income Tax Return. (See the **Instructions for Form 990-T.**)

- Estates
- Partnerships
- REMICs (real estate mortgage investment conduits) (See the **Instructions for Form 1066,** U.S. Real Estate Mortgage Investment Conduit (REMIC) Income Tax Return.)
- Corporations
- Nonprofit organizations (churches, clubs, etc.)
- Farmers' cooperatives
- Plan administrators (A plan administrator is the person or group of persons specified as the administrator by the instrument under which the plan is operated.)

When To Apply for a New EIN

New Business. If you become the new owner of an existing business, **do not** use the EIN of the former owner. **If you already have an EIN, use that number.** If you do not have an EIN, apply for one on this form. If you become the "owner" of a corporation by acquiring its stock, use the corporation's EIN.

Changes in Organization or Ownership. If you already have an EIN, you may need to get a new one if either the organization or ownership of your business changes. If you incorporate a sole proprietorship or form a partnership, you must get a new EIN. However, **do not** apply for a new EIN if:

- You change only the name of your business,
- You elected on **Form 8832,** Entity Classification Election, to change the way the entity is taxed, or
- A partnership terminates because at least 50% of the total interests in partnership capital and profits were sold or exchanged within a 12-month period. (See Regulations section 301.6109-1(d)(2)(iii).) The EIN for the terminated partnership should continue to be used.

Note: *If you are electing to be an "S corporation," be sure you file **Form 2553,** Election by a Small Business Corporation.*

File Only One Form SS-4. File only one Form SS-4, regardless of the number of businesses operated or trade names under which a business operates. However, each corporation in an affiliated group must file a separate application.

EIN Applied for, But Not Received. If you do not have an EIN by the time a return is due, write "Applied for" and the date you applied in the space shown for the number. **Do not** show your social security number (SSN) as an EIN on returns.

If you do not have an EIN by the time a tax deposit is due, send your payment to the Internal Revenue Service Center for your filing area. (See **Where To Apply** below.) Make your check or money order payable to "United States Treasury" and show your name (as shown on Form SS-4), address, type of tax, period covered, and date you applied for an EIN. Send an explanation with the deposit.

For more information about EINs, see **Pub. 583,** Starting a Business and Keeping Records, and **Pub. 1635,** Understanding Your EIN.

How To Apply

You can apply for an EIN either by mail or by telephone. You can get an EIN immediately by calling the Tele-TIN number for the service center for your state, or you can send the completed Form SS-4 directly to the service center to receive your EIN by mail.

Application by Tele-TIN. Under the Tele-TIN program, you can receive your EIN by telephone and use it immediately to file a return or make a payment. To receive an EIN by telephone, complete Form SS-4, then call the Tele-TIN number listed for your state under **Where To Apply.** The person making the call must be authorized to sign the form. (See **Signature** on page 4.)

An IRS representative will use the information from the Form SS-4 to establish your account and assign you an EIN. Write the number you are given on the upper right corner of the form and sign and date it.

*Mail or fax (facsimile) the signed Form SS-4 **within 24 hours** to the Tele-TIN Unit at the service center address for your state.* The IRS representative will give you the fax number. The fax numbers are also listed in Pub. 1635.

Taxpayer representatives can receive their client's EIN by telephone if they first send a fax of a completed **Form 2848,** Power of Attorney and Declaration of Representative, or **Form 8821,** Tax Information Authorization, to the Tele-TIN unit. The Form 2848 or Form 8821 will be used solely to release the EIN to the representative authorized on the form.

Application by Mail. Complete Form SS-4 at least 4 to 5 weeks before you will need an EIN. Sign and date the application and mail it to the service center address for your state. You will receive your EIN in the mail in approximately 4 weeks.

Where To Apply

The Tele-TIN numbers listed below will involve a long-distance charge to callers outside of the local calling area and can be used only to apply for an EIN. **The numbers may change without notice.** Call 1-800-829-1040 to verify a number or to ask about the status of an application by mail.

If your principal business, office or agency, or legal residence in the case of an individual, is located in:	**Call the Tele-TIN number shown or file with the Internal Revenue Service Center at:**
Florida, Georgia, South Carolina	Attn: Entity Control Atlanta, GA 39901 770-455-2360
New Jersey, New York (New York City and counties of Nassau, Rockland, Suffolk, and Westchester)	Attn: Entity Control Holtsville, NY 00501 516-447-4955
New York (all other counties), Connecticut, Maine, Massachusetts, New Hampshire, Rhode Island, Vermont	Attn: Entity Control Andover, MA 05501 978-474-9717
Illinois, Iowa, Minnesota, Missouri, Wisconsin	Attn: Entity Control Stop 6800 2306 E. Bannister Rd. Kansas City, MO 64999 816-926-5999
Delaware, District of Columbia, Maryland, Pennsylvania, Virginia	Attn: Entity Control Philadelphia, PA 19255 215-516-6999
Indiana, Kentucky, Michigan, Ohio, West Virginia	Attn: Entity Control Cincinnati, OH 45999 859-292-5467

Kansas, New Mexico, Oklahoma, Texas	Attn: Entity Control Austin, TX 73301 512-460-7843
Alaska, Arizona, California (counties of Alpine, Amador, Butte, Calaveras, Colusa, Contra Costa, Del Norte, El Dorado, Glenn, Humboldt, Lake, Lassen, Marin, Mendocino, Modoc, Napa, Nevada, Placer, Plumas, Sacramento, San Joaquin, Shasta, Sierra, Siskiyou, Solano, Sonoma, Sutter, Tehama, Trinity, Yolo, and Yuba), Colorado, Idaho, Montana, Nebraska, Nevada, North Dakota, Oregon, South Dakota, Utah, Washington, Wyoming	Attn: Entity Control Mail Stop 6271 P.O. Box 9941 Ogden, UT 84201 801-620-7645
California (all other counties), Hawaii	Attn: Entity Control Fresno, CA 93888 559-452-4010
Alabama, Arkansas, Louisiana, Mississippi, North Carolina, Tennessee	Attn: Entity Control Memphis, TN 37501 901-546-3920
If you have no legal residence, principal place of business, or principal office or agency in any state	Attn: Entity Control Philadelphia, PA 19255 215-516-6999

Specific Instructions

The instructions that follow are for those items that are not self-explanatory. Enter N/A (nonapplicable) on the lines that do not apply.

Line 1. Enter the legal name of the entity applying for the EIN exactly as it appears on the social security card, charter, or other applicable legal document.

Individuals. Enter your first name, middle initial, and last name. If you are a sole proprietor, enter your individual name, not your business name. Enter your business name on line 2. Do not use abbreviations or nicknames on line 1.

Trusts. Enter the name of the trust.

Estate of a decedent. Enter the name of the estate.

Partnerships. Enter the legal name of the partnership as it appears in the partnership agreement. **Do not** list the names of the partners on line 1. See the specific instructions for line 7.

Corporations. Enter the corporate name as it appears in the corporation charter or other legal document creating it.

Plan administrators. Enter the name of the plan administrator. A plan administrator who already has an EIN should use that number.

Line 2. Enter the trade name of the business if different from the legal name. The trade name is the "doing business as" name.

Note: *Use the full legal name on line 1 on all tax returns filed for the entity. However, if you enter a trade name on line 2 and choose to use the trade name instead of the legal name, enter the trade name on all returns you file. To prevent processing delays and errors,* ***always*** *use either the legal name only or the trade name only on all tax returns.*

Line 3. Trusts enter the name of the trustee. Estates enter the name of the executor, administrator, or other fiduciary. If the entity applying has a designated person to receive tax information, enter that person's name as the "care of" person. Print or type the first name, middle initial, and last name.

Line 7. Enter the first name, middle initial, last name, and SSN of a principal officer if the business is a corporation; of a general partner if a partnership; of the owner of a single member entity that is disregarded as an entity separate from its owner; or of a grantor, owner, or trustor if a trust. If the person in question is an alien individual with a previously assigned individual taxpayer identification number (ITIN), enter the ITIN in the space provided, instead of an SSN. You are not required to enter an SSN or ITIN if the reason you are applying for an EIN is to make an entity classification election (see Regulations section 301.7701-1 through 301.7701-3), and you are a nonresident alien with no effectively connected income from sources within the United States.

Line 8a. Check the box that best describes the type of entity applying for the EIN. If you are an alien individual with an ITIN previously assigned to you, enter the ITIN in place of a requested SSN.

Caution: *This is not an election for a tax classification of an entity. See "Limited liability company (LLC)" below.*

If not specifically mentioned, check the "Other" box, enter the type of entity and the type of return that will be filed (for example, common trust fund, Form 1065). Do not enter N/A. If you are an alien individual applying for an EIN, see the **Line 7** instructions above.

Sole proprietor. Check this box if you file Schedule C, C-EZ, or F (Form 1040) and have a qualified plan, or are required to file excise, employment, or alcohol, tobacco, or firearms returns, or are a payer of gambling winnings. Enter your SSN (or ITIN) in the space provided. If you are a nonresident alien with are a nonresident alien with no effectively connected income from sources within the United States, you do not need to enter an SSN or ITIN.

REMIC. Check this box if the entity has elected to be treated as a real estate mortgage investment conduit (REMIC). See the Instructions for Form 1066 for more information.

Other nonprofit organization. Check this box if the nonprofit organization is other than a church or church-controlled organization and specify the type of nonprofit organization (for example, an educational organization).

If the organization also seeks tax-exempt status, you must file either **Package 1023,** Application for Recognition of Exemption, or **Package 1024,** Application for Recognition of Exemption Under Section 501(a). Get **Pub. 557,** Tax Exempt Status for Your Organization, for more information.

Group exemption number (GEN). If the organization is covered by a group exemption letter, enter the four-digit GEN. (Do not confuse the GEN with the nine-digit EIN.) If you do not know the GEN, contact the parent organization. Get Pub. 557 for more information about group exemption numbers.

Withholding agent. If you are a withholding agent required to file Form 1042, check the "Other" box and enter "Withholding agent."

Personal service corporation. Check this box if the entity is a personal service corporation. An entity is a personal service corporation for a tax year only if:

- The principal activity of the entity during the testing period (prior tax year) for the tax year is the performance of personal services substantially by employee-owners, and
- The employee-owners own at least 10% of the fair market value of the outstanding stock in the entity on the last day of the testing period.

Personal services include performance of services in such fields as health, law, accounting, or consulting. For more information about personal service corporations, see the **Instructions for Forms 1120 and 1120-A,** and **Pub. 542,** Corporations.

Limited liability company (LLC). See the definition of limited liability company in the **Instructions for Form 1065,** U.S. Partnership Return of Income. An LLC with two or more members can be a partnership or an association taxable as a corporation. An LLC with a single owner can be an association taxable as a corporation or an entity disregarded as an entity separate from its owner. See Form 8832 for more details.

Note: *A domestic LLC with at least two members that does not file Form 8832 is classified as a partnership for Federal income tax purposes.*

- If the entity is classified as a partnership for Federal income tax purposes, check the "partnership" box.
- If the entity is classified as a corporation for Federal income tax purposes, check the "Other corporation" box and write "limited liability co." in the space provided.
- If the entity is disregarded as an entity separate from its owner, check the "Other" box and write in "disregarded entity" in the space provided.

Plan administrator. If the plan administrator is an individual, enter the plan administrator's SSN in the space provided.

Other corporation. This box is for any corporation other than a personal service corporation. If you check this box, enter the type of corporation (such as insurance company) in the space provided.

Household employer. If you are an individual, check the "Other" box and enter "Household employer" and your SSN. If you are a state or local agency serving as a tax reporting agent for public assistance recipients who become household employers, check the "Other" box and enter "Household employer agent." If you are a trust that qualifies as a household employer, you do not need a separate EIN for reporting tax information relating to household employees; use the EIN of the trust.

QSub. For a qualified subchapter S subsidiary (QSub) check the "Other" box and specify "QSub."

Line 9. Check only **one** box. Do not enter N/A.

Started new business. Check this box if you are starting a new business that requires an EIN. If you check this box, enter the type of business being started. **Do not** apply if you already have an EIN and are only adding another place of business.

Hired employees. Check this box if the existing business is requesting an EIN because it has hired or is hiring employees and is therefore required to file employment tax returns. **Do not** apply if you already have an EIN and are only hiring employees. For information on the applicable employment taxes for family members, see **Circular E,** Employer's Tax Guide (Publication 15).

Created a pension plan. Check this box if you have created a pension plan and need an EIN for reporting purposes. Also, enter the type of plan.

Note: *Check this box if you are applying for a trust EIN when a new pension plan is established.*

Form SS-4 (Rev. 4-2000) Page **4**

Banking purpose. Check this box if you are requesting an EIN for banking purposes only, and enter the banking purpose (for example, a bowling league for depositing dues or an investment club for dividend and interest reporting).

Changed type of organization. Check this box if the business is changing its type of organization, for example, if the business was a sole proprietorship and has been incorporated or has become a partnership. If you check this box, specify in the space provided the type of change made, for example, "from sole proprietorship to partnership."

Purchased going business. Check this box if you purchased an existing business. **Do not** use the former owner's EIN. **Do not** apply for a new EIN if you already have one. Use your own EIN.

Created a trust. Check this box if you created a trust, and enter the type of trust created. For example, indicate if the trust is a nonexempt charitable trust or a split-interest trust.

Note: ***Do not*** *check this box if you are applying for a trust EIN when a new pension plan is established. Check "Created a pension plan."*

Exception. Do **not** file this form for certain grantor-type trusts. The trustee does not need an EIN for the trust if the trustee furnishes the name and TIN of the grantor/owner and the address of the trust to all payors. See the Instructions for Form 1041 for more information.

Other (specify). Check this box if you are requesting an EIN for any other reason, and enter the reason.

Line 10. If you are starting a new business, enter the starting date of the business. If the business you acquired is already operating, enter the date you acquired the business. Trusts should enter the date the trust was legally created. Estates should enter the date of death of the decedent whose name appears on line 1 or the date when the estate was legally funded.

Line 11. Enter the last month of your accounting year or tax year. An accounting or tax year is usually 12 consecutive months, either a calendar year or a fiscal year (including a period of 52 or 53 weeks). A calendar year is 12 consecutive months ending on December 31. A fiscal year is either 12 consecutive months ending on the last day of any month other than December or a 52-53 week year. For more information on accounting periods, see **Pub. 538,** Accounting Periods and Methods.

Individuals. Your tax year generally will be a calendar year.

Partnerships. Partnerships generally must adopt one of the following tax years:

- The tax year of the majority of its partners,
- The tax year common to all of its principal partners,
- The tax year that results in the least aggregate deferral of income, or
- In certain cases, some other tax year.

See the Instructions for Form 1065 for more information.

REMIC. REMICs must have a calendar year as their tax year.

Personal service corporations. A personal service corporation generally must adopt a calendar year unless:

- It can establish a business purpose for having a different tax year, or
- It elects under section 444 to have a tax year other than a calendar year.

Trusts. Generally, a trust must adopt a calendar year except for the following:

- Tax-exempt trusts,
- Charitable trusts, and
- Grantor-owned trusts.

Line 12. If the business has or will have employees, enter the date on which the business began or will begin to pay wages. If the business does not plan to have employees, enter N/A.

Withholding agent. Enter the date you began or will begin to pay income to a nonresident alien. This also applies to individuals who are required to file Form 1042 to report alimony paid to a nonresident alien.

Line 13. For a definition of agricultural labor (farmwork), see **Circular A,** Agricultural Employer's Tax Guide (Publication 51).

Line 14. Generally, enter the exact type of business being operated (for example, advertising agency, farm, food or beverage establishment, labor union, real estate agency, steam laundry, rental of coin-operated vending machine, or investment club). Also state if the business will involve the sale or distribution of alcoholic beverages.

Governmental. Enter the type of organization (state, county, school district, municipality, etc.).

Nonprofit organization (other than governmental). Enter whether organized for religious, educational, or humane purposes, and the principal activity (for example, religious organization- hospital, charitable).

Mining and quarrying. Specify the process and the principal product (for example, mining bituminous coal, contract drilling for oil, or quarrying dimension stone).

Contract construction. Specify whether general contracting or special trade contracting. Also, show the type of work normally performed (for example, general contractor for residential buildings or electrical subcontractor).

Food or beverage establishments. Specify the type of establishment and state whether you employ workers who receive tips (for example, lounge- yes).

Trade. Specify the type of sales and the principal line of goods sold (for example, wholesale dairy products, manufacturer's representative for mining machinery, or retail hardware).

Manufacturing. Specify the type of establishment operated (for example, sawmill or vegetable cannery).

Signature. The application must be signed by (a) the individual, if the applicant is an individual, (b) the president, vice president, or other principal officer, if the applicant is a corporation, (c) a responsible and duly authorized member or officer having knowledge of its affairs, if the applicant is a partnership or other unincorporated organization, or (d) the fiduciary, if the applicant is a trust or an estate.

How To Get Forms and Publications

Phone. You can order forms, instructions, and publications by phone 24 hours a day, 7 days a week. Just call 1-800-TAX-FORM (1-800-829-3676). You should receive your order or notification of its status within 10 workdays.

Personal computer. With your personal computer and modem, you can get the forms and information you need using IRS's Internet Web Site at **www.irs.gov** or File Transfer Protocol at **ftp.irs.gov.**

CD-ROM. For small businesses, return preparers, or others who may frequently need tax forms or publications, a CD-ROM containing over 2,000 tax products (including many prior year forms) can be purchased from the National Technical Information Service (NTIS).

To order **Pub. 1796,** Federal Tax Products on CD-ROM, call **1-877-CDFORMS** (1-877-233-6767) toll free or connect to **www.irs.gov/cdorders**

Privacy Act and Paperwork Reduction Act Notice. We ask for the information on this form to carry out the Internal Revenue laws of the United States. We need it to comply with section 6109 and the regulations thereunder which generally require the inclusion of an employer identification number (EIN) on certain returns, statements, or other documents filed with the Internal Revenue Service. Information on this form may be used to determine which Federal tax returns you are required to file and to provide you with related forms and publications. We disclose this form to the Social Security Administration for their use in determining compliance with applicable laws. We will be unable to issue an EIN to you unless you provide all of the requested information which applies to your entity.

You are not required to provide the information requested on a form that is subject to the Paperwork Reduction Act unless the form displays a valid OMB control number. Books or records relating to a form or its instructions must be retained as long as their contents may become material in the administration of any Internal Revenue law. Generally, tax returns/return information are confidential, as required by section 6103.

The time needed to complete and file this form will vary depending on individual circumstances. The estimated average time is:

Recordkeeping	7 min.
Learning about the law or the form	22 min.
Preparing the form	46 min.
Copying, assembling, and sending the form to the IRS . .	20 min.

If you have comments concerning the accuracy of these time estimates or suggestions for making this form simpler, we would be happy to hear from you. You can write to the Tax Forms Committee, Western Area Distribution Center, Rancho Cordova, CA 95743-0001. **Do not** send the form to this address. Instead, see **Where To Apply** on page 2.

Form **2553**
(Rev. July 1999)
Department of the Treasury
Internal Revenue Service

Election by a Small Business Corporation

(Under section 1362 of the Internal Revenue Code)

▶ See Parts II and III on back and the separate instructions.

▶ The corporation may either send or fax this form to the IRS. See page 1 of the instructions.

OMB No. 1545-0146

Notes: 1. *This election to be an S corporation can be accepted only if all the tests are met under* ***Who may elect*** *on page 1 of the instructions; all signatures in Parts I and III are originals (no photocopies); and the exact name and address of the corporation and other required form information are provided.*

2. *Do not file* ***Form 1120S,*** *U.S. Income Tax Return for an S Corporation, for any tax year before the year the election takes effect.*

3. *If the corporation was in existence before the effective date of this election, see* ***Taxes an S corporation may owe*** *on page 1 of the instructions.*

Part I Election Information

Please Type or Print	Name of corporation (see instructions)	**A Employer identification number**
	Number, street, and room or suite no. (If a P.O. box, see instructions.)	**B** Date incorporated
	City or town, state, and ZIP code	**C** State of incorporation

D Election is to be effective for tax year beginning (month, day, year) . . . . ▶ / /

E Name and title of officer or legal representative who the IRS may call for more information

F Telephone number of officer or legal representative ( )

G If the corporation changed its name or address after applying for the EIN shown in **A** above, check this box . . . . ▶ ☐

H If this election takes effect for the first tax year the corporation exists, enter month, day, and year of the **earliest** of the following: (1) date the corporation first had shareholders, (2) date the corporation first had assets, or (3) date the corporation began doing business . . . . ▶ / /

I Selected tax year: Annual return will be filed for tax year ending (month and day) ▶..

If the tax year ends on any date other than December 31, except for an automatic 52-53-week tax year ending with reference to the month of December, you **must** complete Part II on the back. If the date you enter is the ending date of an automatic 52-53-week tax year, write "52-53-week year" to the right of the date. See Temporary Regulations section 1.441-2T(e)(3).

J Name and address of each shareholder; shareholder's spouse having a community property interest in the corporation's stock; and each tenant in common, joint tenant, and tenant by the entirety. (A husband and wife (and their estates) are counted as one shareholder in determining the number of shareholders without regard to the manner in which the stock is owned.)	**K** Shareholders' Consent Statement. Under penalties of perjury, we declare that we consent to the election of the above-named corporation to be an S corporation under section 1362(a) and that we have examined this consent statement, including accompanying schedules and statements, and to the best of our knowledge and belief, it is true, correct, and complete. We understand our consent is binding and may not be withdrawn after the corporation has made a valid election. (Shareholders sign and date below.)		**L** Stock owned		**M** Social security number or employer identification number (see instructions)	**N** Share-holder's tax year ends (month and day)
	Signature	Date	Number of shares	Dates acquired		

Under penalties of perjury, I declare that I have examined this election, including accompanying schedules and statements, and to the best of my knowledge and belief, it is true, correct, and complete.

Signature of officer ▶ **Title ▶** **Date ▶**

For Paperwork Reduction Act Notice, see page 2 of the instructions. Cat. No. 18629R Form **2553** (Rev. 7-99)

Form 2553 (Rev. 7-99) Page 2

Part II **Selection of Fiscal Tax Year** (All corporations using this part must complete item O and item P, Q, or R.)

O Check the applicable box to indicate whether the corporation is:

1. ☐ A new corporation adopting the tax year entered in item I, Part I.
2. ☐ An existing corporation retaining the tax year entered in item I, Part I.
3. ☐ An existing corporation changing to the tax year entered in item I, Part I.

P Complete item P if the corporation is using the expeditious approval provisions of Rev. Proc. 87-32, 1987-2 C.B. 396, to request **(1)** a natural business year (as defined in section 4.01(1) of Rev. Proc. 87-32) or **(2)** a year that satisfies the ownership tax year test in section 4.01(2) of Rev. Proc. 87-32. Check the applicable box below to indicate the representation statement the corporation is making as required under section 4 of Rev. Proc. 87-32.

1. Natural Business Year ▶ ☐ I represent that the corporation is retaining or changing to a tax year that coincides with its natural business year as defined in section 4.01(1) of Rev. Proc. 87-32 and as verified by its satisfaction of the requirements of section 4.02(1) of Rev. Proc. 87-32. In addition, if the corporation is changing to a natural business year as defined in section 4.01(1), I further represent that such tax year results in less deferral of income to the owners than the corporation's present tax year. I also represent that the corporation is not described in section 3.01(2) of Rev. Proc. 87-32. (See instructions for additional information that must be attached.)

2. Ownership Tax Year ▶ ☐ I represent that shareholders holding more than half of the shares of the stock (as of the first day of the tax year to which the request relates) of the corporation have the same tax year or are concurrently changing to the tax year that the corporation adopts, retains, or changes to per item I, Part I. I also represent that the corporation is not described in section 3.01(2) of Rev. Proc. 87-32.

Note: *If you do not use item P and the corporation wants a fiscal tax year, complete either item Q or R below. Item Q is used to request a fiscal tax year based on a business purpose and to make a back-up section 444 election. Item R is used to make a regular section 444 election.*

Q Business Purpose- To request a fiscal tax year based on a business purpose, you must check box Q1 and pay a user fee. See instructions for details. You may also check box Q2 and/or box Q3.

1. Check here ▶ ☐ if the fiscal year entered in item I, Part I, is requested under the provisions of section 6.03 of Rev. Proc. 87-32. Attach to Form 2553 a statement showing the business purpose for the requested fiscal year. See instructions for additional information that must be attached.

2. Check here ▶ ☐ to show that the corporation intends to make a back-up section 444 election in the event the corporation's business purpose request is not approved by the IRS. (See instructions for more information.)

3. Check here ▶ ☐ to show that the corporation agrees to adopt or change to a tax year ending December 31 if necessary for the IRS to accept this election for S corporation status in the event (1) the corporation's business purpose request is not approved and the corporation makes a back-up section 444 election, but is ultimately not qualified to make a section 444 election, or (2) the corporation's business purpose request is not approved and the corporation did not make a back-up section 444 election.

R Section 444 Election- To make a section 444 election, you must check box R1 and you may also check box R2.

1. Check here ▶ ☐ to show the corporation will make, if qualified, a section 444 election to have the fiscal tax year shown in item I, Part I. To make the election, you must complete **Form 8716,** Election To Have a Tax Year Other Than a Required Tax Year, and either attach it to Form 2553 or file it separately.

2. Check here ▶ ☐ to show that the corporation agrees to adopt or change to a tax year ending December 31 if necessary for the IRS to accept this election for S corporation status in the event the corporation is ultimately not qualified to make a section 444 election.

Part III **Qualified Subchapter S Trust (QSST) Election Under Section 1361(d)(2)***

Income beneficiary's name and address	Social security number
Trust's name and address	Employer identification number

Date on which stock of the corporation was transferred to the trust (month, day, year) . . . . ▶ / /

In order for the trust named above to be a QSST and thus a qualifying shareholder of the S corporation for which this Form 2553 is filed, I hereby make the election under section 1361(d)(2). Under penalties of perjury, I certify that the trust meets the definitional requirements of section 1361(d)(3) and that all other information provided in Part III is true, correct, and complete.

Signature of income beneficiary or signature and title of legal representative or other qualified person making the election | Date

*Use Part III to make the QSST election only if stock of the corporation has been transferred to the trust on or before the date on which the corporation makes its election to be an S corporation. The QSST election must be made and filed separately if stock of the corporation is transferred to the trust after the date on which the corporation makes the S election.

Form **2553** (Rev. 7-99)

Instructions for Form 2553

Department of the Treasury
Internal Revenue Service

(Revised July 1999)

Election by a Small Business Corporation

Section references are to the Internal Revenue Code unless otherwise noted.

General Instructions

Purpose. To elect to be an S corporation, a corporation must file Form 2553. The election permits the income of the S corporation to be taxed to the shareholders of the corporation rather than to the corporation itself, except as noted below under **Taxes an S corporation may owe.**

Who may elect. A corporation may elect to be an S corporation only if it meets all of the following tests:

1. It is a domestic corporation.

2. It has no more than 75 shareholders. A husband and wife (and their estates) are treated as one shareholder for this requirement. All other persons are treated as separate shareholders.

3. Its only shareholders are individuals, estates, exempt organizations described in section 401(a) or 501(c)(3), or certain trusts described in section 1361(c)(2)(A). See the instructions for Part III regarding qualified subchapter S trusts (QSSTs).

A trustee of a trust wanting to make an election under section 1361(e)(3) to be an electing small business trust (ESBT) should see Notice 97-12, 1997-1 C.B. 385. Also see Rev. Proc. 98-23, 1998-10 I.R.B. 30, for guidance on how to convert a QSST to an ESBT. If there was an inadvertent failure to timely file an ESBT election, see the relief provisions under Rev. Proc. 98-55, 1998-46 I.R.B. 27.

4. It has no nonresident alien shareholders.

5. It has only one class of stock (disregarding differences in voting rights). Generally, a corporation is treated as having only one class of stock if all outstanding shares of the corporation's stock confer identical rights to distribution and liquidation proceeds. See Regulations section 1.1361-1(l) for details.

6. It is not one of the following ineligible corporations:

a. A bank or thrift institution that uses the reserve method of accounting for bad debts under section 585;

b. An insurance company subject to tax under the rules of subchapter L of the Code;

c. A corporation that has elected to be treated as a possessions corporation under section 936; or

d. A domestic international sales corporation (DISC) or former DISC.

7. It has a permitted tax year as required by section 1378 or makes a section 444 election to have a tax year other than a permitted tax year. Section 1378 defines a permitted tax year as a tax year ending December 31, or any other tax year for which the corporation establishes a business purpose to the satisfaction of the IRS. See Part II for details on requesting a fiscal tax year based on a business purpose or on making a section 444 election.

8. Each shareholder consents as explained in the instructions for column K.

See sections 1361, 1362, and 1378 for additional information on the above tests.

A parent S corporation can elect to treat an eligible wholly-owned subsidiary as a qualified subchapter S subsidiary (QSSS). If the election is made, the assets, liabilities, and items of income, deduction, and credit of the QSSS are treated as those of the parent. For details, see Notice 97-4, 1997-1 C.B. 351. If the QSSS election was not timely filed, the corporation may be entitled to relief under Rev. Proc. 98-55.

Taxes an S corporation may owe. An S corporation may owe income tax in the following instances:

1. If, at the end of any tax year, the corporation had accumulated earnings and profits, and its passive investment income under section 1362(d)(3) is more than 25% of its gross receipts, the corporation may owe tax on its excess net passive income.

2. A corporation with net recognized built-in gain (as defined in section 1374(d)(2)) may owe tax on its built-in gains.

3. A corporation that claimed investment credit before its first year as an S corporation will be liable for any investment credit recapture tax.

4. A corporation that used the LIFO inventory method for the year immediately preceding its first year as an S corporation may owe an additional tax due to LIFO recapture. The tax is paid in four equal installments, the first of which must be paid by the due date (not including extensions) of the corporation's income tax return for its last tax year as a C corporation.

For more details on these taxes, see the Instructions for Form 1120S.

Where to file. Send or fax this election to the Internal Revenue Service Center listed below. If the corporation files this election by fax, keep the original Form 2553 with the corporation's permanent records.

If the corporation's principal business, office, or agency is located in	Use the following Internal Revenue Service Center address or fax number
New Jersey, New York (New York City and counties of Nassau, Rockland, Suffolk, and Westchester)	Holtsville, NY 00501 (516) 654-6954
New York (all other counties), Connecticut, Maine, Massachusetts, New Hampshire, Rhode Island, Vermont	Andover, MA 05501 (978) 474-5633
Florida, Georgia, South Carolina	Atlanta, GA 39901 (770) 455-2169
Indiana, Kentucky, Michigan, Ohio, West Virginia	Cincinnati, OH 45999 (606) 292-5289
Kansas, New Mexico, Oklahoma, Texas	Austin, TX 73301 (512) 460-4046
Alaska, Arizona, California (counties of Alpine, Amador, Butte, Calaveras, Colusa, Contra Costa, Del Norte, El Dorado, Glenn, Humboldt, Lake, Lassen, Marin, Mendocino, Modoc, Napa, Nevada, Placer, Plumas, Sacramento, San Joaquin, Shasta, Sierra, Siskiyou, Solano, Sonoma, Sutter, Tehama, Trinity, Yolo, and Yuba), Colorado, Idaho, Montana, Nebraska, Nevada, North Dakota, Oregon, South Dakota, Utah, Washington, Wyoming	Ogden, UT 84201 (801) 620-7155
California (all other counties), Hawaii	Fresno, CA 93888 (559) 443-5030
Illinois, Iowa, Minnesota, Missouri, Wisconsin	Kansas City, MO 64999 (816) 823-1975
Alabama, Arkansas, Louisiana, Mississippi, North Carolina, Tennessee	Memphis, TN 37501 (901) 546-3900
Delaware, District of Columbia, Maryland, Pennsylvania, Virginia	Philadelphia, PA 19255 (215) 516-3414

When to make the election. Complete and file Form 2553 **(a)** at any time before the 16th day of the 3rd month of the tax year, if filed during the tax year the election is to take effect, or **(b)** at any time during the preceding tax year. An election made no later than 2 months and 15 days after the beginning of a tax year that is less than 2½ months long is treated as timely made for that tax year. An election made after the 15th day of the 3rd month but before the end of the tax year is effective for the next year. For example, if a calendar tax year corporation makes the election in April 2000, it is effective for the corporation's 2001 calendar tax year.

However, an election made after the due date will be accepted as timely filed if the corporation can show that the failure to file on time was due to reasonable cause. To request relief for a late election, the corporation generally must request a private letter ruling and pay a user fee in accordance with Rev. Proc. 99-1, 1999-1 I.R.B. 6 (or its successor). But if the election is filed within 12 months of its due date and the original due date for filing the corporation's initial Form 1120S has not passed, the ruling and user fee requirements do not apply. To request relief in this case, write "FILED PURSUANT TO REV. PROC. 98-55" at the top of page 1 of Form 2553, attach a statement explaining the reason for failing to file the election on time, and file Form 2553 as otherwise instructed. See Rev. Proc. 98-55 for more details.

See Regulations section 1.1362-6(b)(3)(iii) for how to obtain relief for an inadvertent invalid election if the corporation filed a timely election, but one or more shareholders did not file a timely consent.

Acceptance or nonacceptance of election. The service center will notify the corporation if its election is accepted and when it will take effect. The corporation will also be notified if its election is not accepted. The corporation should generally receive a determination on its election within 60 days after it has filed Form 2553. If box Q1 in Part II is checked on page 2, the corporation will receive a ruling letter from the IRS in Washington, DC, that either approves or denies the selected tax year. When box Q1 is checked, it will generally take an additional 90 days for the Form 2553 to be accepted.

Do not file Form 1120S for any tax year before the year the election takes effect. If the corporation is now required to file **Form 1120,** U.S. Corporation Income Tax Return, or any other applicable tax return, continue filing it until the election takes effect.

Care should be exercised to ensure that the IRS receives the election. If the corporation is not notified of acceptance or nonacceptance of its election within 3 months of date of filing (date mailed), or within 6 months if box Q1 is checked, take follow-up action by corresponding with the service center where the corporation filed the election. If the IRS

Cat. No. 49978N

questions whether Form 2553 was filed, an acceptable proof of filing is **(a)** certified or registered mail receipt (timely postmarked) from the U.S. Postal Service, or its equivalent from a designated private delivery service (see Notice 98-47, 1998-37 I.R.B. 8); **(b)** Form 2553 with accepted stamp; **(c)** Form 2553 with stamped IRS received date; or **(d)** IRS letter stating that Form 2553 has been accepted.

End of election. Once the election is made, it stays in effect until it is terminated. If the election is terminated in a tax year beginning after 1996, the corporation (or a successor corporation) can make another election on Form 2553 only with IRS consent for any tax year before the 5th tax year after the first tax year in which the termination took effect. See Regulations section 1.1362-5 for more details.

Specific Instructions

Part I

Note: *All corporations must complete Part I.*

Name and address of corporation. Enter the true corporate name as stated in the corporate charter or other legal document creating it. If the corporation's mailing address is the same as someone else's, such as a shareholder's, enter "c/o" and this person's name following the name of the corporation. Include the suite, room, or other unit number after the street address. If the Post Office does not deliver to the street address and the corporation has a P.O. box, show the box number instead of the street address. If the corporation changed its name or address after applying for its employer identification number, be sure to check the box in item G of Part I.

Item A. Employer identification number (EIN). If the corporation has applied for an EIN but has not received it, enter "applied for." If the corporation does not have an EIN, it should apply for one on **Form SS-4,** Application for Employer Identification Number. You can order Form SS-4 by calling 1-800-TAX-FORM (1-800-829-3676).

Item D. Effective date of election. Enter the beginning effective date (month, day, year) of the tax year requested for the S corporation. Generally, this will be the beginning date of the tax year for which the ending effective date is required to be shown in item I, Part I. For a new corporation (first year the corporation exists) it will generally be the date required to be shown in item H, Part I. The tax year of a new corporation starts on the date that it has shareholders, acquires assets, or begins doing business, whichever happens first. If the effective date for item D for a newly formed corporation is later than the date in item H, the corporation should file Form 1120 or Form 1120-A for the tax period between these dates.

Column K. Shareholders' Consent Statement. Each shareholder who owns (or is deemed to own) stock at the time the election is made must consent to the election. If the election is made during the corporation's tax year for which it first takes effect, any person who held stock at any time during the part of that year that occurs before the election is made, must consent to the election, even though the person may have sold or transferred his or her stock before the election is made.

An election made during the first 2½ months of the tax year is effective for the following tax year if any person who held stock in the corporation during the part of the tax year before the election was made, and who did not hold stock at the time the election was made, did not consent to the election.

Each shareholder consents by signing and dating in column K or signing and dating a separate consent statement described below.

The following special rules apply in determining who must sign the consent statement.

- If a husband and wife have a community interest in the stock or in the income from it, both must consent.
- Each tenant in common, joint tenant, and tenant by the entirety must consent.
- A minor's consent is made by the minor, legal representative of the minor, or a natural or adoptive parent of the minor if no legal representative has been appointed.
- The consent of an estate is made by the executor or administrator.
- The consent of an electing small business trust is made by the trustee.
- If the stock is owned by a trust (other than an electing small business trust), the deemed owner of the trust must consent. See section 1361(c)(2) for details regarding trusts that are permitted to be shareholders and rules for determining who is the deemed owner.

Continuation sheet or separate consent statement. If you need a continuation sheet or use a separate consent statement, attach it to Form 2553. The separate consent statement must contain the name, address, and EIN of the corporation and the shareholder information requested in columns J through N of Part I. If you want, you may combine all the shareholders' consents in one statement.

Column L. Enter the number of shares of stock each shareholder owns and the dates the stock was acquired. If the election is made during the corporation's tax year for which it first takes effect, do not list the shares of stock for those shareholders who sold or transferred all of their stock before the election was made. However, these shareholders must still consent to the election for it to be effective for the tax year.

Column M. Enter the social security number of each shareholder who is an individual. Enter the EIN of each shareholder that is an estate, a qualified trust, or an exempt organization.

Column N. Enter the month and day that each shareholder's tax year ends. If a shareholder is changing his or her tax year, enter the tax year the shareholder is changing to, and attach an explanation indicating the present tax year and the basis for the change (e.g., automatic revenue procedure or letter ruling request).

Signature. Form 2553 must be signed by the president, treasurer, assistant treasurer, chief accounting officer, or other corporate officer (such as tax officer) authorized to sign.

Part II

Complete Part II if you selected a tax year ending on any date other than December 31 (other than a 52-53-week tax year ending with reference to the month of December).

Box P1. Attach a statement showing separately for each month the amount of gross receipts for the most recent 47 months as required by section 4.03(3) of Rev. Proc. 87-32, 1987-2 C.B. 396. A corporation that does not have a 47-month period of gross receipts cannot establish a natural business year under section 4.01(1).

Box Q1. For examples of an acceptable business purpose for requesting a fiscal tax year, see Rev. Rul. 87-57, 1987-2 C.B. 117.

In addition to a statement showing the business purpose for the requested fiscal year, you must attach the other information necessary to meet the ruling request requirements of Rev. Proc. 99-1 (or its successor). Also attach a statement that shows separately the amount of gross receipts from sales or services (and inventory costs, if applicable) for each of the 36 months preceding the effective date of the election to be an S corporation. If the corporation has been in existence for fewer than 36 months, submit figures for the period of existence.

If you check box Q1, you will be charged a user fee of up to $600 (subject to change—see Rev. Proc. 99-1 or its successor). Do not pay the fee when filing Form 2553. The service center will send Form 2553 to the IRS in Washington, DC, who, in turn, will notify the corporation that the fee is due.

Box Q2. If the corporation makes a back-up section 444 election for which it is qualified, then the election will take effect in the event the business purpose request is not approved. In some cases, the tax year requested under the back-up section 444 election may be different than the tax year requested under business purpose. See **Form 8716,** Election To Have a Tax Year Other Than a Required Tax Year, for details on making a back-up section 444 election.

Boxes Q2 and R2. If the corporation is not qualified to make the section 444 election after making the item Q2 back-up section 444 election or indicating its intention to make the election in item R1, and therefore it later files a calendar year return, it should write "Section 444 Election Not Made" in the top left corner of the first calendar year Form 1120S it files.

Part III

Certain qualified subchapter S trusts (QSSTs) may make the QSST election required by section 1361(d)(2) in Part III. Part III may be used to make the QSST election only if corporate stock has been transferred to the trust on or before the date on which the corporation makes its election to be an S corporation. However, a statement can be used instead of Part III to make the election. If there was an inadvertent failure to timely file a QSST election, see the relief provisions under Rev. Proc. 98-55.

Note: *Use Part III **only** if you make the election in Part I (i.e., Form 2553 cannot be filed with only Part III completed).*

The deemed owner of the QSST must also consent to the S corporation election in column K, page 1, of Form 2553. See section 1361 (c)(2).

Paperwork Reduction Act Notice. We ask for the information on this form to carry out the Internal Revenue laws of the United States. You are required to give us the information. We need it to ensure that you are complying with these laws and to allow us to figure and collect the right amount of tax.

You are not required to provide the information requested on a form that is subject to the Paperwork Reduction Act unless the form displays a valid OMB control number. Books or records relating to a form or its instructions must be retained as long as their contents may become material in the administration of any Internal Revenue law. Generally, tax returns and return information are confidential, as required by section 6103.

The time needed to complete and file this form will depend on individual circumstances. The estimated average time is: **Recordkeeping,** 8 hr., 37 min.; **Learning about the law or the form,** 3 hr., 11 min.; and **Preparing, copying, assembling, and sending the form to the IRS,** 3 hr., 28 min.

If you have comments concerning the accuracy of these time estimates or suggestions for making this form simpler, we would be happy to hear from you. You can write to the Tax Forms Committee, Western Area Distribution Center, Rancho Cordova, CA 95743-0001. **DO NOT** send the form to this address. Instead, see **Where to file** on page 1.

Form **8869** (September 2000)
Department of the Treasury
Internal Revenue Service

Qualified Subchapter S Subsidiary Election

(Under section 1361(b)(3) of the Internal Revenue Code)

OMB No. 1545-1700

Part I Parent S Corporation Making the Election

1a Name of parent	2 Employer identification number (EIN)
b Number, street, and room or suite no. (if a P.O. box, see instructions)	3 Tax year ending (month and day)
c City or town, state, and ZIP code	4 Service center where last return was filed
5 Name of officer or legal representative whom the IRS may call for more information	6 Telephone number of officer or legal representative ( )

Part II Subsidiary Corporation for Which Election is Made (For additional subsidiaries, see instructions.)

7a Name of subsidiary	8 EIN (if any)
b Number, street, and room or suite no. (if a P.O. box, see instructions)	9 Date incorporated
c City or town, state, and ZIP code	10 State of incorporation

11 Date election is to take effect (month, day, year) (see instructions) . . . . . . ▶ / /

12 Did the subsidiary previously file a Federal income tax return? If "Yes," complete lines **13a, 13b,** and **13c** . . . ▶ ☐ Yes ☐ No

13a Service center where last return was filed	13b Tax year ending date of last return (month, day, year) ▶ / /	13c Check type of return filed: ☐ Form 1120 ☐ Form 1120S ☐ Other ▶

14 Was the subsidiary's last return filed as part of a consolidated return? If "Yes," complete lines **15a, 15b,** and **15c** . . . ▶ ☐ Yes ☐ No

15a Name of common parent	15b EIN of common parent	15c Service center where consolidated return was filed

Under penalties of perjury, I declare that I have examined this election, including accompanying schedules and statements, and to the best of my knowledge and belief, it is true, correct, and complete.

Signature of officer of parent corporation ▶	**Title ▶**	**Date ▶**

General Instructions

Section references are to the Internal Revenue Code unless otherwise noted.

Purpose of Form

A parent S corporation uses Form 8869 to elect to treat one or more of its eligible subsidiaries as a qualified subchapter S subsidiary (QSub).

The QSub election results in a deemed liquidation of the subsidiary into the parent. Following the deemed liquidation the QSub is not treated as a separate corporation; all of the subsidiary's assets, liabilities, and items of income, deduction, and credit are treated as those of the parent.

Because the liquidation is a deemed liquidation, ***do not*** *file a* ***Form 966,*** *Corporate Dissolution or Liquidation. However, a final return for the subsidiary may have to be filed if it was a separate corporation prior to the date of liquidation.*

Eligible Subsidiaries

An eligible subsidiary is a domestic corporation whose stock is owned 100% by an S corporation and is **not** one of the following ineligible corporations:

- A bank or thrift institution that uses the reserve method of accounting for bad debts under section 585;
- An insurance company subject to tax under the rules of subchapter L of the Code;
- A corporation that has elected to be treated as a possessions corporation under section 936; or
- A domestic international sales corporation (DISC) or former DISC.

When To Make the Election

The parent S corporation can make the QSub election at any time during the tax year. However, the effective date of the election depends upon when it is filed. See **Effective Date of Election** on page 2.

Where To File

File Form 8869 with the service center where the subsidiary filed its most recent return. However, if the parent S corporation forms a subsidiary, and makes a valid election effective upon formation, submit Form 8869 to the service center where the parent S corporation filed its most recent return.

Acceptance of Election

The service center will notify the corporation if the QSub election is **(a)** accepted and when it will take effect or **(b)** not accepted.

The corporation should generally receive a determination on its election within 60 days after it has filed Form 8869. However, if the corporation is not notified of acceptance or nonacceptance of its election within 3 months of the date of filing (date mailed), take follow-up action by corresponding with the service center where the corporation filed the election.

If the IRS questions whether Form 8869 was filed, an acceptable proof of filing is: **(a)** a certified or registered mail receipt (timely postmarked) from the U.S. Postal Service, or its equivalent from a designated private delivery service (see Notice

For Paperwork Reduction Act Notice, see back of form. Cat. No. 28755K Form **8869** (9-2000)

Form 8869 (9-2000) Page **2**

99-41, 1999-35 I.R.B. 325); **(b)** a Form 8869 with an accepted stamp; **(c)** a Form 8869 with a stamped IRS received date; or **(d)** an IRS letter stating that Form 8869 has been accepted.

Termination of Election

Once the QSub election is made, it remains in effect until terminated. If the election is terminated, IRS consent is generally required for another QSub election with regard to the former QSub (or its successor) for any tax year before the 5th tax year after the 1st tax year in which the termination took effect. See Regulations section 1.1361-5 for more details.

Specific Instructions

Address

Include the suite, room, or other unit number after the street address. If the Post Office does not deliver to the street address and the corporation has a P.O. box, show the box number instead of the street address.

If the subsidiary has the same address as the parent S corporation, enter "Same as parent" in Part II.

If either the parent or subsidiary corporation changes its mailing address after the election is filed, it should notify the IRS by filing **Form 8822,** Change of Address.

Part II

If the QSub election is being made for more than one subsidiary, attach a separate sheet for each subsidiary. Use the same size, format, and line numbers as in Part II of the printed form. Put the parent corporation's name and employer identification number at the top of each sheet.

If the QSub elections are being made effective on the same date for a tiered group of subsidiaries, the parent S corporation may specify the order of the deemed liquidations on an attachment. If no order is specified, the deemed liquidations will be treated as occurring first for the lowest tier subsidiary and proceeding successively upward. See Regulations section 1.1361-4(b)(2).

Note: *A QSub election for a tiered group of subsidiaries may, in certain circumstances, result in the recognition of income. A primary example is excess loss accounts (see Regulations section 1.1502-19).*

Employer Identification Number (EIN)

A QSub is not required to have or use an EIN for Federal tax purposes. If the QSub does not have an EIN, enter "N/A" on line 8.

However, if the QSub has previously filed a return, separately or as part of a consolidated return, and used an EIN, enter that EIN on line 8 and (if applicable) the EIN of its common parent on line 15b. **Note:** *Failure to enter the subsidiary's EIN may result in the service center sending a notice of delinquent filing to the QSub.*

If the QSub wants its own EIN, but does not have one, get **Form SS-4,** Application for Employer Identification Number, for details on how to obtain an EIN immediately by telephone. (**Caution:** *The QSub may use its own EIN only under limited circumstances; see Notice 99-6, 1999-3 I.R.B. 12, for guidance.)* If the QSub has previously applied for an EIN, but has not received it by the time the election is made, write "Applied for" on line 8. **Do not** apply for an EIN more than once. See **Pub. 583,** Starting a Business and Keeping Records, for details.

Effective Date of Election

The effective date of the QSub election entered on line 11 cannot be more than:

1. Two months and 15 days prior to the date of filing the election or

2. Twelve months after the date of filing the election.

If the election specifies a date falling earlier than the date in **1,** it will be treated as being effective 2 months and 15 days prior to the date of filing the election. If the election specifies a date falling later than the date in **2,** it will be treated as being effective 12 months after the date of filing the election.

If no date is specified, the election is effective on the date Form 8869 is filed.

Late Filed Election

If the QSub election is not timely filed for the desired effective date, Rev. Proc. 98-55, 1998-2 C.B. 643, provides relief if the failure to file on time is due to reasonable cause. A corporation with a valid and timely filed S corporation election may be granted additional time to file the QSub election if **all** of the following conditions are met:

- The QSub election is filed within 12 months of the required due date for the desired effective date;
- On the desired effective date, the subsidiary qualifies for QSub status in all respects other than the timeliness of the election; and
- The parent's S corporation tax return due date (excluding extensions) for its first tax year it intended to treat the subsidiary as a QSub has not passed.

If all of the above conditions are met, then file Form 8869, write "FILED PURSUANT TO REV. PROC. 98-55" at the top of page 1, and attach a statement explaining the reason for failing to file the QSub election on time. The service center will review the request for relief and notify the parent corporation if the requirements for granting an extension of time to file the QSub election are satisfied.

If the parent's S corporation election and QSub election are both late, the parent corporation may request relief if the eligibility requirements of Section 4 of Rev. Proc. 98-55 are met. See the revenue procedure for details.

If Rev. Proc. 98-55 does not apply, to obtain relief for a late QSub election the parent corporation must request a private letter ruling and pay a user fee in accordance with Rev. Proc. 2000-1, 2000-1 I.R.B. 4 (or its successor).

Signature

Form 8869 must be signed by the president, treasurer, assistant treasurer, chief accounting officer, or other corporate officer (such as tax officer) authorized to sign the parent's S corporation return.

Paperwork Reduction Act Notice. We ask for the information on this form to carry out the Internal Revenue laws of the United States. You are required to give us the information. We need it to ensure that you are complying with these laws.

You are not required to provide the information requested on a form that is subject to the Paperwork Reduction Act unless the form displays a valid OMB control number. Books or records relating to a form or its instructions must be retained as long as their contents may become material in the administration of any Internal Revenue law. Generally, tax returns and return information are confidential, as required by section 6103.

The time needed to complete and file this form will vary depending on individual circumstances. The estimated average time is:

Recordkeeping . . . . 6 hr., 3 min.
Learning about the law or the form . . . . . . 59 min.
Preparing, copying, assembling, and sending the form to the IRS . . . . 56 min.

If you have comments concerning the accuracy of these time estimates or suggestions for making this form simpler, we would be happy to hear from you. You can write to the Tax Forms Committee, Western Area Distribution Center, Rancho Cordova, CA 95743-0001. **Do not** send the form to this address. Instead, see **Where To File** on page 1.

Form **1120S**

Department of the Treasury
Internal Revenue Service

U.S. Income Tax Return for an S Corporation

▶ **Do not file this form unless the corporation has timely filed Form 2553 to elect to be an S corporation.**
▶ **See separate instructions.**

OMB No. 1545-0130

2000

For calendar year 2000, or tax year beginning , 2000, and ending , 20

A Effective date of election as an S corporation	**Use IRS label. Otherwise, print or type.**	Name	**C Employer identification number**
		Number, street, and room or suite no. (If a P.O. box, see page 11 of the instructions.)	**D** Date incorporated
B Business code no. (see pages 29-31)		City or town, state, and ZIP code	**E** Total assets (see page 11) $

F Check applicable boxes: (1) ☐ Initial return (2) ☐ Final return (3) ☐ Change in address (4) ☐ Amended return
G Enter number of shareholders in the corporation at end of the tax year . . . ▶

Caution: *Include **only** trade or business income and expenses on lines 1a through 21. See page 11 of the instructions for more information.*

Income	**1a**	Gross receipts or sales ___ **b** Less returns and allowances ___ **c** Bal ▶	1c	
	2	Cost of goods sold (Schedule A, line 8)	2	
	3	Gross profit. Subtract line 2 from line 1c	3	
	4	Net gain (loss) from Form 4797, Part II, line 18 *(attach Form 4797)*	4	
	5	Other income (loss) *(attach schedule)*	5	
	6	**Total income (loss).** Combine lines 3 through 5 ▶	6	
Deductions (see page 12 of the instructions for limitations)	**7**	Compensation of officers	7	
	8	Salaries and wages (less employment credits)	8	
	9	Repairs and maintenance	9	
	10	Bad debts	10	
	11	Rents	11	
	12	Taxes and licenses	12	
	13	Interest	13	
	14a	Depreciation *(if required, attach Form 4562)* — 14a		
	b	Depreciation claimed on Schedule A and elsewhere on return — 14b		
	c	Subtract line 14b from line 14a	14c	
	15	Depletion **(Do not deduct oil and gas depletion.)**	15	
	16	Advertising	16	
	17	Pension, profit-sharing, etc., plans	17	
	18	Employee benefit programs	18	
	19	Other deductions *(attach schedule)*	19	
	20	**Total deductions.** Add the amounts shown in the far right column for lines 7 through 19 ▶	20	
	21	Ordinary income (loss) from trade or business activities. Subtract line 20 from line 6	21	
Tax and Payments	**22**	**Tax: a** Excess net passive income tax *(attach schedule)* — 22a		
	b	Tax from Schedule D (Form 1120S) — 22b		
	c	Add lines 22a and 22b (see page 15 of the instructions for additional taxes)	22c	
	23	**Payments: a** 2000 estimated tax payments and amount applied from 1999 return — 23a		
	b	Tax deposited with Form 7004 — 23b		
	c	Credit for Federal tax paid on fuels *(attach Form 4136)* — 23c		
	d	Add lines 23a through 23c	23d	
	24	Estimated tax penalty. Check if Form 2220 is attached ▶ ☐	24	
	25	**Tax due.** If the total of lines 22c and 24 is larger than line 23d, enter amount owed. See page 4 of the instructions for depository method of payment ▶	25	
	26	**Overpayment.** If line 23d is larger than the total of lines 22c and 24, enter amount overpaid ▶	26	
	27	Enter amount of line 26 you want: **Credited to 2001 estimated tax** ▶ **Refunded** ▶	27	

Sign Here

Under penalties of perjury, I declare that I have examined this return, including accompanying schedules and statements, and to the best of my knowledge and belief, it is true, correct, and complete. Declaration of preparer (other than taxpayer) is based on all information of which preparer has any knowledge.

▶ Signature of officer | Date | ▶ Title

Paid Preparer's Use Only

Preparer's signature ▶	Date	Check if self-employed ☐	Preparer's SSN or PTIN
Firm's name (or yours if self-employed), address, and ZIP code ▶		EIN	
		Phone no. ( )	

For Paperwork Reduction Act Notice, see the separate instructions. Cat. No. 11510H Form **1120S** (2000)

Form 1120S (2000) Page **2**

Schedule A Cost of Goods Sold (see page 16 of the instructions)

1	Inventory at beginning of year	1	
2	Purchases	2	
3	Cost of labor	3	
4	Additional section 263A costs *(attach schedule)*	4	
5	Other costs *(attach schedule)*	5	
6	**Total.** Add lines 1 through 5	6	
7	Inventory at end of year	7	
8	**Cost of goods sold.** Subtract line 7 from line 6. Enter here and on page 1, line 2	8	

9a Check all methods used for valuing closing inventory:

(i) ☐ Cost as described in Regulations section 1.471-3

(ii) ☐ Lower of cost or market as described in Regulations section 1.471-4

(iii) ☐ Other (specify method used and attach explanation) ▶ ....

b Check if there was a writedown of "subnormal" goods as described in Regulations section 1.471-2(c) ▶ ☐

c Check if the LIFO inventory method was adopted this tax year for any goods *(if checked, attach Form 970)* ▶ ☐

d If the LIFO inventory method was used for this tax year, enter percentage (or amounts) of closing inventory computed under LIFO **9d**

e Do the rules of section 263A (for property produced or acquired for resale) apply to the corporation? ☐ Yes ☐ No

f Was there any change in determining quantities, cost, or valuations between opening and closing inventory? ☐ Yes ☐ No
If "Yes," attach explanation.

Schedule B Other Information

		Yes	No
1	Check method of accounting: **(a)** ☐ Cash **(b)** ☐ Accrual **(c)** ☐ Other (specify) ▶..........		
2	Refer to the list on pages 29 through 31 of the instructions and state the corporation's principal: **(a)** Business activity ▶ .... **(b)** Product or service ▶		
3	Did the corporation at the end of the tax year own, directly or indirectly, 50% or more of the voting stock of a domestic corporation? (For rules of attribution, see section 267(c).) If "Yes," attach a schedule showing: **(a)** name, address, and employer identification number and **(b)** percentage owned.		
4	Was the corporation a member of a controlled group subject to the provisions of section 1561?		
5	Check this box if the corporation has filed or is required to file **Form 8264,** Application for Registration of a Tax Shelter ▶ ☐		
6	Check this box if the corporation issued publicly offered debt instruments with original issue discount ▶ ☐ If so, the corporation may have to file **Form 8281,** Information Return for Publicly Offered Original Issue Discount Instruments.		
7	If the corporation: **(a)** filed its election to be an S corporation after 1986, **(b)** was a C corporation before it elected to be an S corporation **or** the corporation acquired an asset with a basis determined by reference to its basis (or the basis of any other property) in the hands of a C corporation, and **(c)** has net unrealized built-in gain (defined in section 1374(d)(1)) in excess of the net recognized built-in gain from prior years, enter the net unrealized built-in gain reduced by net recognized built-in gain from prior years (see page 17 of the instructions) ▶ $		
8	Check this box if the corporation had accumulated earnings and profits at the close of the tax year (see page 18 of the instructions) ▶ ☐		

Note: *If the corporation had assets or operated a business in a foreign country or U.S. possession, it may be required to attach* ***Schedule N (Form 1120),*** *Foreign Operations of U.S. Corporations, to this return. See Schedule N for details.*

Schedule K Shareholders' Shares of Income, Credits, Deductions, etc.

		(a) Pro rata share items		**(b)** Total amount
Income (Loss)	1	Ordinary income (loss) from trade or business activities (page 1, line 21)	1	
	2	Net income (loss) from rental real estate activities *(attach Form 8825)*	2	
	3a	Gross income from other rental activities — 3a		
	b	Expenses from other rental activities *(attach schedule)* — 3b		
	c	Net income (loss) from other rental activities. Subtract line 3b from line 3a	3c	
	4	Portfolio income (loss):		
	a	Interest income	4a	
	b	Ordinary dividends	4b	
	c	Royalty income	4c	
	d	Net short-term capital gain (loss) *(attach Schedule D (Form 1120S))*	4d	
	e	Net long-term capital gain (loss) *(attach Schedule D (Form 1120S))*:		
		(1) 28% rate gain (loss) ▶ .... **(2)** Total for year ▶	4e(2)	
	f	Other portfolio income (loss) *(attach schedule)*	4f	
	5	Net section 1231 gain (loss) (other than due to casualty or theft) *(attach Form 4797)*	5	
	6	Other income (loss) *(attach schedule)*	6	

Form **1120S** (2000)

Form 1120S (2000) Page **3**

Schedule K **Shareholders' Shares of Income, Credits, Deductions, etc.** *(continued)*

	(a) Pro rata share items		(b) Total amount
Deductions	**7** Charitable contributions *(attach schedule)*	7	
	8 Section 179 expense deduction *(attach Form 4562)*	8	
	9 Deductions related to portfolio income (loss) (itemize)	9	
	10 Other deductions *(attach schedule)*	10	
Investment Interest	**11a** Interest expense on investment debts	11a	
	b (1) Investment income included on lines 4a, 4b, 4c, and 4f above	11b(1)	
	(2) Investment expenses included on line 9 above	11b(2)	
Credits	**12a** Credit for alcohol used as a fuel *(attach Form 6478)*	12a	
	b Low-income housing credit:		
	(1) From partnerships to which section 42(j)(5) applies for property placed in service before 1990	12b(1)	
	(2) Other than on line 12b(1) for property placed in service before 1990	12b(2)	
	(3) From partnerships to which section 42(j)(5) applies for property placed in service after 1989	12b(3)	
	(4) Other than on line 12b(3) for property placed in service after 1989	12b(4)	
	c Qualified rehabilitation expenditures related to rental real estate activities *(attach Form 3468)*	12c	
	d Credits (other than credits shown on lines 12b and 12c) related to rental real estate activities	12d	
	e Credits related to other rental activities	12e	
	13 Other credits	13	
Adjustments and Tax Preference Items	**14a** Depreciation adjustment on property placed in service after 1986	14a	
	b Adjusted gain or loss	14b	
	c Depletion (other than oil and gas)	14c	
	d (1) Gross income from oil, gas, or geothermal properties	14d(1)	
	(2) Deductions allocable to oil, gas, or geothermal properties	14d(2)	
	e Other adjustments and tax preference items *(attach schedule)*	14e	
Foreign Taxes	**15a** Name of foreign country or U.S. possession ▶		
	b Gross income sourced at shareholder level	15b	
	c Foreign gross income sourced at corporate level:		
	(1) Passive	15c(1)	
	(2) Listed categories *(attach schedule)*	15c(2)	
	(3) General limitation	15c(3)	
	d Deductions allocated and apportioned at shareholder level:		
	(1) Interest expense	15d(1)	
	(2) Other	15d(2)	
	e Deductions allocated and apportioned at corporate level to foreign source income:		
	(1) Passive	15e(1)	
	(2) Listed categories *(attach schedule)*	15e(2)	
	(3) General limitation	15e(3)	
	f Total foreign taxes (check one): ▶ ☐ Paid ☐ Accrued	15f	
	g Reduction in taxes available for credit and gross income from all sources *(attach schedule)*	15g	
Other	**16** Section 59(e)(2) expenditures: **a** Type ▶ .... **b** Amount ▶	16b	
	17 Tax-exempt interest income	17	
	18 Other tax-exempt income	18	
	19 Nondeductible expenses	19	
	20 Total property distributions (including cash) other than dividends reported on line 22 below	20	
	21 Other items and amounts required to be reported separately to shareholders *(attach schedule)*		
	22 Total dividend distributions paid from accumulated earnings and profits	22	
	23 **Income (loss).** (Required only if Schedule M-1 must be completed.) Combine lines 1 through 6 in column (b). From the result, subtract the sum of lines 7 through 11a, 15f, and 16b	23	

Form **1120S** (2000)

Form 1120S (2000) Page **4**

Schedule L — Balance Sheets per Books

Assets	Beginning of tax year (a)	(b)	End of tax year (c)	(d)
1 Cash				
2a Trade notes and accounts receivable				
b Less allowance for bad debts				
3 Inventories				
4 U.S. Government obligations				
5 Tax-exempt securities				
6 Other current assets *(attach schedule)*				
7 Loans to shareholders				
8 Mortgage and real estate loans				
9 Other investments *(attach schedule)*				
10a Buildings and other depreciable assets				
b Less accumulated depreciation				
11a Depletable assets				
b Less accumulated depletion				
12 Land (net of any amortization)				
13a Intangible assets (amortizable only)				
b Less accumulated amortization				
14 Other assets *(attach schedule)*				
15 Total assets				
Liabilities and Shareholders' Equity				
16 Accounts payable				
17 Mortgages, notes, bonds payable in less than 1 year				
18 Other current liabilities *(attach schedule)*				
19 Loans from shareholders				
20 Mortgages, notes, bonds payable in 1 year or more				
21 Other liabilities *(attach schedule)*				
22 Capital stock				
23 Additional paid-in capital				
24 Retained earnings				
25 Adjustments to shareholders' equity *(attach schedule)*				
26 Less cost of treasury stock		( )		( )
27 Total liabilities and shareholders' equity				

Schedule M-1 — Reconciliation of Income (Loss) per Books With Income (Loss) per Return (You are not required to complete this schedule if the total assets on line 15, column (d), of Schedule L are less than $25,000.)

1 Net income (loss) per books		5 Income recorded on books this year not included on Schedule K, lines 1 through 6 (itemize):	
2 Income included on Schedule K, lines 1 through 6, not recorded on books this year (itemize): ----------		a Tax-exempt interest $ ----------	
3 Expenses recorded on books this year not included on Schedule K, lines 1 through 11a, 15f, and 16b (itemize):		6 Deductions included on Schedule K, lines 1 through 11a, 15f, and 16b, not charged against book income this year (itemize):	
a Depreciation $ ----------		a Depreciation $ ----------	
b Travel and entertainment $ ----------		7 Add lines 5 and 6	
4 Add lines 1 through 3		8 Income (loss) (Schedule K, line 23). Line 4 less line 7	

Schedule M-2 — Analysis of Accumulated Adjustments Account, Other Adjustments Account, and Shareholders' Undistributed Taxable Income Previously Taxed (see page 27 of the instructions)

	(a) Accumulated adjustments account	(b) Other adjustments account	(c) Shareholders' undistributed taxable income previously taxed
1 Balance at beginning of tax year			
2 Ordinary income from page 1, line 21			
3 Other additions			
4 Loss from page 1, line 21	( )		
5 Other reductions	( )	( )	
6 Combine lines 1 through 5			
7 Distributions other than dividend distributions			
8 Balance at end of tax year. Subtract line 7 from line 6			

Form **1120S** (2000)

SCHEDULE K-1 (Form 1120S) Department of the Treasury Internal Revenue Service	**Shareholder's Share of Income, Credits, Deductions, etc.** ▶ See separate instructions. For calendar year 2000 or tax year beginning , 2000, and ending , 20	OMB No. 1545-0130 **2000**

Shareholder's identifying number ▶	Corporation's identifying number ▶
Shareholder's name, address, and ZIP code	Corporation's name, address, and ZIP code

A Shareholder's percentage of stock ownership for tax year (see instructions for Schedule K-1) . . . . ▶ .... %

B Internal Revenue Service Center where corporation filed its return ▶ ....

C Tax shelter registration number (see instructions for Schedule K-1) . . . . ▶ ....

D Check applicable boxes: (1) ☐ Final K-1 (2) ☐ Amended K-1

		(a) Pro rata share items		(b) Amount	(c) Form 1040 filers enter the amount in column (b) on:
Income (Loss)	1	Ordinary income (loss) from trade or business activities	1		See pages 4 and 5 of the Shareholder's Instructions for Schedule K-1 (Form 1120S).
	2	Net income (loss) from rental real estate activities	2		
	3	Net income (loss) from other rental activities	3		
	4	Portfolio income (loss):			
	a	Interest	4a		Sch. B, Part I, line 1
	b	Ordinary dividends	4b		Sch. B, Part II, line 5
	c	Royalties	4c		Sch. E, Part I, line 4
	d	Net short-term capital gain (loss)	4d		Sch. D, line 5, col. (f)
	e	Net long-term capital gain (loss):			
		(1) 28% rate gain (loss)	4e(1)		Sch. D, line 12, col. (g)
		(2) Total for year	4e(2)		Sch. D, line 12, col. (f)
	f	Other portfolio income (loss) *(attach schedule)*	4f		(Enter on applicable line of your return.)
	5	Net section 1231 gain (loss) (other than due to casualty or theft)	5		See Shareholder's Instructions for Schedule K-1 (Form 1120S).
	6	Other income (loss) *(attach schedule)*	6		(Enter on applicable line of your return.)
Deductions	7	Charitable contributions *(attach schedule)*	7		Sch. A, line 15 or 16
	8	Section 179 expense deduction	8		See page 6 of the Shareholder's Instructions for Schedule K-1 (Form 1120S).
	9	Deductions related to portfolio income (loss) *(attach schedule)*	9		
	10	Other deductions *(attach schedule)*	10		
Investment Interest	11a	Interest expense on investment debts	11a		Form 4952, line 1
	b	(1) Investment income included on lines 4a, 4b, 4c, and 4f above	11b(1)		See Shareholder's Instructions for Schedule K-1 (Form 1120S).
		(2) Investment expenses included on line 9 above	11b(2)		
Credits	12a	Credit for alcohol used as fuel	12a		Form 6478, line 10
	b	Low-income housing credit:			
		(1) From section 42(j)(5) partnerships for property placed in service before 1990	12b(1)		Form 8586, line 5
		(2) Other than on line 12b(1) for property placed in service before 1990	12b(2)		
		(3) From section 42(j)(5) partnerships for property placed in service after 1989	12b(3)		
		(4) Other than on line 12b(3) for property placed in service after 1989	12b(4)		
	c	Qualified rehabilitation expenditures related to rental real estate activities	12c		See page 7 of the Shareholder's Instructions for Schedule K-1 (Form 1120S).
	d	Credits (other than credits shown on lines 12b and 12c) related to rental real estate activities	12d		
	e	Credits related to other rental activities	12e		
	13	Other credits	13		

For Paperwork Reduction Act Notice, see the Instructions for Form 1120S. Cat. No. 11520D **Schedule K-1 (Form 1120S) 2000**

Schedule K-1 (Form 1120S) (2000) Page 2

		(a) Pro rata share items		(b) Amount	(c) Form 1040 filers enter the amount in column (b) on:
Adjustments and Tax Preference Items	14a	Depreciation adjustment on property placed in service after 1986	14a		See page 7 of the Shareholder's Instructions for Schedule K-1 (Form 1120S) and Instructions for Form 6251
	b	Adjusted gain or loss	14b		
	c	Depletion (other than oil and gas)	14c		
	d	(1) Gross income from oil, gas, or geothermal properties	14d(1)		
		(2) Deductions allocable to oil, gas, or geothermal properties	14d(2)		
	e	Other adjustments and tax preference items *(attach schedule)*	14e		
Foreign Taxes	15a	Name of foreign country or U.S. possession ▶			Form 1116, Part I
	b	Gross income sourced at shareholder level	15b		
	c	Foreign gross income sourced at corporate level:			
		(1) Passive	15c(1)		
		(2) Listed categories *(attach schedule)*	15c(2)		
		(3) General limitation	15c(3)		
	d	Deductions allocated and apportioned at shareholder level:			
		(1) Interest expense	15d(1)		
		(2) Other	15d(2)		
	e	Deductions allocated and apportioned at corporate level to foreign source income:			
		(1) Passive	15e(1)		
		(2) Listed categories *(attach schedule)*	15e(2)		
		(3) General limitation	15e(3)		
	f	Total foreign taxes (check one): ▶ ☐ Paid ☐ Accrued	15f		Form 1116, Part II
	g	Reduction in taxes available for credit and gross income from all sources *(attach schedule)*	15g		See Instructions for Form 1116
Other	16	Section 59(e)(2) expenditures: **a** Type ▶			See Shareholder's Instructions for Schedule K-1 (Form 1120S).
	b	Amount	16b		
	17	Tax-exempt interest income	17		Form 1040, line 8b
	18	Other tax-exempt income	18		See pages 7 and 8 of the Shareholder's Instructions for Schedule K-1 (Form 1120S).
	19	Nondeductible expenses	19		
	20	Property distributions (including cash) other than dividend distributions reported to you on Form 1099-DIV	20		
	21	Amount of loan repayments for "Loans From Shareholders"	21		
	22	Recapture of low-income housing credit:			Form 8611, line 8
	a	From section 42(j)(5) partnerships	22a		
	b	Other than on line 22a	22b		

Supplemental Information

23 Supplemental information required to be reported separately to each shareholder *(attach additional schedules if more space is needed)*:

Schedule K-1 (Form 1120S) 2000

2000

Instructions for Form 1120S

U.S. Income Tax Return for an S Corporation

Section references are to the Internal Revenue Code unless otherwise noted.

Paperwork Reduction Act Notice. We ask for the information on this form to carry out the Internal Revenue laws of the United States. You are required to give us the information. We need it to ensure that you are complying with these laws and to allow us to figure and collect the right amount of tax.

You are not required to provide the information requested on a form that is subject to the Paperwork Reduction Act unless the form displays a valid OMB control number. Books or records relating to a form or its instructions must be retained as long as their contents may become material in the administration of any Internal Revenue law. Generally, tax returns and return information are confidential, as required by section 6103.

The time needed to complete and file this form and related schedules will vary depending on individual circumstances. The estimated average times are:

Form	Recordkeeping	Learning about the law or the form	Preparing the form	Copying, assembling, and sending the form to the IRS
1120S	63 hr., 22 min.	21 hr., 21 min.	39 hr., 9 min.	4 hr., 34 min.
Sch. D (1120S)	10 hr., 31 min.	4 hr., 38 min.	9 hr., 39 min.	1 hr., 20 min.
Sch. K-1 (1120S)	15 hr., 32 min.	10 hr., 25 min.	14 hr., 50 min.	1 hr., 4 min.

If you have comments concerning the accuracy of these time estimates or suggestions for making these forms simpler, we would be happy to hear from you. You can write to the Tax Forms Committee, Western Area Distribution Center, Rancho Cordova, CA 95743-0001. **Do not** send the tax form to this address. Instead, see **Where To File** on page 3.

Contents Page

Contents Page

Contents Page

Changes To Note

- The FSC Repeal and Extraterritorial Income Exclusion Act of 2000 allows a new extraterritorial income exclusion for transactions after September 30, 2000. The exclusion is based on a corporation's qualifying foreign trade income. For more details and to figure the amount of the exclusion, see new **Form 8873,** Extraterritorial Income Exclusion.
- The corporation may need to mail its return to a different service center this year because the IRS has changed the filing location for several areas. If an envelope was received with the tax package, please use it. Otherwise, see **Where To File** on page 3.
- Generally, if a corporation's average annual gross receipts for the 3 prior tax years are $1 million or less, it may be eligible to adopt or change to the cash method of accounting. If the corporation makes this change, it will not be required to account for inventories. Instead, the corporation may treat inventory in the same manner as costs of materials and supplies that are not incidental. For details, see **Schedule A—Cost of Goods Sold**, on page 16.
- If the corporation, at any time during the tax year, had assets or operated a business in a foreign country or U.S. possession, it may be required to attach **Schedule N (Form 1120)**, Foreign

Operations of U.S. Corporations, to this return. See Schedule N for details.

Photographs of Missing Children

The Internal Revenue Service is a proud partner with the National Center for Missing and Exploited Children. Photographs of missing children selected by the Center may appear in instructions on pages that would otherwise be blank. You can help bring these children home by looking at the photographs and calling **1-800-THE-LOST** (1-800-843-5678) if you recognize a child.

Unresolved Tax Issues

If the corporation has attempted to deal with an IRS problem unsuccessfully, it should contact the Taxpayer Advocate. The Taxpayer Advocate independently represents the corporation's interests and concerns within the IRS by protecting its rights and resolving problems that have not been fixed through normal channels.

While Taxpayer Advocates cannot change the tax law or make a technical tax decision, they can clear up problems that resulted from previous contacts and ensure that the corporation's case is given a complete and impartial review.

The corporation's assigned personal advocate will listen to its point of view and will work with the corporation to address its concerns. The corporation can expect the advocate to provide:

- A "fresh look" at a new or on-going problem.
- Timely acknowledgment.
- The name and phone number of the individual assigned to its case.
- Updates on progress.
- Timeframes for action.
- Speedy resolution.
- Courteous service.

When contacting the Taxpayer Advocate, the corporation should provide the following information:

- The corporation's name, address, and employer identification number.
- The name and telephone number of an authorized contact person and the hours he or she can be reached.
- The type of tax return and year(s) involved.
- A detailed description of the problem.
- Previous attempts to solve the problem and the office that had been contacted.
- A description of the hardship the corporation is facing (if applicable).

The corporation may contact a Taxpayer Advocate by calling a toll-free number, **1-877-777-4778.** Persons who have access to TTY/TDD equipment may call 1-800-829-4059 and ask for Taxpayer Advocate assistance. If the corporation prefers, it may call, write, or fax the Taxpayer Advocate office in its area. See **Pub. 1546,** The Taxpayer Advocate Service of the IRS, for a list of addresses and fax numbers.

How To Make a Contribution To Reduce the Public Debt

To make a contribution to reduce the public debt, send a check made payable to the "Bureau of the Public Debt" to Bureau of the Public Debt, Department G, P.O. Box 2188, Parkersburg, WV 26106-2188. Or, enclose a check with Form 1120S. Contributions to reduce the public debt are deductible, subject to the rules and limitations for charitable contributions.

How To Get Forms and Publications

Personal computer. You can access the IRS Web Site 24 hours a day, 7 days a week at **www.irs.gov** to:

- Download forms, instructions, and publications.
- See answers to frequently asked tax questions.
- Search publications on-line by topic or keyword.
- Send us comments or request help by e-mail.
- Sign up to receive local and national tax news by e-mail.

You can also reach us using file transfer protocol at **ftp.irs.gov.**

CD-ROM. Order **Pub. 1796,** Federal Tax Products on CD-ROM, and get:

- Current year forms, instructions, and publications.
- Prior year forms, instructions, and publications.
- Popular tax forms that may be filled in electronically, printed out for submission, and saved for recordkeeping.
- The Internal Revenue Bulletin.

Buy the CD-ROM on the Internet at **www.irs.gov/cdorders** from the National Technical Information Service (NTIS) for $21 (no handling fee) or call **1-877-CDFORMS** (1-877-233-6767) toll free to buy the CD-ROM for $21 (plus a $5 handling fee).

By phone and in person. You can order forms and publications 24 hours a day, 7 days a week, by calling **1-800-TAX-FORM** (1-800-829-3676). You can also get most forms and publications at your local IRS office.

General Instructions

Purpose of Form

Form 1120S is used to report the income, deductions, gains, losses, etc., of a domestic corporation that has elected to be an S corporation by filing **Form 2553,** Election by a Small Business Corporation, and whose election is in effect for the tax year.

Who Must File

A corporation must file Form 1120S if **(a)** it elected to be an S corporation by filing Form 2553, **(b)** the IRS accepted the election, and **(c)** the election remains in effect. **Do not** file Form 1120S for any tax year before the year the election takes effect.

Termination of Election

Once the election is made, it stays in effect until it is terminated. If the election is terminated in a tax year beginning after 1996, the corporation (or a successor corporation) can make another election on Form 2553 only with IRS consent for any tax year before the 5th tax year after the first tax year in which the termination took effect. See Regulations section 1.1362-5 for more details.

An election terminates **automatically** in any of the following cases:

1. The corporation is no longer a small business corporation as defined in section 1361(b). The termination of an election in this manner is effective as of the day on which the corporation no longer meets the definition of a small business corporation. If the election terminates for this reason, attach to Form 1120S for the final year of the S corporation a statement notifying the IRS of the termination and the date it occurred.

2. The corporation, for each of three consecutive tax years, **(a)** has accumulated earnings and profits and **(b)** derives more than 25% of its gross receipts from passive investment income as defined in section 1362(d)(3)(C). The election terminates on the first day of the first tax year beginning after the third consecutive tax year. The corporation must pay a tax for each year it has excess net passive income. See the instructions for line 22a for details on how to figure the tax.

3. The election is revoked. An election may be revoked only with the consent of shareholders who, at the time the revocation is made, hold more than 50% of the number of issued and outstanding shares of stock (including non-voting stock). The revocation may specify an effective revocation date that is on or after the day the revocation is filed. If no date is specified, the revocation is effective at the start of a tax year if the revocation is made on or before the 15th day of the 3rd month of that tax year. If no date is specified and the revocation is made after the 15th day of the 3rd month of the tax year, the revocation is effective at the start of the next tax year.

To revoke the election, the corporation must file a statement with the service center where it filed its election to be an S corporation. In the statement, the corporation must notify the IRS that it is revoking its election to be an S corporation. The statement must be signed by each shareholder who consents to the revocation and contain the information required by Regulations section 1.1362-6(a)(3). A revocation may be rescinded before it takes effect. See Regulations section 1.1362-6(a)(4) for details.

For rules on allocating income and deductions between an S short year and a C short year and other special rules that apply when an election is terminated, see section 1362(e) and Regulations section 1.1362-3.

If an election was terminated under **1** or **2** above, and the corporation believes the termination was inadvertent, the corporation may request permission from the IRS to continue to be treated as an S corporation. See Regulations section 1.1362-4 for the specific requirements that must be met to qualify for inadvertent termination relief.

When To File

In general, file Form 1120S by the 15th day of the 3rd month following the date the corporation's tax year ended as shown at the top of Form 1120S. For calendar year corporations, the due date is March 15, 2001. If the due date falls on a Saturday, Sunday, or legal holiday, file on the next business day. A business day is any day that is not a Saturday, Sunday, or legal holiday.

If the S election was terminated during the tax year, file Form 1120S for the S short year by the due date (including extensions) of the C short year return.

Private Delivery Services

You can use certain private delivery services designated by the IRS to meet the "timely mailing as timely filing/paying" rule for tax returns and payments. The most recent list of designated private delivery services was published by the IRS in August 1999. The list includes only the following:

- Airborne Express (Airborne): Overnight Air Express Service, Next Afternoon Service, Second Day Service.
- DHL Worldwide Express (DHL): DHL "Same Day" Service, DHL USA Overnight.
- Federal Express (FedEx): FedEx Priority Overnight, FedEx Standard Overnight, FedEx 2Day.
- United Parcel Service (UPS): UPS Next Day Air, UPS Next Day Air Saver, UPS 2nd Day Air, UPS 2nd Day Air A.M.

The private delivery service can tell you how to get written proof of the mailing date.

Extension

Use **Form 7004,** Application for Automatic Extension of Time To File Corporation Income Tax Return, to request an automatic 6-month extension of time to file Form 1120S.

Period Covered

File the 2000 return for calendar year 2000 and fiscal years beginning in 2000 and ending in 2001. If the return is for a fiscal year or a short tax year, fill in the tax year space at the top of the form.

Note: *The 2000 Form 1120S may also be used if **(a)** the corporation has a tax year of less than 12 months that begins and ends in 2001 and **(b)** the 2001 Form 1120S is not available by the time the corporation is required to file its return. However, the corporation must show its 2001 tax year on the 2000 Form 1120S and incorporate any tax law changes that are effective for tax years beginning after December 31, 2000.*

Where To File

File your return at the applicable IRS address listed below.

If the corporation's principal business, office, or agency is located in	Use the following Internal Revenue Service Center address
New York *(New York City and counties of Nassau, Rockland, Suffolk, and Westchester)*	Holtsville, NY 00501-0013
New York *(all other counties)*, Connecticut, Maine, Massachusetts, New Hampshire, Rhode Island, Vermont	Andover, MA 05501-0013
Florida, Georgia	Atlanta, GA 39901-0013
Delaware, District of Columbia, Indiana, Kentucky, Maryland, Michigan, New Jersey, North Carolina, Ohio, Pennsylvania, South Carolina, West Virginia, Wisconsin	Cincinnati, OH 45999-0013
Kansas, New Mexico, Oklahoma	Austin, TX 73301-0013
Alaska, Arizona, Arkansas, California *(counties of Alpine, Amador, Butte, Calaveras, Colusa, Contra Costa, Del Norte, El Dorado, Glenn, Humboldt, Lake, Lassen, Marin, Mendocino, Modoc, Napa, Nevada, Placer, Plumas, Sacramento, San Joaquin, Shasta, Sierra, Siskiyou, Solano, Sonoma, Sutter, Tehama, Trinity, Yolo, and Yuba)*, Colorado, Hawaii, Idaho, Iowa, Louisiana, Minnesota, Mississippi, Missouri, Montana, Nebraska, Nevada, North Dakota, Oregon, South Dakota, Texas, Utah, Washington, Wyoming	Ogden, UT 84201-0013
California*(all other counties)*	Fresno, CA 93888-0013
Illinois	Kansas City, MO 64999-0013
Alabama, Tennessee	Memphis, TN 37501-0013
Virginia	Philadelphia, PA 19255-0013

Who Must Sign

The return must be signed and dated by the president, vice president, treasurer, assistant treasurer, chief accounting officer, or any other corporate officer (such as tax officer) authorized to sign. A receiver, trustee, or assignee must sign and date any return he or she is required to file on behalf of a corporation.

If a corporate officer filled in Form 1120S, the Paid Preparer's space under "Signature of officer" should remain blank. If someone prepares Form 1120S and does not charge the corporation, that person should not sign the return. Certain others who prepare Form 1120S should not sign. For example, a regular, full-time employee of the corporation such as a clerk, secretary, etc., should not sign.

Generally, anyone paid to prepare Form 1120S must sign the return and fill in the other blanks in the Paid Preparer's Use Only area of the return.

The preparer required to sign the return **must** complete the required preparer information and:

- Sign it, by hand, in the space provided for the preparer's signature. (Signature stamps or labels are not acceptable.)
- Give a copy of Form 1120S to the taxpayer in addition to the copy filed with the IRS.

Accounting Methods

Figure ordinary income using the method of accounting regularly used in keeping the corporation's books and records. Generally, permissible methods include:

- Cash,
- Accrual, or
- Any other method authorized by the Internal Revenue Code.

In all cases, the method used must clearly reflect income. If inventories are required, the accrual method must be used for sales and purchases of merchandise. See **Schedule A—Cost of Goods Sold** on page 16.

Generally, an S corporation may not use the cash method of accounting if the corporation is a tax shelter (as defined in section 448(d)(3)). See section 448 for details.

Under the accrual method, an amount is includible in income when:

- All the events have occurred that fix the right to receive the income, which is the earliest of the date **(a)** the required performance takes place, **(b)** payment is due, or **(c)** payment is received, and

- The amount can be determined with reasonable accuracy.

See Regulations section 1.451-1(a) for details.

Generally, an accrual basis taxpayer can deduct accrued expenses in the tax year in which:

- All events that determine liability have occurred,
- The amount of the liability can be figured with reasonable accuracy, and
- Economic performance takes place with respect to the expense. There are exceptions for certain items, including recurring expenses. See section 461(h) and the related regulations for the rules for determining when economic performance takes place.

Except for certain home construction contracts and other real property small construction contracts, long-term contracts must generally be accounted for using the percentage of completion method described in section 460.

Mark-to-Market Accounting Method

Dealers in securities must use the "mark-to-market" accounting method described in section 475. Under this method, any security that is inventory to the dealer must be included in inventory at its fair market value. Any security that is not inventory and that is held at the close of the tax year is treated as sold at its fair market value on the last business day of the tax year, and any gain or loss must be taken into account in determining gross income. The gain or loss taken into account is generally treated as ordinary gain or loss. For details, including exceptions, see section 475 and the related regulations.

Dealers in commodities and traders in securities and commodities may elect to use the mark-to-market accounting method. To make the election, the corporation must file a statement describing the election, the first tax year the election is to be effective, and, in the case of an election for traders in securities or commodities, the trade or business for which the election is made. Except for new taxpayers, the statement must be filed by the due date (not including extensions) of the income tax return for the tax year immediately **preceding** the election year and attached to that return, or, if applicable, to a request for an extension of time to file that return. For more details, see Rev. Proc. 99-17, 1999-1 C.B. 503, and sections 475(e) and (f).

Change in Accounting Method

Generally, the corporation must get IRS consent to change its method of accounting used to report taxable income (for income as a whole or for any material item). To do so, it must file **Form 3115,** Application for Change in Accounting Method. For more information, see **Pub. 538,** Accounting Periods and Methods.

Accounting Periods

Generally, an S corporation may not change its accounting period to a tax year that is not a permitted year. A "permitted year" is a calendar year or any other accounting period for which the corporation can establish to the satisfaction of the IRS that there is a business purpose for the tax year.

To change an accounting period, see Regulations section 1.442-1 and **Form 1128,** Application To Adopt, Change, or Retain a Tax Year. Also see Pub. 538.

Election of a Tax Year Other Than a Required Year

Under the provisions of section 444, an S corporation may elect to have a tax year other than a permitted year, but only if the deferral period of the tax year is not longer than the shorter of 3 months or the deferral period of the tax year being changed. This election is made by filing **Form 8716,** Election To Have a Tax Year Other Than a Required Tax Year.

An S corporation may not make or continue an election under section 444 if it is a member of a tiered structure, other than a tiered structure that consists entirely of partnerships and S corporations that have the same tax year. For the S corporation to have a section 444 election in effect, it must make the payments required by section 7519 and file **Form 8752,** Required Payment or Refund Under Section 7519.

A section 444 election ends if an S corporation changes its accounting period to a calendar year or some other permitted year; it is penalized for willfully failing to comply with the requirements of section 7519; or its S election is terminated (unless it immediately becomes a personal service corporation). If the termination results in a short tax year, type or legibly print at the top of the first page of Form 1120S for the short tax year, "SECTION 444 ELECTION TERMINATED."

Rounding Off to Whole Dollars

You may round off cents to whole dollars on your return and accompanying schedules. To do so, drop amounts under 50 cents and increase amounts from 50 to 99 cents to the next higher dollar.

Recordkeeping

The corporation's records must be kept as long as they may be needed for the administration of any provision of the Internal Revenue Code. Usually, records that support an item of income, deduction, or credit on the corporation's return must be kept for 3 years from the date each shareholder's return is due or is filed, whichever is later. Keep records that verify the corporation's basis in property for as long as they are needed to figure the basis of the original or replacement property.

The corporation should also keep copies of any returns it has filed. They help in preparing future returns and in making computations when filing an amended return.

Depository Method of Tax Payment

The corporation must pay the tax due in full no later than the 15th day of the 3rd month after the end of the tax year. The two methods of depositing corporate income taxes are discussed below.

Electronic Deposit Requirement

The corporation must make electronic deposits of **all** depository taxes (such as employment tax, excise tax, and corporate income tax) using the Electronic Federal Tax Payment System (EFTPS) in 2001 if:

- The total deposits of such taxes in 1999 were more than $200,000 or
- The corporation was required to use EFTPS in 2000.

If the corporation is required to use EFTPS and fails to do so, it may be subject to a 10% penalty. If the corporation is not required to use EFTPS, it may participate voluntarily. To enroll in or get more information about EFTPS, call 1-800-555-4477 or 1-800-945-8400.

Depositing on time. For deposits made by EFTPS to be on time, the corporation must initiate the transaction at least 1 business day before the date the deposit is due.

Deposits With Form 8109

If the corporation does not use EFTPS, deposit corporation income tax payments (and estimated tax payments) with **Form 8109,** Federal Tax Deposit Coupon. If you do not have a preprinted Form 8109, use Form 8109-B to make deposits. You can get this form **only** by calling 1-800-829-1040. Be sure to have your employer identification number (EIN) ready when you call.

Do not send deposits directly to an IRS office; otherwise, the corporation may have to pay a penalty. Mail or deliver the completed Form 8109 with the payment to an authorized depositary, i.e., a commercial bank or other financial institution authorized to accept Federal tax deposits.

Make checks or money orders payable to the depositary. To help ensure proper crediting, write the corporation's EIN, the tax period to which the deposit applies, and "Form 1120S" on the check or money order. Be sure to darken the "1120" box on the coupon. Records of these deposits will be sent to the IRS.

For more information on deposits, see the instructions in the coupon booklet (Form 8109) and **Pub. 583,** Starting a Business and Keeping Records.

Estimated Tax

Generally, the corporation must make estimated tax payments for the following taxes if the total of these taxes is $500 or more: **(a)** the tax on certain capital gains, **(b)** the tax on built-in gains, **(c)** the excess net passive income tax, and **(d)** the investment credit recapture tax.

The amount of estimated tax required to be paid annually is the smaller of **(a)** the total of the above taxes shown on the return for the tax year (or if no return is filed, the total of these taxes for the year) or **(b)** the sum of *(i)* the investment credit recapture tax and the built-in gains tax (or the tax on certain capital gains) shown on the return for the tax year (or if no return is filed, the total of these taxes for the year), and *(ii)* any excess net passive income tax shown on the corporation's return for the preceding tax year. If the preceding tax year was less than 12 months, the estimated tax must be determined under **(a).**

The estimated tax is generally payable in four equal installments. However, the corporation may be able to lower the amount of one or more installments by using the annualized income installment method or adjusted seasonal installment method under section 6655(e).

For a calendar year corporation, the payments are due for 2001 by April 16, June 15, September 17, and December 17. For a fiscal year corporation, they are due by the 15th day of the 4th, 6th, 9th, and 12th months of the fiscal year.

The corporation must make the payments using the depository method described above.

Interest and Penalties

Interest

Interest is charged on taxes not paid by the due date, even if an extension of time to file is granted. Interest is also charged from the due date (including extensions) to the date of payment on the failure to file penalty, the accuracy-related penalty, and the fraud penalty. The interest charge is figured at a rate determined under section 6621.

Late Filing of Return

A corporation that does not file its tax return by the due date, including extensions, may have to pay a penalty of 5% a month, or part of a month, up to a maximum of 25%, for each month the return is not filed. The penalty is imposed on the net amount due. The minimum penalty for filing a return more than 60 days late is the smaller of the tax due or $100. The penalty will not be imposed if the corporation can show that the failure to file on time was due to reasonable cause. If the failure is due to reasonable cause, attach an explanation to the return.

Late Payment of Tax

A corporation that does not pay the tax when due generally may have to pay a penalty of ½ of 1% a month or part of a month, up to a maximum of 25%, for each month the tax is not paid. The penalty is imposed on the net amount due.

The penalty will not be imposed if the corporation can show that failure to pay on time was due to reasonable cause.

Failure To Furnish Information Timely

Section 6037(b) requires an S corporation to furnish to each shareholder a copy of the information shown on Schedule K-1 (Form 1120S) that is attached to Form 1120S. Provide Schedule K-1 to each shareholder on or before the day on which the corporation files Form 1120S.

For each failure to furnish Schedule K-1 to a shareholder when due and each failure to include on Schedule K-1 all the information required to be shown (or the inclusion of incorrect information), a $50 penalty may be imposed with regard to each Schedule K-1 for which a failure occurs. If the requirement to report correct information is intentionally disregarded, each $50 penalty is increased to $100 or, if greater, 10% of the aggregate amount of items required to be reported. See sections 6722 and 6724 for more information.

The penalty will not be imposed if the corporation can show that not furnishing information timely was due to reasonable cause and not due to willful neglect.

Trust Fund Recovery Penalty

This penalty may apply if certain excise, income, social security, and Medicare taxes that must be collected or withheld are not collected or withheld, or these taxes are not paid to the IRS. These taxes are generally reported on Forms 720, 941, 943, or 945. The trust fund recovery penalty may be imposed on all persons who are determined by the IRS to have been **responsible** for collecting, accounting for, and paying over these taxes, and who acted willfully in not doing so. The penalty is equal to the unpaid trust fund tax. See the instructions for Form 720, **Pub. 15 (Circular E),** Employer's Tax Guide, or **Pub. 51 (Circular A),** Agricultural Employer's Tax Guide, for more details, including the definition of responsible persons.

Other Forms, Returns, and Statements That May Be Required

- **Schedule N** (Form 1120), Foreign Operations of U.S. Corporations. The corporation may have to file this schedule if it had assets in or operated a business in a foreign country or a U.S. possession.
- **Forms W-2** and **W-3,** Wage and Tax Statement; and Transmittal of Wage and Tax Statements. Use these forms to report wages, tips, other compensation, and withheld income, social security and Medicare taxes for employees.
- **Form 720,** Quarterly Federal Excise Tax Return. Use Form 720 to report environmental taxes, communications and air transportation taxes, fuel taxes, luxury tax on passenger vehicles, manufacturers taxes, ship passenger tax, and certain other excise taxes.

*See **Trust Fund Recovery Penalty** above.*

- **Form 926,** Return by a U.S. Transferor of Property to a Foreign Corporation. Use this form to report certain information required under section 6038B.
- **Form 940** or **Form 940-EZ,** Employer's Annual Federal Unemployment (FUTA) Tax Return. The corporation may be liable for FUTA tax and may have to file Form 940 or 940-EZ if it paid wages of $1,500 or more in any calendar quarter during the calendar year (or the preceding calendar year) or one or more employees worked for the corporation for some part of a day in any 20 different weeks during the calendar year (or the preceding calendar year). A corporate officer who performs substantial services is considered an employee. Except as provided in section 3306(a), reasonable compensation for these services is subject to FUTA tax, no matter what the corporation calls the payments.
- **Form 941,** Employer's Quarterly Federal Tax Return. Employers must file this form quarterly to report income tax withheld on wages and employer and employee social security and Medicare taxes. A corporate officer who performs substantial services is considered an employee. Except as provided in sections 3121(a) and 3401(a), reasonable compensation for these services is subject to employer and employee social security and Medicare taxes and income tax withholding, no matter what the corporation calls the payments. Agricultural employers must file **Form 943,** Employer's Annual Tax Return for Agricultural Employees, instead of Form 941, to report income tax withheld and employer and employee social security and Medicare taxes on farmworkers.

*See **Trust Fund Recovery Penalty** on page 5.*

- **Form 945,** Annual Return of Withheld Federal Income Tax. Use this form to report income tax withheld from nonpayroll payments, including pensions, annuities, IRAs, gambling winnings, and backup withholding.

*See **Trust Fund Recovery Penalty** on page 5.*

- **Form 966,** Corporate Dissolution or Liquidation.
- **Forms 1042** and **1042-S,** Annual Withholding Tax Return for U.S. Source Income of Foreign Persons; and Foreign Person's U.S. Source Income Subject to Withholding. Use these forms to report and transmit withheld tax on payments made to nonresident alien individuals, foreign partnerships, or foreign corporations to the extent such payments constitute gross income from sources within the United States (see sections 861 through 865). For more information, see sections 1441 and 1442, and **Pub. 515,** Withholding of Tax on Nonresident Aliens and Foreign Corporations.
- **Form 1096,** Annual Summary and Transmittal of U.S. Information Returns.
- **Form 1098,** Mortgage Interest Statement. Use this form to report the receipt from any individual of $600 or more of mortgage interest (including points) in the course of the corporation's trade or business.
- **Forms 1099-A, B, C, DIV, INT, LTC, MISC, MSA, OID, PATR, R,** and **S.** You may have to file these information returns to report acquisitions or abandonments of secured property; proceeds from broker and barter exchange transactions; cancellation of debt; certain dividends and distributions; interest payments; payments of long-term care and accelerated death benefits; miscellaneous income payments; distributions from a medical savings account (MSA) or Medicare+Choice MSA; original issue discount; distributions from cooperatives to their patrons; distributions from pensions, annuities, retirement or profit-sharing plans, IRAs, insurance contracts, etc.; and proceeds from real estate transactions. Also use certain of these returns to report amounts that were received as a nominee on behalf of another person.

Use Form 1099-DIV to report actual dividends paid by the corporation. Only distributions from accumulated earnings and profits are classified as dividends. **Do not** issue Form 1099-DIV for dividends received by the corporation that are allocated to shareholders on line 4b of Schedule K-1.

For more information, see the Instructions for Forms 1099, 1098, 5498, and W-2G.

Note: *Every corporation must file Forms 1099-MISC if it makes payments of rents, commissions, or other fixed or determinable income (see section 6041) totaling $600 or more to any one person in the course of its trade or business during the calendar year.*

- **Form 3520,** Annual Return to Report Transactions With Foreign Trust and Receipt of Certain Foreign Gifts. The corporation may have to file this form if it:

1. Directly or indirectly transferred property or money to a foreign trust. For this purpose, any U.S. person who created a foreign trust is considered a transferor.

2. Is treated as the owner of any part of the assets of a foreign trust under the grantor trust rules.

3. Received a distribution from a foreign trust.

For more information, see the Instructions for Form 3520.

Note: *An owner of a foreign trust must ensure that the trust files an annual information return on **Form 3520-A,** Annual Information Return of Foreign Trust With a U.S. Owner.*

- **Form 5471,** Information Return of U.S. Persons With Respect to Certain Foreign Corporations. A corporation may have to file Form 5471 if any of the following apply:

1. It controls a foreign corporation.

2. It acquires, disposes of, or owns 5% or more in value of the outstanding stock of a foreign corporation.

3. It owns stock in a corporation that is a controlled foreign corporation for an uninterrupted period of 30 days or more during any tax year of the foreign corporation, and it owned that stock on the last day of that year.

- **Form 5713,** International Boycott Report. Every corporation that had operations in, or related to, a "boycotting" country, company, or national of a country must file Form 5713 to report those operations and figure the loss of certain tax benefits.
- **Form 8264,** Application for Registration of a Tax Shelter. Tax shelter organizers must file Form 8264 to register tax shelters with the IRS for the purpose of receiving a tax shelter registration number.
- **Form 8271,** Investor Reporting of Tax Shelter Registration Number. Corporations that have acquired an interest in a tax shelter that is required to be registered use Form 8271 to report the tax shelter's registration number. Attach Form 8271 to any return on which a deduction, credit, loss, or other tax benefit attributable to a tax shelter is taken or any income attributable to a tax shelter is reported.
- **Form 8275,** Disclosure Statement. File Form 8275 to disclose items or positions, except those contrary to a regulation, that are not otherwise adequately disclosed on a tax return. The disclosure is made to avoid the parts of the accuracy-related penalty imposed for disregard of rules or substantial understatement of tax. Form 8275 is also used for disclosures relating to preparer penalties for understatements due to unrealistic positions or disregard of rules.
- **Form 8275-R,** Regulation Disclosure Statement, is used to disclose any item on a tax return for which a position has been taken that is contrary to Treasury regulations.
- **Form 8281,** Information Return for Publicly Offered Original Issue Discount Instruments. This form is used by issuers of publicly offered debt instruments having OID to provide the information required by section 1275(c).
- **Forms 8288** and **8288-A,** U.S. Withholding Tax Return for Dispositions by Foreign Persons of U.S. Real Property Interests; and Statement of Withholding on Dispositions by Foreign Persons of U.S. Real Property Interests. Use these forms to report and transmit withheld tax on the sale of U.S. real property by a foreign person. See section 1445 and the related regulations for additional information.
- **Form 8300,** Report of Cash Payments Over $10,000 Received in a Trade or Business. File this form to report the receipt of more than $10,000 in cash or foreign currency in one transaction (or a series of related transactions).
- **Form 8594,** Asset Acquisition Statement. Both the seller and buyer of a group of assets that makes up a trade or business must use this form to report such a sale if goodwill or going concern value attaches, or could attach, to such assets an if the buyer's basis in the assets is determined only by the amount paid for the assets.
- **Form 8697,** Interest Computation Under the Look-Back Method for Completed Long-Term Contracts. Certain S corporations that are not closely held may have to file Form 8697. Form 8697 is used to figure the interest due or to be refunded under the look-back method of section 460(b)(2) on certain long-term contracts that are accounted for under either the percentage of completion-capitalized cost method or the percentage of completion method. Closely held corporations should see the instructions on page 26 for line 23, item 10, of Schedule K-1 for details on the Form 8697 information they must provide to their shareholders.
- **Form 8865,** Return of U.S. Person With Respect To Certain Foreign Partnerships. A corporation may have to file Form 8865 if it:

1. Controlled a foreign partnership (i.e., owned more than a 50% direct or indirect interest in the partnership).

2. Owned at least a 10% direct or indirect interest in a foreign partnership while U.S. persons controlled that partnership.

3. Had an acquisition, disposition, or change in proportional interest of a foreign partnership that:

a. Increased its direct interest to at least 10% or reduced its direct interest of at least 10% to less than 10%.

b. Changed its direct interest by at least a 10% interest.

4. Contributed property to a foreign partnership in exchange for a partnership interest if:

a. Immediately after the contribution, the corporation owned, directly or indirectly, at least a 10% interest in the foreign partnership; or

b. The fair market value of the property the corporation contributed to the foreign partnership in exchange for a partnership interest, when added to other contributions of property made to the foreign partnership during the preceding 12-month period, exceeds $100,000.

Also, the corporation may have to file Form 8865 to report certain dispositions by a foreign partnership of property it previously contributed to that foreign partnership if it was a partner at the time of the disposition.

For more details, including penalties for failing to file Form 8865, see Form 8865 and its separate instructions.

- **Form 8866,** Interest Computation Under the Look-Back Method for Property Depreciated Under the Income Forecast Method. Certain S corporations that are not closely held may have to file Form 8866. Form 8866 is used to figure the interest due or to be refunded under the look-back method of section 167(g)(2) for certain property placed in service after September 13, 1995, and depreciated under the income forecast method. Closely held corporations should see the instructions on page 26 for line 23, item 17, of Schedule K-1 for details on the Form 8866 information they must provide to their shareholders.

Statements

Stock ownership in foreign corporations. If the corporation owned at least 5% in value of the outstanding stock of a foreign personal holding company, and the corporation was required to include in its gross income any undistributed foreign personal holding company income, attach the statement required by section 551(c).

Transfers to a corporation controlled by the transferor. If a person receives stock of a corporation in exchange for property, and no gain or loss is recognized under section 351, the transferor and transferee must each attach to their tax returns the information required by Regulations section 1.351-3.

Assembling the Return

After page 4, Form 1120S, assemble schedules and forms in the following order:

1. Schedule N (Form 1120).

2. Form 4136, Credit for Federal Tax Paid on Fuels.

3. Additional schedules in alphabetical order.

4. Additional forms in numerical order.

To assist us in processing the return, **please complete every applicable entry space on Form 1120S and Schedule K-1.** If you attach statements, do not write "See attached" instead of completing the entry spaces on Form 1120S and Schedule K-1.

If you need more space on the forms or schedules, attach separate sheets and place them at the end of the return. Use the same size and format as on the printed forms. **But show the totals on the printed forms.** Be sure to put the corporation's name and EIN on each sheet.

Amended Return

To correct an error on a Form 1120S already filed, file an amended Form 1120S and check box F(4). If the amended return results in a change to income, or a change in the distribution of any income or other information provided any shareholder, an amended Schedule K-1 (Form 1120S) must also be filed with the amended Form 1120S and given to that shareholder. Be sure to check box D(2) on each Schedule K-1 to indicate that it is an amended Schedule K-1.

A change to the corporation's Federal return may affect its state return. This includes changes made as the result of an IRS examination of Form 1120S. For more information, contact the state tax agency for the state in which the corporation's return was filed.

Passive Activity Limitations

In general, section 469 limits the amount of losses, deductions, and credits that shareholders may claim from "passive activities." The passive activity limitations do not apply to the corporation. Instead, they apply to each shareholder's share of any income or loss and credit attributable to a passive activity. Because the treatment of each shareholder's share of corporate income or loss and credit depends upon the nature of the activity that generated it, the corporation must report income or loss and credits separately for each activity.

The instructions below (pages 7 through 11) and the instructions for Schedules K and K-1 (pages 18 through 26) explain the applicable passive activity limitation rules and specify the type of information the corporation must provide to its shareholders for each activity. If the corporation had more than one activity, it must report information for each activity on an attachment to Schedules K and K-1.

Generally, passive activities include **(a)** activities that involve the conduct of a trade or business in which the shareholder does not materially participate and **(b)** any rental activity (defined on page 8) even if the shareholder materially participates. For exceptions, see **Activities That Are Not Passive Activities** below. The level of each shareholder's participation in an activity must be determined by the shareholder.

The passive activity rules provide that losses and credits from passive activities can generally be applied only against income and tax from passive activities. Thus, passive losses and credits cannot be applied against income from salaries, wages, professional fees, or a business in which the shareholder materially participates; against "portfolio income" (defined on page 9); or against the tax related to any of these types of income.

Special rules require that net income from certain activities that would otherwise be treated as passive income must be recharacterized as nonpassive income for purposes of the passive activity limitations.

To allow each shareholder to apply the passive activity limitations at the individual level, the corporation must report income or loss and credits separately for each of the following: trade or business activities, rental real estate activities, rental activities other than rental real estate, and portfolio income.

Activities That Are Not Passive Activities

Passive activities do not include:

1. Trade or business activities in which the shareholder materially participated for the tax year.

2. Any rental real estate activity in which the shareholder materially participated if the shareholder met both of the following conditions for the tax year:

a. More than half of the personal services the shareholder performed in trades or businesses were performed in real property trades or businesses in which he or she materially participated, **and**

b. The shareholder performed more than 750 hours of services in real property trades or businesses in which he or she materially participated.

For purposes of this rule, each interest in rental real estate is a separate activity unless the shareholder elects to treat all interests in rental real estate as one activity.

If the shareholder is married filing jointly, either the shareholder or his or her spouse must separately meet both conditions **2a** and **b** above, without taking into account services performed by the other spouse.

A real property trade or business is any real property development, redevelopment, construction, reconstruction, acquisition, conversion, rental, operation, management, leasing, or brokerage trade or business. Services the shareholder performed as an employee are not treated as performed in a real property trade or business unless he or she owned more than 5% of the stock in the employer.

3. The rental of a dwelling unit used by a shareholder for personal purposes during the year for more than the **greater of** 14 days or 10% of the number of days that the residence was rented at fair rental value.

4. An activity of trading personal property for the account of owners of interests in the activity. For purposes of this rule, personal property means property that is actively traded, such as stocks, bonds, and other securities. See Temporary Regulations section 1.469-1T(e)(6).

Note: *The section 469(c)(3) exception for a working interest in oil and gas properties does not apply to an S corporation because state law generally limits the liability of shareholders.*

Trade or Business Activities

A trade or business activity is an activity (other than a rental activity or an activity treated as incidental to an activity of holding property for investment) that—

1. Involves the conduct of a trade or business (within the meaning of section 162),

2. Is conducted in anticipation of starting a trade or business, or

3. Involves research or experimental expenditures deductible under section 174 (or that would be if you chose to deduct rather than capitalize them).

If the shareholder does not materially participate in the activity, a trade or business activity of the corporation is a passive activity for the shareholder.

Each shareholder must determine if he or she materially participated in an activity. As a result, while the corporation's overall trade or business income (loss) is reported on page 1 of Form 1120S, the specific income and deductions from each separate trade or business activity must be reported on attachments to Form 1120S. Similarly, while each shareholder's allocable share of the corporation's overall trade or business income (loss) is reported on line 1 of Schedule K-1, each shareholder's allocable share of the income and deductions from each trade or business activity must be reported on attachments to each Schedule K-1. See **Passive Activity Reporting Requirements** on page 10 for more information.

Rental Activities

Generally, except as noted below, if the gross income from an activity consists of amounts paid principally for the use of real or personal tangible property held by the corporation, the activity is a rental activity.

There are several exceptions to this general rule. Under these exceptions, an activity involving the use of real or personal tangible property is **not** a rental activity if any of the following apply:

- The **average period of customer use** (defined below) for such property is 7 days or less.
- The average period of customer use for such property is 30 days or less and **significant personal services** (defined below) are provided by or on behalf of the corporation.
- **Extraordinary personal services** (defined below) are provided by or on behalf of the corporation.
- Rental of the property is treated as **incidental** to a nonrental activity of the corporation under Temporary Regulations section 1.469-1T(e)(3)(vi) and Regulations section 1.469-1(e)(3)(vi).
- The corporation customarily makes the property available during defined business hours for nonexclusive use by various customers.
- The corporation provides property for use in a nonrental activity of a partnership in its capacity as an owner of an interest in such partnership. Whether the corporation provides property used in an activity of a partnership in the corporation's capacity as an owner of an interest in the partnership is based on all the facts and circumstances.

In addition, a guaranteed payment described in section 707(c) is not income from a rental activity under any circumstances.

Average period of customer use. Figure the average period of customer use of property by dividing the total number of days in all rental periods by the number of rentals during the tax year. If the activity involves renting more than one class of property, multiply the average period of customer use of each class by the ratio of the gross rental income from that class to the activity's total gross rental income. The activity's average period of customer use equals the sum of these class-by-class average periods weighted by gross income. See Regulations section 1.469-1(e)(3)(iii).

Significant personal services. Personal services include only services performed by individuals. To determine if personal services are significant personal services, consider all of the relevant facts and circumstances. Relevant facts and circumstances include how often the services are provided, the type and amount of labor required to perform the services, and the value of the services in relation to the amount charged for the use of the property.

The following services are not considered in determining whether personal services are significant:

- Services necessary to permit the lawful use of the rental property.
- Services performed in connection with improvements or repairs to the rental property that extend the useful life of the property substantially beyond the average rental period.
- Services provided in connection with the use of any improved real property that are similar to those commonly provided in connection with long-term rentals of high-grade commercial or residential property. Examples include cleaning and maintenance of common areas, routine repairs, trash collection, elevator service, and security at entrances.

Extraordinary personal services. Services provided in connection with making rental property available for customer use are extraordinary personal services only if the services are performed by individuals and the customers' use of the rental property is incidental to their receipt of the services. For example, a patient's use of a hospital room generally is incidental to the care that the patient receives from the hospital's medical staff. Similarly, a student's use of a dormitory room in a boarding school is incidental to the personal services provided by the school's teaching staff.

Rental property incidental to a nonrental activity. An activity is not a rental activity if the rental of the property is incidental to a nonrental activity, such as the activity of holding property for investment, a trade or business activity, or the activity of dealing in property.

Rental of property is **incidental** to an **activity of holding property for investment** if both of the following apply:

- The main purpose for holding the property is to realize a gain from the appreciation of the property.
- The gross rental income from such property for the tax year is less than 2% of the smaller of the property's unadjusted basis or its fair market value.

Rental of property is **incidental** to a **trade or business activity** if all of the following apply:

- The corporation owns an interest in the trade or business at all times during the year.
- The rental property was mainly used in the trade or business activity during the tax year or during at least 2 of the 5 preceding tax years.
- The gross rental income from the property is less than 2% of the smaller of the property's unadjusted basis or its fair market value.

The sale or exchange of property that is also rented during the tax year (where the gain or loss is recognized) is treated as incidental to the activity of dealing in property if, at the time of the sale or exchange, the property was held primarily for sale to customers in the ordinary course of the corporation's trade or business.

See Temporary Regulations section 1.469-1T(e)(3) and Regulations section 1.469-1(e)(3) for more information on the definition of rental activities for purposes of the passive activity limitations.

Reporting of rental activities. In reporting the corporation's income or losses and credits from rental activities, the corporation must separately report **(a)** rental real estate activities and **(b)** rental activities other than rental real estate activities.

Shareholders who actively participate in a rental real estate activity may be able to deduct part or all of their rental real estate losses (and the deduction equivalent of rental real estate credits) against income (or tax) from nonpassive activities. Generally, the combined amount of rental real estate losses and the deduction equivalent of rental real estate credits from all sources (including rental real estate activities not held through the corporation) that may be claimed is limited to $25,000.

Report rental real estate activity income (loss) on **Form 8825,** Rental Real Estate Income and Expenses of a Partnership or an S Corporation, and on line 2 of Schedules K and K-1, rather than on page 1 of Form 1120S. Report credits related to rental real estate activities on lines 12c and 12d and low-income housing credits on line 12b of Schedules K and K-1.

Report income (loss) from rental activities other than rental real estate on line 3 and credits related to rental activities other than rental real estate on line 12e of Schedules K and K-1.

Portfolio Income

Generally, portfolio income includes all gross income, other than income derived in the ordinary course of a trade or business, that is attributable to interest; dividends; royalties; income from a real estate investment trust, a regulated investment company, a real estate mortgage investment conduit, a common trust fund, a controlled foreign corporation, a qualified electing fund, or a cooperative; income from the disposition of property that produces income of a type defined as portfolio income; and income from the disposition of property held for investment.

Solely for purposes of the preceding paragraph, gross income derived in the ordinary course of a trade or business includes **(and portfolio income, therefore, does not include)** only the following types of income:

- Interest income on loans and investments made in the ordinary course of a trade or business of lending money.
- Interest on accounts receivable arising from the performance of services or the sale of property in the ordinary course of a trade or business of performing such services or selling such property, but only if credit is customarily offered to customers of the business.
- Income from investments made in the ordinary course of a trade or business of furnishing insurance or annuity contracts or reinsuring risks underwritten by insurance companies.
- Income or gain derived in the ordinary course of an activity of trading or dealing in any property if such activity constitutes a trade or business (unless the dealer held the property for investment at any time before such income or gain is recognized).
- Royalties derived by the taxpayer in the ordinary course of a trade or business of licensing intangible property.
- Amounts included in the gross income of a patron of a cooperative by reason of any payment or allocation to the patron based on patronage occurring with respect to a trade or business of the patron.
- Other income identified by the IRS as income derived by the taxpayer in the ordinary course of a trade or business.

See Temporary Regulations section 1.469-2T(c)(3) for more information on portfolio income.

Report portfolio income on line 4 of Schedules K and K-1, rather than on page 1 of Form 1120S.

Report deductions related to portfolio income on line 9 of Schedules K and K-1.

Grouping Activities

Generally, one or more trade or business activities or rental activities may be treated as a single activity if the activities make up an appropriate economic unit for measurement of gain or loss under the passive activity rules. Whether activities make up an appropriate economic unit depends on all the relevant facts and circumstances. The factors given the greatest weight in determining whether activities make up an appropriate economic unit are—

1. Similarities and differences in types of trades or businesses,

2. The extent of common control,

3. The extent of common ownership,

4. Geographical location, and

5. Reliance between or among the activities.

Example. The corporation has a significant ownership interest in a bakery and a movie theater in Baltimore and in a bakery and a movie theater in Philadelphia. Depending on the relevant facts and circumstances, there may be more than one reasonable method for grouping the corporation's activities. For instance, the following groupings may or may not be permissible:

- A single activity,
- A movie theater activity and a bakery activity,
- A Baltimore activity and a Philadelphia activity, or
- Four separate activities.

Once the corporation chooses a grouping under these rules, it must continue using that grouping in later tax years unless a material change in the facts and circumstances makes it clearly inappropriate.

The IRS may regroup the corporation's activities if the corporation's grouping fails to reflect one or more appropriate economic units and one of the primary purposes for the grouping is to avoid the passive activity limitations.

Limitation on grouping certain activities. The following activities may not be grouped together:

1. A rental activity with a trade or business activity unless the activities being grouped together make up an appropriate economic unit, and

a. The rental activity is insubstantial relative to the trade or business activity or vice versa, or

b. Each owner of the trade or business activity has the same proportionate ownership interest in the rental activity. If so, the portion of the rental activity involving the rental of property to be used in the trade or business activity may be grouped with the trade or business activity.

2. An activity involving the rental of real property with an activity involving the rental of personal property (except for personal property provided in connection with real property), or vice versa.

3. Any activity with another activity in a different type of business and in which the corporation holds an interest as a limited partner or as a limited entrepreneur (as defined in section 464(e)(2)) if that other activity engages in holding, producing, or distributing motion picture films or videotapes; farming; leasing section 1245 property; or exploring for or exploiting oil and gas resources or geothermal deposits.

Activities conducted through partnerships. Once a partnership determines its activities under these rules, the corporation as a partner may use these rules to group those activities with:

- Each other,
- Activities conducted directly by the corporation, or
- Activities conducted through other partnerships.

The corporation may not treat as separate activities those activities grouped together by the partnership.

Recharacterization of Passive Income

Under Temporary Regulations section 1.469-2T(f) and Regulations section

1.469-2(f), net passive income from certain passive activities must be treated as nonpassive income. Net passive income is the excess of an activity's passive activity gross income over its passive activity deductions (current year deductions and prior year unallowed losses).

Income from the following six sources is subject to recharacterization. Note that any net passive income recharacterized as nonpassive income is treated as investment income for purposes of figuring investment interest expense limitations if it is from **(a)** an activity of renting substantially nondepreciable property from an equity-financed lending activity or **(b)** an activity related to an interest in a pass-through entity that licenses intangible property.

1. Significant participation passive activities. A significant participation passive activity is any trade or business activity in which the shareholder both participates for more than 100 hours during the tax year and does not materially participate. Because each shareholder must determine his or her level of participation, the corporation will not be able to identify significant participation passive activities.

2. Certain nondepreciable rental property activities. Net passive income from a rental activity is nonpassive income if less than 30% of the unadjusted basis of the property used or held for use by customers in the activity is subject to depreciation under section 167.

3. Passive equity-financed lending activities. If the corporation has net income from a passive equity-financed lending activity, the smaller of the net passive income or equity-financed interest income from the activity is nonpassive income.

Note: *The amount of income from the activities in items **1** through **3** above that any shareholder will be required to recharacterize as nonpassive income may be limited under Temporary Regulations section 1.469-2T(f)(8). Because the corporation will not have information regarding all of a shareholder's activities, it must identify all corporate activities meeting the definitions in items **2** and **3** as activities that may be subject to recharacterization.*

4. Rental activities incidental to a development activity. Net rental activity income is the excess of passive activity gross income from renting or disposing of property over passive activity deductions (current year deductions and prior year unallowed losses) that are reasonably allocable to the rented property. Net rental activity income is nonpassive income for a shareholder if all of the following apply:

- The corporation recognizes gain from the sale, exchange, or other disposition of the rental property during the tax year.
- The use of the item of property in the rental activity started less than 12 months before the date of disposition. The use of an item of rental property begins on the first day on which **(a)** the corporation owns an interest in the property, **(b)** substantially all of the property is either rented or held out for rent and ready to be rented, and **(c)** no significant value-enhancing services remain to be performed.
- The shareholder materially participated or significantly participated for any tax year in an activity that involved the performing of services to enhance the value of the property (or any other item of property, if the basis of the property disposed of is determined in whole or in part by reference to the basis of that item of property).

Because the corporation cannot determine a shareholder's level of participation, the corporation must identify net income from property described above (without regard to the shareholder's level of participation) as income that may be subject to recharacterization.

5. Activities involving property rented to a nonpassive activity. If a taxpayer rents property to a trade or business activity in which the taxpayer materially participates, the taxpayer's net rental activity income (defined in item 4) from the property is nonpassive income.

6. Acquisition of an interest in a pass-through entity that licenses intangible property. Generally, net royalty income from intangible property is nonpassive income if the taxpayer acquired an interest in the pass-through entity after it created the intangible property or performed substantial services or incurred substantial costs in developing or marketing the intangible property.

Net royalty income is the excess of passive activity gross income from licensing or transferring any right in intangible property over passive activity deductions (current year deductions and prior year unallowed losses) that are reasonably allocable to the intangible property.

See Temporary Regulations section 1.469-2T(f)(7)(iii) for exceptions to this rule.

Passive Activity Reporting Requirements

To allow shareholders to correctly apply the passive activity loss and credit limitation rules, any corporation that carries on more than one activity must:

1. Provide an attachment for each activity conducted through the corporation that identifies the type of activity conducted (trade or business, rental real estate, rental activity other than rental real estate, or investment).

2. On the attachment for each activity, provide a schedule, using the same line numbers as shown on Schedule K-1, detailing the net income (loss), credits, and all items required to be separately stated under section 1366(a)(1) from each trade or business activity, from each rental real estate activity, from each rental activity other than a rental real estate activity, and from investments.

3. Identify the net income (loss) and the shareholder's share of corporation interest expense from each activity of renting a dwelling unit that any shareholder uses for personal purposes during the year for more than the greater of 14 days or 10% of the number of days that the residence is rented at fair rental value.

4. Identify the net income (loss) and the shareholder's share of interest expense from each activity of trading personal property conducted through the corporation.

5. For any gain (loss) from the disposition of an interest in an activity or of an interest in property used in an activity (including dispositions before 1987 from which gain is being recognized after 1986):

a. Identify the activity in which the property was used at the time of disposition;

b. If the property was used in more than one activity during the 12 months preceding the disposition, identify the activities in which the property was used and the adjusted basis allocated to each activity; and

c. For gains only, if the property was substantially appreciated at the time of the disposition and the applicable holding period specified in Regulations section 1.469-2(c)(2)(iii)(A) was not satisfied, identify the amount of the nonpassive gain and indicate whether or not the gain is investment income under Regulations section 1.469-2(c)(2)(iii)(F).

6. Specify the amount of gross portfolio income, the interest expense properly allocable to portfolio income, and expenses other than interest expense that are clearly and directly allocable to portfolio income.

7. Identify the ratable portion of any section 481 adjustment (whether a net positive or a net negative adjustment) allocable to each corporate activity.

8. Identify any gross income from sources specifically excluded from passive activity gross income, including:

a. Income from intangible property, if the shareholder is an individual whose personal efforts significantly contributed to the creation of the property;

b. Income from state, local, or foreign income tax refunds; and

c. Income from a covenant not to compete, if the shareholder is an individual who contributed the covenant to the corporation.

9. Identify any deductions that are not passive activity deductions.

10. If the corporation makes a full or partial disposition of its interest in another entity, identify the gain (loss) allocable to each activity conducted through the entity, and the gain allocable to a passive activity that would have been recharacterized as nonpassive gain had the corporation disposed of its interest in property used in the activity (because the property was substantially appreciated at the time of the disposition, and the gain represented more than 10% of the shareholder's total gain from the disposition).

11. Identify the following items that may be subject to the recharacterization rules under Temporary Regulations section 1.469-2T(f) and Regulations section 1.469-2(f):

a. Net income from an activity of renting substantially nondepreciable property;

b. The smaller of equity-financed interest income or net passive income from an equity-financed lending activity;

c. Net rental activity income from property developed (by the shareholder or the corporation), rented, and sold within 12 months after the rental of the property commenced;

d. Net rental activity income from the rental of property by the corporation to a trade or business activity in which the shareholder had an interest (either directly or indirectly); and

e. Net royalty income from intangible property if the shareholder acquired the shareholder's interest in the corporation after the corporation created the intangible property or performed substantial services or incurred substantial costs in developing or marketing the intangible property.

12. Identify separately the credits from each activity conducted by or through the corporation.

Specific Instructions

General Information

Name, Address, and Employer Identification Number

Use the label that was mailed to the corporation. Cross out any errors and print the correct information on the label.

Name. If the corporation did not receive a label, print or type the corporation's true name (as set forth in the corporate charter or other legal document creating it).

Address. Include the suite, room, or other unit number after the street address. If a preaddressed label is used, include the information on the label. If the Post Office does not deliver to the street address and the corporation has a P.O. box, show the box number instead of the street address.

If the corporation changes its mailing address after filing its return, it can notify the IRS by filing **Form 8822,** Change of Address.

Employer identification number (EIN). Show the correct EIN in item C on page 1 of Form 1120S.

Item B—Business Code No.

See the **Codes for Principal Business Activity** on pages 29 through 31 of these instructions.

Item E—Total Assets

Enter the corporation's total assets at the end of the tax year, as determined by the accounting method regularly used in maintaining the corporation's books and records. If there were no assets at the end of the tax year, enter the total assets as of the beginning of the tax year. If the S election terminated during the tax year, see the instructions for Schedule L on page 27 for special rules that may apply when figuring the corporation's year-end assets.

Item F—Initial Return, Final Return, Change in Address, and Amended Return

If this is the corporation's first return, check box F(1). If the corporation has ceased to exist, check box F(2). Also check box D(1) on each Schedule K-1 to indicate that it is a final Schedule K-1. Indicate a change in address by checking box F(3). If this amends a previously filed return, check box F(4). If Schedules K-1 are also being amended, check box D(2) on each Schedule K-1.

Income

CAUTION *Report only trade or business activity income or loss on lines 1a through 6.* ***Do not report rental activity income or portfolio income or loss on these lines.*** *(See* ***Passive Activity Limitations*** *beginning on page 7 for definitions of rental income and portfolio income.) Rental activity income and portfolio income are reported on Schedules K and K-1 (rental real estate activities are also reported on Form 8825).*

Do not include any tax-exempt income on lines 1 through 5. A corporation that receives any exempt income other than interest, or holds any property or engages in an activity that produces exempt income, reports this income on line 18 of Schedules K and K-1.

Report tax-exempt interest income, including exempt-interest dividends received as a shareholder in a mutual fund or other regulated investment company, on line 17 of Schedules K and K-1.

See **Deductions** beginning on page 12 for information on how to report expenses related to tax-exempt income.

If the S corporation has had debt discharged resulting from a title 11 bankruptcy proceeding, or while insolvent, see **Form 982,** Reduction of Tax Attributes Due to Discharge of Indebtedness, and **Pub. 908,** Bankruptcy Tax Guide.

Line 1—Gross Receipts or Sales

Enter gross receipts or sales from all trade or business operations except those you report on lines 4 and 5. In general, advance payments are reported in the year of receipt. To report income from long-term contracts, see section 460. For special rules for reporting certain advance payments for goods and long-term contracts, see Regulations section 1.451-5. For permissible methods for reporting certain advance payments for services by an accrual method corporation, see Rev. Proc. 71-21,1971-2 C.B. 549.

Installment sales. Generally, the installment method cannot be used for:

- Sales of property after December 16, 1999, that would otherwise be reported under the accrual method of accounting.
- Dealer dispositions of property. A "dealer disposition" is any disposition of:

1. Personal property by a person who regularly sells or otherwise disposes of property of the same type on the installment plan or

2. Real property held for sale to customers in the ordinary course of the taxpayer's trade or business.

Exception. These restrictions on using the installment method do not apply to dispositions of property used or produced in a farming business or sales of timeshares and residential lots for which the corporation elects to pay interest under section 453(l)(3).

Enter on line 1a the gross profit on collections from installment sales for any of the following:

- Dealer dispositions of property before March 1, 1986.
- Dispositions of property used or produced in the trade or business of farming.
- Certain dispositions of timeshares and residential lots reported under the installment method.

Attach a schedule showing the following information for the current and the 3 preceding years:

- Gross sales.
- Cost of goods sold.
- Gross profits.
- Percentage of gross profits to gross sales.
- Amount collected.
- Gross profit on the amount collected.

Line 2—Cost of Goods Sold

See the instructions for Schedule A on page 16.

Line 4—Net Gain (Loss) From Form 4797

Include only ordinary gains or losses from the sale, exchange, or involuntary conversion of assets used in a trade or business activity. Ordinary gains or losses from the sale, exchange, or involuntary conversions of assets used in rental activities are reported separately on Schedule K as part of the net income (loss) from the rental activity in which the property was used.

A corporation that is a partner in a partnership must include on **Form 4797,** Sales of Business Property, its share of ordinary gains (losses) from sales, exchanges, or involuntary or compulsory conversions (other than casualties or thefts) of the partnership's trade or business assets.

Do not include any recapture of the section 179 expense deduction. See the instructions on page 25 for Schedule K-1, line 23, item 3, and the Instructions for Form 4797 for more information.

Line 5—Other Income (Loss)

Enter on line 5 trade or business income (loss) that is not included on lines 1a through 4. Examples of such income include:

- Interest income derived in the ordinary course of the corporation's trade or business, such as interest charged on receivable balances.
- Recoveries of bad debts deducted in earlier years under the specific charge-off method.
- Taxable income from insurance proceeds.
- The amount of credit figured on **Form 6478,** Credit for Alcohol Used as Fuel.
- All section 481(a) income adjustments resulting from changes in accounting methods (show the computation on an attached schedule).

The corporation must also include in other income the:

- Recapture amount under section 280F if the business use of listed property drops to 50% or less. To figure the recapture amount, the corporation must complete Part IV of Form 4797.
- Recapture of any deduction previously taken under section 179A. The S corporation may have to recapture part or all of the benefit of any allowable deduction for qualified clean-fuel vehicle property (or clean-fuel vehicle refueling property), if the property ceases to qualify for the deduction within 3 years after the date it was placed in service. See **Pub. 535,** Business Expenses, for details on how to figure the recapture.

If "other income" consists of only one item, identify it by showing the account caption in parentheses on line 5. A separate schedule need not be attached to the return in this case.

Do not net any expense item (such as interest) with a similar income item. Report all trade or business expenses on lines 7 through 19.

Do not include items requiring separate computations by shareholders that must be reported on Schedules K and K-1. See the instructions for Schedules K and K-1 beginning on page 18.

Ordinary Income (Loss) From a Partnership, Estate, or Trust

Enter the ordinary trade or business income (loss) from a partnership shown on Schedule K-1 (Form 1065), from an estate or trust shown on Schedule K-1 (Form 1041), or from a foreign partnership, estate, or trust. Show the partnership's, estate's, or trust's name, address, and EIN (if any) on a separate statement attached to this return. If the amount entered is from more than one source, identify the amount from each source

Do not include portfolio income or rental activity income (loss) from a partnership, estate, or trust on this line. Instead, report these amounts on the applicable lines of Schedules K and K-1, or on line 20a of Form 8825 if the amount is from a rental real estate activity.

Ordinary income or loss from a partnership that is a publicly traded partnership is not reported on this line. Instead, report the amount separately on line 6 of Schedules K and K-1.

Treat shares of other items separately reported on Schedule K-1 issued by the other entity as if the items were realized or incurred by the S corporation.

If there is a loss from a partnership, the amount of the loss that may be claimed is subject to the at-risk and basis limitations as appropriate.

If the tax year of the S corporation does not coincide with the tax year of the partnership, estate, or trust, include the ordinary income (loss) from the other entity in the tax year in which the other entity's tax year ends.

Deductions

*Report **only** trade or business activity expenses on lines 7 through 19.*

Do not report rental activity expenses or deductions allocable to portfolio income on these lines. Rental activity expenses are separately reported on Form 8825 or line 3 of Schedules K and K-1. Deductions allocable to portfolio income are separately reported on line 9 of Schedules K and K-1. See **Passive Activity Limitations** beginning on page 7 for more information on rental activities and portfolio income.

Do not report any nondeductible amounts (such as expenses connected with the production of tax-exempt income) on lines 7 through 19. Instead, report nondeductible expenses on line 19 of Schedules K and K-1. If an expense is connected with both taxable income and nontaxable income, allocate a reasonable part of the expense to each kind of income.

Limitations on Deductions

Section 263A uniform capitalization rules. The uniform capitalization rules of section 263A require corporations to capitalize or include in inventory costs certain costs incurred in connection with:

- The production of real and tangible personal property held in inventory or held for sale in the ordinary course of business.
- Real property or personal property (tangible and intangible) acquired for resale.
- The production of real property and tangible personal property by a corporation for use in its trade or business or in an activity engaged in for profit.

The costs required to be capitalized under section 263A are not deductible until the property to which the costs relate is sold, used, or otherwise disposed of by the corporation.

Exceptions. Section 263A **does not** apply to:

- Personal property acquired for resale if the taxpayer's average annual gross receipts for the 3 prior tax years are $10 million or less.
- Timber.
- Most property produced under a long-term contract.
- Certain property produced in a farming business. See page 13.

The corporation must report the following costs separately to the shareholders for purposes of determinations under section 59(e):

- Research and experimental costs under section 174.
- Intangible drilling costs for oil, gas, and geothermal property.
- Mining exploration and development costs.
- Inventory of a cash method corporation that does not account for inventories. See **Pub. 553,** Highlights of 2000 Tax Changes.

Tangible personal property produced by a corporation includes a film, sound recording, video tape, book, or similar property.

Corporations subject to the rules are required to capitalize not only direct costs but an allocable portion of most indirect costs (including taxes) that benefit the assets produced or acquired for resale or are incurred by reason of the performance of production or resale activities.

For inventory, some of the ***indirect costs*** that must be capitalized are:

- Administration expenses.
- Taxes.

- Depreciation.
- Insurance.
- Compensation paid to officers attributable to services.
- Rework labor.
- Contributions to pension, stock bonus, and certain profit-sharing, annuity, or deferred compensation plans.

Regulations section 1.263A-1(e)(3) specifies other indirect costs that relate to production or resale activities that must be capitalized and those that may be currently deducted.

Interest expense paid or incurred during the production period of designated property must be capitalized and is governed by special rules. For more details, see Regulations sections 1.263A-8 through 1.263A-15.

For more details on the uniform capitalization rules, see Regulations sections 1.263A-1 through 1.263A-3.

Special rules for certain corporations engaged in farming. For S corporations not required to use the accrual method of accounting, the rules of section 263A **do not** apply to expenses of raising any—

- Animal or
- Plant that has a preproductive period of 2 years or less.

Shareholders of S corporations not required to use the accrual method of accounting may elect to currently deduct the preproductive period expenses of certain plants that have a preproductive period of more than 2 years. Because each shareholder makes the election to deduct these expenses, the corporation should not capitalize them. Instead, the corporation should report the expenses separately on line 21 of Schedule K and each shareholder's pro rata share on line 23 of Schedule K-1.

See sections 263A(d) and (e) and Regulations section 1.263A-4 for definitions and other details.

Transactions between related taxpayers. Generally, an accrual basis S corporation may deduct business expenses and interest owed to a related party (including any shareholder) **only** in the tax year of the corporation that includes the day on which the payment is includible in the income of the related party. See section 267 for details.

Section 291 limitations. If the S corporation was a C corporation for any of the 3 immediately preceding years, the corporation may be required to adjust deductions allowed to the corporation for depletion of iron ore and coal, and the amortizable basis of pollution control facilities. See section 291 to determine the amount of the adjustment.

Business start-up expenses. Business start-up expenses must be capitalized. An election may be made to amortize them over a period of not less than 60 months. See section 195 and Regulations section 1.195-1.

Reducing certain expenses for which credits are allowable. For each credit listed below, the corporation must reduce the otherwise allowable deductions for expenses used to figure the credit by the amount of the current year credit.

1. The work opportunity credit,

2. The welfare-to-work credit,

3. The credit for increasing research activities,

4. The enhanced oil recovery credit,

5. The disabled access credit,

6. The empowerment zone employment credit,

7. The Indian employment credit,

8. The credit for employer social security and Medicare taxes paid on certain employee tips, and

9. The orphan drug credit.

If the corporation has any of these credits, be sure to figure each current year credit before figuring the deductions for expenses on which the credit is based.

Line 7—Compensation of Officers and Line 8—Salaries and Wages

Enter on line 7 the total compensation of all officers paid or incurred in the trade or business activities of the corporation. Enter on line 8 the amount of salaries and wages paid or incurred to employees (other than officers) during the tax year in the trade or business activities of the corporation.

Reduce the amounts on lines 7 and 8 by any applicable employment credits from **Form 5884,** Work Opportunity Credit, **Form 8861,** Welfare-to-Work Credit, **Form 8844,** Empowerment Zone Employment Credit, and **Form 8845,** Indian Employment Credit. See the instructions for these forms for more information.

Include fringe benefit expenditures made on behalf of officers and employees owning more than 2% of the corporation's stock. Also report these fringe benefits as wages in box 1 of Form W-2. Do not include amounts paid or incurred for fringe benefits of officers and employees owning 2% or less of the corporation's stock. These amounts are reported on line 18, page 1, of Form 1120S. See the instructions for that line for information on the types of expenditures that are treated as fringe benefits and for the stock ownership rules.

Report amounts paid for health insurance coverage for a more than 2% shareholder (including that shareholder's spouse and dependents) as an information item in box 14 of that shareholder's Form W-2. For 2000, a more than 2% shareholder may be allowed to deduct up to 60% of such amounts on Form 1040, line 28.

Do not include amounts reported elsewhere on the return, such as salaries and wages included in cost of goods sold, elective contributions to a section 401(k) cash or deferred arrangement, or amounts contributed under a salary reduction SEP agreement or a SIMPLE IRA plan.

If a shareholder or a member of the family of one or more shareholders of the corporation renders services or furnishes capital to the corporation for which reasonable compensation is not paid, the IRS may make adjustments in the items taken into account by such individuals and the value of such services or capital. See section 1366(e).

Line 9—Repairs and Maintenance

Enter the costs of incidental repairs and maintenance, such as labor and supplies, that do not add to the value of the property or appreciably prolong its life, but only to the extent that such costs relate to a trade or business activity and are not claimed elsewhere on the return. New buildings, machinery, or permanent improvements that increase the value of the property are not deductible. They are chargeable to capital accounts and may be depreciated or amortized.

Line 10—Bad Debts

Enter the total debts that became worthless in whole or in part during the year, but only to the extent such debts relate to a trade or business activity. Report deductible nonbusiness bad debts as a short-term capital loss on Schedule D (Form 1120S).

Cash method taxpayers cannot take a bad debt deduction unless the amount was previously included in income.

Line 11—Rents

If the corporation rented or leased a vehicle, enter the total annual rent or lease expense paid or incurred in the trade or business activities of the corporation. Also complete Part V of **Form 4562,** Depreciation and Amortization. If the corporation leased a vehicle for a term of 30 days or more, the deduction for vehicle lease expense may have to be reduced by an amount called the **inclusion amount.** The corporation may have an inclusion amount if—

The lease term began:	And the vehicle's fair market value on the first day of the lease exceeded:
After 12/31/98	$15,500
After 12/31/96 but before 1/1/99	$15,800
After 12/31/94 but before 1/1/97	$15,500
After 12/31/93 but before 1/1/95	$14,600

If the lease term began before January 1, 1994, see **Pub. 463,** Travel, Entertainment, Gift, and Car Expenses, to find out if the corporation has an inclusion amount.

See Pub. 463 for instructions on figuring the inclusion amount.

Line 12—Taxes and Licenses

Enter taxes and licenses paid or incurred in the trade or business activities of the corporation, if not reflected in cost of goods sold. Federal import duties and Federal excise and stamp taxes are deductible only if paid or incurred in carrying on the trade or business of the corporation.

Do not deduct the following taxes on line 12:

- State and local sales taxes paid or incurred in connection with the acquisition or disposition of business property. These taxes must be added to the cost of the property, or in the case of a disposition, subtracted from the amount realized.
- Taxes assessed against local benefits that increase the value of the property assessed, such as for paving, etc.
- Federal income taxes, or taxes reported elsewhere on the return.
- Section 901 foreign taxes. Report these taxes separately on line 15f, Schedule K.
- Taxes allocable to a rental activity. Taxes allocable to a rental real estate activity are reported on Form 8825. Taxes allocable to a rental activity other than a rental real estate activity are reported on line 3b of Schedule K.
- Taxes allocable to portfolio income. Report these taxes separately on line 9 of Schedules K and K-1.
- Taxes paid or incurred for the production or collection of income, or for the management, conservation, or maintenance of property held to produce income. Report these taxes separately on line 10 of Schedules K and K-1.

See section 263A(a) for information on capitalization of allocable costs (including taxes) for any property.

Line 13—Interest

Include on line 13 only interest incurred in the trade or business activities of the corporation that is not claimed elsewhere on the return. **Do not** include interest expense:

- On debt used to purchase rental property or debt used in a rental activity. Interest allocable to a rental real estate activity is reported on Form 8825 and is used in arriving at net income (loss) from rental real estate activities on line 2 of Schedules K and K-1. Interest allocable to a rental activity other than a rental real estate activity is included on line 3b of Schedule K and is used in arriving at net income (loss) from a rental activity (other than a rental real estate activity). This net amount is reported on line 3c of Schedule K and line 3 of Schedule K-1.
- Clearly and directly allocable to portfolio or investment income. This interest expense is reported separately on line 11a of Schedule K.
- On debt proceeds allocated to distributions made to shareholders during the tax year. Instead, report such interest on line 10 of Schedules K and K-1. To determine the amount to allocate to distributions to shareholders, see Notice 89-35, 1989-1 C.B. 675.
- On debt required to be allocated to the production of designated property. Interest allocable to designated property produced by an S corporation for its own use or for sale must instead be capitalized. The corporation must also capitalize any interest on debt allocable to an asset used to produce designated property. A shareholder may have to capitalize interest that the shareholder incurs during the tax year for the production expenditures of the S corporation. Similarly, interest incurred by an S corporation may have to be capitalized by a shareholder for the shareholder's own production expenditures. The information required by the shareholder to properly capitalize interest for this purpose must be provided by the corporation on an attachment for line 23 of Schedule K-1. See section 263A(f) and Regulations sections 1.263A-8 through 1.263A-15 for additional information, including the definition of "designated property."

Special rules apply to:

- Allocating interest expense among activities so that the limitations on passive activity losses, investment interest, and personal interest can be properly figured. Generally, interest expense is allocated in the same manner as debt is allocated. Debt is allocated by tracing disbursements of the debt proceeds to specific expenditures. Temporary Regulations section 1.163-8T gives rules for tracing debt proceeds to expenditures.
- Prepaid interest, which generally can only be deducted over the period to which the prepayment applies. See section 461(g) for details.
- Limit the interest deduction if the corporation is a policyholder or beneficiary with respect to a life insurance, endowment, or annuity contract issued after June 8, 1997. For details, see section 264(f). Attach a statement showing the computation of the deduction.

Line 14—Depreciation

Enter on line 14a only the depreciation claimed on assets used in a trade or business activity. See the Instructions for Form 4562 or **Pub. 946,** How To Depreciate Property, to figure the amount of depreciation to enter on this line. Complete and attach Form 4562 only if the corporation placed property in service during the tax year or claims depreciation on any car or other listed property.

Do not include any section 179 expense deduction on this line. This amount is not deductible by the corporation. Instead, it is passed through to the shareholders on line 8 of Schedule K-1.

Line 15—Depletion

If the corporation claims a deduction for timber depletion, complete and attach **Form T,** Forest Activities Schedules.

Do not deduct depletion for oil and gas properties. Each shareholder figures depletion on these properties under section 613A(c)(11). See the instructions on page 25 for Schedule K-1, line 23, item 2, for information on oil and gas depletion that must be supplied to the shareholders by the corporation.

Line 17—Pension, Profit-Sharing, etc., Plans

Enter the deductible contributions not claimed elsewhere on the return made by the corporation for its employees under a qualified pension, profit-sharing, annuity, or simplified employee pension (SEP) or SIMPLE plan, and under any other deferred compensation plan.

If the corporation contributes to an individual retirement arrangement (IRA) for employees, include the contribution in salaries and wages on page 1, line 8, or Schedule A, line 3, and not on line 17.

Employers who maintain a pension, profit-sharing, or other funded deferred compensation plan, whether or not qualified under the Internal Revenue Code and whether or not a deduction is claimed for the current tax year, generally must file the applicable form listed below.

- **Form 5500,** Annual Return/Report of Employee Benefit Plan. File this form for a plan that is not a one-participant plan (see below).
- **Form 5500-EZ,** Annual Return of One-Participant (Owners and Their Spouses) Retirement Plan. File this form for a plan that only covers the owner (or the owner and his or her spouse) but only if the owner (or the owner and his or her spouse) owns the entire business.

There are penalties for failure to file these forms on time and for overstating the pension plan deduction.

Line 18—Employee Benefit Programs

Enter amounts for fringe benefits paid or incurred on behalf of employees owning 2% or less of the corporation's stock. These fringe benefits include **(a)** employer contributions to certain accident and health plans, **(b)** the cost of up to $50,000 of group-term life insurance on an employee's life, and **(c)** meals and lodging furnished for the employer's convenience.

Do not deduct amounts that are an incidental part of a pension, profit-sharing, etc., plan included on line 17 or amounts reported elsewhere on the return.

Report amounts paid on behalf of more than 2% shareholders on line 7 or 8, whichever applies. A shareholder is considered to own more than 2% of the corporation's stock if that person owns on any day during the tax year more than 2% of the outstanding stock of the corporation or stock possessing more than 2% of the combined voting power of all stock of the corporation. See section 318 for attribution rules.

Line 19—Other Deductions

Attach your own schedule listing by type and amount all allowable deductions related to a trade or business activity **only** for which there is no separate line on page 1 of Form 1120S. Enter the total on this line. Examples of other deductions include:

- Amortization (except as noted below)—see the Instructions for Form 4562 for more information. Complete and attach Form 4562 if the corporation is claiming amortization of costs that began during the tax year.
- Insurance premiums.
- Legal and professional fees.
- Supplies used and consumed in the business.
- Utilities.

Also, see **Special Rules** below for limits on certain other deductions.

Do not deduct on line 19:

- Items that must be reported separately on Schedules K and K-1.
- Qualified expenditures to which an election under section 59(e) may apply. See the instructions on page 25 for lines 16a and 16b of Schedule K-1 for details on treatment of these items.
- Amortization of reforestation expenditures under section 194. The corporation can elect to amortize up to $10,000 of qualified reforestation expenditures paid or incurred during the tax year. However, the amortization is not deducted by the corporation but the amortizable basis is instead separately allocated among the shareholders. See the instructions on page 26 for Schedule K-1, line 23, item 18 and Pub. 535 for more details.
- Fines or penalties paid to a government for violating any law. Report these expenses on Schedule K, line 19.
- Expenses allocable to tax-exempt income. Report these expenses on Schedule K, line 19.
- Net operating losses as provided by section 172 or the special deductions in sections 241 through 249 (except the election to amortize organizational expenditures under section 248). These deductions cannot be claimed by an S corporation.

Note: *Shareholders are allowed, subject to limitations, to deduct from gross income the corporation's net operating loss. See section 1366.*

Special Rules

Travel, meals, and entertainment. Subject to limitations and restrictions discussed below, a corporation can deduct ordinary and necessary travel, meals, and entertainment expenses paid or incurred in its trade or business. Special rules apply to deductions for gifts, skybox rentals, luxury water travel, convention expenses, and entertainment tickets. See section 274 and Pub. 463 for more details.

Travel. The corporation cannot deduct travel expenses of any individual accompanying a corporate officer or employee, including a spouse or dependent of the officer or employee, unless:

- That individual is an employee of the corporation, and
- His or her travel is for a bona fide business purpose and would otherwise be deductible by that individual.

Meals and entertainment. Generally, the corporation can deduct only 50% of the amount otherwise allowable for meals and entertainment expenses. In addition (subject to exceptions under section 274(k)(2)):

- Meals must not be lavish or extravagant,
- A bona fide business discussion must occur during, immediately before, or immediately after the meal; and
- An employee of the corporation must be present at the meal.

See section 274(n)(3) for a special rule that applies to expenses for meals consumed by individuals subject to the hours of service limits of the Department of Transportation.

Membership dues. The corporation may deduct amounts paid or incurred for membership dues in civic or public service organizations, professional organizations (such as bar and medical associations), business leagues, trade associations, chambers of commerce, boards of trade, and real estate boards. However, no deduction is allowed if a principal purpose of the organization is to entertain, or provide entertainment facilities for, members or their guests. In addition, corporations may not deduct membership dues in any club organized for business, pleasure, recreation, or other social purpose. This includes country clubs, golf and athletic clubs, airline and hotel clubs, and clubs operated to provide meals under conditions favorable to business discussion.

Entertainment facilities. The corporation cannot deduct an expense paid or incurred for a facility (such as a yacht or hunting lodge) used for an activity usually considered entertainment, amusement, or recreation.

Note: *The corporation may be able to deduct otherwise nondeductible meals, travel, and entertainment expenses if the amounts are treated as compensation and reported on Form W-2 for an employee or on Form 1099-MISC for an independent contractor.*

Lobbying expenses. Do not deduct amounts paid or incurred to participate or intervene in any political campaign on behalf of a candidate for public office, or to influence the general public regarding legislative matters, elections, or referendums. In addition, corporations generally cannot deduct expenses paid or incurred to influence Federal or state legislation, or to influence the actions or positions of certain Federal executive branch officials. However, certain in-house lobbying expenditures that do not exceed $2,000 are deductible. See section 162(e) for more details.

Clean-fuel vehicles and certain refueling property. A deduction is allowed for part of the cost of qualified clean-fuel vehicle property and qualified clean-fuel vehicle refueling property placed in service during the tax year. For more details, see section 179A and Pub. 535.

Certain corporations engaged in farming. Section 464(f) limits the deduction for certain expenditures of S corporations engaged in farming that use the cash method of accounting, and whose prepaid farm supplies are more than 50% of other deductible farming expenses. Prepaid farm supplies include expenses for feed, seed, fertilizer, and similar farm supplies not used or consumed during the year. They also include the cost of poultry that would be allowable as a deduction in a later tax year if the corporation were to **(a)** capitalize the cost of poultry bought for use in its farm business and deduct it ratably over the lesser of 12 months or the useful life of the poultry and **(b)** deduct the cost of poultry bought for resale in the year it sells or otherwise disposes of it. If the limit applies, the corporation can deduct prepaid farm supplies that do not exceed 50% of its other deductible farm expenses in the year of payment. The excess is deductible only in the year the corporation uses or consumes the supplies (other than poultry, which is deductible as explained above). For exceptions and more details on these rules, see **Pub. 225,** Farmer's Tax Guide.

Line 21—Ordinary Income (Loss)

Enter this income or loss on line 1 of Schedule K. Line 21 income is not used in figuring the tax on line 22a or 22b. See the instructions for line 22a for figuring taxable income for purposes of line 22a or 22b tax.

Tax and Payments

Line 22a—Excess Net Passive Income Tax

If the corporation has always been an S corporation, the excess net passive income tax does not apply.

If the corporation has accumulated earnings and profits (E&P) at the close of its tax year, has passive investment income for the tax year that is in excess of 25% of gross receipts, **and** has taxable income at year-end, the corporation must pay a tax on the excess net passive income. Complete lines 1 through 3 and line 9 of the worksheet below to make this determination. If line 2 is greater than line 3 and the corporation has taxable income (see instructions for line 9 of worksheet), it must pay the tax. Complete a separate schedule using the format of lines 1 through 11 of the worksheet below to figure the tax. Enter the tax on line 22a, page 1, Form 1120S, and attach the computation schedule to Form 1120S.

Reduce each item of passive income passed through to shareholders by its portion of tax on line 22a. See section 1366(f)(3).

Line 22b—Tax From Schedule D (Form 1120S)

If the corporation elected to be an S corporation before 1987 (or elected to be an S corporation during 1987 or 1988 and qualifies for transitional relief from the built-in gains tax), see instructions for Part III of Schedule D (Form 1120S) to determine if the corporation is liable for the capital gains tax.

If the corporation made its election to be an S corporation after 1986, see the instructions for Part IV of Schedule D to determine if the corporation is liable for the built-in gains tax.

Note: *For purposes of line 21 of Part III and line 27 of Part IV of Schedule D, taxable income is defined in section 1375(b)(1)(B) and is generally figured in the same manner as taxable income for line 9 of the line 22a worksheet below.*

Line 22c

Include in the total for line 22c the following:

Investment credit recapture tax. The corporation is liable for investment credit recapture attributable to credits allowed for tax years for which the corporation was not an S corporation. Figure the corporation's investment credit recapture tax by completing **Form 4255,** Recapture of Investment Credit.

To the left of the line 22c total, enter the amount of recapture tax and "Tax From Form 4255." Attach Form 4255 to Form 1120S.

LIFO recapture tax. The corporation may be liable for the additional tax due to LIFO recapture under Regulations section 1.1363-2 if—

- The corporation used the LIFO inventory pricing method for its last tax year as a C corporation, or
- A C corporation transferred LIFO inventory to the corporation in a nonrecognition transaction in which those assets were transferred basis property.

The additional tax due to LIFO recapture is figured for the corporation's last tax year as a C corporation or for the tax year of the transfer, whichever applies. See the Instructions for Forms 1120 and 1120-A to figure the tax. The tax is paid in four equal installments. The C corporation must pay the first installment by the due date (not including extensions) of Form 1120 for the corporation's last tax year as a C corporation or for the tax year of the transfer, whichever applies. The S corporation must pay each of the remaining installments by the due date (not including extensions) of Form 1120S for the 3 succeeding tax years. Include this year's installment in the total amount to be entered on line 22c. To the left of the total on line 22c, enter the installment amount and "LIFO tax."

Interest due under the look-back method for completed long-term contracts. If the corporation owes interest, attach **Form 8697,** Interest Computation Under the Look-Back Method for Completed Long-Term Contracts. To the left of the total on line 22c, enter the amount owed and "From Form 8697."

Interest due under the look-back method for property depreciated under the income forecast method. If the corporation owes interest, attach **Form 8866,** Interest Computation Under the Look-Back Method for Property Depreciated Under the Income Forecast Method. To the left of the total on line 22c, enter the amount owed and "From Form 8866."

Line 23d

If the S corporation is a beneficiary of a trust and the trust makes a section 643(g) election to credit its estimated tax payments to its beneficiaries, include the corporation's share of the payment (reported to the corporation on Schedule K-1 (Form 1041)) in the total amount entered on line 23d. Also, to the left of line 23d, enter "T" and the amount of the payment.

Line 24—Estimated Tax Penalty

A corporation that fails to make estimated tax payments when due may be subject to an underpayment penalty for the period of underpayment. Use **Form 2220,** Underpayment of Estimated Tax by Corporations, to see if the corporation owes a penalty and to figure the amount of the penalty. If you attach Form 2220 to Form 1120S, be sure to check the box on line 24 and enter the amount of any penalty on this line.

Schedule A—Cost of Goods Sold

Generally, inventories are required at the beginning and end of each tax year if the production, purchase, or sale of merchandise is an income-producing factor. See Regulations section 1.471-1.

However, if a corporation's average annual gross receipts for the 3 prior tax years are $1 million or less and the corporation is an eligible taxpayer that adopts or changes to the cash method of accounting, it will not be required to account for inventories. If the corporation is not required to account for inventories and does not want to do so, it must treat

Worksheet for Line 22a

1. Enter gross receipts for the tax year (see section 1362(d)(3)(B) for gross receipts from the sale of capital assets)* . . . . ______
2. Enter passive investment income as defined in section 1362(d)(3)(C)* . . . ______
3. Enter 25% of line 1 (If line 2 is less than line 3, stop here. You are not liable for this tax.) . . . . ______
4. Excess passive investment income- Subtract line 3 from line 2 . . . ______
5. Enter deductions directly connected with the production of income on line 2 (see section 1375(b)(2))* . . . ______
6. Net passive income- Subtract line 5 from line 2 . . . . ______
7. Divide amount on line 4 by amount on line 2 . . . . ______%
8. Excess net passive income- Multiply line 6 by line 7. . . . . ______
9. Enter taxable income (see instructions for taxable income below) . . . ______
10. Enter smaller of line 8 or line 9 . ______
11. Excess net passive income tax- Enter 35% of line 10. Enter here and on line 22a, page 1, Form 1120S . . . ______

*Income and deductions on lines 1, 2, and 5 are from total operations for the tax year. This includes applicable income and expenses from page 1, Form 1120S, as well as those reported separately on Schedule K. See section 1375(b)(4) for an exception regarding lines 2 and 5.

Line 9 of Worksheet—Taxable income

Line 9 taxable income is defined in Regulations section 1.1374-1(d). Figure this income by completing lines 1 through 28 of **Form 1120,** U.S. Corporation Income Tax Return. Include the Form 1120 computation with the worksheet computation you attach to Form 1120S. You do not have to attach the schedules, etc., called for on Form 1120. However, you may want to complete certain Form 1120 schedules, such as Schedule D (Form 1120) if you have capital gains or losses.

inventory in the same manner as costs of materials and supplies that are not incidental. Under this rule, inventory costs for raw materials purchased for use in producing finished goods and merchandise purchased for resale are deductible in the year the finished goods or merchandise are sold (or, if later, the year the corporation paid for the raw materials or merchandise). Enter amounts paid for all raw materials and merchandise during the tax year on line 2. The amount the corporation can deduct for the tax year is figured on line 8.

If the corporation wants to change to the cash method of accounting, it must file Form 3115. It may also have to make an adjustment to prevent amounts of income or expense from being duplicated or omitted. This is called a section 481(a) adjustment, which is taken into account over a period not to exceed 4 years. For example, if the corporation accrued sales in 1999 for which it received payment in 2000, it must report those sales in both years as a result of changing its accounting method and will make a section 481(a) adjustment to prevent duplication of income. See Rev. Proc. 99-49, 1999-52 I.R.B. 725, to figure the amount of this adjustment for the tax year. Include any positive section 481(a) adjustment on page 1, line 5. If the section 481(a) adjustment is negative, report it page 1, line 19.

For eligibility requirements and further details on changing to the cash method of accounting, see Pub. 553.

Section 263A Uniform Capitalization Rules

The uniform capitalization rules of section 263A are discussed under **Limitations on Deductions** on page 12. See those instructions before completing Schedule A.

Line 1–Inventory at Beginning of Year

If the corporation is changing its method of accounting from accrual to cash for the current tax year and it does not want to account for inventories, it must refigure last year's closing inventory using the cash method and enter the result on line 1. If there is a difference between the closing inventory and the refigured amount, attach an explanation and take it into account when figuring the corporation's section 481(a) adjustment (explained above).

Line 4—Additional Section 263A Costs

An entry is required on this line only for corporations that have elected a simplified method of accounting.

For corporations that have elected the simplified production method, additional section 263A costs are generally those costs, other than interest, that were not capitalized under the corporation's method of accounting immediately prior to the effective date of section 263A that are required to be capitalized under section 263A. For new corporations, additional section 263A costs are the costs, other than interest, that must be capitalized under section 263A, but which the corporation would not have been required to capitalize if it had existed before the effective date of section 263A. For more details, see Regulations section 1.263A-2(b).

For corporations that have elected the simplified resale method, additional section 263A costs are generally those costs incurred with respect to the following categories:

- Off-site storage or warehousing;
- Purchasing;
- Handling, such as processing, assembly, repackaging, and transporting; and
- General and administrative costs (mixed service costs).

For more details, see Regulations section 1.263A-3(d).

Enter on line 4 the balance of section 263A costs paid or incurred during the tax year not includable on lines 2, 3, and 5.

Line 5—Other Costs

Enter on line 5 any other inventoriable costs paid or incurred during the tax year not entered on lines 2 through 4.

Line 7—Inventory at End of Year

See Regulations sections 1.263A-1 through 1.263A-3 for details on figuring the costs to be included in ending inventory.

If the corporation is using the cash method of accounting and it does not want to account for inventories, enter on line 7 the portion of its raw materials and merchandise purchased for resale that are included on line 6 and were not sold during the year.

Lines 9a Through 9e—Inventory Valuation Methods

Inventories can be valued at:

- Cost.
- Cost or market value (whichever is lower).
- Any other method approved by the IRS that conforms to the requirements of the applicable regulations.

However, the corporation is required to use cost if it is using the cash method of accounting.

Producers whose average annual gross receipts are $1 million or less that use the cash method of accounting and choose not to account for inventories may currently deduct expenditures for direct labor and all indirect costs that would otherwise be included in inventory costs.

The average cost (rolling average) method of valuing inventories generally does not conform to the requirements of the regulations. See Rev. Rul. 71-234, 1971-1 C.B. 148.

Corporations that use erroneous valuation methods must change to a method permitted for Federal income tax purposes. To make this change, use Form 3115.

On line 9a, check the method(s) used for valuing inventories. Under "lower of cost or market," *market* (for normal goods) means the current bid price prevailing on the inventory valuation date for the particular merchandise in the volume usually purchased by the taxpayer. For a manufacturer, market applies to the basic elements of cost—raw materials, labor, and burden. If section 263A applies to the taxpayer, the basic elements of cost must reflect the current bid price of all direct costs and all indirect costs properly allocable to goods on hand at the inventory date.

Inventory may be valued below cost when the merchandise is unsalable at normal prices or unusable in the normal way because the goods are "subnormal" due to damage, imperfections, shop wear, etc., within the meaning of Regulations section 1.471-2(c). These goods may be valued at a current bona fide selling price minus direct cost of disposition (but not less than scrap value) if such a price can be established.

If this is the first year the last-in, first-out (LIFO) inventory method was either adopted or extended to inventory goods not previously valued under the LIFO method provided in section 472, attach **Form 970,** Application To Use LIFO Inventory Method, or a statement with the information required by Form 970. Also check the LIFO box on line 9c. On line 9d, enter the amount or the percent of total closing inventories covered under section 472. Estimates are acceptable.

If the corporation has changed or extended its inventory method to LIFO and has had to "write up" its opening inventory to cost in the year of election, report the effect of this write-up as income (line 5, page 1) proportionately over a 3-year period that begins with the tax year of the election (section 472(d)).

See Pub. 538 for more information on inventory valuation methods.

Schedule B—Other Information

Be sure to answer the questions and provide other information in items 1 through 8.

Line 7

Complete line 7 if the corporation **(a)** filed its election to be an S corporation after 1986; **(b)** was a C corporation before it elected to be an S corporation **or** the corporation acquired an asset with a basis determined by reference to its basis (or the basis of any other property) in the hands of a C corporation; and **(c)** has net unrealized built-in gain (defined below) in excess of the net recognized built-in gain from prior years.

The corporation is liable for section 1374 tax if **(a), (b),** and **(c)** above apply and it has a net recognized built-in gain (section 1374(d)(2)) for its tax year.

Section 633(d)(8) of the Tax Reform Act of 1986 provides transitional relief from the built-in gains tax for certain corporations that elected to be S corporations in 1987 or 1988. See the instructions for Part IV of Schedule D (Form 1120S) for more information.

The corporation's net unrealized built-in gain is the amount, if any, by which the fair market value of the assets of the corporation at the beginning of its first S corporation year (or as of the date the assets were acquired, for any asset with a basis determined by reference to its basis (or the basis of any other property) in the hands of a C corporation) exceeds the aggregate adjusted basis of such assets at that time.

Enter on line 7 the corporation's net unrealized built-in gain reduced by the net recognized built-in gain for prior years. See sections 1374(c)(2) and (d)(1).

Line 8

Check the box on line 8 if the corporation was a C corporation in a prior year and has accumulated earnings and profits (E&P) at the close of its 2000 tax year. For details on figuring accumulated E&P, see section 312. If the corporation has accumulated E&P, it may be liable for tax imposed on excess net passive income. See the instructions for line 22a, page 1, of Form 1120S for details on this tax.

General Instructions for Schedules K and K-1—Shareholders' Shares of Income, Credits, Deductions, etc.

Purpose of Schedules

The corporation is liable for taxes on lines 22a, 22b, and 22c, page 1, Form 1120S. Shareholders are liable for income tax on their shares of the corporation's income (reduced by any taxes paid by the corporation on income) and must include their share of the income on their tax return whether or not it is distributed to them. Unlike most partnership income, S corporation income is **not** self-employment income and is not subject to self-employment tax.

Schedule K is a summary schedule of all the shareholders' shares of the corporation's income, deductions, credits, etc. Schedule K-1 shows each shareholder's separate share. Attach a copy of each shareholder's Schedule K-1 to the Form 1120S filed with the IRS. Keep a copy as a part of the corporation's records, and give each shareholder a separate copy.

The total pro rata share items (column (b)) of all Schedules K-1 should equal the amount reported on the same line of Schedule K. Lines 1 through 20 of Schedule K correspond to lines 1 through 20 of Schedule K-1. Other lines do not correspond, but instructions explain the differences.

Be sure to give each shareholder a copy of the Shareholder's Instructions for Schedule K-1 (Form 1120S). These instructions are available separately from Schedule K-1 at most IRS offices.

Note: *Instructions that apply only to line items reported on Schedule K-1 may be prepared and given to each shareholder instead of the instructions printed by the IRS.*

Substitute Forms

The corporation **does not** need IRS approval to use a substitute Schedule K-1 if it is an exact copy of the IRS schedule, **or** if it contains only those lines the taxpayer is required to use, and the lines have the same numbers and titles and are in the same order as on the IRS Schedule K-1. In either case, the substitute schedule must include the OMB number and either **(a)** the Shareholder's Instructions for Schedule K-1 (Form 1120S) or **(b)** instructions that apply to the items reported on Schedule K-1 (Form 1120S).

The corporation must request IRS approval to use other substitute Schedules K-1. To request approval, write to Internal Revenue Service, Attention: Substitute Forms Program Coordinator, W:CAR:MP:FP:S:CS, 1111 Constitution Avenue, NW, Washington, DC 20224.

The corporation may be subject to a penalty if it files a substitute Schedule K-1 that does not conform to the specifications of Rev. Proc. 2000-19, 2000-12 I.R.B. 785.

Shareholder's Pro Rata Share Items

General Rule

Items of income, loss, deductions, etc., are allocated to a shareholder on a daily basis, according to the number of shares of stock held by the shareholder on each day during the tax year of the corporation. See the instructions for item A.

A shareholder who disposes of stock is treated as the shareholder for the day of disposition. A shareholder who dies is treated as the shareholder for the day of the shareholder's death.

Special Rules

Termination of shareholder's interest. If a shareholder terminates his or her interest in a corporation during the tax year, the corporation, with the consent of all affected shareholders (including the one whose interest is terminated), may elect to allocate income and expenses, etc., as if the corporation's tax year consisted of 2 separate tax years, the first of which ends on the date of the shareholder's termination.

To make the election, the corporation must attach a statement to a timely filed original or amended Form 1120S for the tax year for which the election is made. In the statement, the corporation must state that it is electing under section 1377(a)(2) and Regulations section 1.1377-1(b) to treat the tax year as if it consisted of 2 separate tax years. The statement must also explain how the shareholder's entire interest was terminated (e.g., sale or gift), and state that the corporation and each affected shareholder consent to the corporation making the election. A corporate officer must sign the statement under penalties of perjury on behalf of the corporation. A single statement may be filed for all terminating elections made for the tax year. If the election is made, write "Section 1377(a)(2) Election Made" at the top of each affected shareholder's Schedule K-1.

For more details on the election, see Regulations section 1.1377-1(b).

Qualifying dispositions. If a qualifying disposition takes place during the tax year, the corporation may make an irrevocable election to allocate income and expenses, etc., as if the corporation's tax year consisted of 2 tax years, the first of which ends on the close of the day on which the qualifying disposition occurs. A qualifying disposition is:

1. A disposition by a shareholder of at least 20% of the corporation's outstanding stock in one or more transactions in any 30-day period during the tax year,

2. A redemption treated as an exchange under section 302(a) or 303(a) of at least 20% of the corporation's outstanding stock in one or more transactions in any 30-day period during the tax year, or

3. An issuance of stock that equals at least 25% of the previously outstanding stock to one or more new shareholders in any 30-day period during the tax year.

To make the election, the corporation must attach a statement to a timely filed original or amended Form 1120S for the tax year for which the election is made. In the statement, the corporation must state that it is electing under Regulations section 1.1368-1(g)(2)(i) to treat the tax year as if it consisted of separate tax years. The statement must also give the facts relating to the qualifying disposition (e.g., sale, gift, stock issuance, or redemption), and state that each shareholder who held stock in the corporation during the tax year consents to the election. A corporate officer must sign the statement under penalties of perjury on behalf of the corporation. A single election statement may be filed for all elections made under this special rule for the tax year.

For more details on the election, see Regulations section 1.1368-1(g)(2).

Specific Instructions (Schedule K Only)

Enter the total amount for each applicable line item on Schedule K.

Specific Instructions (Schedule K-1 Only)

General Information

On each Schedule K-1, complete the date spaces at the top; enter the names, addresses, and identifying numbers of the shareholder and corporation; complete items A through D; and enter the shareholder's pro rata share of each item. **Schedule K-1 must be prepared and given to each shareholder on or before the day on which Form 1120S is filed.**

Note: *Space has been provided on line 23 (Supplemental Information) of Schedule K-1 for the corporation to provide additional information to shareholders. This space, if sufficient, should be used in place of any attached schedules required for any lines on Schedule K-1, or other amounts not shown on lines 1 through 22 of Schedule K-1. Please be sure to identify the applicable line number next to the information entered below line 23.*

Special Reporting Requirements for Corporations With Multiple Activities

If items of income, loss, deduction, or credit from more than one activity (determined for purposes of the passive activity loss and credit limitations) are reported on lines 1, 2, or 3 of Schedule K-1, the corporation must provide information for each activity to its shareholders. See **Passive Activity Reporting Requirements** on page 10 for details on the reporting requirements.

Special Reporting Requirements for At-Risk Activities

If the corporation is involved in one or more at-risk activities for which a loss is reported on Schedule K-1, the corporation must report information separately for each at-risk activity. See section 465(c) for a definition of at-risk activities.

For each at-risk activity, the following information must be provided on an attachment to Schedule K-1:

1. A statement that the information is a breakdown of at-risk activity loss amounts.

2. The identity of the at-risk activity; the loss amount for the activity; other income and deductions; and other information that relates to the activity.

Specific Items

Item A

If there was no change in shareholders or in the relative interest in stock the shareholders owned during the tax year, enter the percentage of total stock owned by each shareholder during the tax year. For example, if shareholders X and Y each owned 50% for the entire tax year, enter 50% in item A for each shareholder. Each shareholder's pro rata share items (lines 1 through 20 of Schedule K-1) are figured by multiplying the Schedule K amount on the corresponding line of Schedule K by the percentage in item A.

If there was a change in shareholders or in the relative interest in stock the shareholders owned during the tax year, each shareholder's percentage of ownership is weighted for the number of days in the tax year that stock was owned. For example, A and B each held 50% for half the tax year and A, B, and C held 40%, 40%, and 20%, respectively, for the remaining half of the tax year. The percentage of ownership for the year for A, B, and C is figured as follows and is then entered in item A.

	a	b	c (a × b)	
	% of total stock owned	% of tax year held	% of ownership for the year	
A	50 40	50 50	25 +20	45
B	50 40	50 50	25 +20	45
C	20	50	10	10
Total				100%

If there was a change in shareholders or in the relative interest in stock the shareholders owned during the tax year, each shareholder's pro rata share items generally are figured by multiplying the Schedule K amount by the percentage in item A. However, if a shareholder terminated his or her entire interest in the corporation during the year or a qualifying disposition took place, the corporation may elect to allocate income and expenses, etc., as if the tax year consisted of 2 tax years, the first of which ends on the day of the termination or qualifying disposition. See **Special Rules** on page 18 for more details. Each shareholder's pro rata share items are figured separately for each period on a daily basis, based on the percentage of stock held by the shareholder on each day.

Item B

Enter the Internal Revenue Service Center address where the Form 1120S, to which a copy of this K-1 was attached, was or will be filed.

Item C

If the corporation is a registration-required tax shelter or has invested in a registration-required tax shelter, it must enter its tax shelter registration number in item C. Also, a corporation that has invested in a registration-required shelter must furnish a copy of its Form 8271 to its shareholders. See Form 8271 for more details.

Specific Instructions (Schedules K and K-1, Except as Noted)

Income (Loss)

Reminder: Before entering income items on Schedule K or K-1, be sure to reduce the items of income for the following:

1. Built-in gains tax (Schedule D, Part IV, line 33). Each recognized built-in gain item (within the meaning of section 1374(d)(3)) is reduced by its proportionate share of the built-in gains tax.

2. Capital gains tax (Schedule D, Part III, line 25). The section 1231 gain included on line 5 or 6 of Schedule K is reduced by this tax.

3. Excess net passive income tax (line 22a, page 1, Form 1120S). Each item of passive investment income (within the meaning of section 1362(d)(3)(C)) is reduced by its proportionate share of the net passive income tax.

Line 1—Ordinary Income (Loss) From Trade or Business Activities

Enter the amount from line 21, page 1. Enter the income or loss without reference to **(a)** shareholders' basis in the stock of the corporation and in any indebtedness of the corporation to the shareholders (section 1366(d)), **(b)** shareholders' at-risk limitations, and **(c)** shareholders' passive activity limitations. These limitations, if applicable, are determined at the shareholder level.

If the corporation is involved in more than one trade or business activity, see **Passive Activity Reporting Requirements** on page 10 for details on the information to be reported for each activity. If an at-risk activity loss is reported on line 1, see **Special Reporting Requirements for At-Risk Activities** on this page.

Line 2—Net Income (Loss) From Rental Real Estate Activities

Enter the net income or loss from rental real estate activities of the corporation from **Form 8825,** Rental Real Estate Income and Expenses of a Partnership or an S Corporation. Each Form 8825 has space for reporting the income and expenses of up to eight properties.

If the corporation has income or loss from more than one rental real estate activity reported on line 2, see **Passive**

Activity Reporting Requirements on page 10 for details on the information to be reported for each activity. If an at-risk activity loss is reported on line 2, see **Special Reporting Requirements for At-Risk Activities** on page 19.

Line 3—Income and Expenses of Other Rental Activities

Enter on lines 3a and 3b of Schedule K (line 3 of Schedule K-1) the income and expenses of rental activities other than those reported on Form 8825. If the corporation has more than one rental activity reported on line 3, see **Passive Activity Reporting Requirements** on page 10 for details on the information to be reported for each activity. If an at-risk activity loss is reported on line 3, see **Special Reporting Requirements for At-Risk Activities** on page 19. Also see **Rental activities** on page 8 for a definition and other details on other rental activities.

Lines 4a Through 4f—Portfolio Income (Loss)

Enter portfolio income (loss) on lines 4a through 4f. See **Portfolio income** on page 9 for the definition of portfolio income. Do not reduce portfolio income by deductions allocated to it. Report such deductions (other than interest expense) on line 9 of Schedules K and K-1. Interest expense allocable to portfolio income is generally investment interest expense and is reported on line 11a of Schedules K and K-1.

Lines 4a and 4b. Enter only taxable interest and ordinary dividends that are portfolio income. Interest income derived in the ordinary course of the corporation's trade or business, such as interest charged on receivable balances, is reported on line 5, page 1, Form 1120S. See Temporary Regulations section 1.469-2T(c)(3).

Lines 4d, 4e(1), and 4e(2). Enter on line 4d the gain or loss that is portfolio income (loss) from Schedule D (Form 1120S), line 6. Enter on line 4e(1) the gain or loss that is portfolio income (loss) from Schedule D (Form 1120S), line 13. Enter on line 4e(2) the gain or loss that is portfolio income (loss) from Schedule D (Form 1120S), line 14.

If any gain or loss from lines 6, 13, and 14 of Schedule D is not portfolio income (e.g., gain or loss from the disposition of nondepreciable personal property used in a trade or business), do not report this income or loss on lines 4d(2), 4e(1), and 4e(2). Instead, report it on line 6 of Schedules K and K-1. If the income or loss is attributable to more than one activity, report the income or loss amount separately for each activity on an attachment to Schedule K-1 and identify the activity to which the income or loss relates.

Line 4f. Enter any other portfolio income not reported on lines 4a through 4e.

If the corporation holds a residual interest in a REMIC, report on an attachment for line 4f each shareholder's share of taxable income (net loss) from the REMIC (line 1b of Schedule Q (Form 1066)); excess inclusion (line 2c of Schedule Q (Form 1066)); and section 212 expenses (line 3b of Schedule Q (Form 1066)). Because Schedule Q (Form 1066) is a quarterly statement, the corporation must follow the Schedule Q (Form 1066) Instructions for Residual Interest Holder to figure the amounts to report to shareholders for the corporation's tax year.

Line 5—Net Section 1231 Gain (Loss) (Other Than Due to Casualty or Theft)

Enter the net section 1231 gain (loss) (excluding net gain from involuntary conversions due to casualty or theft) from Form 4797, line 7, column (g). Report net gain or loss from involuntary conversions due to casualty or theft on line 6.

If the corporation is involved in more than one trade or business or rental activity, see **Passive Activity Reporting Requirements** on page 10 for details on the information to be reported for each activity. If an at-risk activity loss is reported on line 5, see **Special Reporting Requirements for At-Risk Activities** on page 19.

Line 6—Other Income (Loss)

Enter any other item of income or loss not included on lines 1 through 5. Items to be reported on line 6 include:

- Recoveries of tax benefit items (section 111).
- Gambling gains and losses (section 165(d)).
- Gains from the disposition of an interest in oil, gas, geothermal, or other mineral properties (section 1254).
- Net gain (loss) from involuntary conversions due to casualty or theft. The amount for this item is shown on **Form 4684,** Casualties and Thefts, line 38a or 38b.
- Any net gain or loss from section 1256 contracts from **Form 6781,** Gains and Losses From Section 1256 Contracts and Straddles.
- Gain from the sale or exchange of qualified small business stock (as defined in the Instructions for Schedule D) that is eligible for the 50% section 1202 exclusion. To be eligible for the section 1202 exclusion, the stock must have been held by the corporation for more than 5 years. Corporate shareholders are not eligible for the section 1202 exclusion. Additional limitations apply at the shareholder level. Report each shareholder's share of section 1202 gain on Schedule K-1. Each shareholder will determine if he or she qualifies for the section 1202 exclusion. Report on an attachment to Schedule K-1 for each sale or exchange the name of the qualified small business that issued the stock, the shareholder's share of the corporation's adjusted basis and sales price of the stock, and the dates the stock was bought and sold.
- Gain eligible for section 1045 rollover (replacement stock purchased by the corporation). Include only gain from the sale or exchange of qualified small business stock (as defined in the Instructions for Schedule D) that was deferred by the corporation under section 1045 and reported on Schedule D. See the Instructions for Schedule D for more details. Corporate shareholders are not eligible for the section 1045 rollover. Additional limitations apply at the shareholder level. Report each shareholder's share of the gain eligible for section 1045 rollover on Schedule K-1. Each shareholder will determine if he or she qualifies for the rollover. Report on an attachment to Schedule K-1 for each sale or exchange the name of the qualified small business that issued the stock, the shareholder's share of the corporation's adjusted basis and sales price of the stock, and the dates the stock was bought and sold.
- Gain eligible for section 1045 rollover (replacement stock not purchased by the corporation). Include only gain from the sale or exchange of qualified small business stock (as defined in the Instructions for Schedule D) the corporation held for more than 6 months but that **was not** deferred by the corporation under section 1045. See the Instructions for Schedule D for more details. A shareholder (other than a corporation) may be eligible to defer his or her pro rata share of this gain under section 1045 if he or she purchases other qualified small business stock during the 60-day period that began on the date the stock was sold by the corporation. Additional limitations apply at the shareholder level. Report on an attachment to Schedule K-1 for each sale or exchange the name of the qualified small business that issued the stock, the shareholder's share of the corporation's adjusted basis and sales price of the stock, and the dates the stock was bought and sold.

If the corporation is involved in more than one trade or business or rental activity, see **Passive Activity Reporting Requirements** on page 10 for details on the information to be reported for each activity. If an at-risk activity loss is reported on line 6, see **Special Reporting Requirements for At-Risk Activities** on page 19.

Deductions

Line 7—Charitable Contributions

Enter the amount of charitable contributions paid during the tax year. On an attachment to Schedules K and K-1, show separately the dollar amount of contributions subject to each of the 50%, 30%, and 20% of adjusted gross income limits. For additional information, see **Pub. 526,** Charitable Contributions.

CAUTION *An accrual basis S corporation **may not** elect to treat a contribution as having been paid in the tax year the board of directors authorizes the payment if the contribution is not actually paid until the next tax year.*

Generally, no deduction is allowed for any contribution of $250 or more unless the corporation obtains a written acknowledgment from the charitable organization that shows the amount of cash contributed, describes any property contributed, and gives an estimate of the value of any goods or services provided in return for the contribution. The acknowledgment must be obtained by the due date (including extensions) of the corporation's return, or if earlier, the date the corporation files its return. Do not attach the acknowledgment to the tax return, but keep it with the corporation's records. These rules apply in addition to the filing requirements for Form 8283 described below.

Certain contributions made to an organization conducting lobbying activities are not deductible. See section 170(f)(9) for more details.

If the corporation contributes property other than cash and the deduction claimed for such property exceeds $500, complete **Form 8283,** Noncash Charitable Contributions, and attach it to Form 1120S. The corporation must give a copy of its Form 8283 to every shareholder if the deduction for any item or group of similar items of contributed property exceeds $5,000, even if the amount allocated to any shareholder is $5,000 or less.

If the deduction for an item or group of similar items of contributed property is $5,000 or less, the corporation must report each shareholder's pro rata share of the amount of noncash contributions to enable individual shareholders to complete their own Forms 8283. See the Instructions for Form 8283 for more information.

If the corporation made a qualified conservation contribution under section 170(h), also include the fair market value of the underlying property before and after the donation, as well as the type of legal interest contributed, and describe the conservation purpose furthered by the donation. Give a copy of this information to each shareholder.

Line 8—Section 179 Expense Deduction

An S corporation may elect to expense part of the cost of certain tangible property that the corporation purchased during the tax year for use in its trade or business or certain rental activities. See the Instructions for Form 4562 for more information.

Complete Part I of Form 4562 to figure the corporation's section 179 expense deduction. The corporation does not claim the deduction itself, but instead passes it through to the shareholders. Attach Form 4562 to Form 1120S and show the total section 179 expense deduction on Schedule K, line 8. Report each individual shareholder's pro rata share on Schedule K-1, line 8. Do not complete line 8 of Schedule K-1 for any shareholder that is an estate or trust.

If the corporation is an enterprise zone business, also report on an attachment to Schedules K and K-1 the cost of section 179 property placed in service during the year that is qualified zone property.

See the instructions for line 23 of Schedule K-1, item 3, for any recapture of a section 179 amount.

Line 9—Deductions Related to Portfolio Income (Loss)

Enter on line 9 the deductions clearly and directly allocable to portfolio income (other than interest expense). Interest expense related to portfolio income is investment interest expense and is reported on line 11a of Schedules K and K-1. Generally, the line 9 expenses are section 212 expenses and are subject to section 212 limitations at the shareholder level.

Note: *No deduction is allowed under section 212 for expenses allocable to a convention, seminar, or similar meeting. Because these expenses are not deductible by shareholders, the corporation does not report these expenses on line 9 or line 10. The expenses are nondeductible and are reported as such on line 19 of Schedules K and K-1.*

Line 10—Other Deductions

Enter any other deductions not included on lines 7, 8, 9, and 15f. On an attachment, identify the deduction and amount, and if the corporation has more than one activity, the activity to which the deduction relates.

Examples of items to be reported on an attachment to line 10 include:

- Amounts (other than investment interest required to be reported on line 11a of Schedules K and K-1) paid by the corporation that would be allowed as itemized deductions on a shareholder's income tax return if they were paid directly by a shareholder for the same purpose. These amounts include, but are not limited to, expenses under section 212 for the production of income other than from the corporation's trade or business.
- Any penalty on early withdrawal of savings not reported on line 9 because the corporation withdrew funds from its time savings deposit before its maturity.
- Soil and water conservation expenditures (section 175).
- Expenditures paid or incurred for the removal of architectural and transportation barriers to the elderly and disabled that the corporation has elected to treat as a current expense. See section 190.
- Contributions to a capital construction fund.
- Interest expense allocated to debt-financed distributions. See Notice 89-35, 1989-1 C.B. 675, for more information.
- If there was a gain (loss) from a casualty or theft to property not used in a trade or business or for income producing purposes, provide each shareholder with the needed information to complete Form 4684.

Investment Interest

Lines 11a and 11b must be completed for all shareholders.

Line 11a—Investment Interest Expense

Include on this line the interest properly allocable to debt on property held for investment purposes. Property held for investment includes property that produces income (unless derived in the ordinary course of a trade or business) from interest, dividends, annuities, or royalties; and gains from the disposition of property that produces those types of income or is held for investment.

Investment interest expense **does not** include interest expense allocable to a passive activity.

Report investment interest expense only on line 11a of Schedules K and K-1.

The amount on line 11a will be deducted by individual shareholders on Schedule A (Form 1040), line 13, after applying the investment interest expense limitations of section 163(d).

For more information, see **Form 4952,** Investment Interest Expense Deduction.

Lines 11b(1) and 11b(2)—Investment Income and Expenses

Enter on line 11b(1) only the investment income included on lines 4a, b, c, and f of Schedule K-1. Do not include other portfolio gains or losses on this line.

Enter on line 11b(2) only the investment expense included on line 9 of Schedule K-1.

If there are other items of investment income or expense included in the amounts that are required to be passed through separately to the shareholders on Schedule K-1, such as net short-term capital gain or loss, net long-term capital gain or loss, and other portfolio gains or losses, give each shareholder a schedule identifying these amounts.

Investment income includes gross income from property held for investment, the excess of net gain attributable to the disposition of property held for investment over net capital gain from the disposition of property held for investment, and any net capital gain from the disposition of property held for investment that each shareholder elects to include in investment income under section 163(d)(4)(B)(iii). Generally, investment income and investment expenses do not include any income or expenses from a passive activity. See Regulations section 1.469-2(f)(10) for exceptions.

Property subject to a net lease is not treated as investment property because it is subject to the passive loss rules. Do not reduce investment income by losses from passive activities.

Investment expenses are deductible expenses (other than interest) directly connected with the production of investment income. See the Instructions for Form 4952 for more information on investment income and expenses.

Credits

Note: *If the corporation has credits from more than one trade or business activity on line 12a or 13, or from more than one rental activity on line 12b, 12c, 12d, or 12e, it must report separately on an attachment to Schedule K-1, the amount of each credit and provide any other applicable activity information listed in* ***Passive Activity Reporting Requirements*** *on page 10. However,* ***do not*** *attach* ***Form 3800,*** *General Business Credit, to Form 1120S.*

Line 12a—Credit for Alcohol Used as Fuel

Enter on line 12a of Schedule K the credit for alcohol used as fuel attributable to trade or business activities. Enter on line 12d or 12e the credit for alcohol used as fuel attributable to rental activities. Figure the credit on **Form 6478,** Credit for Alcohol Used as Fuel, and attach it to Form 1120S. The credit must be included in income on page 1, line 5, of Form 1120S. See section 40(f) for an election the corporation can make to have the credit not apply.

Enter each shareholder's share of the credit for alcohol used as fuel on line 12a, 12d, or 12e of Schedule K-1.

If this credit includes the small ethanol producer credit, identify on a statement attached to each Schedule K-1 **(a)** the amount of the small producer credit included in the total credit allocated to the shareholder, **(b)** the number of gallons of qualified ethanol fuel production allocated to the shareholder, and **(c)** the shareholder's pro rata share, in gallons, of the corporation's productive capacity for alcohol.

Line 12b—Low-Income Housing Credit

Section 42 provides for a credit that may be claimed by owners of low-income residential rental buildings. If shareholders are eligible to claim the low-income housing credit, complete the applicable parts of **Form 8586,** Low-Income Housing Credit, and attach it to Form 1120S. Enter the credit figured by the corporation on Form 8586, and any low-income housing credit received from other entities in which the corporation is allowed to invest, on the applicable line as explained below. The corporation must also complete and attach **Form 8609,** Low-Income Housing Credit Allocation Certification, and **Schedule A (Form 8609),** Annual Statement, to Form 1120S. See the Instructions for Form 8586 and Form 8609 for information on completing these forms.

Line 12b(1). If the corporation invested in a partnership to which the provisions of section 42(j)(5) apply, report on line 12b(1) the credit the partnership reported to the corporation on line 12a(1) of Schedule K-1 (Form 1065). If the corporation invested **before 1990** in a section 42(j)(5) partnership, also include on this line any credit the partnership reported to the corporation on line 12a(3) of Schedule K-1 (Form 1065).

Line 12b(2). Report on line 12b(2) any low-income housing credit for property placed in service before 1990 and not reported on line 12b(1). This includes any credit from a building placed in service before 1990 in a project owned by the corporation and any credit from a partnership reported to the corporation on line 12a(2) of Schedule K-1 (Form 1065). Also include on this line any credit from a partnership reported to the corporation on line 12a(4) of Schedule K-1 (Form 1065), if the corporation invested in that partnership **before 1990.**

Line 12b(3). If the corporation invested **after 1989** in a partnership to which the provisions of section 42(j)(5) apply, report on line 12b(3) the credit the partnership reported to the corporation on line 12a(3) of Schedule K-1 (Form 1065).

Line 12b(4). Report on line 12b(4) any low-income housing credit for property placed in service after 1989 and not reported on any other line. This includes any credit from a building placed in service after 1989 in a project owned by the corporation and any credit from a partnership reported to the corporation on line 12a(4) of Schedule K-1 (Form 1065), if the corporation invested in that partnership **after 1989.**

Line 12c—Qualified Rehabilitation Expenditures Related to Rental Real Estate Activities

Enter total qualified rehabilitation expenditures related to rental real estate activities of the corporation. For line 12c of Schedule K, complete the applicable lines of **Form 3468,** Investment Credit, that apply to qualified rehabilitation expenditures for property related to rental real estate activities of the corporation for which income or loss is reported on line 2 of Schedule K. See Form 3468 for details on qualified rehabilitation expenditures. Attach Form 3468 to Form 1120S.

For line 12c of Schedule K-1, enter each shareholder's pro rata share of the expenditures. On the dotted line to the left of the entry space for line 12c, enter the line number of Form 3468 on which the shareholder should report the expenditures. If there is more than one type of expenditure, or the expenditures are from more than one line 2 activity, report this information separately for each expenditure or activity on an attachment to Schedules K and K-1.

Note: *Qualified rehabilitation expenditures* ***not*** *related to rental real estate activities must be listed separately on line 23 of Schedule K-1.*

Line 12d—Credits (Other Than Credits Shown on Lines 12b and 12c) Related to Rental Real Estate Activities

Enter on line 12d any other credit (other than credits on lines 12b and 12c) related to rental real estate activities. On the dotted line to the left of the entry space for line 12d, identify the type of credit. If there is more than one type of credit or the credit is from more than one line 2 activity, report this information separately for each credit or activity on an attachment to Schedules K and K-1. These credits may include any type of credit listed in the instructions for line 13.

Line 12e—Credits Related to Other Rental Activities

Enter on line 12e any credit related to other rental activities for which income or loss is reported on line 3 of Schedules K and K-1. On the dotted line to the left of the entry space for line 12e, identify the type of credit. If there is more than one type of credit or the credit is from more than one line 3 activity, report this information separately for each credit or activity on an attachment to Schedules K and K-1. These credits may include any type of credit listed in the instructions for line 13.

Line 13—Other Credits

Enter on line 13 any other credit, except credits or expenditures shown or listed for lines 12a through 12e of Schedules K and K-1 or the credit for Federal tax paid on fuels (which is reported on line 23c of page 1). On the dotted line to the left of the entry space for line 13, identify the type of credit. If there is more than one type of credit or the credit is from more than one activity, report this information separately for each credit or activity on an attachment to Schedules K and K-1.

The credits to be reported on line 13 and other required attachments follow.

- Credit for backup withholding on dividends, interest, or patronage dividends.
- Nonconventional source fuel credit. Figure this credit on a separate schedule

and attach it to Form 1120S. See section 29 for rules on figuring the credit.

- Qualified electric vehicle credit (Form 8834).
- Unused investment credit from cooperatives. If the corporation is a member of a cooperative that passes an unused investment credit through to its members, the credit is in turn passed through to the corporation's shareholders.
- Work opportunity credit (Form 5884).
- Welfare-to-work credit (Form 8861).
- Credit for increasing research activities (Form 6765).
- Enhanced oil recovery credit (Form 8830).
- Disabled access credit (Form 8826).
- Renewable electricity production credit (Form 8835).
- Empowerment zone employment credit (Form 8844).
- Indian employment credit (Form 8845).
- Credit for employer social security and Medicare taxes paid on certain employee tips (Form 8846).
- Orphan drug credit (Form 8820).
- Credit for contributions to selected community development corporations (Form 8847).
- General credits from an electing large partnership.

See the instructions on page 25 for line 21 (Schedule K) and line 23 (Schedule K-1) to report expenditures qualifying for the **(a)** rehabilitation credit not related to rental real estate activities, **(b)** energy credit, or **(c)** reforestation credit.

Adjustments and Tax Preference Items

Lines 14a through 14e must be completed for all shareholders.

Enter items of income and deductions that are adjustments or tax preference items for the alternative minimum tax (AMT). See **Form 6251,** Alternative Minimum Tax—Individuals, or Schedule I of **Form 1041,** U.S. Income Tax Return for Estates and Trusts, to determine the amounts to enter and for other information.

Do not include as a tax preference item any qualified expenditures to which an election under section 59(e) may apply. Because these expenditures are subject to an election by each shareholder, the corporation cannot figure the amount of any tax preference related to them. Instead, the corporation must pass through to each shareholder on lines 16a and 16b of Schedule K-1 the information needed to figure the deduction.

Line 14a—Depreciation Adjustment on Property Placed in Service After 1986

Figure the adjustment for line 14a based only on tangible property placed in service after 1986 (and tangible property placed in service after July 31, 1986, and before 1987 for which the corporation elected to use the general depreciation system). **Do not** make an adjustment for motion picture films, videotapes, sound recordings, certain public utility property (as defined in section 168(f)(2)), property depreciated under the unit-of-production method (or any other method not expressed in a term of years), or qualified Indian reservation property.

For property placed in service **before 1999**, refigure depreciation for the AMT as follows (using the same convention used for the regular tax):

- For section 1250 property (generally, residential rental and nonresidential real property), use the straight line method over 40 years.
- For tangible property (other than section 1250 property) depreciated using the straight line method for the regular tax, use the straight line method over the property's class life. Use 12 years if the property has no class life.
- For any other tangible property, use the 150% declining balance method, switching to the straight line method the first tax year it gives a larger deduction, over the property's AMT class life. Use 12 years if the property has no class life.

Note: *See Pub. 946 for a table of class lives.*

For property placed in service **after 1998**, refigure depreciation for the AMT **only** for property depreciated for the regular tax using the 200% declining balance method. For the AMT, use the 150% declining balance method, switching to the straight line method the first tax year it gives a larger deduction, and the same convention and recovery period used for the regular tax.

Figure the adjustment by subtracting the AMT deduction for depreciation from the regular tax deduction and enter the result on line 14a. If the AMT deduction is more than the regular tax deduction, enter the difference as a negative amount. Depreciation capitalized to inventory must also be refigured using the AMT rules. Include on this line the current year adjustment to income, if any, resulting from the difference.

Line 14b—Adjusted Gain or Loss

If the corporation disposed of any tangible property placed in service after 1986 (or after July 31, 1986, if an election was made to use the General Depreciation System), or if it disposed of a certified pollution control facility placed in service after 1986, refigure the gain or loss from the disposition using the adjusted basis for the AMT. The property's adjusted basis for the AMT is its cost or other basis minus all depreciation or amortization deductions allowed or allowable for the AMT during the current tax year and previous tax years. Enter on this line the difference between the regular tax gain (loss) and the AMT gain (loss). If the AMT gain is less than the regular tax gain, OR the AMT loss is more than the regular tax loss, OR there is an AMT loss and a regular tax gain, enter the difference as a negative amount.

If any part of the adjustment is allocable to net short-term capital gain (loss), net long-term capital gain (loss), or net section 1231 gain (loss), attach a schedule that identifies the amount of the adjustment allocable to each type of gain or loss. For a net long-term capital gain (loss), also identify the amount of the adjustment that is 28% rate gain (loss). For a net section 1231 gain (loss), also identify the amount of adjustment that is unrecaptured section 1250 gain.

No schedule is required if the adjustment is allocable solely to ordinary gain (loss).

Line 14c—Depletion (Other Than Oil and Gas)

Do not include any depletion on oil and gas wells. The shareholders must figure their depletion deductions and preference items separately under section 613A.

Refigure the depletion deduction under section 611 for mines, wells (other than oil and gas wells), and other natural deposits for the AMT. Percentage depletion is limited to 50% of the taxable income from the property as figured under section 613(a), using only income and deductions for the AMT. Also, the deduction is limited to the property's adjusted basis at the end of the year, as refigured for the AMT. Figure this limit separately for each property. When refiguring the property's adjusted basis, take into account any AMT adjustments made this year or in previous years that affect basis (other than the current year's depletion).

Enter the difference between the regular tax and AMT deduction. If the AMT deduction is greater, enter the difference as a negative amount.

Lines 14d(1) and 14d(2)

Generally, the amounts to be entered on these lines are only the income and deductions for oil, gas, and geothermal properties that are used to figure the amount on line 21, page 1, Form 1120S.

If there are any items of income or deductions for oil, gas, and geothermal properties included in the amounts that are required to be passed through separately to the shareholders on Schedule K-1, give each shareholder a schedule that shows, for the line on which the income or deduction is included, the amount of income or deductions included in the total amount for that line. Do not include any of these direct pass-through amounts on line 14d(1) or 14d(2). The shareholder is told in the Shareholder's Instructions for Schedule K-1 (Form 1120S) to adjust the amounts on lines 14d(1) and 14d(2) for any other income or deductions from oil, gas, or geothermal properties included on lines 2 through 10 and 23 of Schedule K-1 in order to determine the total income and deductions from oil, gas, and geothermal properties for the corporation.

Figure the amounts for lines 14d(1) and 14d(2) separately for oil and gas properties that are not geothermal deposits and for all properties that are geothermal deposits.

Give the shareholders a schedule that shows the separate amounts included in the computation of the amounts on lines 14d(1) and 14d(2).

Line 14d(1)—Gross income from oil, gas, and geothermal properties. Enter the total amount of gross income (within the meaning of section 613(a)) from all oil, gas, and geothermal properties received or accrued during the tax year and included on page 1, Form 1120S.

Line 14d(2)—Deductions allocable to oil, gas, and geothermal properties. Enter the amount of any deductions allowed for the AMT that are allocable to oil, gas, and geothermal properties.

Line 14e—Other Adjustments and Tax Preference Items

Attach a schedule that shows each shareholder's share of other items not shown on lines 14a through 14d(2) that are adjustments or tax preference items or that the shareholder needs to complete Form 6251 or Schedule I of Form 1041. See these forms and their instructions to determine the amount to enter. Other adjustments or tax preference items include the following:

- Accelerated depreciation of real property under pre-1987 rules.
- Accelerated depreciation of leased personal property under pre-1987 rules.
- Long-term contracts entered into after February 28, 1986. Except for certain home construction contracts, the taxable income from these contracts must be figured using the percentage of completion method of accounting for the AMT.
- Losses from tax shelter farm activities. No loss from any tax shelter farm activity is allowed for the AMT.

Foreign Taxes

Lines 15a through 15g must be completed if the corporation has foreign income, deductions, or losses, or has paid or accrued foreign taxes. See **Pub. 514,** Foreign Tax Credit for Individuals, for more information.

Line 15a—Name of Foreign Country or U.S. Possession

Enter the name of the foreign country or U.S. possession from which the corporation had income or to which the corporation paid or accrued taxes. If the corporation had income from, or paid or accrued taxes to, **more than one** foreign country or U.S. possession, enter **"See attached"** and attach a schedule for each country for lines 15a through 15g.

Line 15b—Gross Income Sourced at Shareholder Level

Enter the total gross income of the corporation that is required to be sourced at the shareholder level. This includes income from the sale of most personal property other than inventory, depreciable property, and certain intangible property. See Pub. 514 and section 865 for details. Attach a schedule showing the following information:

- The amount of this gross income (without regard to its source) in each category identified in the instructions for line 15c, including each of the listed categories.
- Specifically identify gains on the sale of personal property other than inventory, depreciable property, and certain intangible property on which a foreign tax of 10% or more was paid or accrued. Also list losses on the sale of such property if the foreign country would have imposed a 10% or higher tax had the sale resulted in a gain. See **Sales or Exchanges of Certain Personal Property** in Pub. 514 and section 865.

Line 15c—Foreign Gross Income Sourced at Corporate Level

Separately report gross income from sources outside the United States by category of income as follows. See Pub.514 for information on the categories of income.

Line 15c(1). Passive foreign source income.

Line 15c(2). Attach a schedule showing the amount of foreign source income included in each of the following listed categories of income:

- Financial services income;
- High withholding tax interest;
- Shipping income;
- Dividends from each noncontrolled section 902 corporation;
- Dividends from a domestic international sales corporation (DISC) or a former DISC;
- Distributions from a foreign sales corporation (FSC) or a former FSC;
- Section 901(j) income; and
- Certain income re-sourced by treaty.

Line 15c(3). General limitation foreign source income (all other foreign source income).

Line 15d—Deductions Allocated and Apportioned at Shareholder Level

Enter on line 15d(1) the corporation's total interest expense (including interest equivalents under Temporary Regulations section 1.861-9T(b)). Do not include interest directly allocable under Temporary Regulations section 1.861-10T to income from a specific property. This type of interest is allocated and apportioned at the corporate level and is included on lines 15e(1) through (3). On line 15d(2), enter the total of all other deductions or losses that are required to be allocated at the shareholder level. For example, include on line 15d(2) research and experimental expenditures (see Regulations section 1.861-17(f)).

Line 15e—Deductions Allocated and Apportioned at Corporate Level to Foreign Source Income

Separately report corporate deductions that are apportioned at the corporate level to **(1)** passive foreign source income, **(2)** each of the listed foreign categories of income, and **(3)** general limitation foreign source income (see the instructions for line 15c). See Pub. 514 for more information.

Line 15f—Total Foreign Taxes

Enter in U.S. dollars the total foreign taxes (described in section 901 or section 903) that were paid or accrued by the corporation (according to its method of accounting for such taxes). Translate these amounts into U.S. dollars by using the applicable exchange rate (see Pub. 514).

Attach a schedule reporting the following information:

1. The total amount of foreign taxes (including foreign taxes on income sourced at the shareholder level) relating to each category of income (see instructions for line 15c).

2. The dates on which the taxes were paid or accrued, the exchange rates used, and the amounts in both foreign currency and U.S. dollars, for:

- Taxes withheld at source on interest.
- Taxes withheld at source on dividends.
- Taxes withheld at source on rents and royalties.
- Other foreign taxes paid or accrued.

Line 15g—Reduction in Taxes Available for Credit and Gross Income From All Sources

Attach a schedule showing:

- The corporation's gross income from all sources, including all U.S. and foreign source income.
- The total reductions in taxes available for credit.

Separately show the reductions for:

- Taxes on foreign mineral income (section 901(e)).
- Taxes on foreign oil and gas extraction income (section 907(a)).
- Taxes attributable to boycott operations (section 908).
- Failure to timely file (or furnish all of the information required on) Forms 5471 and 8865.
- Any other items (specify).

Other

Lines 16a and 16b—Section 59(e)(2) Expenditures

Generally, section 59(e) allows each shareholder to make an election to deduct the shareholder's pro rata share of the corporation's otherwise deductible qualified expenditures ratably over 10 years (3 years for circulation expenditures), beginning with the tax year in which the expenditures were made (or for intangible drilling and development costs, over the 60-month period beginning with the month in which such costs were paid or incurred). The term "qualified expenditures" includes only the following types of expenditures paid or incurred during the tax year:

- Circulation expenditures.
- Research and experimental expenditures.
- Intangible drilling and development costs.
- Mining exploration and development costs.

If a shareholder makes the election, the above items are not treated as tax preference items.

Because the shareholders are generally allowed to make this election, the corporation cannot deduct these amounts or include them as adjustments or tax preference items on Schedule K-1. Instead, on lines 16a and 16b of Schedule K-1, the corporation passes through the information the shareholders need to figure their separate deductions.

On line 16a, enter the type of expenditures claimed on line 16b. Enter on line 16b the qualified expenditures paid or incurred during the tax year to which an election under section 59(e) may apply. Enter this amount for all shareholders whether or not any shareholder makes an election under section 59(e). If the expenditures are for intangible drilling and development costs, enter the month in which the expenditures were paid or incurred (after the type of expenditures on line 16a). If there is more than one type of expenditure included in the total shown on line 16b (or intangible drilling and development costs were paid or incurred for more than 1 month), report this information separately for each type of expenditure (or month) on an attachment to Schedules K and K-1.

Line 17—Tax-Exempt Interest Income

Enter on line 17 tax-exempt interest income, including any exempt-interest dividends received from a mutual fund or other regulated investment company. This information must be reported by individuals on line 8b of Form 1040. Generally, the basis of the shareholder's stock is increased by the amount shown on this line under section 1367(a)(1)(A).

Line 18—Other Tax-Exempt Income

Enter on line 18 all income of the corporation exempt from tax other than tax-exempt interest (e.g., life insurance proceeds). Generally, the basis of the shareholder's stock is increased by the amount shown on this line under section 1367(a)(1)(A).

Line 19—Nondeductible Expenses

Enter on line 19 nondeductible expenses paid or incurred by the corporation. Do not include separately stated deductions shown elsewhere on Schedules K and K-1, capital expenditures, or items for which the deduction is deferred to a later tax year. Generally, the basis of the shareholder's stock is decreased by the amount shown on this line under section 1367(a)(2)(D).

Line 20

Enter total distributions made to each shareholder other than dividends reported on line 22 of Schedule K. Noncash distributions of appreciated property are valued at fair market value. See **Distributions** on page 27 for the ordering rules on distributions.

Line 21 (Schedule K Only)

Attach a statement to Schedule K to report the corporation's total income, expenditures, or other information for items 1 through 19 of the line 23 (Schedule K-1 Only) instruction below.

Line 22 (Schedule K Only)

Enter total dividends paid to shareholders from accumulated earnings and profits. Report these dividends to shareholders on Form 1099-DIV. Do not report them on Schedule K-1.

Lines 22a and 22b (Schedule K-1 Only)—Recapture of Low-Income Housing Credit

If recapture of part or all of the low-income housing credit is required because **(a)** prior year qualified basis of a building decreased or **(b)** the corporation disposed of a building or part of its interest in a building, see **Form 8611,** Recapture of Low-Income Housing Credit. The instructions for Form 8611 indicate when Form 8611 is completed by the corporation and what information is provided to shareholders when recapture is required.

Note: *If a shareholder's ownership interest in a building decreased because of a transaction at the shareholder level, the corporation must provide the necessary information to the shareholder to enable the shareholder to figure the recapture.*

If the corporation filed **Form 8693,** Low-Income Housing Credit Disposition Bond, to avoid recapture of the low-income housing credit, no entry should be made on line 22 of Schedule K-1.

See Form 8586, Form 8611, and section 42 for more information.

Supplemental Information

Line 23 (Schedule K-1 Only)

Enter in the line 23 Supplemental Information space of Schedule K-1, or on an attached schedule if more space is needed, each shareholder's share of any information asked for on lines 1 through 22 that is required to be reported in detail, and items **1** through **20** below. Please identify the applicable line number next to the information entered in the Supplemental Information space. Show income or gains as a positive number. Show losses in parentheses.

1. Taxes paid on undistributed capital gains by a regulated investment company or a real estate investment trust (REIT). As a shareholder of a regulated investment company or a REIT, the corporation will receive notice on **Form 2439,** Notice to Shareholder of Undistributed Long-Term Capital Gains, of the amount of tax paid on undistributed capital gains.

2. Gross income and other information relating to oil and gas well properties that are reported to shareholders to allow them to figure the depletion deduction for oil and gas well properties. See section 613A(c)(11) for details.

The corporation cannot deduct depletion on oil and gas wells. Each shareholder must determine the allowable amount to report on his or her return. See Pub. 535 for more information.

3. Recapture of section 179 expense deduction. For property placed in service after 1986, the section 179 deduction is recaptured at any time the business use of property drops to 50% or less. Enter the amount originally passed through and the corporation's tax year in which it was passed through. Inform the shareholder if the recapture amount was caused by the disposition of the section 179 property. See section 179(d)(10) for more information. Do not include this amount on line 4 or 5, page 1, Form 1120S.

4. Recapture of certain mining exploration expenditures (section 617).

5. Any information or statements the corporation is required to furnish to shareholders to allow them to comply with requirements under section 6111 (registration of tax shelters) or section 6662(d)(2)(B)(ii) (regarding adequate disclosure of items that may cause an understatement of income tax).

6. If the corporation is involved in farming or fishing activities, report the gross income from these activities to shareholders.

7. Any information needed by a shareholder to compute the interest due under section 453(l)(3). If the corporation elected to report the dispositions of certain timeshares and residential lots on the installment method, each shareholder's tax liability must be increased by the shareholder's pro rata share of the interest on tax attributable to the installment payments received during the tax year.

8. Any information needed by a shareholder to compute the interest due under section 453A(c). If an obligation arising from the disposition of property to which section 453A applies is outstanding at the close of the year, each shareholder's tax liability must be increased by the tax due under section 453A(c) on the shareholder's pro rata share of the tax deferred under the installment method.

9. Any information needed by a shareholder to properly capitalize interest as required by section 263A(f). See **Section 263A uniform capitalization rules** on page 12 for more information.

10. If the corporation is a closely held S corporation (defined in section 460(b)) and it entered into any long-term contracts after February 28, 1986, that are accounted for under either the percentage of completion-capitalized cost method or the percentage of completion method, it must attach a schedule to Form 1120S showing the information required in items (a) and (b) of the instructions for lines 1 and 3 of Part II for **Form 8697,** Interest Computation Under the Look-Back Method for Completed Long-Term Contracts. It must also report the amounts for Part II, lines 1 and 3, to its shareholders. See the Instructions for Form 8697 for more information.

11. Expenditures qualifying for the **(a)** rehabilitation credit not related to rental real estate activities, **(b)** energy credit, or **(c)** reforestation credit. Complete and attach Form 3468 to Form 1120S. See Form 3468 and related instructions for information on eligible property and the lines on Form 3468 to complete. Do not include that part of the cost of the property the corporation has elected to expense under section 179. Attach to each Schedule K-1 a separate schedule in a format similar to that shown on Form 3468 detailing each shareholder's pro rata share of qualified expenditures. Also indicate the lines of Form 3468 on which the shareholders should report these amounts.

12. Recapture of investment credit. Complete and attach **Form 4255,** Recapture of Investment Credit, when investment credit property is disposed of, or it no longer qualifies for the credit, before the end of the recapture period or the useful life applicable to the property. State the type of property at the top of Form 4255, and complete lines 2, 4, and 5, whether or not any shareholder is subject to recapture of the credit. Attach to each Schedule K-1 a separate schedule providing the information the corporation is required to show on Form 4255, but list only the shareholder's pro rata share of the cost of the property subject to recapture. Also indicate the lines of Form 4255 on which the shareholders should report these amounts.

The corporation itself is liable for investment credit recapture in certain cases. See the instructions for line 22c, page 1, Form 1120S, for details.

13. Any information needed by a shareholder to compute the recapture of the qualified electric vehicle credit. See Pub. 535 for more information.

14. Any information a shareholder may need to figure recapture of the Indian employment credit. Generally, if the corporation terminates a qualified employee less than 1 year after the date of initial employment, any Indian employment credit allowed for a prior tax year by reason of wages paid or incurred to that employee must be recaptured. For details, see section 45A(d).

15. Nonqualified withdrawals by the corporation from a capital construction fund.

16. Unrecaptured section 1250 gain. Figure this amount for each section 1250 property in Part III of Form 4797 (except property for which gain is reported using the installment method on Form 6252) for which you had an entry in Part I of Form 4797 by subtracting line 26g of Form 4797 from the **smaller** of line 22 or line 24 of Form 4797. Figure the total of these amounts for all section 1250 properties. Generally, the result is the corporation's unrecaptured section 1250 gain. However, if the corporation is reporting gain on the installment method for a section 1250 property held more than 1 year, see the next paragraph to figure the unrecaptured section 1250 gain on that property allocable to this tax year. Report each shareholder's pro rata share of the total amount as "Unrecaptured section 1250 gain."

The total unrecaptured section 1250 gain for an installment sale of section 1250 property held more than 1 year is figured in a manner similar to that used in the preceding paragraph. However, the total unrecaptured section 1250 gain must be allocated to the installment payments received from the sale. To do so, the corporation generally must treat the gain allocable to each installment payment as unrecaptured section 1250 gain until all such gain has been used in full. Figure the unrecaptured section 1250 gain for installment payments received during the tax year as the **smaller** of **(a)** the amount from line 26 or line 37 of Form 6252 (whichever applies) or **(b)** the total unrecaptured section 1250 gain for the sale reduced by all gain reported in prior years (excluding section 1250 ordinary income recapture). However, if the corporation chose not to treat all of the gain from payments received after May 6, 1997, and before August 24, 1999, as unrecaptured section 1250 gain, use only the amount the corporation chose to treat as unrecaptured section 1250 gain for those payments to reduce the total unrecaptured section 1250 gain remaining to be reported for the sale.

If the corporation received a Schedule K-1 or Form 1099-DIV from an estate, a trust, a REIT, or a mutual fund reporting "unrecaptured section 1250 gain," **do not** add it to the corporation's own unrecaptured section 1250 gain. Instead, report it as a separate amount. For example, if the corporation received a Form 1099-DIV from a REIT with unrecaptured section 1250 gain, report it as "Unrecaptured section 1250 gain from a REIT."

Also report as a separate amount any gain from the sale or exchange of an interest in a partnership attributable to unrecaptured section 1250 gain. See Regulations section 1.1(h)-1 and attach a statement required under Regulations section 1.1(h)-1(e).

17. If the corporation is a closely held S corporation (defined in section 460(b)(4)) and it depreciated certain property placed in service after September 13, 1995, under the income forecast method, it must attach to Form 1120S the information specified in the instructions for Form 8866, line 2, for the 3rd and 10th tax years beginning after the tax year the property was placed in service. It must also report the line 2 amounts to its shareholders. See the Instructions for Form 8866 for more details.

18. Amortization of reforestation expenditures. Report the amortizable basis and year in which the amortization began for the current year and the 7 preceding years. For limits that may apply, see section 194 and Pub. 535.

19. Any information needed by a shareholder to figure the interest due under section 1260(b). If any portion of a constructive ownership transaction was open in any prior year, each shareholder's tax liability must be increased by the shareholder's pro rata share of interest due on any deferral of gain recognition. See section 1260(b) for details, including how to figure the interest.

20. Any other information the shareholders need to prepare their tax returns.

Specific Instructions

Schedule L—Balance Sheets per Books

The balance sheets should agree with the corporation's books and records. Include certificates of deposit as cash on line 1 of Schedule L.

If the S election terminated during the tax year, the year-end balance sheet generally should agree with the books and records at the end of the C short year. However, if the corporation elected under section 1362(e)(3) to have items assigned to each short year under normal tax accounting rules, the year-end balance sheet should agree with the books and records at the end of the S short year.

Line 5—Tax-Exempt Securities

Include on this line—

1. State and local government obligations, the interest on which is excludible from gross income under section 103(a), and

2. Stock in a mutual fund or other regulated investment company that distributed exempt-interest dividends during the tax year of the corporation.

Line 24—Retained Earnings

If the corporation maintains separate accounts for appropriated and unappropriated retained earnings, it may want to continue such accounting for purposes of preparing its financial balance sheet. Also, if the corporation converts to C corporation status in a subsequent year, it will be required to report its appropriated and unappropriated retained earnings on separate lines of Schedule L of Form 1120.

Line 25—Adjustments to Shareholders' Equity

Some examples of adjustments to report on this line include:

- Unrealized gains and losses on securities held "available for sale."
- Foreign currency translation adjustments.
- The excess of additional pension liability over unrecognized prior service cost.
- Guarantees of employee stock (ESOP) debt.
- Compensation related to employee stock award plans.

If the total adjustment to be entered is a negative amount, enter the amount in parentheses.

Schedule M-1—Reconciliation of Income (Loss) per Books With Income (Loss) per Return

Line 3b—Travel and Entertainment

Include on this line the part of the cost of meals and entertainment not allowed under section 274(n); expenses for the use of an entertainment facility; the part of business gifts over $25; expenses of an individual allocable to conventions on cruise ships over $2,000; employee achievement awards over $400; the part of the cost of entertainment tickets that exceeds face value (also subject to 50% disallowance); the part of the cost of skyboxes that exceeds the face value of nonluxury box seat tickets; the part of the cost of luxury water travel not allowed under section 274(m); expenses for travel as a form of education; nondeductible club dues; and other travel and entertainment expenses not allowed as a deduction.

Schedule M-2—Analysis of Accumulated Adjustments Account, Other Adjustments Account, and Shareholders' Undistributed Taxable Income Previously Taxed

Column (a)—Accumulated Adjustments Account

The accumulated adjustments account (AAA) is an account of the S corporation that generally reflects the accumulated undistributed net income of the corporation for the corporation's post-1982 years. S corporations with accumulated E&P must maintain the AAA to determine the tax effect of distributions during S years and the post-termination transition period. An S corporation without accumulated E&P does not need to maintain the AAA in order to determine the tax effect of distributions. Nevertheless, if an S corporation without accumulated E&P engages in certain transactions to which section 381(a) applies, such as a merger into an S corporation with accumulated E&P, the S corporation must be able to calculate its AAA at the time of the merger for purposes of determining the tax effect of post-merger distributions. Therefore, it is recommended that the AAA be maintained by all S corporations.

On the first day of the corporation's first tax year as an S corporation, the balance of the AAA is zero. At the end of the tax year, adjust the AAA for the items for the tax year as explained below and in the order listed.

1. Increase the AAA by income (other than tax-exempt income) and the excess of the deduction for depletion over the basis of the property subject to depletion (unless the property is an oil and gas property the basis of which has been allocated to shareholders).

2. Generally, decrease the AAA by deductible losses and expenses, nondeductible expenses (other than expenses related to tax-exempt income and Federal taxes attributable to a C corporation tax year), and the sum of the shareholders' deductions for depletion for any oil or gas property held by the corporation as described in section 1367(a)(2)(E). However, if the total decreases under **2** exceeds the total increases under **1** above, the excess is a "net negative adjustment." If the corporation has a net negative adjustment, **do not** take it into account under **2.** Instead, take it into account only under **4** below.

3. Decrease AAA (but not below zero) by property distributions (other than dividend distributions from accumulated E&P), unless the corporation elects to reduce accumulated E&P first. See **Distributions** below for definitions and other details.

4. Decrease AAA by any net negative adjustment. For adjustments to the AAA for redemptions, reorganizations, and corporate separations, see Regulations section 1.1368-2(d).

Note: *The AAA may have a negative balance at year end. See section 1368(e).*

Column (b)—Other Adjustments Account

The other adjustments account is adjusted for tax-exempt income (and related expenses) and Federal taxes attributable to a C corporation tax year. After these adjustments are made, the account is reduced for any distributions made during the year. See **Distributions** below.

Column (c)—Shareholders' Undistributed Taxable Income Previously Taxed

The shareholders' undistributed taxable income previously taxed account, also called previously taxed income (PTI), is maintained only if the corporation had a balance in this account at the start of its 2000 tax year. If there is a beginning balance for the 2000 tax year, no adjustments are made to the account except to reduce the account for distributions made under section 1375(d) (as in effect before the enactment of the Subchapter S Revision Act of 1982). See **Distributions** below for the order of distributions from the account.

Each shareholder's right to nontaxable distributions from PTI is personal and cannot be transferred to another person. The corporation is required to keep records of each shareholder's net share of PTI.

Distributions

General rule. Unless the corporation makes one of the elections described below, property distributions (including cash) are applied in the following order to reduce accounts of the S corporation that are used to figure the tax effect of distributions made by the corporation to its shareholders:

1. Reduce the AAA determined without regard to any net negative adjustment for the tax year (but not below zero). If distributions during the tax year exceed the AAA at the close of the tax year determined without regard to any net negative adjustment for the tax year, the AAA is allocated pro rata to each distribution made during the tax year. See section 1368(c).

2. Reduce shareholders' PTI account for any section 1375(d) (as in effect before 1983) distributions. A distribution from the PTI account is tax free to the extent of a shareholder's basis in his or her stock in the corporation.

3. Reduce accumulated E&P. Generally, the S corporation has accumulated E&P only if it has not distributed E&P accumulated in prior years when the S corporation was a C corporation (section 1361(a)(2)). See section 312 for information on E&P. The only adjustments that can be made to the accumulated E&P of an S corporation are **(a)** reductions for dividend distributions; **(b)** adjustments for redemptions, liquidations, reorganizations, etc.; and **(c)** reductions for investment credit recapture tax for which the corporation is liable. See sections 1371(c) and (d)(3).

4. Reduce the other adjustments account.

5. Reduce any remaining shareholders' equity accounts.

Elections relating to source of distributions. The corporation may modify the above ordering rules by making one or more of the following elections:

1. ***Election to distribute accumulated E&P first.*** If the corporation has accumulated E&P and wants to distribute this E&P before making distributions from the AAA, it may elect to do so with the consent of all its affected shareholders (section 1368(e)(3)(B)). This election is irrevocable and applies only for the tax year for which it is made. For details on making the election, see **Statement regarding elections** below.

2. ***Election to make a deemed dividend.*** If the corporation wants to distribute all or part of its accumulated E&P through a deemed dividend, it may elect to do so with the consent of all its affected shareholders (section 1368(e)(3)(B)). Under this election, the corporation will be treated as also having made the election to distribute accumulated E&P first. The amount of the deemed dividend cannot exceed the accumulated E&P at the end of the tax year, reduced by any actual distributions of accumulated E&P made during the tax year. A deemed dividend is treated as if it were a pro rata distribution of money to the shareholders, received by the shareholders, and immediately contributed back to the corporation, all on the last day of the tax year. This election is irrevocable and applies only for the tax year for which it is made. For details on making the election, see **Statement regarding elections** below.

3. ***Election to forego PTI.*** If the corporation wants to forego distributions of PTI, it may elect to do so with the consent of all its affected shareholders (section 1368(e)(3)(B)). Under this election, paragraph 2 under the **General rule** above does not apply to any distribution made during the tax year. This election is irrevocable and applies only for the tax year for which it is made. For details on making the election, see **Statement regarding elections** below.

Statement regarding elections. To make any of the above elections, the corporation must attach a statement to a timely filed original or amended Form 1120S for the tax year for which the election is made. In the statement, the corporation must identify the election it is making and must state that each shareholder consents to the election. A corporate officer must sign the statement under penalties of perjury on behalf of the corporation. The statement of election to make a deemed dividend must include the amount of the deemed dividend distributed to each shareholder.

Example

The following example shows how the Schedule M-2 accounts are adjusted for items of income (loss), deductions, and distributions reported on Form 1120S. In this example, the corporation has no PTI or accumulated E&P.

Items per return are:

1. Page 1, line 21 income—$10,000

2. Schedule K, line 2 loss—($3,000)

3. Schedule K, line 4a income—$4,000

4. Schedule K, line 4b income—$16,000

5. Schedule K, line 7 deduction—$24,000

6. Schedule K, line 10 deduction—$3,000

7. Schedule K, line 13 work opportunity credit—$6,000

8. Schedule K, line 17 tax-exempt interest—$5,000

9. Schedule K, line 19 nondeductible expenses—$6,000 (reduction in salaries and wages for work opportunity credit), and

10. Schedule K, line 20 distributions—$65,000.

Based on return items 1 through 10 and starting balances of zero, the columns for the AAA and the other adjustments account are completed as shown in the Schedule M-2 Worksheet below.

For the AAA, the worksheet line 3—$20,000 amount is the total of the Schedule K, lines 4a and 4b income of $4,000 and $16,000. The worksheet line 5—$36,000 amount is the total of the Schedule K, line 2 loss of ($3,000), line 7 deduction of $24,000, line 10 deduction of $3,000, and the line 19 nondeductible expenses of $6,000. The worksheet line 7 is zero. The AAA at the end of the tax year (figured without regard to distributions and the net negative adjustment of $6,000) is zero, and distributions cannot reduce the AAA below zero.

For the other adjustments account, the worksheet line 3 amount is the Schedule K, line 17, tax-exempt interest income of $5,000. The worksheet line 7 amount is $5,000, reducing the other adjustments account to zero. The remaining $60,000 of distributions are not entered on Schedule M-2.

Schedule M-2 Worksheet

		(a) Accumulated adjustments account	(b) Other adjustments account	(c) Shareholders' undistributed taxable income previously taxed
1	Balance at beginning of tax year	-0-	-0-	
2	Ordinary income from page 1, line 21	10,000		
3	Other additions	20,000	5,000	
4	Loss from page 1, line 21	( )		
5	Other reductions	(36,000)	( )	
6	Combine lines 1 through 5	(6,000)	5,000	
7	Distributions other than dividend distributions	-0-	5,000	
8	Balance at end of tax year. Subtract line 7 from line 6	(6,000)	-0-	

Codes for Principal Business Activity

This list of principal business activities and their associated codes is designed to classify an enterprise by the type of activity in which it is engaged to facilitate the administration of the Internal Revenue Code. These principal business activity codes are based on the North American Industry Classification System.

Using the list of activities and codes below, determine from which activity the company derives the largest percentage of its "total receipts." Total receipts is defined as the sum of gross receipts or sales (page 1, line 1a), all other income (page 1, lines 4 and 5), income (receipts only) reported on Schedule K, lines 3a and 4a through 4f, and income (receipts only) reported on Form 8825, lines 2, 19, and 20a. If the company purchases raw materials and supplies them to a subcontractor to produce the finished product, but retains title to the product, the company is considered a manufacturer and must use one of the manufacturing codes (311110-339900).

Once the principal business activity is determined, enter the six-digit code from the list below on page 1, item B. Also enter a brief description of the business activity on page 2, Schedule B, line 2(a) and the principal product or service of the business on line 2(b).

Agriculture, Forestry, Fishing and Hunting

Code

Crop Production

111100 Oilseed & Grain Farming
111210 Vegetable & Melon Farming (including potatoes & yams)
111300 Fruit & Tree Nut Farming
111400 Greenhouse, Nursery, & Floriculture Production
111900 Other Crop Farming (including tobacco, cotton, sugarcane, hay, peanut, sugar beet & all other crop farming)

Animal Production

112111 Beef Cattle Ranching & Farming
112112 Cattle Feedlots
112120 Dairy Cattle & Milk Production
112210 Hog & Pig Farming
112300 Poultry & Egg Production
112400 Sheep & Goat Farming
112510 Animal Aquaculture (including shellfish & finfish farms & hatcheries)
112900 Other Animal Production

Forestry and Logging

113110 Timber Tract Operations
113210 Forest Nurseries & Gathering of Forest Products
113310 Logging

Fishing, Hunting and Trapping

114110 Fishing
114210 Hunting & Trapping

Support Activities for Agriculture and Forestry

115110 Support Activities for Crop Production (including cotton ginning, soil preparation, planting, & cultivating)
115210 Support Activities for Animal Production
115310 Support Activities For Forestry

Mining

211110 Oil & Gas Extraction
212110 Coal Mining
212200 Metal Ore Mining
212310 Stone Mining & Quarrying
212320 Sand, Gravel, Clay, & Ceramic & Refractory Minerals Mining & Quarrying
212390 Other Nonmetallic Mineral Mining & Quarrying
213110 Support Activities for Mining

Utilities

221100 Electric Power Generation, Transmission & Distribution
221210 Natural Gas Distribution
221300 Water, Sewage & Other Systems

Construction

Code

Building, Developing, and General Contracting

233110 Land Subdivision & Land Development
233200 Residential Building Construction
233300 Nonresidential Building Construction

Heavy Construction

234100 Highway, Street, Bridge, & Tunnel Construction
234900 Other Heavy Construction

Special Trade Contractors

235110 Plumbing, Heating, & Air-Conditioning Contractors
235210 Painting & Wall Covering Contractors
235310 Electrical Contractors
235400 Masonry, Drywall, Insulation, & Tile Contractors
235500 Carpentry & Floor Contractors
235610 Roofing, Siding, & Sheet Metal Contractors
235710 Concrete Contractors
235810 Water Well Drilling Contractors
235900 Other Special Trade Contractors

Manufacturing

Food Manufacturing

311110 Animal Food Mfg
311200 Grain & Oilseed Milling
311300 Sugar & Confectionery Product Mfg
311400 Fruit & Vegetable Preserving & Specialty Food Mfg
311500 Dairy Product Mfg
311610 Animal Slaughtering and Processing
311710 Seafood Product Preparation & Packaging
311800 Bakeries & Tortilla Mfg
311900 Other Food Mfg (including coffee, tea, flavorings & seasonings)

Beverage and Tobacco Product Manufacturing

312110 Soft Drink & Ice Mfg
312120 Breweries
312130 Wineries
312140 Distilleries
312200 Tobacco Manufacturing

Textile Mills and Textile Product Mills

313000 Textile Mills
314000 Textile Product Mills

Apparel Manufacturing

315100 Apparel Knitting Mills
315210 Cut & Sew Apparel Contractors
315220 Men's & Boys' Cut & Sew Apparel Mfg
315230 Women's & Girls' Cut & Sew Apparel Mfg

Code

315290 Other Cut & Sew Apparel Mfg
315990 Apparel Accessories & Other Apparel Mfg

Leather and Allied Product Manufacturing

316110 Leather & Hide Tanning & Finishing
316210 Footwear Mfg (including rubber & plastics)
316990 Other Leather & Allied Product Mfg

Wood Product Manufacturing

321110 Sawmills & Wood Preservation
321210 Veneer, Plywood, & Engineered Wood Product Mfg
321900 Other Wood Product Mfg

Paper Manufacturing

322100 Pulp, Paper, & Paperboard Mills
322200 Converted Paper Product Mfg

Printing and Related Support Activities

323100 Printing & Related Support Activities

Petroleum and Coal Products Manufacturing

324110 Petroleum Refineries (including integrated)
324120 Asphalt Paving, Roofing, & Saturated Materials Mfg
324190 Other Petroleum & Coal Products Mfg

Chemical Manufacturing

325100 Basic Chemical Mfg
325200 Resin, Synthetic Rubber, & Artificial & Synthetic Fibers & Filaments Mfg
325300 Pesticide, Fertilizer, & Other Agricultural Chemical Mfg
325410 Pharmaceutical & Medicine Mfg
325500 Paint, Coating, & Adhesive Mfg
325600 Soap, Cleaning Compound, & Toilet Preparation Mfg
325900 Other Chemical Product & Preparation Mfg

Plastics and Rubber Products Manufacturing

326100 Plastics Product Mfg
326200 Rubber Product Mfg

Nonmetallic Mineral Product Manufacturing

327100 Clay Product & Refractory Mfg
327210 Glass & Glass Product Mfg
327300 Cement & Concrete Product Mfg
327400 Lime & Gypsum Product Mfg
327900 Other Nonmetallic Mineral Product Mfg

Primary Metal Manufacturing

331110 Iron & Steel Mills & Ferroalloy Mfg
331200 Steel Product Mfg from Purchased Steel
331310 Alumina & Aluminum Production & Processing
331400 Nonferrous Metal (except Aluminum) Production & Processing
331500 Foundries

Fabricated Metal Product Manufacturing

332110 Forging & Stamping
332210 Cutlery & Handtool Mfg
332300 Architectural & Structural Metals Mfg
332400 Boiler, Tank, & Shipping Container Mfg
332510 Hardware Mfg
332610 Spring & Wire Product Mfg
332700 Machine Shops; Turned Product; & Screw, Nut, & Bolt Mfg
332810 Coating, Engraving, Heat Treating, & Allied Activities
332900 Other Fabricated Metal Product Mfg

Code

Machinery Manufacturing

333100 Agriculture, Construction, & Mining Machinery Mfg
333200 Industrial Machinery Mfg
333310 Commercial & Service Industry Machinery Mfg
333410 Ventilation, Heating, Air-Conditioning, & Commercial Refrigeration Equipment Mfg
333510 Metalworking Machinery Mfg
333610 Engine, Turbine & Power Transmission Equipment Mfg
333900 Other General Purpose Machinery Mfg

Computer and Electronic Product Manufacturing

334110 Computer & Peripheral Equipment Mfg
334200 Communications Equipment Mfg
334310 Audio & Video Equipment Mfg
334410 Semiconductor & Other Electronic Component Mfg
334500 Navigational, Measuring, Electromedical, & Control Instruments Mfg
334610 Manufacturing & Reproducing Magnetic & Optical Media

Electrical Equipment, Appliance, and Component Manufacturing

335100 Electric Lighting Equipment Mfg
335200 Household Appliance Mfg
335310 Electrical Equipment Mfg
335900 Other Electrical Equipment & Component Mfg

Transportation Equipment Manufacturing

336100 Motor Vehicle Mfg
336210 Motor Vehicle Body & Trailer Mfg
336300 Motor Vehicle Parts Mfg
336410 Aerospace Product & Parts Mfg
336510 Railroad Rolling Stock Mfg
336610 Ship & Boat Building
336990 Other Transportation Equipment Mfg

Furniture and Related Product Manufacturing

337000 Furniture & Related Product Manufacturing

Miscellaneous Manufacturing

339110 Medical Equipment & Supplies Mfg
339900 Other Miscellaneous Manufacturing

Wholesale Trade

Wholesale Trade, Durable Goods

421100 Motor Vehicle & Motor Vehicle Parts & Supplies Wholesalers
421200 Furniture & Home Furnishing Wholesalers
421300 Lumber & Other Construction Materials Wholesalers
421400 Professional & Commercial Equipment & Supplies Wholesalers
421500 Metal & Mineral (except Petroleum) Wholesalers
421600 Electrical Goods Wholesalers
421700 Hardware, & Plumbing & Heating Equipment & Supplies Wholesalers
421800 Machinery, Equipment, & Supplies Wholesalers
421910 Sporting & Recreational Goods & Supplies Wholesalers
421920 Toy & Hobby Goods & Supplies Wholesalers
421930 Recyclable Material Wholesalers
421940 Jewelry, Watch, Precious Stone, & Precious Metal Wholesalers
421990 Other Miscellaneous Durable Goods Wholesalers

Code

Wholesale Trade, Nondurable Goods
422100 Paper & Paper Product Wholesalers
422210 Drugs & Druggists' Sundries Wholesalers
422300 Apparel, Piece Goods, & Notions Wholesalers
422400 Grocery & Related Product Wholesalers
422500 Farm Product Raw Material Wholesalers
422600 Chemical & Allied Products Wholesalers
422700 Petroleum & Petroleum Products Wholesalers
422800 Beer, Wine, & Distilled Alcoholic Beverage Wholesalers
422910 Farm Supplies Wholesalers
422920 Book, Periodical, & Newspaper Wholesalers
422930 Flower, Nursery Stock, & Florists' Supplies Wholesalers
422940 Tobacco & Tobacco Product Wholesalers
422950 Paint, Varnish, & Supplies Wholesalers
422990 Other Miscellaneous Nondurable Goods Wholesalers

Retail Trade

Motor Vehicle and Parts Dealers
441110 New Car Dealers
441120 Used Car Dealers
441210 Recreational Vehicle Dealers
441221 Motorcycle Dealers
441222 Boat Dealers
441229 All Other Motor Vehicle Dealers
441300 Automotive Parts, Accessories, & Tire Stores

Furniture and Home Furnishings Stores
442110 Furniture Stores
442210 Floor Covering Stores
442291 Window Treatment Stores
442299 All Other Home Furnishings Stores

Electronics and Appliance Stores
443111 Household Appliance Stores
443112 Radio, Television, & Other Electronics Stores
443120 Computer & Software Stores
443130 Camera & Photographic Supplies Stores

Building Material and Garden Equipment and Supplies Dealers
444110 Home Centers
444120 Paint & Wallpaper Stores
444130 Hardware Stores
444190 Other Building Material Dealers
444200 Lawn & Garden Equipment & Supplies Stores

Food and Beverage Stores
445110 Supermarkets and Other Grocery (except Convenience) Stores
445120 Convenience Stores
445210 Meat Markets
445220 Fish & Seafood Markets
445230 Fruit & Vegetable Markets
445291 Baked Goods Stores
445292 Confectionery & Nut Stores
445299 All Other Specialty Food Stores
445310 Beer, Wine, & Liquor Stores

Health and Personal Care Stores
446110 Pharmacies & Drug Stores
446120 Cosmetics, Beauty Supplies, & Perfume Stores
446130 Optical Goods Stores
446190 Other Health & Personal Care Stores

Gasoline Stations
447100 Gasoline Stations (including convenience stores with gas)

Code

Clothing and Clothing Accessories Stores
448110 Men's Clothing Stores
448120 Women's Clothing Stores
448130 Children's & Infants' Clothing Stores
448140 Family Clothing Stores
448150 Clothing Accessories Stores
448190 Other Clothing Stores
448210 Shoe Stores
448310 Jewelry Stores
448320 Luggage & Leather Goods Stores

Sporting Goods, Hobby, Book, and Music Stores
451110 Sporting Goods Stores
451120 Hobby, Toy, & Game Stores
451130 Sewing, Needlework, & Piece Goods Stores
451140 Musical Instrument & Supplies Stores
451211 Book Stores
451212 News Dealers & Newsstands
451220 Prerecorded Tape, Compact Disc, & Record Stores

General Merchandise Stores
452110 Department stores
452900 Other General Merchandise Stores

Miscellaneous Store Retailers
453110 Florists
453210 Office Supplies & Stationery Stores
453220 Gift, Novelty, & Souvenir Stores
453310 Used Merchandise Stores
453910 Pet & Pet Supplies Stores
453920 Art Dealers
453930 Manufactured (Mobile) Home Dealers
453990 All Other Miscellaneous Store Retailers (including tobacco, candle, & trophy shops)

Nonstore Retailers
454110 Electronic Shopping & Mail-Order Houses
454210 Vending Machine Operators
454311 Heating Oil Dealers
454312 Liquefied Petroleum Gas (Bottled Gas) Dealers
454319 Other Fuel Dealers
454390 Other Direct Selling Establishments (including door-to-door retailing, frozen food plan providers, party plan merchandisers, & coffee-break service providers)

Transportation and Warehousing

Air, Rail, and Water Transportation
481000 Air Transportation
482110 Rail Transportation
483000 Water Transportation

Truck Transportation
484110 General Freight Trucking, Local
484120 General Freight Trucking, Long-distance
484200 Specialized Freight Trucking

Transit and Ground Passenger Transportation
485110 Urban Transit Systems
485210 Interurban & Rural Bus Transportation
485310 Taxi Service
485320 Limousine Service
485410 School & Employee Bus Transportation
485510 Charter Bus Industry
485990 Other Transit & Ground Passenger Transportation

Pipeline Transportation
486000 Pipeline Transportation

Scenic & Sightseeing Transportation
487000 Scenic & Sightseeing Transportation

Code

Support Activities for Transportation
488100 Support Activities for Air Transportation
488210 Support Activities for Rail Transportation
488300 Support Activities for Water Transportation
488410 Motor Vehicle Towing
488490 Other Support Activities for Road Transportation
488510 Freight Transportation Arrangement
488990 Other Support Activities for Transportation

Couriers and Messengers
492110 Couriers
492210 Local Messengers & Local Delivery

Warehousing and Storage
493100 Warehousing & Storage (except lessors of miniwarehouses & self-storage units)

Information

Publishing Industries
511110 Newspaper Publishers
511120 Periodical Publishers
511130 Book Publishers
511140 Database & Directory Publishers
511190 Other Publishers
511210 Software Publishers

Motion Picture and Sound Recording Industries
512100 Motion Picture & Video Industries (except video rental)
512200 Sound Recording Industries

Broadcasting and Telecommunications
513100 Radio & Television Broadcasting
513200 Cable Networks & Program Distribution
513300 Telecommunications (including paging, cellular, satellite, & other telecommunications)

Information Services and Data Processing Services
514100 Information Services (including news syndicates, libraries, & on-line information services)
514210 Data Processing Services

Finance and Insurance

Depository Credit Intermediation
522110 Commercial Banking
522120 Savings Institutions
522130 Credit Unions
522190 Other Depository Credit Intermediation

Nondepository Credit Intermediation
522210 Credit Card Issuing
522220 Sales Financing
522291 Consumer Lending
522292 Real Estate Credit (including mortgage bankers & originators)
522293 International Trade Financing
522294 Secondary Market Financing
522298 All Other Nondepository Credit Intermediation

Activities Related to Credit Intermediation
522300 Activities Related to Credit Intermediation (including loan brokers)

Securities, Commodity Contracts, and Other Financial Investments and Related Activities
523110 Investment Banking & Securities Dealing
523120 Securities Brokerage
523130 Commodity Contracts Dealing
523140 Commodity Contracts Brokerage

Code

523210 Securities & Commodity Exchanges
523900 Other Financial Investment Activities (including portfolio management & investment advice)

Insurance Carriers and Related Activities
524140 Direct Life, Health, & Medical Insurance & Reinsurance Carriers
524150 Direct Insurance & Reinsurance (except Life, Health & Medical) Carriers
524210 Insurance Agencies & Brokerages
524290 Other Insurance Related Activities

Funds, Trusts, and Other Financial Vehicles
525100 Insurance & Employee Benefit Funds
525910 Open-End Investment Funds (Form 1120-RIC)
525920 Trusts, Estates, & Agency Accounts
525930 Real Estate Investment Trusts (Form 1120-REIT)
525990 Other Financial Vehicles

For 551111 "Offices of Bank Holding Companies" and 551112 "Offices of Other Holding Companies," see **Management of Companies (Holding Companies)** on the next page.

Real Estate and Rental and Leasing

Real Estate
531110 Lessors of Residential Buildings & Dwellings
531114 Cooperative Housing
531120 Lessors of Nonresidential Buildings (except Miniwarehouses)
531130 Lessors of Miniwarehouses & Self-Storage Units
531190 Lessors of Other Real Estate Property
531210 Offices of Real Estate Agents & Brokers
531310 Real Estate Property Managers
531320 Offices of Real Estate Appraisers
531390 Other Activities Related to Real Estate

Rental and Leasing Services
532100 Automotive Equipment Rental & Leasing
532210 Consumer Electronics & Appliances Rental
532220 Formal Wear & Costume Rental
532230 Video Tape & Disc Rental
532290 Other Consumer Goods Rental
532310 General Rental Centers
532400 Commercial & Industrial Machinery & Equipment Rental & Leasing

Lessors of Nonfinancial Intangible Assets (except copyrighted works)
533110 Lessors of Nonfinancial Intangible Assets (except copyrighted works)

Professional, Scientific, and Technical Services

Legal Services
541110 Offices of Lawyers
541190 Other Legal Services

Accounting, Tax Preparation, Bookkeeping, and Payroll Services
541211 Offices of Certified Public Accountants
541213 Tax Preparation Services
541214 Payroll Services
541219 Other Accounting Services

Architectural, Engineering, and Related Services
541310 Architectural Services

Code	
541320	Landscape Architecture Services
541330	Engineering Services
541340	Drafting Services
541350	Building Inspection Services
541360	Geophysical Surveying & Mapping Services
541370	Surveying & Mapping (except Geophysical) Services
541380	Testing Laboratories

Specialized Design Services

Code	
541400	Specialized Design Services (including interior, industrial, graphic, & fashion design)

Computer Systems Design and Related Services

Code	
541511	Custom Computer Programming Services
541512	Computer Systems Design Services
541513	Computer Facilities Management Services
541519	Other Computer Related Services

Other Professional, Scientific, and Technical Services

Code	
541600	Management, Scientific, & Technical Consulting Services
541700	Scientific Research & Development Services
541800	Advertising & Related Services
541910	Marketing Research & Public Opinion Polling
541920	Photographic Services
541930	Translation & Interpretation Services
541940	Veterinary Services
541990	All Other Professional, Scientific, & Technical Services

Management of Companies (Holding Companies)

Code	
551111	Offices of Bank Holding Companies
551112	Offices of Other Holding Companies

Administrative and Support and Waste Management and Remediation Services

Administrative and Support Services

Code	
561110	Office Administrative Services
561210	Facilities Support Services
561300	Employment Services
561410	Document Preparation Services
561420	Telephone Call Centers
561430	Business Service Centers (including private mail centers & copy shops)
561440	Collection Agencies
561450	Credit Bureaus
561490	Other Business Support Services (including repossession services, court reporting, & stenotype services)
561500	Travel Arrangement & Reservation Services
561600	Investigation & Security Services
561710	Exterminating & Pest Control Services
561720	Janitorial Services
561730	Landscaping Services
561740	Carpet & Upholstery Cleaning Services
561790	Other Services to Buildings & Dwellings
561900	Other Support Services (including packaging & labeling services, & convention & trade show organizers)

Waste Management and Remediation Services

Code	
562000	Waste Management & Remediation Services

Educational Services

Code	
611000	Educational Services (including schools, colleges, & universities)

Health Care and Social Assistance

Offices of Physicians and Dentists

Code	
621111	Offices of Physicians (except mental health specialists)
621112	Offices of Physicians, Mental Health Specialists
621210	Offices of Dentists

Offices of Other Health Practitioners

Code	
621310	Offices of Chiropractors
621320	Offices of Optometrists
621330	Offices of Mental Health Practitioners (except Physicians)
621340	Offices of Physical, Occupational & Speech Therapists, & Audiologists
621391	Offices of Podiatrists
621399	Offices of All Other Miscellaneous Health Practitioners

Outpatient Care Centers

Code	
621410	Family Planning Centers
621420	Outpatient Mental Health & Substance Abuse Centers
621491	HMO Medical Centers
621492	Kidney Dialysis Centers
621493	Freestanding Ambulatory Surgical & Emergency Centers
621498	All Other Outpatient Care Centers

Medical and Diagnostic Laboratories

Code	
621510	Medical & Diagnostic Laboratories

Home Health Care Services

Code	
621610	Home Health Care Services

Other Ambulatory Health Care Services

Code	
621900	Other Ambulatory Health Care Services (including ambulance services & blood & organ banks)

Hospitals

Code	
622000	Hospitals

Nursing and Residential Care Facilities

Code	
623000	Nursing & Residential Care Facilities

Social Assistance

Code	
624100	Individual & Family Services
624200	Community Food & Housing, & Emergency & Other Relief Services
624310	Vocational Rehabilitation Services
624410	Child Day Care Services

Arts, Entertainment, and Recreation

Performing Arts, Spectator Sports, and Related Industries

Code	
711100	Performing Arts Companies
711210	Spectator Sports (including sports clubs & racetracks)
711300	Promoters of Performing Arts, Sports, & Similar Events
711410	Agents & Managers for Artists, Athletes, Entertainers, & Other Public Figures
711510	Independent Artists, Writers, & Performers

Museums, Historical Sites, and Similar Institutions

Code	
712100	Museums, Historical Sites, & Similar Institutions

Amusement, Gambling, and Recreation Industries

Code	
713100	Amusement Parks & Arcades
713200	Gambling Industries
713900	Other Amusement & Recreation Industries (including golf courses, skiing facilities, marinas, fitness centers, & bowling centers)

Accommodation and Food Services

Accommodation

Code	
721110	Hotels (except casino hotels) & Motels
721120	Casino Hotels
721191	Bed & Breakfast Inns
721199	All Other Traveler Accommodation
721210	RV (Recreational Vehicle) Parks & Recreational Camps
721310	Rooming & Boarding Houses

Food Services and Drinking Places

Code	
722110	Full-Service Restaurants
722210	Limited-Service Eating Places
722300	Special Food Services (including food service contractors & caterers)
722410	Drinking Places (Alcoholic Beverages)

Other Services

Repair and Maintenance

Code	
811110	Automotive Mechanical & Electrical Repair & Maintenance
811120	Automotive Body, Paint, Interior, & Glass Repair
811190	Other Automotive Repair & Maintenance (including oil change & lubrication shops & car washes)
811210	Electronic & Precision Equipment Repair & Maintenance
811310	Commercial & Industrial Machinery & Equipment (except Automotive & Electronic) Repair & Maintenance
811410	Home & Garden Equipment & Appliance Repair & Maintenance
811420	Reupholstery & Furniture Repair
811430	Footwear & Leather Goods Repair
811490	Other Personal & Household Goods Repair & Maintenance

Personal and Laundry Services

Code	
812111	Barber Shops
812112	Beauty Salons
812113	Nail Salons
812190	Other Personal Care Services (including diet & weight reducing centers)
812210	Funeral Homes & Funeral Services
812220	Cemeteries & Crematories
812310	Coin-Operated Laundries & Drycleaners
812320	Drycleaning & Laundry Services (except Coin-Operated)
812330	Linen & Uniform Supply
812910	Pet Care (except Veterinary) Services
812920	Photofinishing
812930	Parking Lots & Garages
812990	All Other Personal Services

Religious, Grantmaking, Civic, Professional, and Similar Organizations

Code	
813000	Religious, Grantmaking, Civic, Professional, & Similiar Organizations (including condominium and homeowners associations)

Index

APPENDIX D
LIMITED LIABILITY COMPANY DOCUMENTS AND FORMS

These forms refer to *partnerships* and *partners*. Because partnership is the default classification of LLCs, they apply to LLCs also. In other words, read *member* for *partner* and *limited liability company* for *partnership*.

LLC FORMS TO FILE WITH YOUR STATE

To facilitate comparison of S corporations and LLCs, we continued to use Virginia forms as examples. That is, you can compare the forms for S corporations and LLCs in the same state, and you can compare two states by comparing these forms with those in the example in Chapter 6.

As for S corporations, check with the secretary of state or other appropriate agency in your state for the forms and instructions. It will be the same state agency for both S corporations and LLCs.

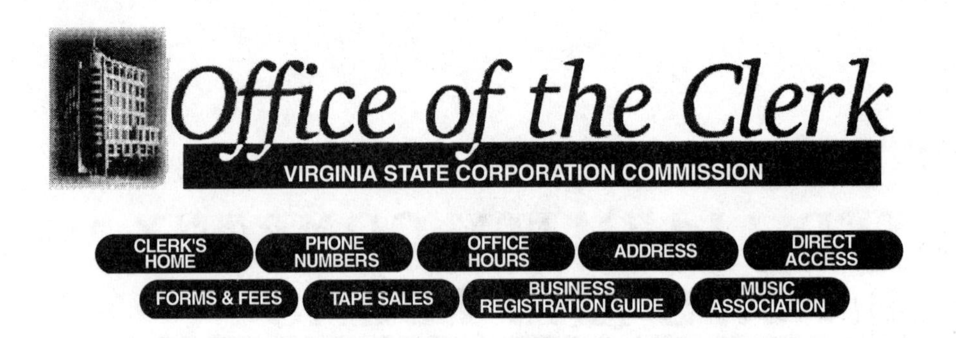

Limited Liability Company Form/Fee Schedule

SCC FORM #	TITLE OF FORM LIMITED LIABILITY COMPANIES	FILING FEE (IF APPLICABLE) & COMMENTS
LLC-1010.1	**Conversion of Partnership to Limited Liability Company**	$100
LLC-1011	**Articles of Organization**	$100
LLC-1011.1	**Guide For Certificate of Correction to The Articles of Organization of a Domestic Limited Liability Company**	$25
LLC-1013	**Application for Reservation or Renewal of Reservation of Limited Liability Company Name**	$10 for Reservation, effective for 120 days $10 for Renewal of Reservation, renewal can be filed up to 30 days prior to expiration of reservation
LLC-1014	**Guide for Articles of Amendment to Articles of Organization or Amended and Restated Articles of Organization**	$25
LLC-1016	**Statement of Change of Registered Agent/Registered Office of a Limited Liability Company**	No fee. Contact the Clerk's Office to obtain a pre-printed form LLC-1016.
LLC-1017	**Statement of Resignation of Registered Agent of a Limited Liability Company**	No fee.
LLC-1050	**Certificate of Cancellation of Limited Liability Company**	$25

LLC-1050.1	**Articles of Reinstatement of a Domestic Limited Liability Company (Voluntarily Canceled)**	Contact the Clerk's Office Call Center for filing fee inquiries.
LLC-1052	**Application for Registration as a Foreign Limited Liability Company**	$100
LLC-1055	**Certificate of Correction for a Foreign Limited Liability Company**	$25
LLC-1056	**Cancellation of Certificate of Registration as a Foreign Limited Liability Company**	$25
LLC-1103	**Articles of Organization for a Professional Limited Liability Company**	$100

(07/2000)

LLC-1011
(07/00)

COMMONWEALTH OF VIRGINIA
STATE CORPORATION COMMISSION

ARTICLES OF ORGANIZATION OF A DOMESTIC LIMITED LIABILITY COMPANY

Pursuant to Chapter 12 of Title 13.1 of the Code of Virginia the undersigned states as follows:

1. The name of the limited liability company is

____.

(The name must contain the words "limited company" or "limited liability company" or their abbreviations "L.C.", "LC", "L.L.C." or "LLC")

2. A. The registered agent's name is _______________________________
whose business office is identical with the registered office.

B. The registered agent is (mark appropriate box)
(1) an <u>INDIVIDUAL</u> who is a resident of Virginia **and**
[ ] a member/manager of the limited liability company
[ ] an officer/director of a corporate member/manager of the limited liability company
[ ] a general partner of a general or limited partnership member/manager of the limited liability company
[ ] a trustee of a trust that is a member of the limited liability company
[ ] a member of the Virginia State Bar

OR

(2) [ ] a professional corporation, professional limited liability company or registered limited liability partnership registered with the Virginia State Bar under § 54.1-3902 of the Code of Virginia.

3. The address of the initial registered office in Virginia is

____
(number/street)

_______________________________ VA ______________,
(city or town) (zip)

located in the [ ] city **or** [ ] county of _______________________________.

4. The post office address of the principal office is

____
(number/street)

____
(city or town) (state) (zip)

5. Signature:

_______________________________ _______________
(organizer) (date)

____
(printed name)

SEE INSTRUCTIONS ON THE REVERSE

INSTRUCTIONS

§ 13.1-1003 of the Code of Virginia requires that this document be in the English language, typewritten or printed in black, legible and reproducible.

The registered office must include the complete post office address, including a street address, if any, or a rural route and box number. Also, state the name of the city or county in which the office is physically located. Cities and counties in Virginia are separate local jurisdictions.

The document must be executed in the name of the limited liability company by the person forming the company (see § 13.1-1003 of the Code of Virginia).

Submit the original articles to the Clerk of the State Corporation Commission, 1300 E. Main Street, Tyler Building, 1st Floor, Richmond, Virginia 23219 or P. O. Box 1197, Richmond, Virginia 23218-1197, along with a filing fee check for **$100.00** payable to the State Corporation Commission. **PLEASE DO NOT SEND CASH**. If you have questions, call (804) 371-9733.

LLC-1010.1
(07/00)

COMMONWEALTH OF VIRGINIA
STATE CORPORATION COMMISSION

ARTICLES OF ORGANIZATION FOR CONVERSION OF A DOMESTIC OR FOREIGN PARTNERSHIP OR LIMITED PARTNERSHIP TO A LIMITED LIABILITY COMPANY

Pursuant to Chapter 12 of Title 13.1 of the Code of Virginia the undersigned states as follows:

1. The name of the former [ ] partnership **or** [ ] limited partnership is **(mark one)**

____.

2. If the former partnership or limited partnership is a registered limited liability partnership, the date and place of filing of the initial registration as or statement of registered limited liability partnership are

date: ____________________; place of filing: ______________________________.

3. The name of the limited liability company is

____.

(The name must contain the words "limited company" or "limited liability company" or their abbreviations "L.C.," "LC," "L.L.C.," or "LLC.")

4. A. The registered agent's name is ______________________________
whose business office is identical with the registered office.

B. The registered agent is (mark appropriate box)
(1) an <u>INDIVIDUAL</u> who is a resident of Virginia <u>**and**</u>
[ ] a member/manager of the limited liability company
[ ] an officer/director of a corporate member/manager of the limited liability company
[ ] a general partner of a general or limited partnership member/manager of the limited liability company
[ ] a trustee of a trust that is a member of the limited liability company
[ ] a member of the Virginia State Bar

OR

(2) [ ] a professional corporation, professional limited liability company or registered limited liability partnership registered with the Virginia State Bar under § 54.1-3902 of the Code of Virginia.

5. The address of the initial registered office in Virginia is

____
(number/street)

_______________________________ VA ______________,
(city or town) (zip)

located in the [ ] city **or** [ ] county of ______________________________.

6. The post office address of the principal office is

____
(number/street)

____
(city or town) (state) (zip)

7. Signature:

______________________________ ______________________
(organizer) (date)

____
(printed name)

SEE INSTRUCTIONS ON THE REVERSE

INSTRUCTIONS

§ 13.1-1003 of the Code of Virginia requires that this document be in the English language, typewritten or printed in black, legible and reproducible.

The registered office address must include the complete post office address, including a street address, if any, or a rural route and box number. Also, state the name of the city or county in which the office is physically located. Cities and counties in Virginia are separate local jurisdictions.

The document must be executed in the name of the limited liability company by the person forming the company (see § 13.1-1003 of the Code of Virginia).

Submit the original articles to the Clerk of the State Corporation Commission, 1300 E. Main Street, Tyler Building, 1st Floor, Richmond, Virginia 23219 or P.O. Box 1197, Richmond, Virginia 23218-1197, along with a filing fee check for **$100.00** payable to the State Corporation Commission. **PLEASE DO NOT SEND CASH**. If you have questions, call (804) 371-9733.

CHECKLIST FOR PREPARATION OF OPERATING AGREEMENT BETWEEN MEMBERS OF A LIMITED LIABILITY COMPANY (LLC)

This checklist is designed for use by prospective members of an LLC. Your attorney may have other questions and should incorporate technical aspect of partnership taxation into the final agreement.

____ 1. Name of LLC.

____ 2. Address and telephone number of principal office.

____ 3. Employer identification number, if already assigned by IRS.

____ 4. Date on which company will terminate (this may not be necessary to list in all states).

____ 5. Initial manager(s) of the company.

____ 6. Registered agent (usually this is the company's attorney).

____ 7. Description of business (this may or may not be necessary for state registration purposes, but it needs to be in your attorney's file).

____ 8. The names of the members, the percentage of interest in the LLC each is to have, and the amount of capital each is to contribute (percentage of interest and capital contributions do not have to be equal between members).

____ 9. Type of contribution of each member (cash, personal property, real estate, or services). For property, include description and fair market value. For services, specify extent in terms of results or time.

____ 10. Distribution of items of income and loss (a list of each member with the percentage of each item):

a. Operating income.

b. Operating loss.

c. Gain from sale of assets.

d. Loss from sale of assets.

____ 11. Voting rights regarding:

a. Selection of management.

b. Distributions to members.

____ 12. Description of management areas

a. Description of routine functions about which management is to make decisions.

b. Major areas on which entire membership (or a fraction of membership) is to make decisions (acquisition and sales of major assets, substantial contractual arrangements, etc.).

____ 13. Compensation of managers who are also members.

____ 14. Restrictions, if any, on members engaging in competitive or related businesses.

____ 15. Restrictions, if any, on members dealing at arms-length with the LLC.

____ 16. Designation of "tax-matters partner." (IRS requires this name to be recorded on the annual partnership return. It is the person the IRS will contact in the event of audit or other tax matter.)

____ 17. Restrictions on transfer of member interests (required to qualify for partnership taxation).

____ 18. Events that will terminate the LLC and optional procedure for continuing the LLC instead of terminating it (be certain they meet minimum requirements for taxation as partnership).

____ 19. Events that will cause a member's interest to be bought by the LLC (such as death, insolvency, incompetency, or other specified event).

____ 20. How to compute the price at which a member's interest would be purchased by the LLC.

____ 21. Method by which operating agreement can be amended.

THE IRS FORMS

If the LLC is a new business, it will need to file a Form SS-4, Application for Employer Identification Number. On the other hand, if it's an existing partnership converting to an LLC, the IRS will view it as a continuing partnership, so no new Form SS-4 is necessary. If you're a sole proprietor converting to an LLC (in those states that permit that), the IRS will still consider you a sole proprietorship so you continue using the same identification number and do not file a Form SS-4.

If you are converting a corporation to an LLC, that involves liquidating the corporation and starting a new enterprise as an LLC (partnership to the IRS). You then need to file a Form SS-4 to obtain a new identification number for your new partnership. Of course, if you are the sole stockholder of your corporation and are converting to an LLC, you'll need an identification number as a sole proprietorship.

Remember that the fact that the IRS views your LLC as a partnership or a sole proprietorship does not affect the limited liability of the LLC. Limited liability is generally determined by state statute, while the IRS is concerned with liability for federal taxes.

For an LLC, there is no equivalent of a Form 2553 that elects S corporation tax status. Filing the first partnership income tax return establishes your partnership with the IRS.

Form **1065**
Department of the Treasury
Internal Revenue Service

U.S. Return of Partnership Income

For calendar year 2000, or tax year beginning .... , 2000, and ending .... , 20.... .
▶ See separate instructions.

OMB No. 1545-0099

2000

A Principal business activity	Use the IRS label. Otherwise, print or type.	Name of partnership	D Employer identification number
B Principal product or service		Number, street, and room or suite no. If a P.O. box, see page 13 of the instructions.	E Date business started
C Business code number		City or town, state, and ZIP code	F Total assets (see page 13 of the instructions) $

G Check applicable boxes: (1) ☐ Initial return (2) ☐ Final return (3) ☐ Change in address (4) ☐ Amended return
H Check accounting method: (1) ☐ Cash (2) ☐ Accrual (3) ☐ Other (specify) ▶..........
I Number of Schedules K-1. Attach one for each person who was a partner at any time during the tax year ▶..........

Caution: *Include **only** trade or business income and expenses on lines 1a through 22 below. See the instructions for more information.*

Income	1a	Gross receipts or sales	1a			
	b	Less returns and allowances	1b		1c	
	2	Cost of goods sold (Schedule A, line 8)			2	
	3	Gross profit. Subtract line 2 from line 1c			3	
	4	Ordinary income (loss) from other partnerships, estates, and trusts *(attach schedule)*			4	
	5	Net farm profit (loss) *(attach Schedule F (Form 1040))*			5	
	6	Net gain (loss) from Form 4797, Part II, line 18			6	
	7	Other income (loss) *(attach schedule)*			7	
	8	**Total income (loss).** Combine lines 3 through 7			8	
Deductions (see page 14 of the instructions for limitations)	9	Salaries and wages (other than to partners) (less employment credits)			9	
	10	Guaranteed payments to partners			10	
	11	Repairs and maintenance			11	
	12	Bad debts			12	
	13	Rent			13	
	14	Taxes and licenses			14	
	15	Interest			15	
	16a	Depreciation (if required, attach Form 4562)	16a			
	b	Less depreciation reported on Schedule A and elsewhere on return	16b		16c	
	17	Depletion **(Do not deduct oil and gas depletion.)**			17	
	18	Retirement plans, etc.			18	
	19	Employee benefit programs			19	
	20	Other deductions *(attach schedule)*			20	
	21	**Total deductions.** Add the amounts shown in the far right column for lines 9 through 20			21	
	22	**Ordinary income (loss)** from trade or business activities. Subtract line 21 from line 8			22	

Sign Here

Under penalties of perjury, I declare that I have examined this return, including accompanying schedules and statements, and to the best of my knowledge and belief, it is true, correct, and complete. Declaration of preparer (other than general partner or limited liability company member) is based on all information of which preparer has any knowledge.

▶ Signature of general partner or limited liability company member ▶ Date

Paid Preparer's Use Only

Preparer's signature ▶	Date	Check if self-employed ▶ ☐	Preparer's SSN or PTIN
Firm's name (or yours if self-employed), address, and ZIP code ▶		EIN ▶	
		Phone no. ( )	

For Paperwork Reduction Act Notice, see separate instructions. Cat. No. 11390Z Form **1065** (2000)

Form 1065 (2000) Page 2

Schedule A **Cost of Goods Sold** (see page 17 of the instructions)

1	Inventory at beginning of year	1	
2	Purchases less cost of items withdrawn for personal use	2	
3	Cost of labor	3	
4	Additional section 263A costs *(attach schedule)*	4	
5	Other costs *(attach schedule)*	5	
6	**Total.** Add lines 1 through 5	6	
7	Inventory at end of year	7	
8	**Cost of goods sold.** Subtract line 7 from line 6. Enter here and on page 1, line 2	8	

9a Check all methods used for valuing closing inventory:

(i) ☐ Cost as described in Regulations section 1.471-3

(ii) ☐ Lower of cost or market as described in Regulations section 1.471-4

(iii) ☐ Other (specify method used and attach explanation) ▶ ....

b Check this box if there was a writedown of "subnormal" goods as described in Regulations section 1.471-2(c). ▶ ☐

c Check this box if the LIFO inventory method was adopted this tax year for any goods *(if checked, attach Form 970)*. ▶ ☐

d Do the rules of section 263A (for property produced or acquired for resale) apply to the partnership? ☐ **Yes** ☐ **No**

e Was there any change in determining quantities, cost, or valuations between opening and closing inventory? ☐ **Yes** ☐ **No**
If "Yes," attach explanation.

Schedule B **Other Information**

		Yes	No
1	What type of entity is filing this return? Check the applicable box: **a** ☐ Domestic general partnership **b** ☐ Domestic limited partnership **c** ☐ Domestic limited liability company **d** ☐ Domestic limited liability partnership **e** ☐ Foreign partnership **f** ☐ Other ▶		
2	Are any partners in this partnership also partnerships?		
3	During the partnership's tax year, did the partnership own any interest in another partnership or in any foreign entity that was disregarded as an entity separate from its owner under Regulations sections 301.7701-2 and 301.7701-3? If yes, see instructions for required attachment		
4	Is this partnership subject to the consolidated audit procedures of sections 6221 through 6233? If "Yes," see **Designation of Tax Matters Partner** below		
5	Does this partnership meet **all three** of the following requirements? **a** The partnership's total receipts for the tax year were less than $250,000; **b** The partnership's total assets at the end of the tax year were less than $600,000; **and** **c** Schedules K-1 are filed with the return and furnished to the partners on or before the due date (including extensions) for the partnership return. If "Yes," the partnership is not required to complete Schedules L, M-1, and M-2; Item F on page 1 of Form 1065; or Item J on Schedule K-1		
6	Does this partnership have any foreign partners?		
7	Is this partnership a publicly traded partnership as defined in section 469(k)(2)?		
8	Has this partnership filed, or is it required to file, **Form 8264,** Application for Registration of a Tax Shelter?		
9	At any time during calendar year 2000, did the partnership have an interest in or a signature or other authority over a financial account in a foreign country (such as a bank account, securities account, or other financial account)? See page 19 of the instructions for exceptions and filing requirements for Form TD F 90-22.1. If "Yes," enter the name of the foreign country. ▶		
10	During the tax year, did the partnership receive a distribution from, or was it the grantor of, or transferor to, a foreign trust? If "Yes," the partnership may have to file Form 3520. See page 19 of the instructions		
11	Was there a distribution of property or a transfer (e.g., by sale or death) of a partnership interest during the tax year? If "Yes," you may elect to adjust the basis of the partnership's assets under section 754 by attaching the statement described under **Elections Made By the Partnership** on page 7 of the instructions		
12	Enter the number of Forms 8865 attached to this return ▶		

Designation of Tax Matters Partner (see page 19 of the instructions)

Enter below the general partner designated as the tax matters partner (TMP) for the tax year of this return:

Name of designated TMP ▶ Identifying number of TMP ▶

Address of designated TMP ▶

Form **1065** (2000)

Form 1065 (2000) Page 3

Schedule K — Partners' Shares of Income, Credits, Deductions, etc.

	(a) Distributive share items		(b) Total amount
Income (Loss)	1 Ordinary income (loss) from trade or business activities (page 1, line 22)	1	
	2 Net income (loss) from rental real estate activities *(attach Form 8825)*	2	
	3a Gross income from other rental activities — 3a		
	b Expenses from other rental activities *(attach schedule)* — 3b		
	c Net income (loss) from other rental activities. Subtract line 3b from line 3a	3c	
	4 Portfolio income (loss): a Interest income	4a	
	b Ordinary dividends	4b	
	c Royalty income	4c	
	d Net short-term capital gain (loss) *(attach Schedule D (Form 1065))*	4d	
	e Net long-term capital gain (loss) *(attach Schedule D (Form 1065))*:		
	(1) 28% rate gain (loss) ▶ .... (2) Total for year ▶	4e(2)	
	f Other portfolio income (loss) *(attach schedule)*	4f	
	5 Guaranteed payments to partners	5	
	6 Net section 1231 gain (loss) (other than due to casualty or theft) *(attach Form 4797)*	6	
	7 Other income (loss) *(attach schedule)*	7	
Deductions	8 Charitable contributions *(attach schedule)*	8	
	9 Section 179 expense deduction *(attach Form 4562)*	9	
	10 Deductions related to portfolio income (itemize)	10	
	11 Other deductions *(attach schedule)*	11	
Credits	12a Low-income housing credit:		
	(1) From partnerships to which section 42(j)(5) applies for property placed in service before 1990	12a(1)	
	(2) Other than on line 12a(1) for property placed in service before 1990	12a(2)	
	(3) From partnerships to which section 42(j)(5) applies for property placed in service after 1989	12a(3)	
	(4) Other than on line 12a(3) for property placed in service after 1989	12a(4)	
	b Qualified rehabilitation expenditures related to rental real estate activities *(attach Form 3468)*	12b	
	c Credits (other than credits shown on lines 12a and 12b) related to rental real estate activities	12c	
	d Credits related to other rental activities	12d	
	13 Other credits	13	
Investment Interest	14a Interest expense on investment debts	14a	
	b (1) Investment income included on lines 4a, 4b, 4c, and 4f above	14b(1)	
	(2) Investment expenses included on line 10 above	14b(2)	
Self-Employment	15a Net earnings (loss) from self-employment	15a	
	b Gross farming or fishing income	15b	
	c Gross nonfarm income	15c	
Adjustments and Tax Preference Items	16a Depreciation adjustment on property placed in service after 1986	16a	
	b Adjusted gain or loss	16b	
	c Depletion (other than oil and gas)	16c	
	d (1) Gross income from oil, gas, and geothermal properties	16d(1)	
	(2) Deductions allocable to oil, gas, and geothermal properties	16d(2)	
	e Other adjustments and tax preference items *(attach schedule)*	16e	
Foreign Taxes	17a Name of foreign country or U.S. possession ▶		
	b Gross income sourced at partner level	17b	
	c Foreign gross income sourced at partnership level:		
	(1) Passive ▶ ...... (2) Listed categories *(attach schedule)* ▶ ...... (3) General limitation ▶	17c(3)	
	d Deductions allocated and apportioned at partner level:		
	(1) Interest expense ▶ ...... (2) Other ▶	17d(2)	
	e Deductions allocated and apportioned at partnership level to foreign source income:		
	(1) Passive ▶ ...... (2) Listed categories *(attach schedule)* ▶ ...... (3) General limitation ▶	17e(3)	
	f Total foreign taxes (check one): ▶ Paid ☐ Accrued ☐	17f	
	g Reduction in taxes available for credit and gross income from all sources *(attach schedule)*	17g	
Other	18 Section 59(e)(2) expenditures: a Type ▶ ...... b Amount ▶	18b	
	19 Tax-exempt interest income	19	
	20 Other tax-exempt income	20	
	21 Nondeductible expenses	21	
	22 Distributions of money (cash and marketable securities)	22	
	23 Distributions of property other than money	23	
	24 Other items and amounts required to be reported separately to partners *(attach schedule)*		

Form **1065** (2000)

Form 1065 (2000) Page **4**

Analysis of Net Income (Loss)

1 Net income (loss). Combine Schedule K, lines 1 through 7 in column (b). From the result, subtract the sum of Schedule K, lines 8 through 11, 14a, 17f, and 18b						**1**	
2 Analysis by partner type:	**(i)** Corporate	**(ii)** Individual (active)	**(iii)** Individual (passive)	**(iv)** Partnership	**(v)** Exempt organization	**(vi)** Nominee/Other	
a General partners							
b Limited partners							

Schedule L — Balance Sheets per Books (Not required if Question 5 on Schedule B is answered "Yes.")

Assets	Beginning of tax year (a)	Beginning of tax year (b)	End of tax year (c)	End of tax year (d)
1 Cash				
2a Trade notes and accounts receivable				
b Less allowance for bad debts				
3 Inventories				
4 U.S. government obligations				
5 Tax-exempt securities				
6 Other current assets *(attach schedule)*				
7 Mortgage and real estate loans				
8 Other investments *(attach schedule)*				
9a Buildings and other depreciable assets				
b Less accumulated depreciation				
10a Depletable assets				
b Less accumulated depletion				
11 Land (net of any amortization)				
12a Intangible assets (amortizable only)				
b Less accumulated amortization				
13 Other assets *(attach schedule)*				
14 **Total** assets				
Liabilities and Capital				
15 Accounts payable				
16 Mortgages, notes, bonds payable in less than 1 year				
17 Other current liabilities *(attach schedule)*				
18 All nonrecourse loans				
19 Mortgages, notes, bonds payable in 1 year or more				
20 Other liabilities *(attach schedule)*				
21 Partners' capital accounts				
22 **Total** liabilities and capital				

Schedule M-1 — Reconciliation of Income (Loss) per Books With Income (Loss) per Return

(Not required if Question 5 on Schedule B is answered "Yes." See page 30 of the instructions.)

1 Net income (loss) per books		**6** Income recorded on books this year not included on Schedule K, lines 1 through 7 (itemize): **a** Tax-exempt interest $	
2 Income included on Schedule K, lines 1 through 4, 6, and 7, not recorded on books this year (itemize):		**7** Deductions included on Schedule K, lines 1 through 11, 14a, 17f, and 18b, not charged against book income this year (itemize): **a** Depreciation $	
3 Guaranteed payments (other than health insurance)			
4 Expenses recorded on books this year not included on Schedule K, lines 1 through 11, 14a, 17f, and 18b (itemize): **a** Depreciation $ **b** Travel and entertainment $		**8** Add lines 6 and 7	
		9 Income (loss) (Analysis of Net Income (Loss), line 1). Subtract line 8 from line 5	
5 Add lines 1 through 4			

Schedule M-2 — Analysis of Partners' Capital Accounts (Not required if Question 5 on Schedule B is answered "Yes.")

1 Balance at beginning of year		**6** Distributions: **a** Cash	
2 Capital contributed during year		**b** Property	
3 Net income (loss) per books		**7** Other decreases (itemize):	
4 Other increases (itemize):			
		8 Add lines 6 and 7	
5 Add lines 1 through 4		**9** Balance at end of year. Subtract line 8 from line 5	

Form **1065** (2000)

SCHEDULE K-1 (Form 1065)
Department of the Treasury
Internal Revenue Service

Partner's Share of Income, Credits, Deductions, etc.

▶ See separate instructions.

For calendar year 2000 or tax year beginning , 2000, and ending , 20

OMB No. 1545-0099

2000

Partner's identifying number ▶

Partner's name, address, and ZIP code

Partnership's identifying number ▶

Partnership's name, address, and ZIP code

A This partner is a ☐ general partner ☐ limited partner ☐ limited liability company member

B What type of entity is this partner? ▶

C Is this partner a ☐ domestic or a ☐ foreign partner?

D Enter partner's percentage of:

	(i) Before change or termination	(ii) End of year
Profit sharing	%	%
Loss sharing	%	%
Ownership of capital	%	%

E IRS Center where partnership filed return:

F Partner's share of liabilities (see instructions):

Nonrecourse . . . . $

Qualified nonrecourse financing . $

Other . . . . $

G Tax shelter registration number . ▶

H Check here if this partnership is a publicly traded partnership as defined in section 469(k)(2) . . . . . ☐

I Check applicable boxes: (1) ☐ Final K-1 (2) ☐ Amended K-1

J Analysis of partner's capital account:

(a) Capital account at beginning of year	(b) Capital contributed during year	(c) Partner's share of lines 3, 4, and 7, Form 1065, Schedule M-2	(d) Withdrawals and distributions	(e) Capital account at end of year (combine columns (a) through (d))
			( )	

		(a) Distributive share item		(b) Amount	(c) 1040 filers enter the amount in column (b) on:
Income (Loss)	1	Ordinary income (loss) from trade or business activities	1		See page 6 of Partner's Instructions for Schedule K-1 (Form 1065).
	2	Net income (loss) from rental real estate activities	2		
	3	Net income (loss) from other rental activities	3		
	4	Portfolio income (loss):			
	a	Interest	4a		Sch. B, Part I, line 1
	b	Ordinary dividends	4b		Sch. B, Part II, line 5
	c	Royalties	4c		Sch. E, Part I, line 4
	d	Net short-term capital gain (loss)	4d		Sch. D, line 5, col. (f)
	e	Net long-term capital gain (loss):			
		(1) 28% rate gain (loss)	4e(1)		Sch. D, line 12, col. (g)
		(2) Total for year	4e(2)		Sch. D, line 12, col. (f)
	f	Other portfolio income (loss) *(attach schedule)*	4f		Enter on applicable line of your return.
	5	Guaranteed payments to partner	5		See page 6 of Partner's Instructions for Schedule K-1 (Form 1065).
	6	Net section 1231 gain (loss) (other than due to casualty or theft)	6		
	7	Other income (loss) *(attach schedule)*	7		Enter on applicable line of your return.
Deductions	8	Charitable contributions (see instructions) *(attach schedule)*	8		Sch. A, line 15 or 16
	9	Section 179 expense deduction	9		See pages 7 and 8 of Partner's Instructions for Schedule K-1 (Form 1065).
	10	Deductions related to portfolio income *(attach schedule)*	10		
	11	Other deductions *(attach schedule)*	11		
Credits	12a	Low-income housing credit:			
		(1) From section 42(j)(5) partnerships for property placed in service before 1990	12a(1)		Form 8586, line 5
		(2) Other than on line 12a(1) for property placed in service before 1990	12a(2)		
		(3) From section 42(j)(5) partnerships for property placed in service after 1989	12a(3)		
		(4) Other than on line 12a(3) for property placed in service after 1989	12a(4)		
	b	Qualified rehabilitation expenditures related to rental real estate activities	12b		See page 8 of Partner's Instructions for Schedule K-1 (Form 1065).
	c	Credits (other than credits shown on lines 12a and 12b) related to rental real estate activities	12c		
	d	Credits related to other rental activities	12d		
	13	Other credits	13		

For Paperwork Reduction Act Notice, see Instructions for Form 1065. Cat. No. 11394R **Schedule K-1 (Form 1065) 2000**

Schedule K-1 (Form 1065) 2000 Page **2**

	(a) Distributive share item		(b) Amount	(c) 1040 filers enter the amount in column (b) on:
Investment Interest	**14a** Interest expense on investment debts	14a		Form 4952, line 1
	b (1) Investment income included on lines 4a, 4b, 4c, and 4f	14b(1)		See page 9 of Partner's Instructions for Schedule K-1 (Form 1065).
	(2) Investment expenses included on line 10	14b(2)		
Self-employment	**15a** Net earnings (loss) from self-employment	15a		Sch. SE, Section A or B
	b Gross farming or fishing income	15b		See page 9 of Partner's Instructions for Schedule K-1 (Form 1065).
	c Gross nonfarm income	15c		
Adjustments and Tax Preference Items	**16a** Depreciation adjustment on property placed in service after 1986	16a		See page 9 of Partner's Instructions for Schedule K-1 (Form 1065) and Instructions for Form 6251.
	b Adjusted gain or loss	16b		
	c Depletion (other than oil and gas)	16c		
	d (1) Gross income from oil, gas, and geothermal properties	16d(1)		
	(2) Deductions allocable to oil, gas, and geothermal properties	16d(2)		
	e Other adjustments and tax preference items *(attach schedule)*	16e		
Foreign Taxes	**17a** Name of foreign country or U.S. possession ▶			Form 1116, Part I
	b Gross income sourced at partner level	17b		
	c Foreign gross income sourced at partnership level:			
	(1) Passive	17c(1)		
	(2) Listed categories *(attach schedule)*	17c(2)		
	(3) General limitation	17c(3)		
	d Deductions allocated and apportioned at partner level:			
	(1) Interest expense	17d(1)		
	(2) Other	17d(2)		
	e Deductions allocated and apportioned at partnership level to foreign source income:			
	(1) Passive	17e(1)		
	(2) Listed categories *(attach schedule)*	17e(2)		
	(3) General limitation	17e(3)		
	f Total foreign taxes (check one): ▶ ☐ Paid ☐ Accrued	17f		Form 1116, Part II
	g Reduction in taxes available for credit and gross income from all sources *(attach schedule)*	17g		See Instructions for Form 1116.
Other	**18** Section 59(e)(2) expenditures: **a** Type ▶			See page 9 of Partner's Instructions for Schedule K-1 (Form 1065).
	b Amount	18b		
	19 Tax-exempt interest income	19		Form 1040, line 8b
	20 Other tax-exempt income	20		See pages 9 and 10 of Partner's Instructions for Schedule K-1 (Form 1065).
	21 Nondeductible expenses	21		
	22 Distributions of money (cash and marketable securities)	22		
	23 Distributions of property other than money	23		
	24 Recapture of low-income housing credit:			
	a From section 42(j)(5) partnerships	24a		Form 8611, line 8
	b Other than on line 24a	24b		

Supplemental Information

25 Supplemental information required to be reported separately to each partner *(attach additional schedules if more space is needed):*

....

....

....

....

....

....

Schedule K-1 (Form 1065) 2000

Instructions for Form 1065, U.S. Return of Partnership Income

The instructions for this form are longer and probably even more confusing than those for the Form 1120S, U.S. Income Tax Return for an S Corporation. If you think that an LLC might better suit your needs for a business form, order these instructions from the IRS. Parts of this publication are clear, and you may find those sections helpful.

APPENDIX E
RECORDS TO BE KEPT AND INFORMATION TO BE FILED

IRS Regulation Sec. 1.351-3 Records to be kept and information to be filed.

(a) Every person who received the stock or securities of a controlled corporation, or other property as part of the consideration, in exchange for property under section 351, shall file with his income tax return for the taxable year in which the exchange is consummated a complete statement of all facts pertinent to such exchange, including—

(1) A description of the property transferred, or of his interest in such property, together with a statement of the cost or other basis thereof, adjusted to the date of transfer.

(2) With respect to stock of the controlled corporation received in the exchange, a statement of—
(i) The kind of stock and preferences, if any;
(ii) The number of shares of each class received; and
(iii) The fair market value per share of each class at the date of the exchange.

(3) With respect to securities of the controlled corporation received in the exchange, a statement of—
(i) The principal amount and terms; and
(ii) The fair market value at the date of exchange.

(4) The amount of money received, if any.

(5) With respect to other property received—
(i) A complete description of each separate item;
(ii) The fair market value of each separate item at the date of exchanges; and

(iii) In the case of a corporate shareholder, the adjusted basis of the other property in the hands of the controlled corporation immediately before the distribution of such other property to the corporate shareholder in connection with the exchange.

(6) With respect to liabilities of the transferors assumed by the controlled corporation, a statement of—

(i) The nature of the liabilities.

(ii) When and under what circumstances created;

(iii) The corporate business reason for assumption by the controlled corporation; and

(iv) Whether such assumption eliminates the transferor's primary liability.

(b) Every such controlled corporation shall file with its income tax return for the taxable year in which the exchange is consummated—

(1) A complete description of all the property received from the transferors.

(2) A statement of the cost or other basis thereof in the hands of the transferors adjusted to the date of transfer.

(3) The following information with respect to the capital stock of the controlled corporation—

(i) The total issued and outstanding capital stock immediately prior to and immediately after the exchange, with a complete description of each class of stock,

(ii) The classes of stock and number of shares issued to each transferor in the exchange, and the number of shares of each class of stock owned by each transferor immediately prior to and immediately after the exchange, and

(iii) The fair market value of the capital stock as of the date of exchange which was issued to each transferor.

(4) The following information with respect to securities of the controlled corporation—

(i) The principal amount and terms of all securities outstanding immediately prior to and immediately after the exchange,

(ii) The principal amount and terms of securities issued to each transferor in the exchange, with a statement showing each transferor's holdings of securities of the controlled corporation immediately prior to and immediately after the exchange,

(iii) The fair market value of the securities issued to the transferors on the date of the exchange, and

(iv) A statement as to whether the securities issued in the exchange are subordinated in any way to other claims against the controlled corporation.

(5) The amount of money, if any, which passed to each of the transferors in connection with the transaction.

(6) With respect to other property which passed to each transferor—

(i) A complete description of each separate item;

(ii) The fair market value of each separate item at the date of exchange, and

(iii) In the case of a corporate transferor, the adjusted basis of each separate item in the hands of the controlled corporation immediately before the distribution of such other property to the corporate transferor in connection with the exchange.

(7) The following information as to the transferor's liabilities assumed by the controlled corporation in the exchange—

(i) The amount and a description thereof,

(ii) When and under what circumstances created, and

(iii) The corporate business reason or reasons for assumption by the controlled corporation.

(c) Permanent records in substantial form shall be kept by every taxpayer who participates in the type of exchange described in section 351, showing the information listed above, in order to facilitate the determination of gain or loss from a subsequent disposition of stock or securities and other property, if any, received in the exchange.

INDEX